Masonry Estimating

by

Rynold V. Kolkoski

The Aberdeen Group®

426 S. Westgate St., Addison, Illinois 60101

ACKNOWLEDGMENTS

Certainly it can be recalled that knowledge comes from teachers and books . . . and experience. This author wishes to acknowledge the source of much of the information compiled in this book and appreciates having access to all this useful information.

AA Wire Products Company
Chicago, Illinois

American Insurance Association
Chicago, Illinois

American Society for Testing and Materials
Philadelphia, Pennsylvania

Atlas Minerals & Chemicals, Inc.
Mertztown, Pennsylvania

Brick Institute of America
Reston, Virginia

The Burns & Russell Co.
Baltimore, Maryland

The Donley Brothers Co.
Cleveland, Ohio

The Dow Chemical Company
Midland, Michigan

Dur-O-Wall, Inc.
Arlington Heights, Illinois

Glen-Gery Corporation
Wyomissing, Pennsylvania

Grace Construction Products Division
Cambridge, Massachusetts

Hanley Company
Summerville, Pennsylvania

Heckmann Building Products, Inc.
Chicago, Illinois

Hohmann & Barnard, Inc.
Hauppauge, New York

Indiana Limestone Institute
Bedford, Indiana

Interpave Corp.
Cincinnati, Ohio

Merry Companies
Augusta, Georgia

Morgen Manufacturing Co.
Yankton, South Dakota

National Concrete Masonry Association
Herndon, Virginia

National Fireproofing Corp.
Pittsburgh, Pennsylvania

Patent Scaffolding Co.
Cleveland, Ohio

Paver Systems Incorporated
Cincinnati, Ohio

Pittsburgh Corning Corp.
Pittsburgh, Pennsylvania

The Process Solvent Company, Inc.
Kansas City, Kansas

The Proudfoot Company, Inc.
Greenwich, Connecticut

Reading Concrete Products Corp.
Cincinnati, Ohio

Robinson Brick Company
Denver, Colorado

Solite
Richmond, Virginia

Stark Ceramics, Inc.
Canton, Ohio

Structural Clay Products Institute
Washington, D.C.

TY-WALL
Birmingham, Alabama

Unit Masonry Association
Cincinnati, Ohio

Victor Oolitic Stone Company
Bloomington, Indiana

Waco Scaffold & Shoring Company
Cleveland, Ohio

The W.H. Anderson Co.
Cincinnati, Ohio

Whitacre-Greer
Waynesburg, Ohio

Williams Products, Inc.
Troy, Michigan

W.R. Meadows, Inc.
Elgin, Illinois

ISBN 0-924659-74-2

Item No. 560

Library of Congress Cataloging-in-Publication Data

Kolkoski, Rynold V.
    Masonry estimating / by Rynold V. Kolkoski.
        p.   cm.
    Originally published: Carlsbad, CA : Craftsman Book Co., 1988.
    Includes index.
    ISBN 0-924659-74-2 (pbk.)
    1. Masonry—Estimates.   I. Title.
TH5330.K65 1995
    693'.1—dc20   95-13384
                                                                    CIP

Cover photography courtesy of:

Left: Rainguard Products Company
Center: Brick Institute of America
Right: Richard Steiger

CONTENTS

CHAPTER ONE

About the Book

his manual will give you the information you need to estimate brick, block, or nearly any type of unit masonry. The information here is straight to the point, easy to understand, but complete enough to guide you through just about any quantity take-off and estimate. Whether you're an experienced masonry estimating ''pro'' or a beginning estimator just learning the fine points, this book should become the most useful reference in your professional library.

Throughout this book my emphasis will be on estimating accuracy. The dictionary defines the word *estimate* as meaning:

to form an approximate idea of . . .
to form a general opinion about . . .
a calculation not professedly exact . . .

Don't you believe it! Any masonry cost estimate prepared by a competent professional estimator has to be more than ''approximate'' or a ''general opinion . . . not professedly exact.'' Your estimates should be as exact as the information available permits. I'll emphasize accuracy again and again in this manual. Good estimates aren't plagued with guesses, allowances, approximations, and assumptions. The procedures I recommend will help you compile good estimates, time after time after time.

The most important part of masonry estimating is the quantity take-off — reading from the plans the dimensions and descriptions for masonry work to be done. Many bids are won and lost in the take-off. You'll probably use the same labor rates and have the same material costs as most of the other masonry contractors in your area. Many times the difference between your bid and the competition will be in the take-off itself. If you don't have an accurate take-off, you can't have an accurate estimate. And the only way to get work at a decent profit is with competitive bids based on accurate estimates.

This chapter is a broad-brush introduction to quantity take-off procedures. I'll explain a few of the basic principles and provide some background information. In the next chapter we'll get down to specifics.

I'm going to assume that you've worked with masonry plans and understand the abbreviations and notations designers use. If you're new to plan reading, there are many good books on the subject. Your local bookstore will probably have one or two, or should be able to order the book you need. If not, there's an order form bound into the back of this manual that lists books you may want to order.

What the Estimator Brings to the Job

Good masonry estimators have patience and endurance. Digging into a set of plans can be tedious and monotonous work. You've got to discover every last bit of masonry in the job. There's no substitute for taking the time and trouble to be thorough. Discovering those hidden masonry items in a set of plans may keep you from being a low bidder, but no one wants to be low bidder on a money-losing job.

Careful estimators do more than discover the masonry work others overlook. They also find the "outs" and deductions that give them a competitive advantage — and the job at a good profit. I'll show you how to spot legitimate cost savings in most masonry jobs.

Background
Patience and endurance alone won't make you a good masonry estimator. You also need knowledge and skill. You have to be familiar with masonry materials and construction procedures. And you have to know how to read and interpret construction drawings, including the civil, architectural, structural and mechanical sheets. It takes imagination and skill to visualize all the components of an intricate masonry design, to understand the composite structure of the building and to interpret the intent of the architect correctly. Some of this comes only with experience. But don't worry. Even if you've never worked on a masonry job, I'll provide most of the information you need to compile accurate estimates.

A good background in mathematics will be useful, of course. But nothing beyond high school math will be necessary to follow my explanations. If you've had courses in mechanical drawing, have studied the properties of materials, and have served an apprenticeship under an experienced estimator, you're several steps ahead. If you don't have this experience, no problem. I'll explain everything you need to know.

The Right Information

To prepare an estimate, you need complete bid information and an accurate masonry quantity survey (take-off). You also need to know your costs: labor and materials, equipment rental rates, prevailing payroll taxes, insurance and fringe benefits.

An experienced estimator won't submit a competitive bid on an incomplete set of plans. Neither should you. You bid what's in the plans, specifications, addenda, and special information letters. There's no need to speculate about what else may be in the job. You'll see unbiddable plans occasionally. I'll show you how to identify them. If you don't understand how the work will be done, ask for information from the architect or the job superintendent or *don't bid*. It's as simple as that.

Doing the Take-Off

I'll start by introducing you to the three forms I use for take-offs. Figure 1-1 is the *masonry specification take-off sheet.* Figure 1-2 is the *take-off sheet.* Figure 1-3 is the *summary sheet* where totals from all other pages are brought together. You'll use these forms again later. Most of this book is an explanation of how to use these documents. For now, just look them over and compare them with other estimating forms you've seen.

I suggest that you follow a simple convention when noting dimensions on your take-off sheet. Look at Figure 1-4. Under the heading *4'' face brick,* every wall is indentified by two numbers, a height and a length. In Figure 1-4 the 4'' face brick wall is made up of three different areas. One area is 9'4'' high and 130'0'' long, another portion of the wall is 8'0'' high and 40'0'' long, and the third part is only 6'8'' high and 28'0'' long. The overall length of the wall is 198 feet. Notice also that I've written the inches as superscript numbers with a line under them. This helps avoid confusion and reduces the chance of an error. I suggest that you follow the same system when listing dimensions on your take-off sheet.

Wall heights will be shown on the drawings. The lengths are scaled from the floor plans. I suggest that you measure each wall section and list it on your take-off sheet. Then go back to the plans and use a colored pencil to put a check mark through that wall section. That reduces the chance of listing any wall twice. When all walls have been checked on the plans, you can be sure none have been omitted.

In Figure 1-5, each wall height has been multiplied by the wall length to find the wall area. At the bottom of the column, the number *1720* is the sum of all wall areas. After doing these calculations, I recommend that you verify wall heights and lengths once more. Take another look at the wall sections and check the total length. Either roll a measuring wheel (map measure) over the marked floor plans or use an architect's scale to determine the dimensions. If there's a discrepancy of more than 2% (2 feet in each 100 feet), measure again.

MASONRY QUANTITY SURVEYS

DATE

SHEET ____ OF ____

EST. BY

BID DUE

BLDG. _______________________ OWNER _______________________

LOCATION _______________________ ARCHITECT _______________________

PLAN NOS. ____________ DATE ____________ GEN. CONTR. _______________________

Specification Section ____________ Date ____________ Addenda ____________

Face Brick	Size		Allowance				
Common Brick	Size		Material				
Glazed Tile	Size		Material				
Concrete Block	Size		Material				
Exp. Joints	Type		Material				
Control Joints	Type		Material				
Fill	Walls		Material				
Flashing	Furnished By		Material				
Caulking	Furnished By		Material				
Parging	Thickness						
Anchors	Type	Galv.	WT.	Spacing	H	V	
Ties	Type	Galv.	WT.	Spacing	H	V	
Reinforcing	Type	Galv.	WT.	Spacing	V		
PC Concrete	Sills	Copings	Lintels	Facing			
Stone	Sills	Copings	Trim	Facing			
Bond Beams	Fill Furn. By						
P.C. Lintels							
Cleaning	Materials						
Workmanship	Bond		Joints				
Waterproofing							
Special							
Alternates							

Masonry specification take-off sheet
Figure 1-1

MASONRY QUANTITY SURVEYS

DATE
SHEET   OF
EST. BY
BID DUE

BLDG. _______________________   OWNER _______________________

LOCATION _______________________   ARCHITECT _______________________

PLAN NOS. _______________ DATE _______________   GEN. CONTR. _______________________

Take-off sheet
Figure 1-2

MASONRY QUANTITY SURVEYS

DATE

SHEET   OF

EST. BY

BID DUE

BLDG. ____________________   OWNER____________________

LOCATION ____________________   ARCHITECT____________________

PLAN NOS. ___________ DATE ___________   GEN. CONTR. ____________________

ITEM	UNIT	QUANTITY	MATERIAL		LABOR		WORK	TOTAL
			Unit	Amount	Unit	Amount		

Summary sheet
Figure 1-3

MASONRY QUANTITY SURVEYS

123 Beech Drive
Cincinnati, OH 45123

DATE
SHEET   OF
EST. BY
BID DUE

BLDG. _______________________   OWNER _______________________

LOCATION _______________________   ARCHITECT _______________________

PLAN NOS. _______________ DATE _______________   GEN. CONTR. _______________________

			4" FACE BRICK						
			9⁴ (HEIGHT)						
			130⁰ (LENGTH)						
130 40 28 198			8⁰ (HEIGHT) 40⁰ (LENGTH)						
WHEEL 200			6⁸ (HEIGHT) 28⁰ (LENGTH)						

Sample face brick take-off
Figure 1-4

MASONRY QUANTITY SURVEYS

123 Beech Drive
Cincinnati, OH 45123

DATE

SHEET   OF

EST. BY

BID DUE

BLDG. ___________________________   OWNER ___________________________

LOCATION ___________________________   ARCHITECT ___________________________

PLAN NOS. ___________ DATE ___________   GEN. CONTR. ___________________________

4" F.BRK.

9⅓
130⁰
1213.3

130
40
28
198

8⁰
40⁰
320

WHEEL
200

6⅝
28⁰
186.7

1720

OUTS

DR 3⁰ × 7⁰   ①   21
WD 4⁰ × 6⁰   ③   48

69

1651

Sample face brick take-off
Figure 1-5

Tools of the estimating trade
Figure 1-6

The next step is to find the *outs*. These are wall openings - areas that don't have to be filled with brick, block or other unit masonry. Note the outs listed at the bottom left of Figure 1-5. Record the outs and deduct the area from the total wall area to find the net wall area. In Figure 1-5, the outs will be 69 square feet, leaving a wall area of 1651 square feet (1720 less 69).

This system is uncomplicated, easy to follow, and less likely to yield mistakes. It makes checking easy when your estimate is passed to another estimator for verification. It simplifies the recording of outs and makes it more likely that you'll remember how the estimate was compiled weeks later when work actually begins.

Equipment You'll Need
The only equipment you'll need is a flat 1/8'' - 1/4'' scale, an architect's scale, a map measure for checking measurements, some colored marking pencils and a calculator. For some civil drawings you'll need an engineer's scale that shows feet and hundredths of a foot rather than feet and inches. And, of course, this book should be close at hand. Figure 1-6 shows some of the estimating tools you'll need.

Masonry Descriptions and Specifications
This book describes all the masonry units and accessories you're likely to need to complete any job. I'll explain what you need to know about how unit masonry is made.

I've also included drawings that show masonry unit sizes and shapes. You'll also find here concise specifications for most brick and block.

Mortar, Masonry Accessories and Wall Treatments

Mortar is an important item in masonry estimating. That's why I've included tables showing the quantity of mortar required for the various masonry units. You'll learn an easy way to figure the mortar quantity needed for your job.

I'll discuss the accessories involved in masonry estimating: reinforcing, anchors, control joints, flashing, insulation, and so on. You'll find sketches and tables that make it easier to include the accessories in your quantity survey.

Information about the various wall treatments is included — caulking, waterproofing, parging, jointing, pointing, and cleaning, with helpful hints and tables for determining quantities.

Production Rates

Labor is a key cost on every masonry job. That makes your labor estimate an important part of every bid. The labor cost for any job depends on how many units your crew can lay in each hour and day. Good masonry estimators can predict quite accurately how many brick or block a work crew can lay in a day. Of course, productivity varies with the crew, working conditions and the type of job.

In later chapters you'll find production tables for most types of masonry. These are the figures I use. They're good estimates for *my* crews and the type of jobs my crews handle. They may or may not apply on your jobs. The best estimate for your work is based on productivity records from your jobs. You'll never find any figures that are better. But if you don't yet have your own labor productivity records, use mine. I'll also explain how to modify production rates for unusual working conditions.

Miscellaneous Items

In the back of this book there's a glossary and an appendix that includes abbreviations and weights of materials. Page through it so you have a general idea of what's there. Then, when you need the information, you'll know where to find it.

Some of the information in this book you may already have seen in masonry text books, manufacturers' pamphlets and technical articles. You probably have some of it lying around on your desk already. I've included it here to make this a complete reference. You don't have to go rummaging around in your files to find what you need.

A Sample Take-Off

The book ends with plans and details for a small office building and a detailed, step-by-step sample take-off. It takes you through all the stages of preparing a masonry estimate, from a preliminary abstract of the specifications to the final summary and pricing. There's no better way to learn than by doing. I suggest that you estimate the office building yourself. Work carefully. Do the best you can. Then compare your estimate with my estimate.

Finally, there's an actual take-off and estimate of a six-story college campus building. The bid I show was actually submitted for construction of Carlin Hall.

Having provided that brief introduction, it's time to get down to work. We'll start with a look at block and tile.

CHAPTER TWO

Block and Structural Tile

Estimating unit masonry is a broad topic. There's a lot to learn. But I can simplify it for you by breaking the subject down into manageable chunks. In this chapter I'll explain how to take off material quantities for block, including concrete block, structural clay tile, glazed block, glass block and gypsum block. In later chapters I'll show how to prepare material take-offs for other types of masonry. After covering material take-off, I'll describe how to figure labor costs, add overhead, contingency and then build profit into your bids.

Let's start with some definitions.

Concrete Block

Concrete masonry units are made mainly of portland cement, graded aggregates and water. Regular- or normal-weight block uses aggregates such as sand and gravel, crushed stone, and air-cooled blast furnace slag. Aggregates for lightweight block include expanded shale, clay, slate, expanded blast-furnace slag, sintered fly ash, coal cinders, and natural lightweight materials such as pumice and scoria. Manufacturers use whatever aggregate is available at reasonable cost in their area.

The term *concrete block* is sometimes used to designate *only* regular weight block. But I'll use the term *concrete block* to include all regular and lightweight block made from any of the aggregates listed above.

Sizes

Concrete masonry units are available in many sizes, shapes, colors, textures, and profiles. The most common block has a face size of 8'' x 16'' and may be 4'', 6'', 8'', 10'' or 12'' thick. Other sizes and shapes are available to fit almost any situation. Special shapes can be made on request. Figure 2-1 shows typical concrete masonry units.

Types

The type of aggregate used in block determines the texture in the plain block. The manufacturer may also split or score the face to make many other attractive textures. Various types of fluting provide designers with a choice of profiles.

Special block are available for sound absorption, for copings, sills, chimneys, paving, pilasters, and so on. There are too many types and variations for me to show even a representative sample of the block that are available. But the concrete block dealers in your area will be more than happy to supply brochures that describe the block they sell. Stock up on product literature the next time you visit your dealer.

ASTM Specifications

Concrete masonry units are manufactured to conform to the requirements of the American Society for Testing and Materials (ASTM). ASTM standards classify concrete masonry units according to type and weight class.

The standards specify the minimum net area compressive strength in psi (pounds per square inch) that units must meet to comply. Compressive strength requirements are higher for load-bearing units (ASTM C 55 and C 90) than for non-loadbearing units (C 129).

The type of unit is indicated either as Type I, moisture-controlled, or Type II, non-moisture-controlled.

ASTM C 55, the standard for concrete building brick and larger architectural facing units, also includes grade designations. Grade "N" is for use as facing units in exterior walls and where high strength and resistance to moisture penetration and severe frost action are needed. Grade "S" is for general use and where moderate resistance to moisture and frost action is needed.

Familiarize yourself with these ASTM specifications:

ASTM C 90
Hollow Load-Bearing Concrete Masonry Units

ASTM C 55
Concrete Building Brick

ASTM C 129
Hollow Non-Load-Bearing Concrete Masonry Units

ASTM C 33
Normal-Weight, (Heavy) Aggregates

ASTM C 331
Lightweight Aggregates

It's important for every estimator to understand the full meaning of the ASTM code numbers. When an architect specifies the block in a certain area "shall be in accordance with ASTM Specification C 90, Type I," he's telling you:

1) The block have to be manufactured of materials that conform to ASTM Specification C 90.

2) Type I tells you the blocks must conform to specific ASTM moisture content requirements.

3) This ASTM designation also tells you the weight limitations and the minimum thickness of shell and web.

I've never seen a set of specifications that explained exactly what the ASTM numbers mean. You won't either. In fact, you don't need to know all the details about each ASTM specification. Your only responsibility is to be sure your dealer's quote is based on the right block.

Of course, block manufacturers have to know what these specifications require. They make block to meet each ASTM specification and will, if requested, certify in writing that their block complies.

Notice that ASTM specifications don't say anything about block weight, color, surface texture, fire resistance, thermal transmission or acoustical properties.

Block Variations

Figure 2-1 shows the more common concrete masonry units. You won't use all of these block on any job, of course. The usual job needs only a few different types of block.

Most concrete block look about the same. But there are many variations from one manufacturer to another. One key variation is the *coring*. Whether the block is two-core or three-core will have a great effect on its loadbearing capacity. Three-core block are much stronger.

A wall is strongest when the cores and webs (walls dividing the cores) are in vertical alignment. If the webs aren't vertically aligned, bearing strength comes from the exterior walls (shells) only.

Another important variation is the shell and web thickness. The thicker the shell and web, the lower the percentage of void, the higher the bearing strength, the greater the weight. Weight of materials used to manufacture the block affects the insulating value and the fire rating.

Figure 2-2 summarizes some key facts about heavyweight and lightweight block. Some of the data in this table comes from manufacturers' brochures. The rest has been calculated from manufacturers' data. This information may not be accurate for block made by manufacturers in your area. But if you find the information in Figure 2-2 to be useful, make up a similar table for the type of block you use. Block manufacturers should be able to supply the data you need.

You'll find that a table like Figure 2-2 is very useful when estimating concrete block. The columns headed *Width, Cores, Percent solid and Shell thickness* are based on data supplied by the block manufacturer. The other columns were calculated from this basic information.

Since you'll probably want to make a table like Figure 2-2 based on data that applies to the block you use, I'll explain how it's done. Notice there's a letter or number in brackets at the bottom of all columns. The columns that have a letter in brackets at the bottom have figures supplied by block manufacturers. Columns with numbers in brackets at the bottom were calculated from manufacturers' data. The paragraphs below explain how to do these calculations.

1) *Gross Volume in Cubic Feet and Volume of Voids:* The gross volume is determined by multiplying the depth by the height by the length, using the actual dimensions, then dividing the result by 1728, the number of cubic inches in a cubic foot. Here's the calculation for a block with nominal dimensions of 8 x 8 x 16 and actual dimensions of 7⅝ x 7⅝ x 15⅝:

$$\frac{7.625 \times 7.625 \times 15.625}{1728} = .526 \text{ CF}$$

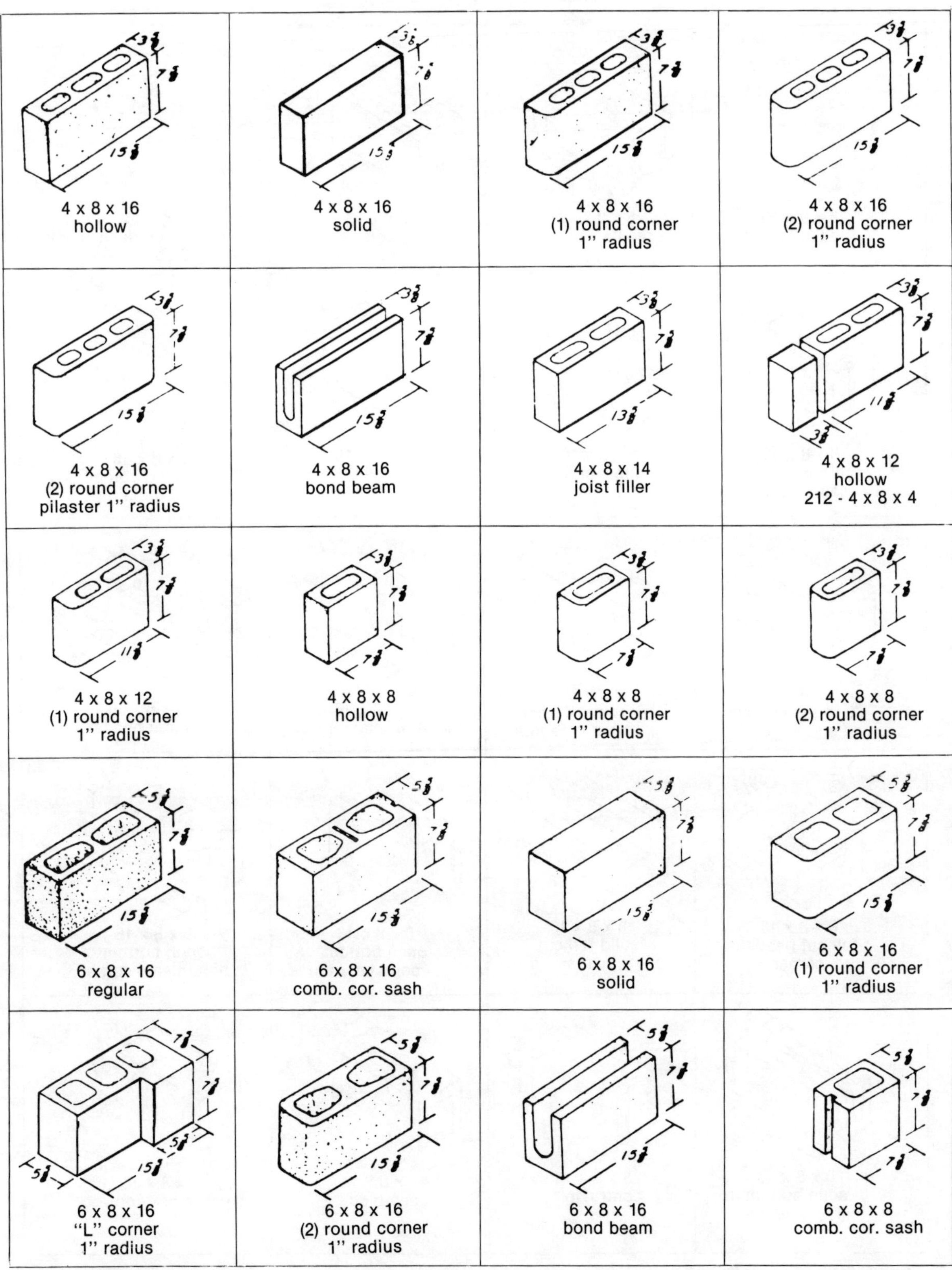

Courtesy: Reading Concrete Products

Typical concrete masonry units
Figure 2-1

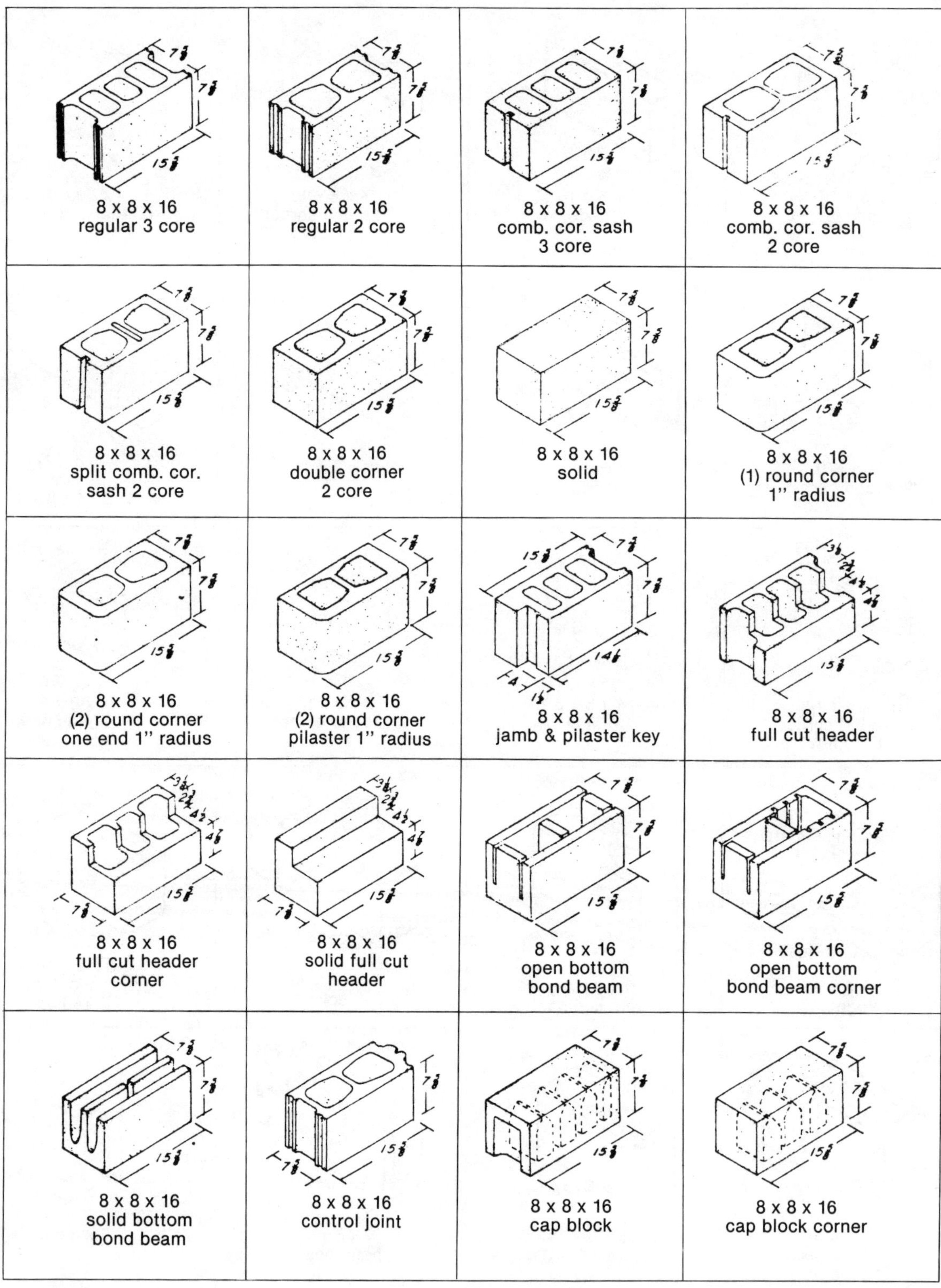

Courtesy: Reading Concrete Products

Typical concrete masonry units
Figure 2-1 (continued)

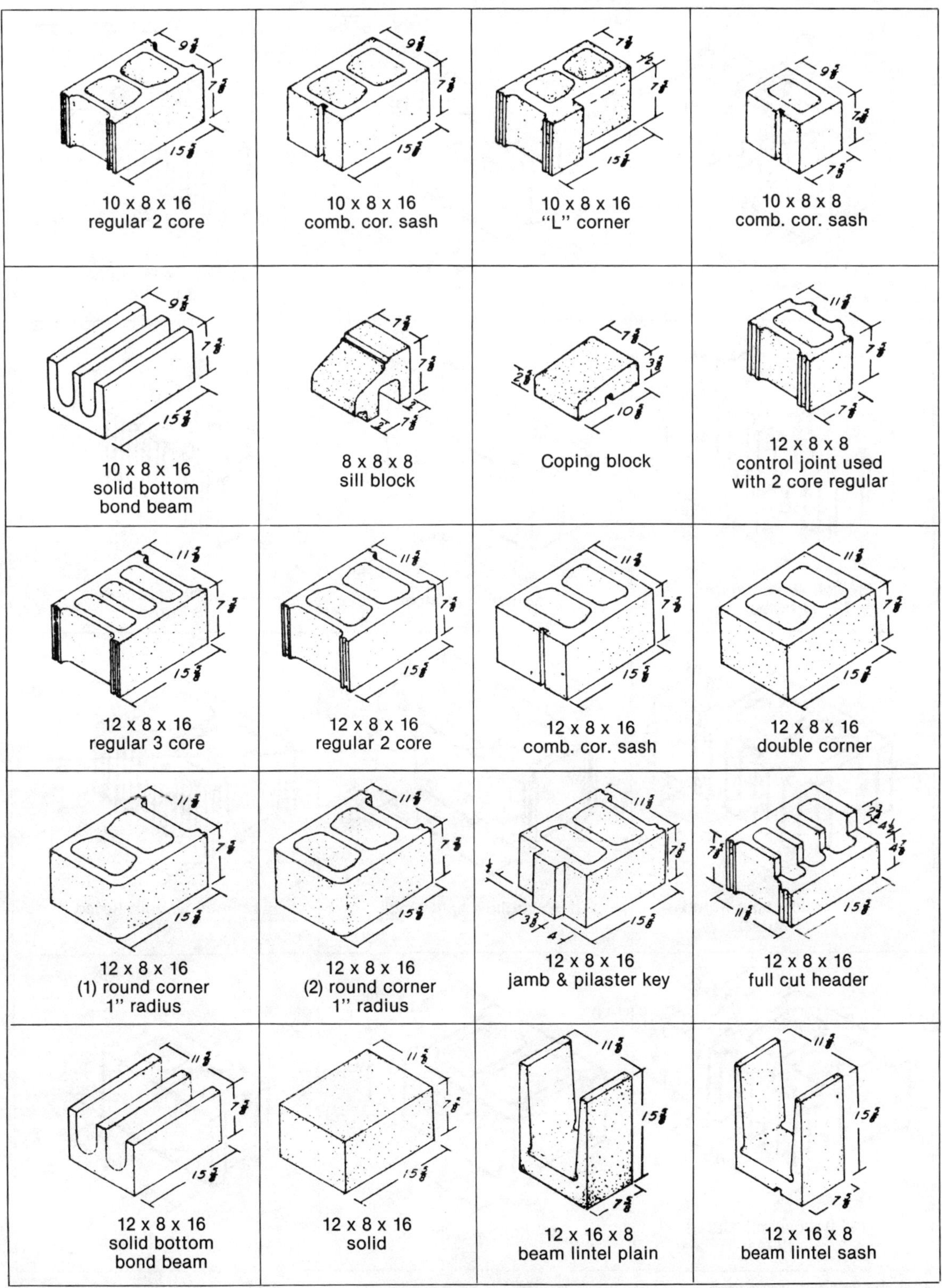

Typical concrete masonry units
Figure 2-1 (continued)

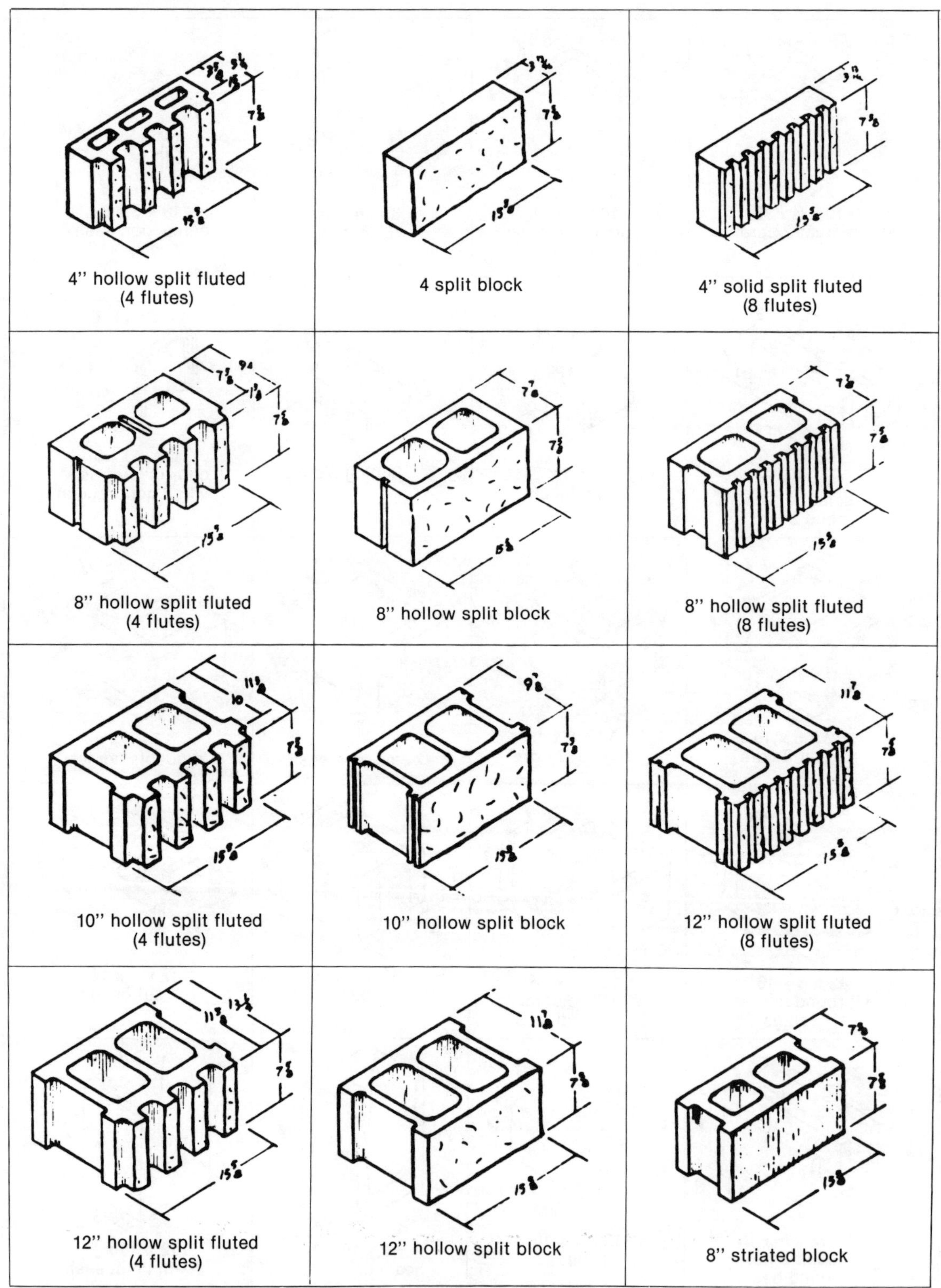

Courtesy: Reading Concrete Products

Typical concrete masonry units
Figure 2-1 (continued)

Width x 8 x 16 inches	Cores	Concrete Block								Heavyweight CMU			Lightweight CMU		
		Gross volume (CF)	Volume of voids (CF)	Percent solid	Equiv. thickness (inches)	Shell thickness (inches)	Mortar (CY/M)	* Fill (CY/M)		Weight @ 133# /CF	Fire rating (FR) hours	Prod. running bond exposed	Weight @ 94# /CF	Fire rating (FR) hours	Prod. running bond exposed
4	3	.250	.067	73.5	2.66	1.000	1.02	2.5		25	¾	166	18	1	180
6	2	.388	.141	63.6	3.57	1.250	1.15	5.3		33	1	148	24	1½	168
8	2	.526	.257	51.2	3.90	1.250	1.15	9.6		36	1½	140	26	2	163
8	3	.526	.221	58.0	4.42	1.250	1.15	8.2		41	2	124	29	2½	157
10	2	.664	.320	51.8	4.98	1.500	1.28	11.9		46	2	107	33	3	148
12	2	.802	.435	45.8	5.32	1.500	1.28	16.2		49	3	100	35	4	143
12	3	.802	.354	55.9	6.49	1.500	1.28	13.2		60	4	84	43	4	117
8	2	.526	.208	60.5	4.61	1.500	1.28	7.8		43	2	117	30	3	155
8	2	.526	.181	65.7	5.00	1.750	1.40	6.8		46	3	107	33	3	148
8	3	.526	.132	75.0	5.71	2.125	1.60	4.9		53	3	91	38	4	134
12	3	.802	.337	58.0	6.74	1.750	1.40	12.5		62	4	83	44	4	113
6	3	.388	.097	75.0	4.21	1.875	1.47	3.6		39	2	131	28	2	159
12	2	.802	.201	75.0	8.71	3.375	2.23	7.5		80	4	71	57	4	86
4	0	.250	.000	100.0	3.62	—	1.18	—		34	1½	145	24	2	168
6	0	.388	.000	100.0	5.62	—	1.69	—		52	3	92	37	4	137
8	0	.526	.000	100.0	7.62	—	2.20	—		70	4	78	50	4	97
12	0	.802	.000	100.0	11.62	—	3.22	—		107	4	54	76	4	74
8	Ivany	.526	.305	42.0	3.20	1.250	1.15	11.3		30	—	155	21	—	174
12	Ivany	.802	.529	34.0	3.95	1.250	1.15	19.6		37	—	137	26	—	163
(A)	(B)	(1)	(1a)	(C)	(2)	(D)	(3)	(4)		(5)	(6)	(7)	(5)	(6)	(7)

Data in columns A, B, C, and D furnished by the block manufacturer.
Data in columns 1 through 7 was calculated from manufacturer's data.

Concrete block data
Figure 2-2

* Does not allow for fill at joints and waste. Add 7% to quantities for block laid in the wall.

Then find the volume of voids by multiplying the gross volume by the percent of solid, and subtracting the answer from the gross volume. For example, let's find the volume of voids in a 12'' block with a gross volume of 0.802 CF and a percent solid of 45.8:

$$.802 - (.802 \times .458) = .435 \text{ CF}$$

You can use this information to determine the equivalent thickness and fire rating, and the amount of mortar required per 1000 (M) blocks.

2) *Equivalent Thickness (E.T.) in Inches:* Find the E.T. by multiplying the actual thickness of the block by the percent solid. Equivalent thickness is an important measure of fire resistance. We'll talk more about the fire ratings in Chapter 10. Here's how you would calculate equivalent thickness for a 6'' concrete block that's 63.6% solid:

$$5.625 \times .636 = 3.57''$$

3) *Mortar, Cubic Yards per 1000 Blocks:* This column shows the cubic yards of mortar required to lay 1000 units. In Chapter 5 I'll explain how to compute these quantities. According to this table, it will take 1.02 cubic yards of mortar to lay 1000 4'' blocks.

4) *Fill, Cubic Yards per 1000 Blocks:* This column shows the cubic yards of material required to fill the cores of 1000 units. The fill can be grout, sand, concrete or granular insulation. The table shows that fill required for 1000 12'' concrete blocks, 45.8% solid, would be 16.2 cubic yards. *

5) *Weight, in Pounds:* The weight of the unit depends on the actual net volume times the weight of material used to make the block. For example, the weight of a 6'' heavyweight concrete masonry unit (HWCMU), 63.6% solid, is:

$$.388 \times .636 \times 133 = 33 \text{ lbs}$$

The weight of a 12'' lightweight concrete masonry unit (LWCMU), 45.8 % solid, is:

$$.802 \times .458 \times 94 = 35 \text{ lbs}$$

6) *Fire Rating in Hours:* The fire rating, in many codes, is determined by the equivalent thickness. I'll explain this in Chapter 10. Using this table, the fire rating for a 12'' LWCMU, 45.8% solid, is 4 hours.

7) *Production:* This is the number of units a bricklayer can lay in one day. The production for most common concrete units is on the table. Chapter 8 explains how to determine production rates. Using this table, you find the production for 8'' LWCMU, 58% solid, is 157 pieces a day.

* Does not allow for fill at joints and waste. Add 7% to quantities for block laid in the wall.

Figure 2-3 shows properties of some common concrete masonry wall panels. Be familiar with these panels so you can discuss them with architects, engineers, material suppliers and owners. It's an important part of your education as an estimator. The block you use may not be identical to the block identified in Figure 2-3. But you can use Figure 2-3 as a guide when developing similar data for your own use.

Figure 2-4 shows typical details of corner construction of concrete masonry walls of various thicknesses. These show the special, and more expensive, masonry units used for each type of corner. And of course, labor costs will be higher. You can often compensate for this extra cost by lapping at the corners when you do the lineal measurements in your take-off.

The Take-Off

Most estimators take off concrete block in square feet and then convert to pieces for pricing. But you can take off in lineal feet, cubic feet, cubic yards or square yards. I'll do the calculations in square feet.

Suppose we want to find the square feet of block in a masonry wall. We'll start with the height and the length in feet. For example, assume the masonry wall is 8'8" high and 21'4" long. The area is:

$$8'8" = 8.667'$$
$$21'4" = 21.334'$$
$$8.667 \times 21.334 = 185 \text{ SF}$$

Here's how to record it on the take-off sheet:

$$
\begin{array}{ll}
8\frac{8}{} & \text{(height)} \\
21\frac{4}{} & \text{(length)} \\
\boxed{185} & \text{(extension)} \\
\times\ 1.125 & \text{(conversion factor)} \\
\hline
209 & \text{(pieces)}
\end{array}
$$

The circle around the 185 indicates that it's an extension (the product of multiplying two numbers). The conversion factor is the number of pieces in one square foot. Here's how you find it:

$$\frac{144}{8 \times 16} = \frac{144}{128} = 1.125$$

Eight times 16 is 128. Divide 128 into 144 (the number of square inches in one foot) and you get 1.125. That's the number of 8" by 16" blocks needed for one square foot of wall.

Abbreviations

LWMCU . . . . Light weight concrete masonry units	**W** . . . . Weight per square foot of wall surface
HWCMU . . . . Heavyweight concrete masonry units	**STC** . . . Sound transmission class (average decibel loss of sound passing through the wall)
LFV . . . . Loose fill — vermiculite	**R** . . . . Thermal resistance (SF x HRS x F/BTU)
LFP . . . . Loose fill — perlite	**U** . . . . . Thermal transfer coefficient (BTU/SF x HRS x F)
FIP . . . . Foam in place - urea formaldehyde	**M** . . . . Mass coefficient for correcting "U" value based on thermal cycling
PSMI . . . . Polystyrene foam bead molded inserts	
PSB . . . . Polystyrene bead foam board	**MU** . . . . M x U
PSE . . . . Polystyrene extruded foam board	**SF** . . . . Square feet
PU . . . . Polyurethane foam board	**°F** . . . . Degrees Fahrenheit
PIC . . . . Polyisocyanurate foam board — foil backed	**HRS** . . . . Hours
SGT . . . . Structural glazed tile	**GLCMU** . . . . Glazed concrete masonry unit
FR . . . . Fire rating	

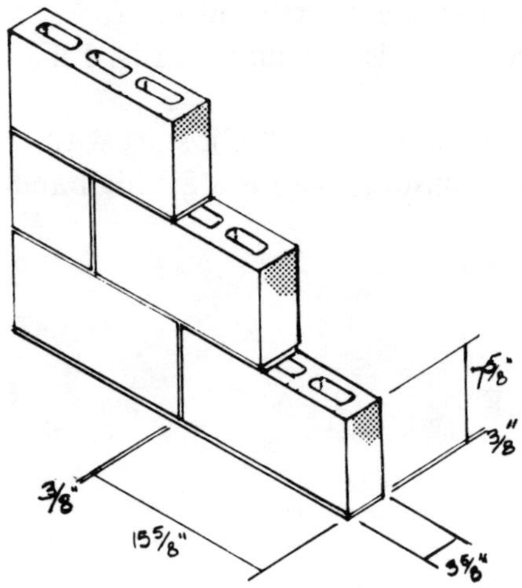

Description
4" LWCMU	8 x 16	
4" HWCMU	8 x 16	

Properties
	LW	HW
FR	1	¾
W	26	37
STC Paint	43	44
STC No paint	40	45
R	2.07	1.57
U	0.48	0.64
MU	0.47	0.61

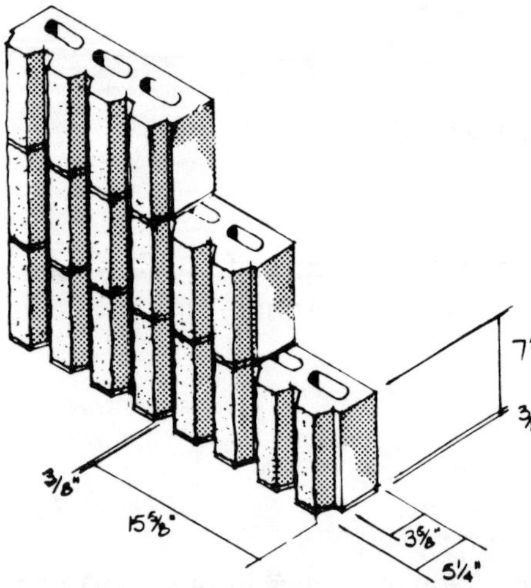

Description
4" HWCMU 4-flute	8 x 16

Properties
FR	1
W	52
STC Paint	. . .
STC No paint	. . .
R	1.57
U	0.64
MU	0.60

Typical wall panels
Figure 2-3

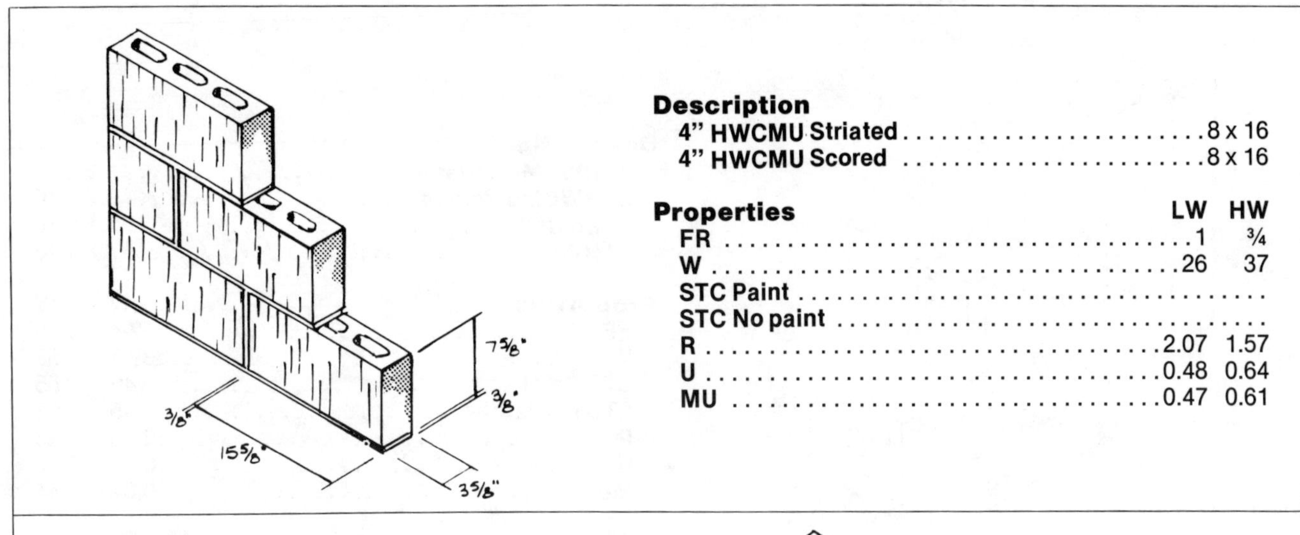

Description

4" HWCMU Striated . . . . 8 x 16
4" HWCMU Scored . . . . 8 x 16

Properties	**LW**	**HW**
FR	1	¾
W	26	37
STC Paint		
STC No paint		
R	2.07	1.57
U	0.48	0.64
MU	0.47	0.61

Description

4" HWCMU Split . . . . 8 x 16

Properties

FR 1½
W 44
STC Paint . . . .
STC No paint . . . .
R 1.39
U 0.72
MU 0.68

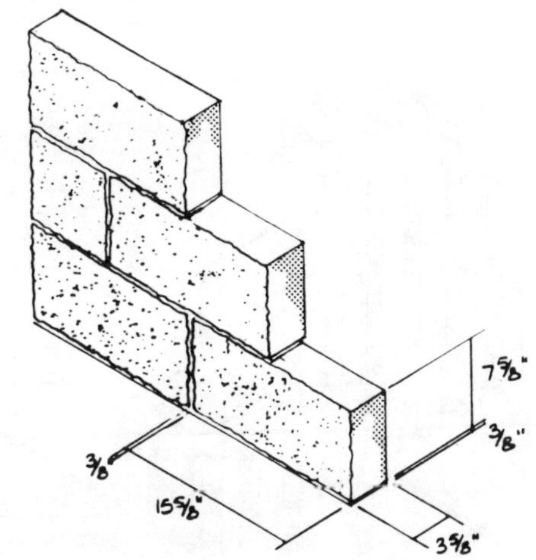

Description

10" HWCMU 4-flute . . . . 8 x 16

Properties

FR 3
W 80
STC Paint . . . . 55 +
STC No paint . . . . 50 +
R 2.28
U 0.44
MU 0.39

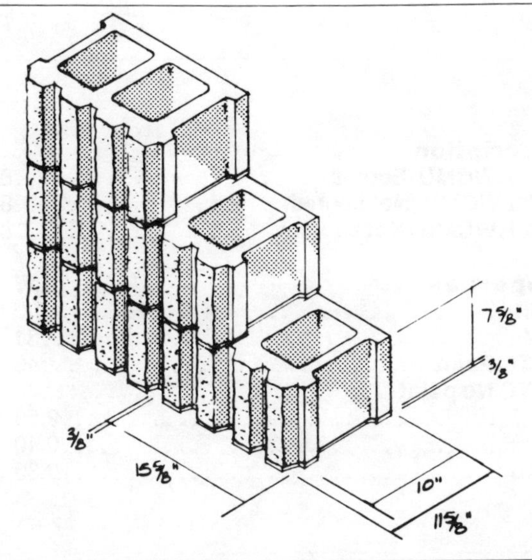

Typical wall panels
Figure 2-3 (continued)

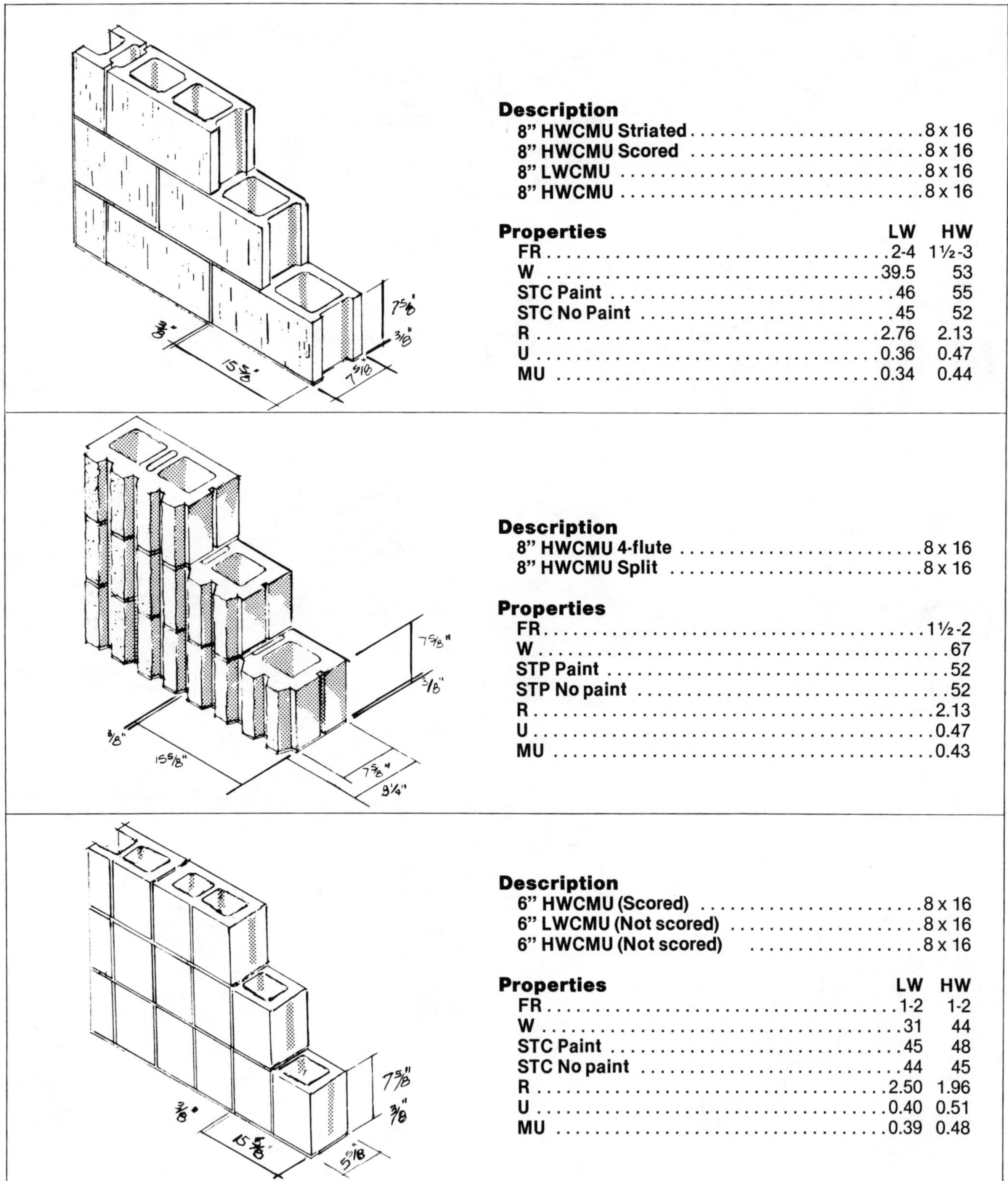

Typical wall panels
Figure 2-3 (continued)

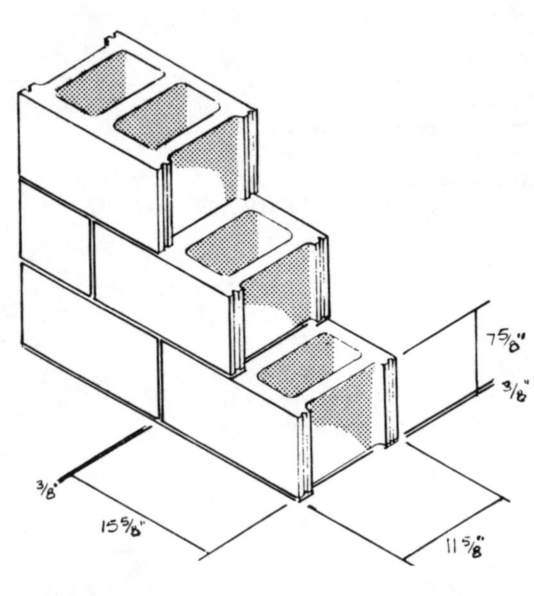

Description

12" LWCMU	8 x 16
12" HWCMU	8 x 16

Properties

	LW	HW
FR	4	3-4
W	53	70
STC Paint	50 +	55 +
STC No paint	45	52
R	2.99	2.33
U	0.34	0.43
MU	0.32	0.39

Description

12" HWCMU 4-flute	8 x 16

Properties

FR	3
W	85
STC Paint	55 +
STC No paint	52
R	2.33
U	0.43
MU	0.38

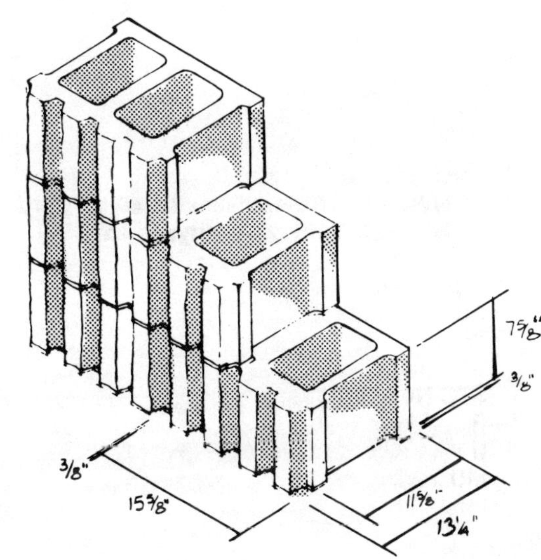

Description

4" HWCMU Split, 8" LWCMU
4" HWCMU 4-flute, 8" LWCMU
4" Face brick (2⅔ x 8), 8" LWCMU
4" Face brick (4 x 12), 8" LWCMU

Properties

FR	4
W	81
STC Paint	55 +
STC No paint	50 +
R	4.17
U	0.24
MU	0.21

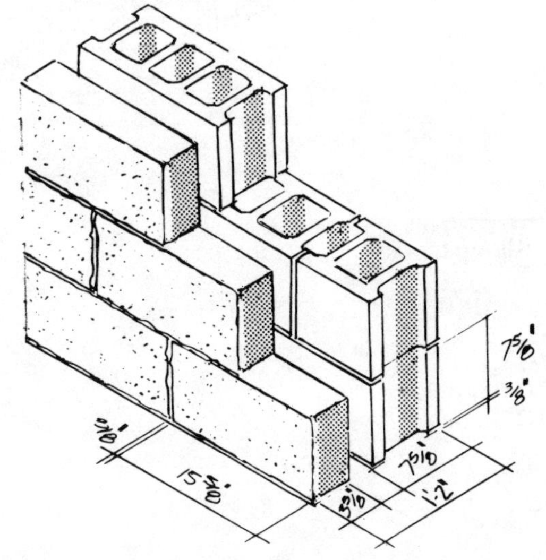

Typical wall panels
Figure 2-3 (continued)

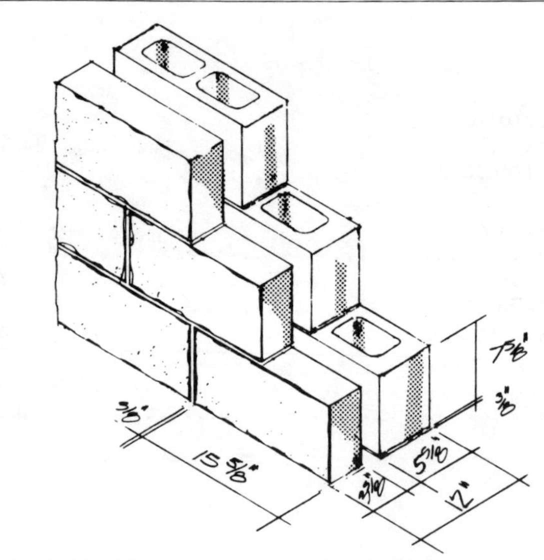

Description
4" HWCMU (Split), 2" cavity, 6" LWCMU
4" HWCMU (4-flute), 2" cavity, 6" LWCMU
4" Face brick (2⅔ x 8), 2" cavity, 6" LWCMU
4" Face brick (4 x 12), 2" cavity, 6" LWCMU

Properties
FR	4
W	70
STC Paint	55 +
STC No paint	50
R	3.37
U	0.30
MU	0.27

Description
4" HWCMU 4-flute, 2" cavity, 4" LWCMU
4" HWCMU Split, 2" cavity, 4" LWCMU

Properties
FR	3-4
W	64
STC paint	55
STC No paint	50
R	3.81
U	0.26
MU	0.24

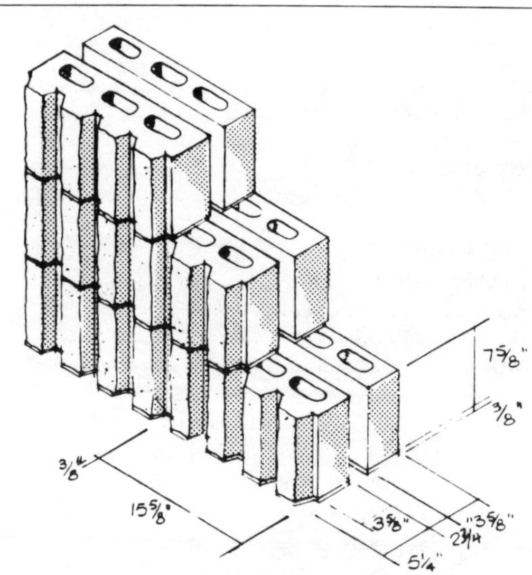

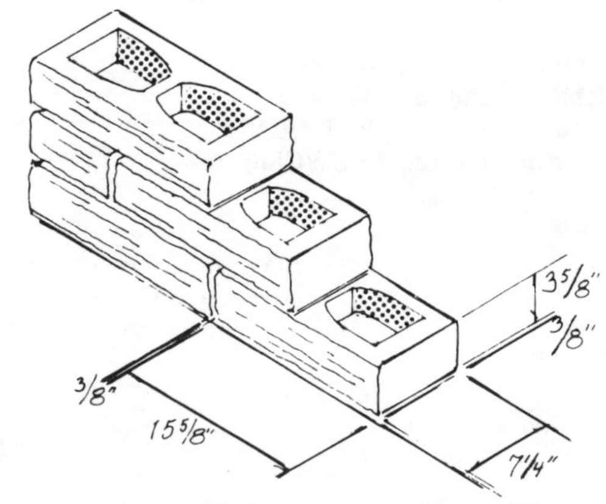

Description
8" Slump block .... 4 x 16

Properties
FR	3
W	51.7
STC Paint	55
STC No paint	52
R	2.13
U	0.47
MU	0.44

Typical wall panels
Figure 2-3 (continued)

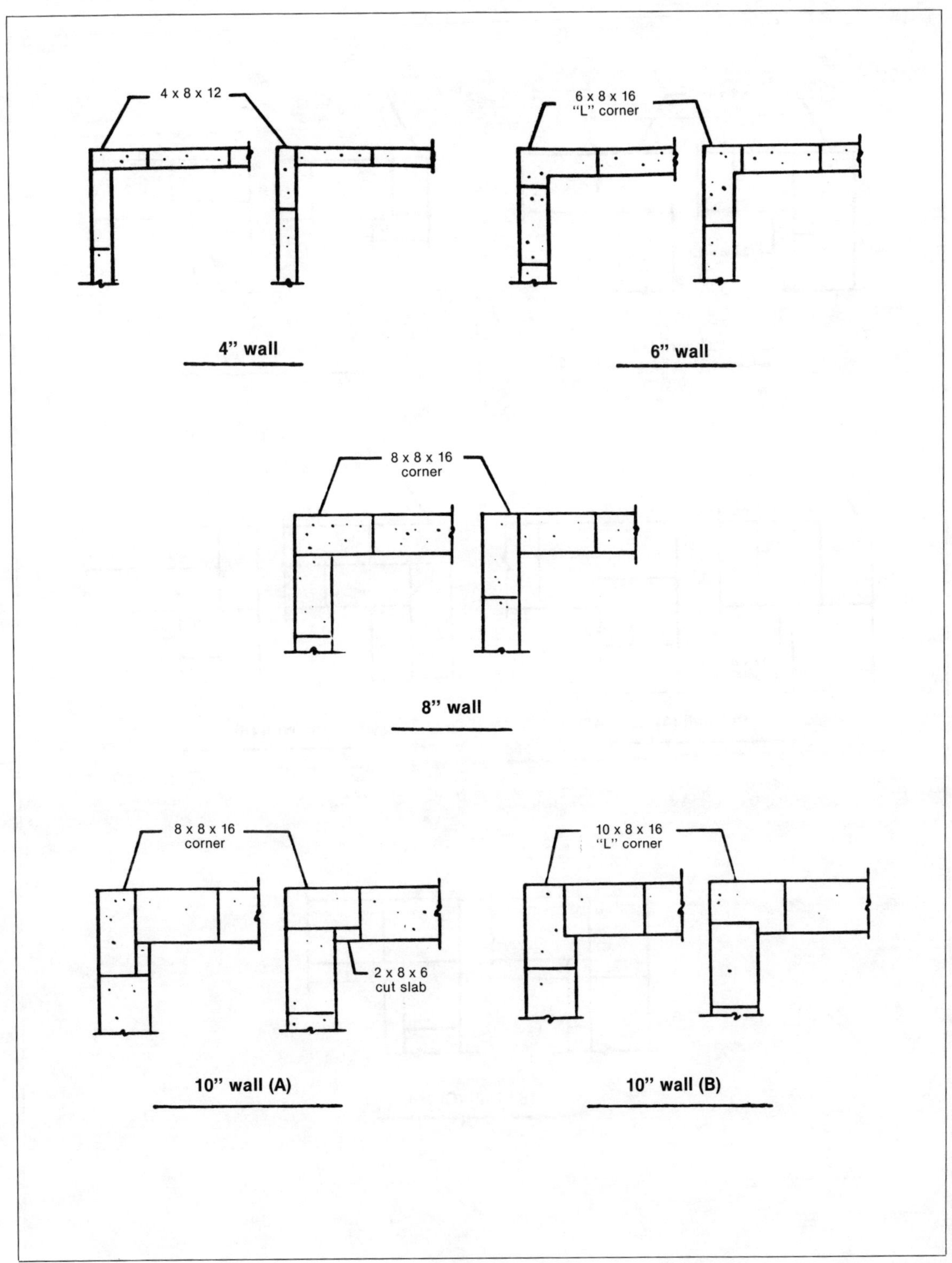

Typical corner construction for concrete masonry walls
Figure 2-4

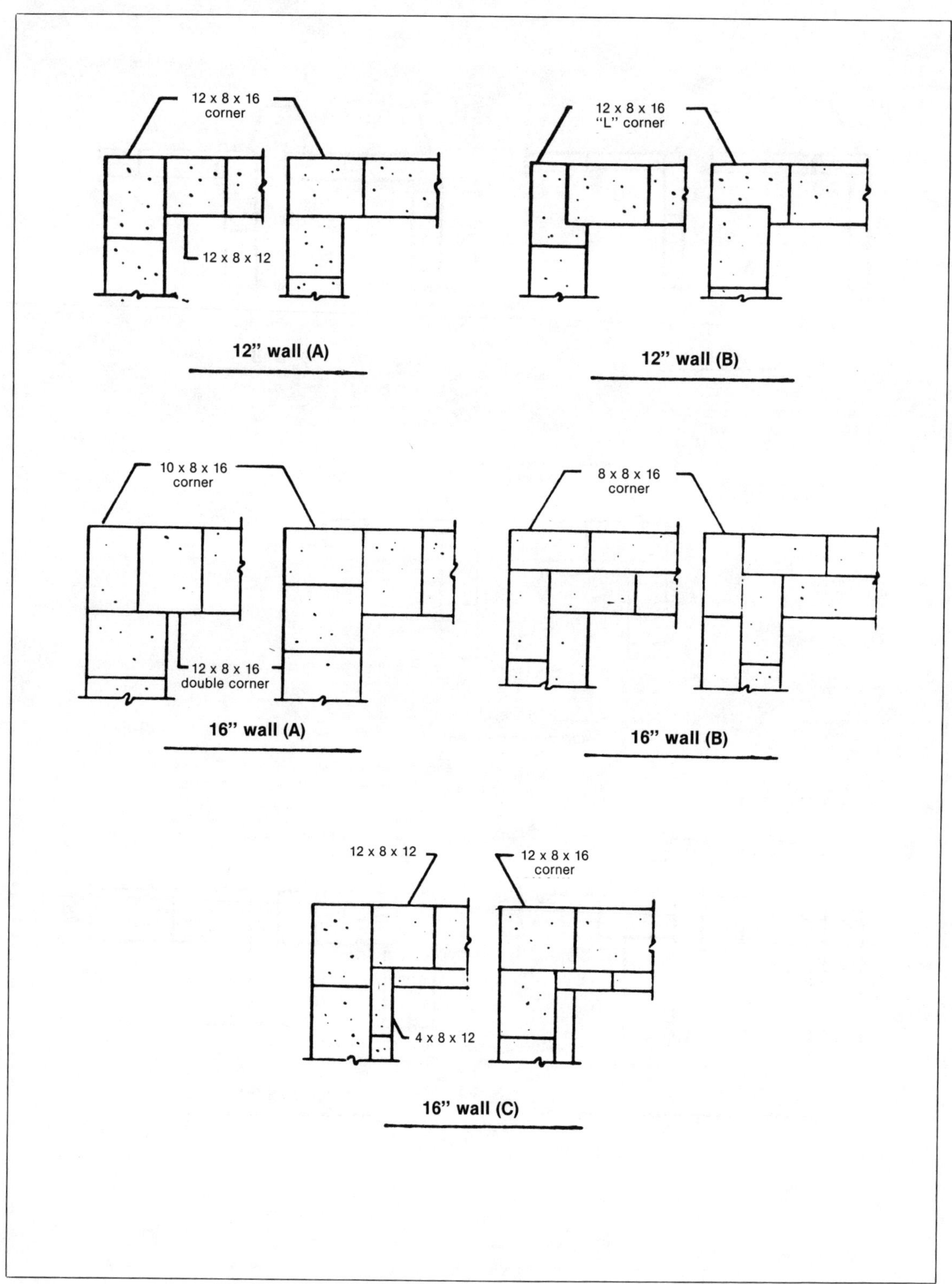

Typical corner construction for concrete masonry walls
Figure 2-4 (continued)

A Sample Take-Off

Figures 2-5 through 2-7 show the masonry specifications, a floor plan, and details of wall sections for a simple concrete block building. The wall sections (Figure 2-7) show the concrete block that are used and how they're built into the wall. The detail drawings in Figure 2-7 are identified as sections A, B, and C. Notice on Figure 2-6 the same letters are shown on lines that cut through the wall. Those lines show where the section views apply. Let's see how we would take off this job.

Step 1: Finding the materials needed— Look at wall section C (Figure 2-7). Note that the wall is made up of several different types of blocks:

- The bond beam unit (at the top of the wall)
- The standard 8 x 8 x 16 block
- The solid 4 x 4 x 16 filler block
- The solid 12 x 8 x 16 block
- The standard 12 x 8 x 16 block

Wall sections A and B have the same blocks as section C but include the lintel and sill block that are needed at doors and windows. These three sections show the types of blocks you'll have to record on the take-off sheet. First record the column headings for the five types of block shown in section C, Figure 2-7.

Bond Beam	8x8x16 CB	4x4x16 Solid CB	12x8x16 Solid CB	12x8x16 CB	

We'll also need the lintel and sill blocks shown in sections A and B, but let's start with the most common block.

Step 2: Determining the height— We'll begin by calculating the wall area for each of the five types of block listed above. To find the area, we need to know the height and length for each type of block shown in section C, Figure 2-7.

- The height of the bond beam unit is 0'8''.

- The height of the standard 8 x 8 x 16 CB blocks is 10'8''. (To find that, subtract 0'8'' from 11'4''.)

- The height of the solid 4 x 4 x 16 filler block is 0'4''.

- The height of the solid 12 x 8 x 16 block is 0'8''.

- The height of the standard 12 x 8 x 16 blocks is 2'8''. (Subtract 0'8'' from 3'4''.)

List these heights on your take-off sheet:

Bond Beam	8x8x16 CB	4x4x16 Solid CB	12x8x16 Solid CB	12x8x16 CB	
0⁸	10⁸	0⁴	0⁸	2⁸	

MASONRY QUANTITY SURVEYS
123 Beech Drive
Cincinnati, OH 45123

DATE

SHEET ___ OF ___

EST. BY *RVK*

BID DUE

BLDG. ____________________________ OWNER ____________________________

LOCATION ____________________________ ARCHITECT ____________________________

PLAN NOS. ____________ DATE ____________ GEN. CONTR. ____________________________

Specification Section ____________ Date ____________ Addenda ____________

Face Brick	Size	Allowance	
Common Brick	Size	Material	
Glazed Tile	Size	Material	
Concrete Block	Size *8 x 8 x 16* / *12 x 8 x 16*	Material *LWCMU* / *HWCMU*	
Exp. Joints	Type	Material	
Control Joints	Type	Material	
Fill	Walls	Material	
Flashing	Furnished By	Material	
Caulking	Furnished By	Material	
Parging	Thickness		

Anchors	Type	Galv.	WT.	Spacing	H	V
Anchors	Type	Galv.	WT.	Spacing	H	V
Ties	Type	Galv.	WT.	Spacing	H	V
Reinforcing *(8") (12")*	Type *TRUSS*	Galv. ✓	WT. *9 GA.*	Spacing		*16* V

PC Concrete	Sills ✓	Copings	Lintels ✓	Facing
Stone	Sills	Copings	Trim	Facing

Bond Beams ____ Fill Furn. By *MASON @ TOP COURSE*

P.C. Lintels ____ *OVER DOORS AND WINDOWS*

Cleaning ____ Materials

Workmanship ____ Bond *RUNNING* Joints *3/8" CONCAVE*

Waterproofing ____ *NONE*

Special ____
4 x 4 x 16 SOLID CB HW
12 x 8 x 16 " " "

Alternates ____

Sample abstract of specifications
Figure 2-5

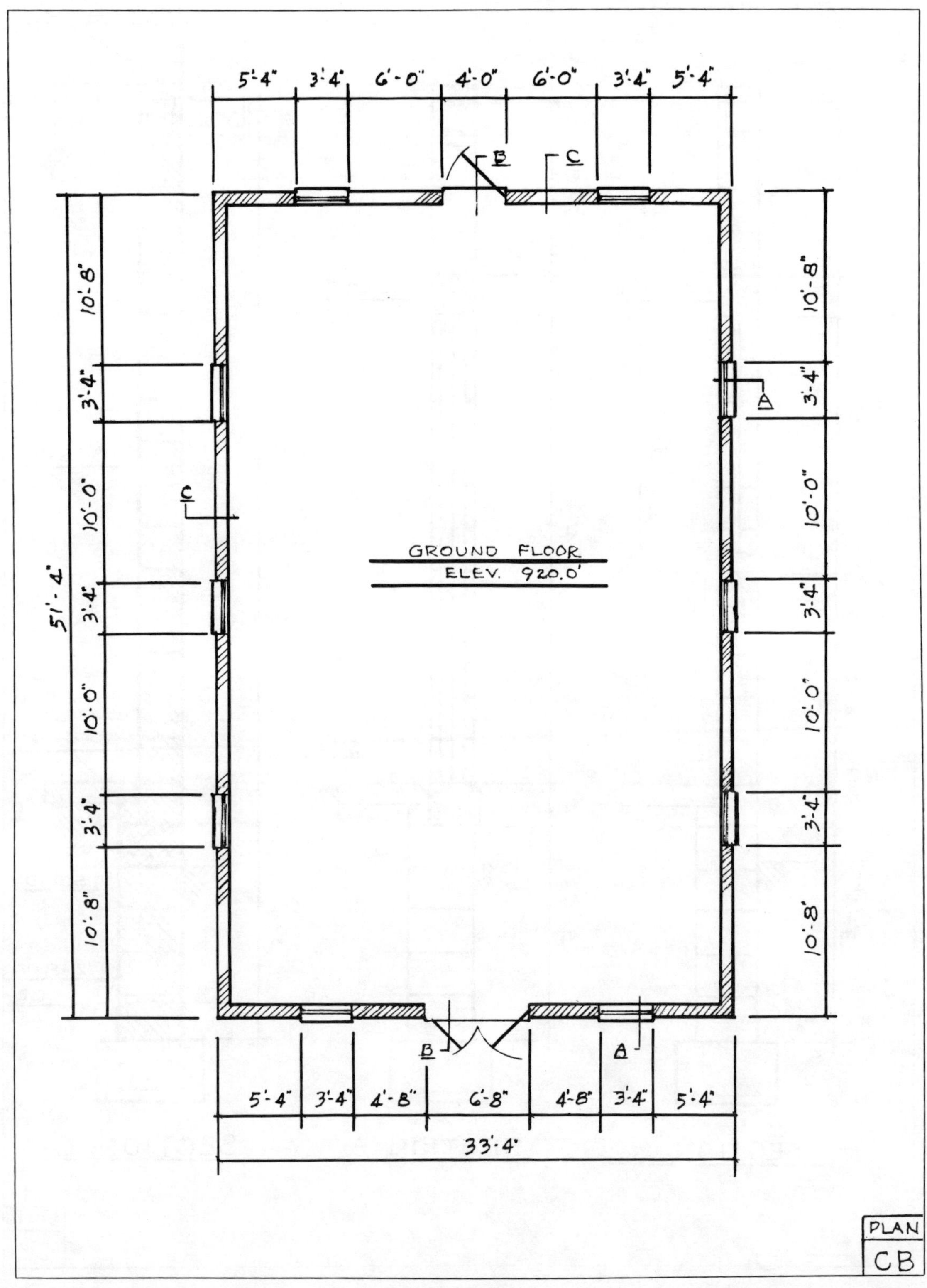

Sample floor plan
Figure 2-6

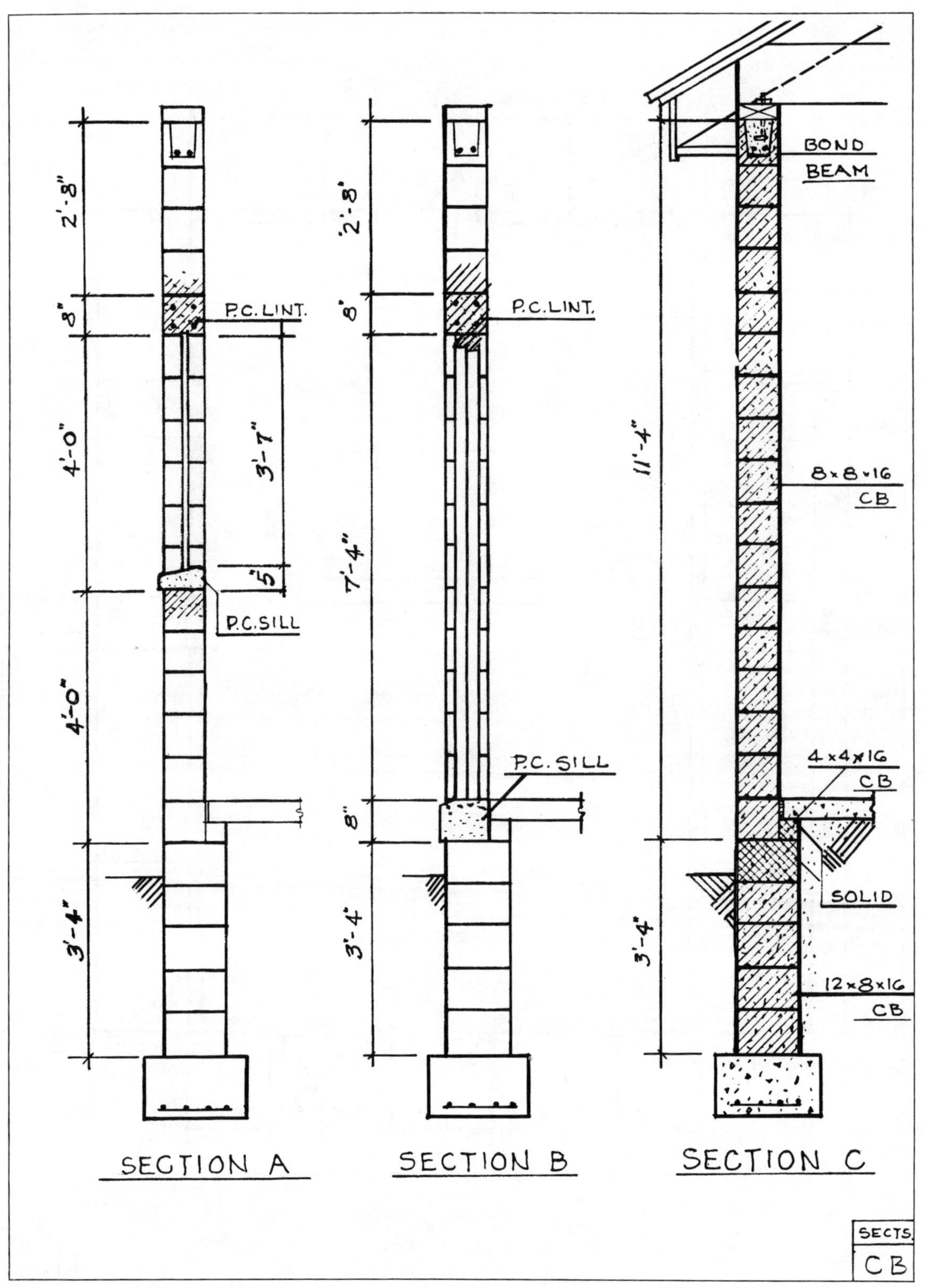

Wall section details
Figure 2-7

***Step 3: Determining the length*—** Next, find the wall lengths for each type of block. Because this is a simple plan and section C applies to the entire perimeter of the building, it's easy to find the lengths. Just add up the four wall lengths.

$$
\begin{array}{c}
33'\ 4'' \\
51'\ 4'' \\
33'\ 4'' \\
51'\ 4'' \\
\hline
168'16'' \quad \text{or} \quad 169'4''
\end{array}
$$

Add the accumulated lengths to the take-off sheet:

		BOND BEAM	8 x 8 x 16	4 x 4 x 16	12 x 8 x 16	12 x 8 x 16			
			CB	Solid CB	Solid CB	CB			
		08'	10⁸	0⁴	0⁸	0⁸			
		169±	169±	169±	169±	169±			

Notice that these figures ignore the outs for windows and doors. We'll figure the outs later and subtract them from our total.

Measuring and checking: On floor plans, the most common scales are 1/8'' equals 1'0'' or 1/4'' equals 1'0''. Details are usually drawn to a larger scale, ranging from 1/2'' equals 1'0'' to 3'' equals 1'0''.

You can use a flexible tape measure to scale the dimensions, but I don't recommend it.

For larger floor plans, it's more convenient to find wall lengths by measuring with an architect's scale. If you choose to scale off lengths on the floor plan, be sure to use the right scale. There are flat scales that show from two to four scales, or triangular scales that show eleven scales on their six edges.

I like the flat scale that's shaped like a parallelogram. It's graduated in 1/8's on one side and 1/4's on the opposite side. It's simple, so you're less likely to make a mistake. It has the scales you need most often, and it fits nicely in a briefcase. You can also use it to measure large scale details. For instance, if a detail is drawn to a scale of 1½'' equals 1'0'', each 1/8'' on the flat scale equals 1''. At a scale of 3'' equals 1'0'', each 1/4'' equals 1''.

Most plans are drawn to scale very accurately. But plans can shrink when reproduced. You'll always be working from a reproduction. If your copy has shrunk, *the plans are no longer to scale.* It's always wise to check the accuracy of the blueprint you're working on. To check plan accuracy, find some known distance on the plans. A long wall would be a good choice. Then measure the same distance with your scale. If there's a difference, the plan is no longer in scale.

A plan that's reproduced *only 2%* smaller than the original can cost you *a lot* of money if you don't notice the shrinkage. If an exterior wall is 1,000 feet long, 2% shrinkage is 20 linear feet. Multiplied by a wall height of 15 feet, your estimate would come up 300 square feet short. If your wall cost is $14 a square foot, that's a $4,200 mistake.

If you're measuring hundreds of linear feet on a plan, it's good practice to check the overall measurement with a plan measuring wheel (map measure). Many drafting supply stores sell these handy gadgets. It's easy to overlook a small section of wall or make a mistake in calculations when adding the length of many wall sections. A plan measure will help find an error because you just roll the wheel along the entire wall length. If there's a difference of more than 2% between the calculated length and the figure your plan measure shows, something's wrong.

You'll occasionally come across a drawing with the letters *N.T.S.* next to it. That means *not to scale.* Use the dimensions given on the plans for these drawings. Don't try to measure distances on a N.T.S. plan.

Step 4: Extensions— Now you're ready to start figuring areas. Multiply the height by the length and circle the product. Of course, first you'll have to convert from inches to decimal fractions of a foot. Just divide the number of inches by 12 to convert from inches to decimals, and round to three places. For example, 10'8'' times 169'4'' converts to 10.667' times 169.333'. The answer is 1806.28 square feet, which we've rounded to 1807. Your estimate should look like this:

		BOND BEAM	8 x 8 x 16 CB	4 x 4 x 16 Solid CB	12 x 8 x 16 Solid CB	12 x 8 x 16 CB				
		0⁸ / 169⁴	10⁸ / 169⁴	0⁴ / 169⁴	0⁸ / 169⁴	2⁸ / 169⁴				
		(113)	(1807)	(57)	(113)	(452)				

Step 5: Shortcuts— Although the take-off we've just done is accurate, it should be clear to you that some shortcuts are possible. You can eliminate unnecessary calculations with a few simple changes. Here's another version of the take-off we just did, using the shortcuts I recommend:

		BOND BEAM	8 x 8 x 16 CB	4 x 4 x 16 Solid CB EXTRA	12 x 8 x 16 Solid CB D.O.	12 x 8 x 16 CB				
		D.O.								
		LF / 169⁴	11⁴ / 169⁴	LF / 169⁴	LF / 169⁴	3⁴ / 169⁴				
			(1920)			(565)				

If you're uncomfortable using these shortcuts, stick to the long way, at least for a while. But whether you use them or not, you should understand them. Here's an explanation of the shortcuts shown above.

The bond beam is made up of units the same size as standard concrete block used in the wall. The difference is that the bond beams have a trough to hold concrete and steel rods. For take-off purposes, you can include this bond beam unit in the area with the standard stretcher units. It costs more to lay bond beams, so you should identify the block, even though the quantity is included with the other wall units. In the take-off, I've marked this unit "Bond Beam, D.O., LF." The D.O. stands for *difference only*. Since this unit is only one course high, you can eliminate the extension (113 in the long form) and just use the lineal feet dimension.

The 4 x 4 x 16 filler block is only one course high. You can eliminate the extension (57 in the long form) and use the lineal feet dimension only. Because this unit isn't included with other block, I've marked it *extra* instead of D.O., as under the bond beam.

You can include the 12 x 8 x 16 solid concrete block in the area with the standard units and mark it "12 x 8 x 16 Solid CB, D.O., LF." Since this occurs in only one course, I've eliminated the extension (113 in the long form) and used the lineal feet only.

Of course, you don't have to go through all the steps I've just gone through. Once you're comfortable with this method of take-off, you can go directly to Step 5. Your quantity take-off sheet will look like Figure 2-8.

As you get more estimating experience, you'll find other convenient shortcuts. But don't ever sacrifice accuracy and clarity for speed. Work carefully and make the estimate easy to understand so another estimator can check it.

Step 6: Lintels and sills— In column 9 of Figure 2-8, show the number and length of the lintels, one over each opening. Don't forget to add the extra 8" bearing to the width of the opening. In columns 10 and 11, record the precast sills.

Step 7: Outs— Now you've got the measurements and areas you need to finish the take-off. The final step is to figure the *outs* — the openings in the masonry wall — so you can deduct these areas from the total. The plan in Figure 2-6 shows two doors (4'0" and 6'8" wide) and ten windows (3'4" wide). Look at the wall sections in Figure 2-7 to find the heights. To make the deduction accurate, include the precast lintels and sills. This makes the height for the windows 4'8". The total height for the doors is 8'8".

A brief description of the outs is shown midway down in column 1. Column 2 shows the dimensions, while column 5 carries the extensions. Subtract the area of the outs, 246 square feet, from the total area of 8 x 8 x 16 concrete block. That reduces the area of block to 1,674 square feet.

Step 8: Converting to pieces— Some of the items on the take-off sheet are purchased by the piece and some by the lineal foot. To convert the area in square feet to the number of pieces needed, you'll use a conversion factor. Notice in columns 5 and 8, the factor is 1.125. In columns 6 and 7, it's 0.75. The row of numbers below the heavy lines shows the number of pieces or the number of lineal feet to order.

At the bottom of the sheet, in columns 5 and 8, there's information on the reinforcing shown in Figure 2-5. We'll go into detail on estimating reinforcing, along with other masonry accessories, in Chapter 6.

MASONRY QUANTITY SURVEYS

123 Beech Drive
Cincinnati, OH 45123

DATE
SHEET   OF
EST. BY
BID DUE

BLDG. ___________________________   OWNER ___________________________

LOCATION ___________________________   ARCHITECT ___________________________

PLAN NOS. ______________ DATE ______________   GEN. CONTR. ___________________________

①	②	③	④	⑤	⑥	⑦	⑧	⑨	⑩	⑪	⑫
			BOND BEAM D.D.	8x8x16 CB	4x4x16 Solid CB EXTRA	12x8x16 Solid CB D.D.	12x8x16 CB	8x8 P.C. LINT	8x8 P.C. SILL	5x8 P.C. SILL	
			LF	SF 11±	LF	LF	SF 3±	LF	LF	LF	
			169±	169±	169±	169±	169±				
				(1920)			(565)				
DOOR 6⁸x8⁸				① 57				① 8	① 7		
" 4⁰x8⁸				① 34				① 6	① 4		
WIND. 3⁴x4⁸				⑩ 155				⑩ 47		⑩ 34	
				246				61	11		
				1674 x1.125	170 x.75	170 x.75	565 x1.125				
			170	1884	128	128	636	61	11	34	
			✓	✓	✓	✓	✓	✓	✓	✓	
				8" REIN. x.7 1319 LF			12" REIN. x.7 446 LF				
				✓							

Complete take-off sheet
Figure 2-8

Recap and Summary

Because this is a simple job, all of the material take-off is on one sheet. If material take-off required several pages, page totals would be brought forward to a material recap sheet. In this case, all of the figures on the bottom line can be transferred directly to the summary sheet for pricing.

There's a detailed explanation of the take-off, material recap and summary for a more complicated building in Chapter 11.

Structural Clay Tile

Few masonry estimators figure very many new structural clay tile jobs. I'm not going to go into the same detail about clay tile that I did with concrete block. But there are many structurally sound, beautiful masonry buildings constructed with hollow clay tile that will have to be repaired or remodeled. You should know something about this type of construction.

Structural clay tile is one of the more durable building materials. It's a die-extruded product made from burned clays. Earlier in this century it was used as a back-up block for exterior walls, for partition walls, for furring, for fireproofing of structural steel members, as a filler in certain types of floor construction and — don't forget — chimney brick. Structural clay block had the advantage of being relatively cheap to manufacture and cheap to install because the units are much larger than brick.

Structural clay tile can't be used where there's danger of earthquakes because it doesn't provide enough resistance to horizontal movement. Even outside of seismic zones, structural clay block has been replaced by concrete block for most applications.

Structural clay tile is lightweight, fireproof, rotproof, rustproof, termite-proof, immune to decay from contact with water or chemicals and most important of all, it expands and contracts very little.

Expansion and Contraction

All building materials contract and expand as the temperature changes. The amount of contraction and expansion varies with the amount of temperature change and can be estimated fairly accurately. Figure 2-9 shows how much some common building materials change in size as the temperature changes. Notice that burned clay tile has one of the lowest coefficients of expansion of all masonry materials.

Most building materials expand with increases in moisture content and contract with water loss. Clay products expand slowly when wet, and, unlike most other materials, don't shrink when dry at atmospheric temperatures. Concrete, on the other hand, also expands with moisture, but it contracts as the moisture is lost. This shrinkage continues indefinitely, although it slows with time. Many fine clay walls have been ruined by the relative difference in the rate of expansion and contraction between clay and concrete.

Fire Resistance

Hollow clay tile resists the spread of fire. Figure 2-10 shows clay tile used as fireproofing for a structural steel beam. Clay tile was once the most popular fireproofing material. Today, it has been replaced by other materials in most construction.

Material	Average Coefficient of lineal thermal expansion, in millionths (0.000001) per degree fahrenheit	Thermal expansion, inches per 100 feet for 100°F temperature increase (to closest 1/16 inch)	
Clay Masonry			
Clay or shale brick	3.6	0.43	(7/16)
Fire clay brick or tile	2.5	0.30	(5/16)
Clay or shale tile	3.3	0.40	(3/8)
Concrete Masonry			
Dense aggregate	5.2	0.62	(5/8)
Cinder aggregate	3.1	0.37	(3/8)
Expanded-shale aggregate	4.3	0.52	(1/2)
Expanded-slag aggregate	4.6	0.55	(9/16)
Pumice or cinder aggregate	4.1	0.49	(1/2)
Stone			
Granite	4.7	0.56	(9/16)
Limestone	4.4	0.53	(1/2)
Marble	7.3	0.88	(7/8)
Concrete			
Gravel aggregate	6.0	0.72	(3/4)
Lightweight, structural	4.5	0.54	(9/16)
Metal			
Aluminum	12.8	1.54	(1 9/16)
Bronze	10.1	1.21	(1 3/16)
Stainless steel	9.6	1.15	(1 1/8)
Structural steel	6.7	0.80	(13/16)
Wood, parallel to fiber			
Fir	2.1	0.25	(1/4)
Maple	3.6	0.43	(7/16)
Oak	2.7	0.32	(5/16)
Pine	3.6	0.43	(7/16)
Wood, perpendicular to fiber			
Fir	32.0	3.84	(3 13/16)
Maple	27.0	3.24	(3 1/4)
Oak	30.0	3.60	(3 5/8)
Pine	19.0	2.28	(2 1/4)
Plaster			
Gypsum aggregate	7.6	0.91	(15/16)
Perlite aggregate	5.2	0.62	(5/8)
Vermiculite aggregate	5.9	0.71	(11/16)

Thermal movement
Figure 2-9

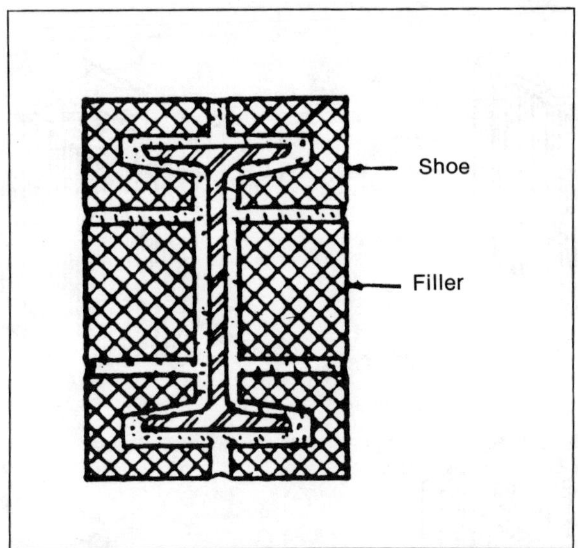

Clay tile used as beam fireproofing
Figure 2-10

Sizes

Common face dimensions for back-up tile are 5'' x 12'' and 8'' x 12''. They can be made in thicknesses of 4'', 6'', 8'' and 12''. Partition and furring tile have face dimensions of 12'' x 12'' and can be made in thicknesses of 2'' (split), 2'', 3'', 4'', 5'', 6'', 8'', 10'', and 12''. See Figure 2-11.

Dimensions

The way clay tile dimensions are listed on plans is very important. Besides giving the actual measurements, the arrangement of dimensions will tell you whether the unit will be laid on its end or side. Look at Figure 2-12.

- The first dimension is the through-the-wall thickness.

- The second dimension is either the height or the length, depending on whether the unit will be used in side construction or end construction.

- The third dimension is the cut-off length.

Here are the proper designations of a tile measuring 3¾'' thick, 7¾'' high, 12'' long:
For *side* construction: 3¾'' x 7¾'' x 12''
For *end* construction: 3¾'' x 12'' x 7¾''

Need More Information?

If you have a question on structural clay tile, the best source for information is:

Brick Institute of America
11490 Commerce Park Drive
Reston, VA 22091

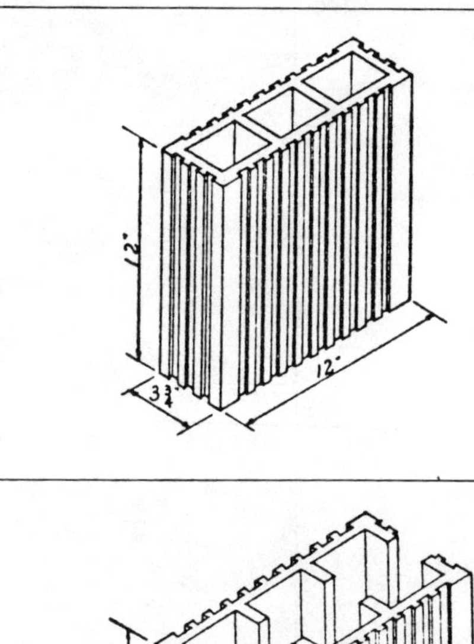

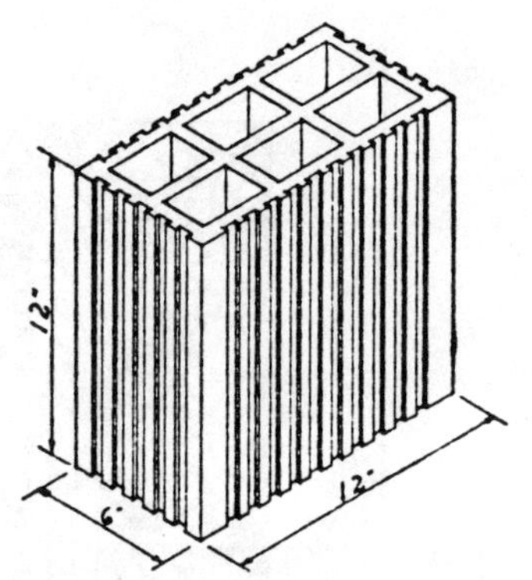

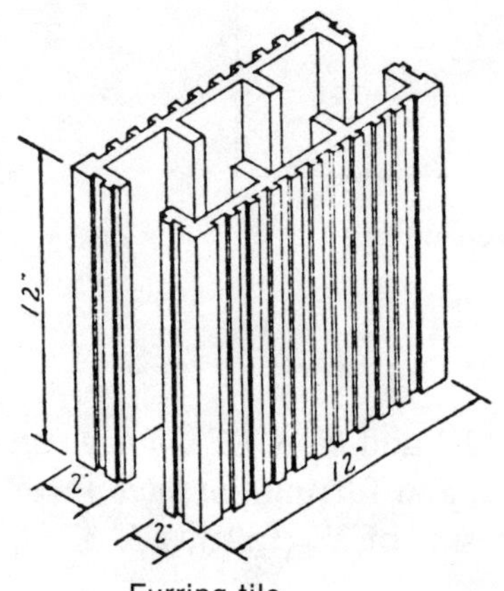

Furring tile

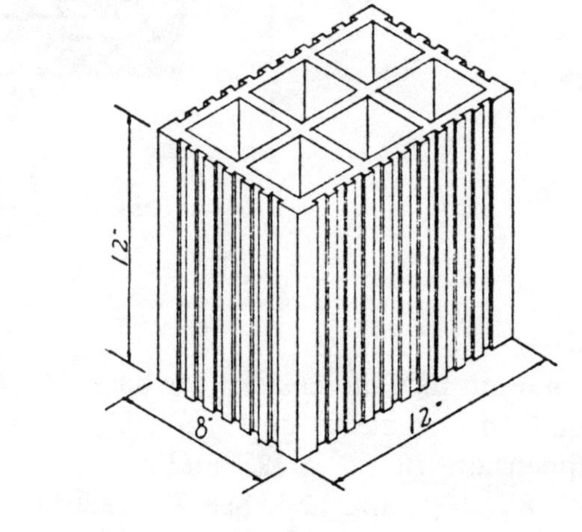

Unit size	Partition tile			Load-bearing tile	
	Horizontal or vertical cell	Number cells	Weight (lbs.)	Number cells	Weight (lbs.)
2 x 12 x 12	VC	3	15	--	--
2 x 12 x 12 Furr.	VC	--	9	--	--
3 x 12 x 12	VC	3	15	--	--
3¾ x 12 x 12	VC	--	--	3	20
4 x 12 x 12	VC	3	16	--	--
5 x 12 x 12	VC	3	20	--	--
6 x 12 x 12	VC	3	22	6	30
8 x 12 x 12	VC	6	30	6	36
10 x 12 x 12	VC	6	35	6	42
12 x 12 x 12	VC	6	40	6	48

Finish available:
1. Scored four sides for plaster.
2. Smooth one side and one end. S1S1E.
3. Smooth four sides. S4S.

Sizes of hollow clay tile
Figure 2-11

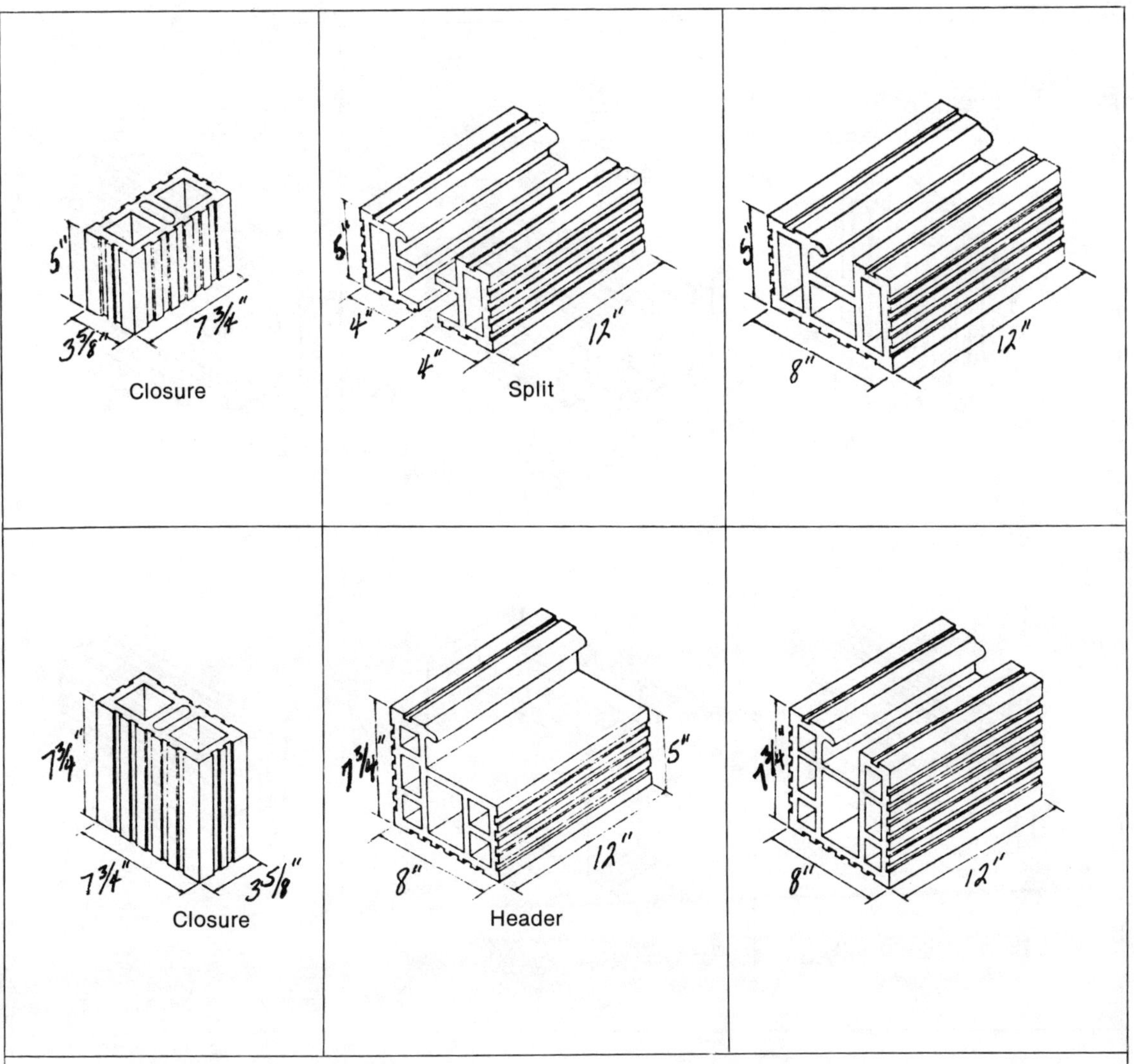

Speed tile			
Unit size	Horizontal or vertical cell	Number cells	Weight (lbs.)
8 x 5 x 12	HC	3	16
8 x 7¾ x 12	HC	7	24
8 x 7¾ x 12 Hdr.	HC	6	20
3 ⅝ x 5 x 7¾	VC	3	6
3 ⅝ x 7¾ x 7¾	VC	3	8

Speed tile furnished scored for plaster both sides; or smooth one side, scored one side; or smooth both sides.

Courtesy: Merry Companies

Sizes of hollow clay tile
Figure 2-11 (continued)

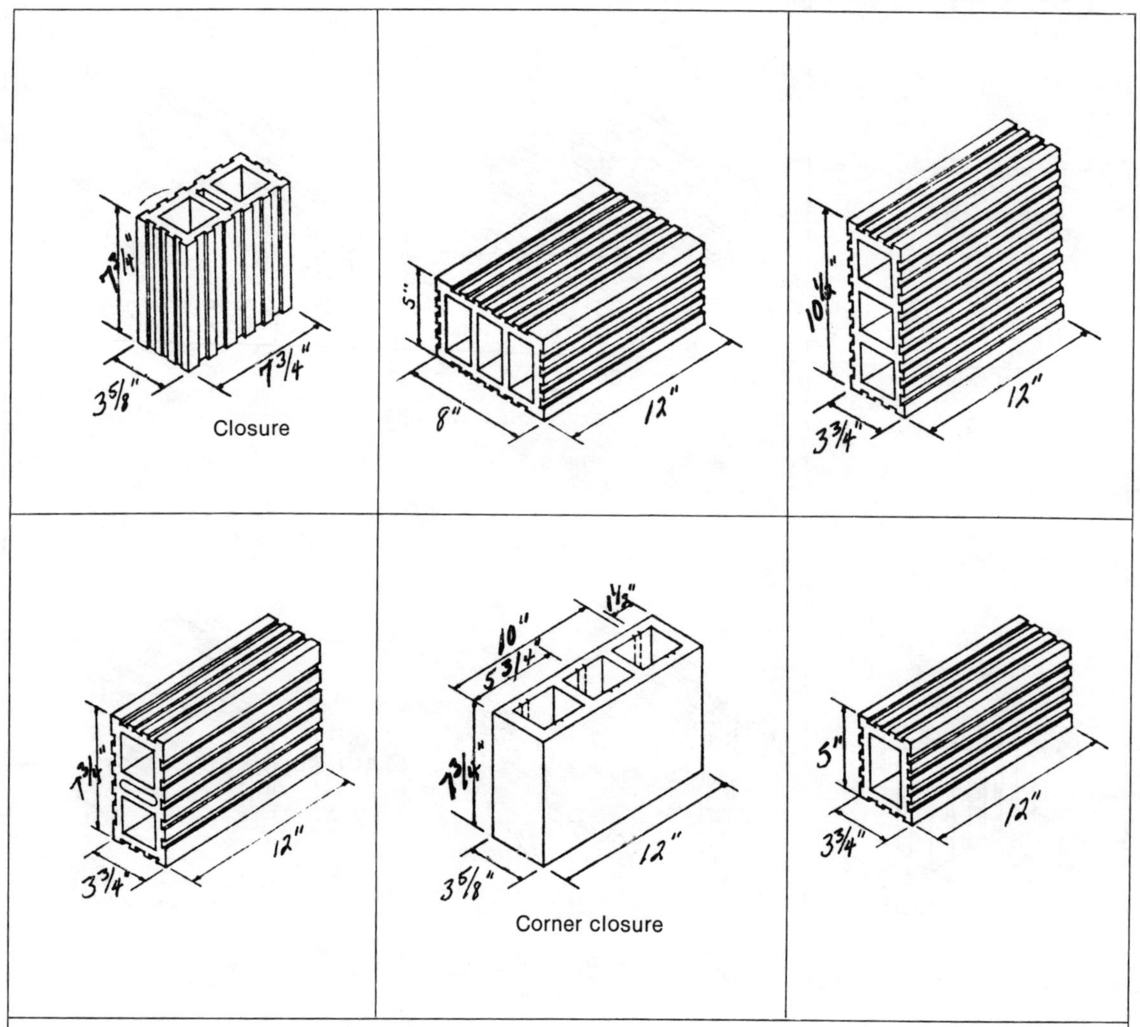

Cavity Wall Back-up Tile

Unit size	Construction	Number cells	Weight (lbs.)
3¾ x 7¾ x 12	HC	3	12
3¾ x 5 x 12	HC	1	9
8 x 5 x 12	HC	3	16
3¾ x 10½ x 12	HC	3	18
3⅝ x 7¾ x 12	VC	3	13.5
3⅝ x 7¾ x 7¾	VC	3	8

All of the above back-up units, except 10½" tile, furnished smooth one or two sides, or scored two sides.

Sizes of hollow clay tile
Figure 2-11 (continued)

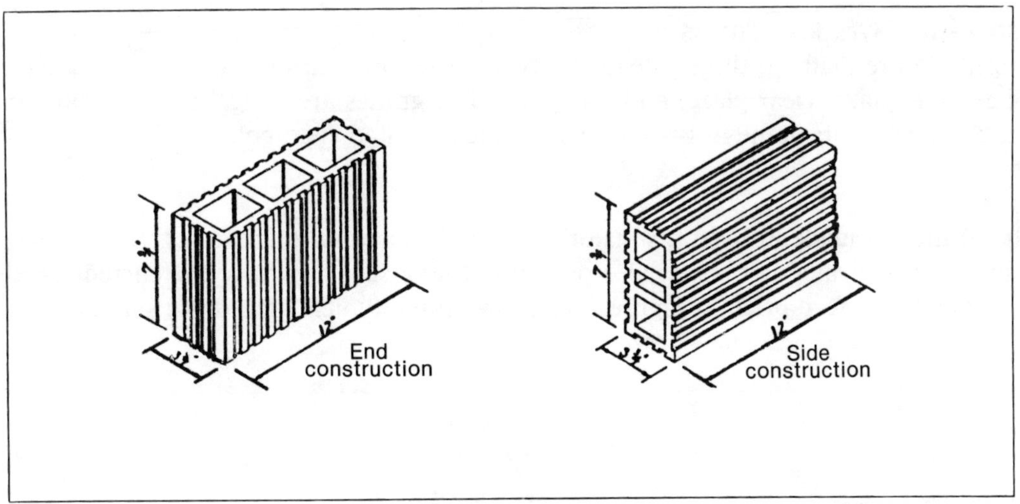

Courtesy: Merry Companies

Dimensions denote use of clay tile
Figure 2-12

Estimating

As I said at the beginning of this section, I'm not going to explain how to do a detailed estimate of clay tile work. You'll probably never need to estimate a new clay tile building. Anyhow, the procedure is nearly the same as estimating concrete block.

But you may be asked to estimate clay tile repair or remodeling work. When that happens, your first problem will be to find replacement materials. Clay tile is still made, but only on special order and only in limited quantities. Many brick manufacturers make panel brick (8 x 8 or 12 x 12) that can be substituted where only small quantities are needed.

If clay tile is available and if you decide to use it on the job, the first step will be to make a good quantity survey. Because this is repair or remodeling work, you'll have to go directly to the job site. Don't expect the architect to put all the details on the plan. Take good measurements, make notes and sketches that describe the conditions, dimensions, access to work, scaffolding needed, and anything else that's relevant. Quantities of structural tile are usually measured in square feet and converted to pieces for pricing.

Structural Glazed Tile

Structural glazed tile is still used occasionally in commercial buildings. It's made from de-aired clay that has been molded into the desired shape. The tile is sprayed with a glazing mixture on one face, two faces, or one face and one end, depending on the intended use. The spray is a mixture of metallic oxides, chemicals and ground clay. When fired in a kiln, this surface turns hard and glossy and will resist abrasion and wear. Glazed tile never needs painting and will remain easy to clean for years.

Categories, Grades, Colors

Glazed tile are made in three categories, two grades and various colors. The categories are ceramic glaze, clear glaze, and salt glaze. The grades are either select or standard quality. The colors come in two groups, trim colors and field colors.

Sizes

Glazed tile are made in several sizes or series and in several thicknesses. Some sizes and shapes will be available on special order only. Make sure you have the current catalog and price list before pricing. Figure 2-13 shows some typical glazed tile shapes.

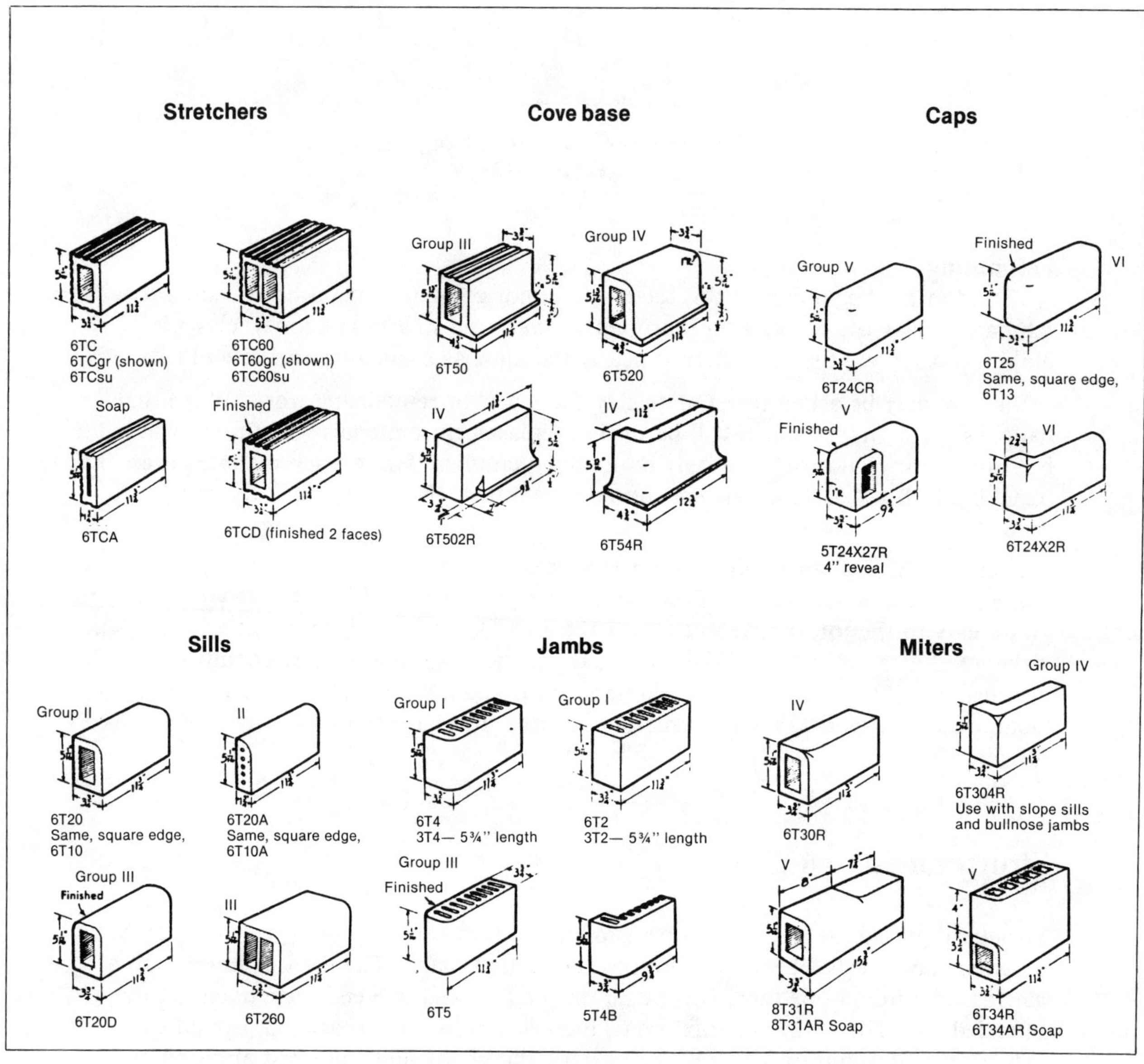

Structural glazed tile basic shapes — 6T series
Figure 2-13

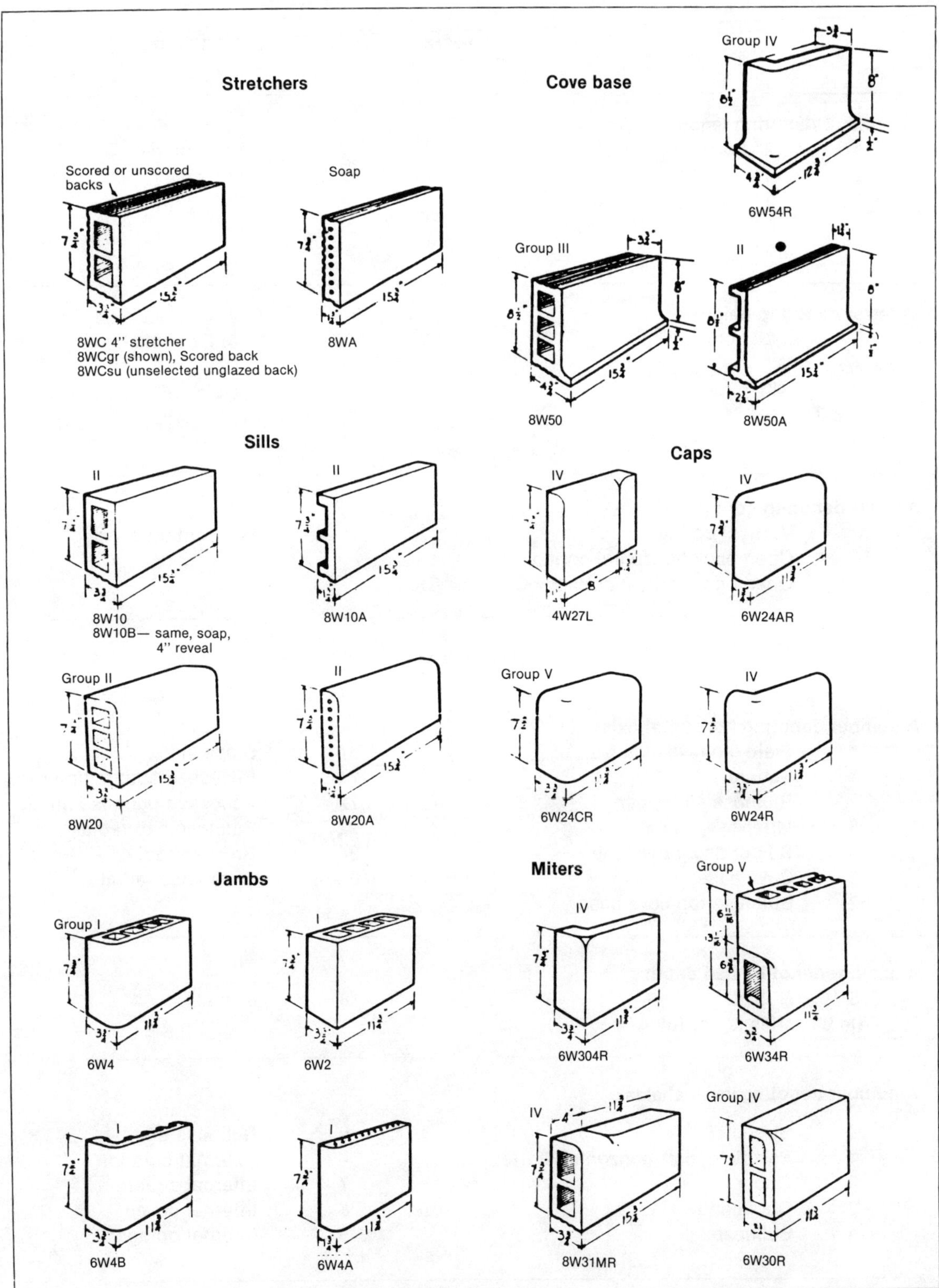

Structural glazed tile basic shapes — 8W series
Figure 2-13 (continued)

Prefix

A number denoting length

1	2" nominal		6	12" nominal
2	4"		7	14"
3	6"		8	16"
4	8"		9	18"
5	10"			

A letter denoting height

S	$2\frac{2}{3}$" nominal		N	$6\frac{2}{3}$" nominal
J	3"		W	8"
P	4"		U	$2\frac{2}{3}$"
D & T	$5\frac{1}{3}$"		Y	12"
M	6"		Z	24"

A letter denoting coring

X	Vertical coring		C	Horizontal coring
H	Open back horizontal coring			
V	Open back vertical coring			

Number

A number denoting horizontal axis

*	Field (no reveal)		7	Slope sill
1	Square sill		71	Recessed square lintel
2	Bullnose sill or cap		72	Recessed bullnose lintel
3	Miter		92	Bullnose cap radial
4	Box or decorative cap		94	Box cap radial
5	Cove base		95	Cove base radial
52	Bullnose top cove base			

A number denoting bed depth

6	6" bed		8	8" bed
(The 90 series is not full 4" bed)				

A number denoting vertical axis

0	Stretcher		5	Bullnose end
1	Part field, part horizontal starter		6	External octagon
2	Quoin		7	Internal square
3	Quoin end		8	Internal coved
4	Bullnose		9	Internal octagon

Structural glazed tile nomenclature
Figure 2-14

Suffix

A letter denoting return and reveal and sometimes bed depth

A	2" bed with no return or reveal following	6, 7, 8, 9
	2" reveal following	0
	2" return and reveal following	2, 4
B	2" bed with 4" return and no reveal following	0
	2" bed with 4" return and 2" reveal following	2, 4
C	4" bed with 4" return and 4" reveal following	2, 4
E	2" bed with 6" return and no reveal following	2, 4
F	4" bed with 6" return and no reveal following	2, 4
J	2" bed with 8" return and no reveal following	2, 4
K	4" bed with 8" return and no reveal following	2, 4

A letter or letters denoting back face

sm	Unselected glazed back	su	Unselected, unglazed back
gr	Scored or grooved back	D	Two faced

A letter denoting right or left
When required

R	Right	L	Left

Certain composite numbers are marked by use of a prefix, both numbers joined by X and a suffix.

Vertical axis numbers 6, 7, 8, 9 are always made 2" bed and the suffix A is dropped.

Vertical axis numbers 2 and 4 when used with horizontal axis numbers 1, 2, 4, 5 and 52 are regularly made 4" return, 2" reveal and 2" bed and suffix B is dropped. For 4" reveal and bed in these units use suffix C.

Starters are designed by adding 0 in front of the vertical axis number from which they start. For example 5 cove base plus 04 bullnose starter equals 504.

A right or left hand shape is the long leg extending from a corner or an opening and applies to the last vertical axis number if more than one used.

X denotes blank.

Structural glazed tile nomenclature
Figure 2-14 (continued)

Nomenclature

Glazed tile are identified by a *prefix, number,* and a *suffix.* The prefix denotes face size and coring (*6TC*). The number refers to the horizontal or vertical axis and bed depth (*4DC60*). The suffix identifies the return, reveal, back face and right- or left-handed shape (*6W24CR*). Figure 2-14 shows the prefix, number and suffix codes.

Let's take an example. Look at Figure 2-15. The glazed tile shown is called 6T504AR. In the prefix, the 6 indicates a 12'' length. The T indicates a height of 5'⅓''.

In the number, 5 indicates cove base; 0 indicates starter; 4 indicates bullnose end.

In the suffix, A indicates a 2'' return and reveal following 4, and R shows that it's a right hand unit.

Using the chart, you can identify the correct code number for any structural glazed tile.

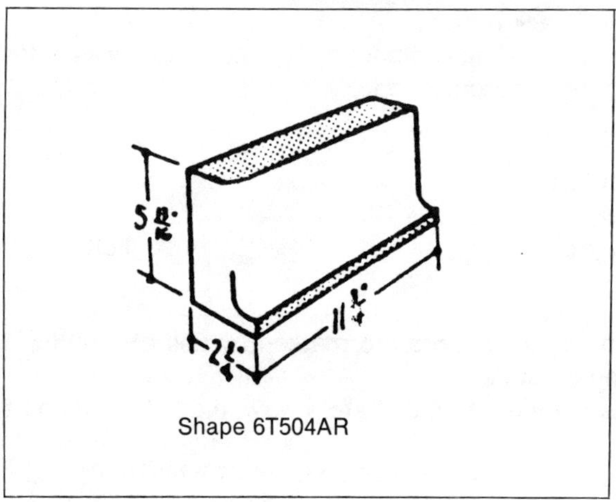

Illlustration of nomenclature
Figure 2-15

Estimating

Estimating glazed tile is a little more difficult than concrete block or structural clay tile. I'll present a simple take-off and estimate at the end of this section. In Chapter 11, there's a more detailed masonry take-off and estimate that shows how to measure and record glazed tile quantities.

The field (full size stretcher tile) is usually measured in square feet and converted to pieces. Take additional measurements at corners, angles, sills, jambs, heads, ledges, caps, and so on. These measurements are usually taken in lineal feet with an additional allowance at corners and angles. The additional allowance should cover the cost of the special shapes at these points, over and above the cost of the field tile. This add-on cost will be identified as *difference only* (D.O.) in the take-off and summary. See Figure 2-16.

Figure 2-17 shows typical details of glazed tile walls. Be sure you know what units are to be used — 8W series, 6T, whether it's stack bond or running bond, the various shapes in both series, and if units will be cut on the job. These details are usually not shown on the architect's drawings, so it's up to the masonry contractor to provide them. The cost of any special units and the extra labor should appear in your estimate.

MASONRY QUANTITY SURVEYS

123 Beech Drive
Cincinnati, OH 45123

DATE
SHEET   OF
EST. BY
BID DUE

BLDG. ___________________________   OWNER_______________________

LOCATION ________________________   ARCHITECT____________________

PLAN NOS. ___________ DATE ________   GEN. CONTR. _________________

ITEM	UNIT	QUANTITY	MATERIAL		LABOR		WORK	TOTAL
			Unit	Amount	Unit	Amount		
COVE BASE (8W50A) D.O.	*PCS.*							

D.O. cost on take-off sheet
Figure 2-16

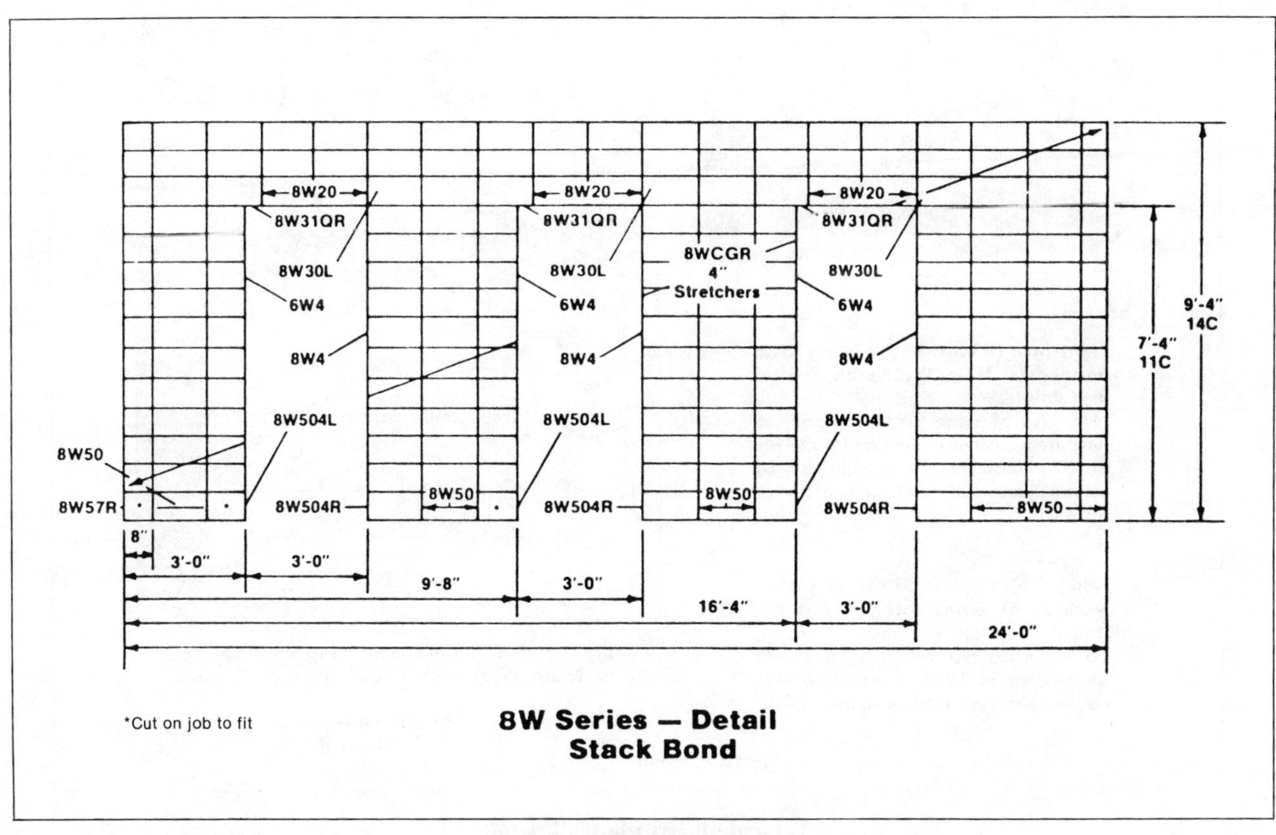

Typical glazed tile wall detail
Figure 2-17

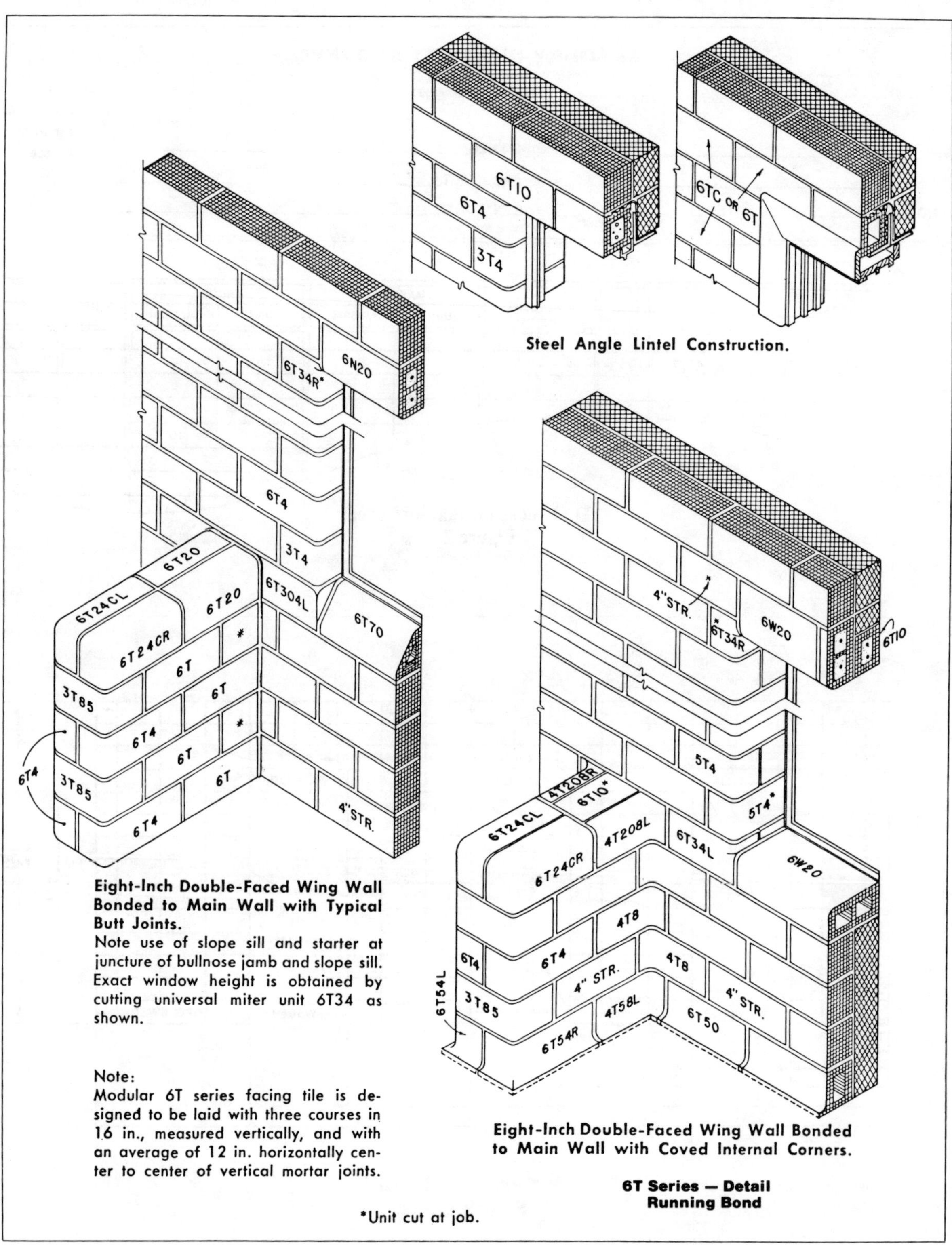

Eight-Inch Double-Faced Wing Wall Bonded to Main Wall with Typical Butt Joints.

Note use of slope sill and starter at juncture of bullnose jamb and slope sill. Exact window height is obtained by cutting universal miter unit 6T34 as shown.

Note:

Modular 6T series facing tile is designed to be laid with three courses in 16 in., measured vertically, and with an average of 12 in. horizontally center to center of vertical mortar joints.

Eight-Inch Double-Faced Wing Wall Bonded to Main Wall with Coved Internal Corners.

6T Series — Detail Running Bond

*Unit cut at job.

Typical glazed tile wall detail
Figure 2-17 (continued)

Figure 2-18 shows typical tile sizes, weights, fire ratings, U-values, mortar requirements and production rates for structural glazed tile. Figure 2-19 describes the more common units and lists physical properties.

The Sample Estimate

We'll use a simple plan (Figure 2-20) for this estimate. It shows that six walls have 2'' glazed tile and two walls have 4'' glazed tile. Conveniently, all six walls are 7'0'' long. Section X shows that the glazed tile height is 8'8''.

Let's do a take-off for the tile only. Later I'll show you how to combine the concrete block and glazed tile in a single estimate. As I describe how the estimate is made, follow along on the take-off sheet, Figure 2-21.

STRUCTURAL GLAZED TILE

Unit	Nominal size	Weight (lbs)	Fire rating	U value	Mortar CY/M	Production
6THA	2 x 5 x 12	6.0	--	--	0.34	150
6TCA	2 x 5 x 12	6.0	--	--	0.32	150
6TCgr	4 x 5 x 12	10.2	1[1]	0.40	0.47	150
6TCD	4 x 5 x 12	10.2	--	0.40	0.47	140
6TC60gr	6 x 5 x 12	16.0	1[2]	0.35	0.63	137
6TC80gr	8 x 5 x 12	26.0	2[2]	--	0.78	110
Gr. I	--	--	--	--	--	135
Gr. II	--	--	--	--	--	135
Gr. III	--	--	--	--	--	128
Gr. IV	--	--	--	--	--	120
Gr. V	--	--	--	--	--	113
Gr. VI	--	--	--	--	--	105
8WHA	2 x 8 x 16	13.6	--	--	0.41	142
8WCA	2 x 8 x 16	13.6	--	--	0.41	142
8WCgr	4 x 8 x 16	21.0	1[1]	0.40	0.59	126
8WCD	4 x 8 x 16	21.0	--	0.40	0.59	113
Gr. I	--	--	--	--	--	113
Gr. II	--	--	--	--	--	113
Gr. III	--	--	--	--	--	107
Gr. IV	--	--	--	--	--	101
Gr. V	--	--	--	--	--	95

[1] With ¾'' plaster

[2] 2 cells in wall thickness

Structural glazed tile — general information
Figure 2-18

Abbreviations

FR . . . . .Fire rating

W . . . . .Weight per square foot of wall surface

STC . . .Sound transmission class (average decibel loss of sound passing through the wall)

R . . . . .Thermal resistance (SF x HRS x F/BTU)

U . . . . . .Thermal transfer coefficient (BTU/SF x HRS x F)

M . . . . .Mass coefficient for correcting "U" value based on thermal cycling

MU . . . . .M x U

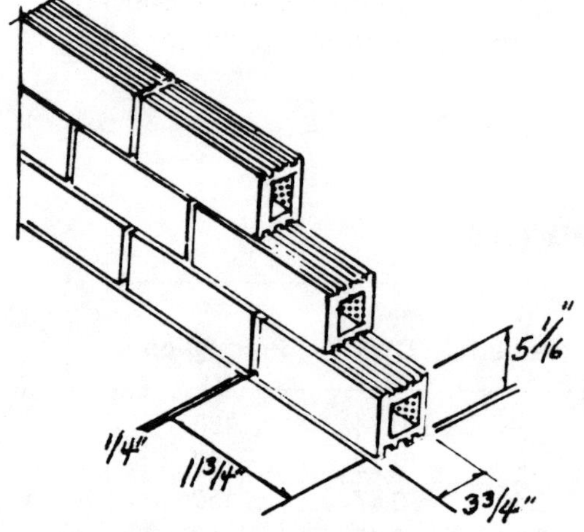

Description

2" Structural glazed tile	5⅓ x 12
4" Structural glazed tile	5⅓ x 12
6" Structural glazed tile	5⅓ x 12

Properties

	2"	4"	6"
FR			1
W	16.5	30	41
STC Paint			
STC No paint		45	47
R		2.50	2.86
U		0.40	0.35
MU		0.39	0.33

Description

2" SGT	8 x 16
4" SGT	8 x 16
6" SGT	8 x 16

Properties

	2"	4"	6"
FR			1
W	16.5	30	41
STC Paint			
STC No Paint		45	47
R		2.50	2.86
U		0.40	0.35
MU		0.39	0.33

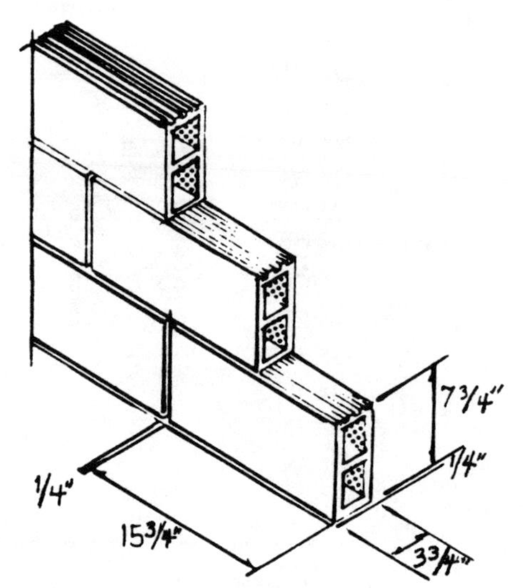

Structural glazed tile — physical properties
Figure 2-19

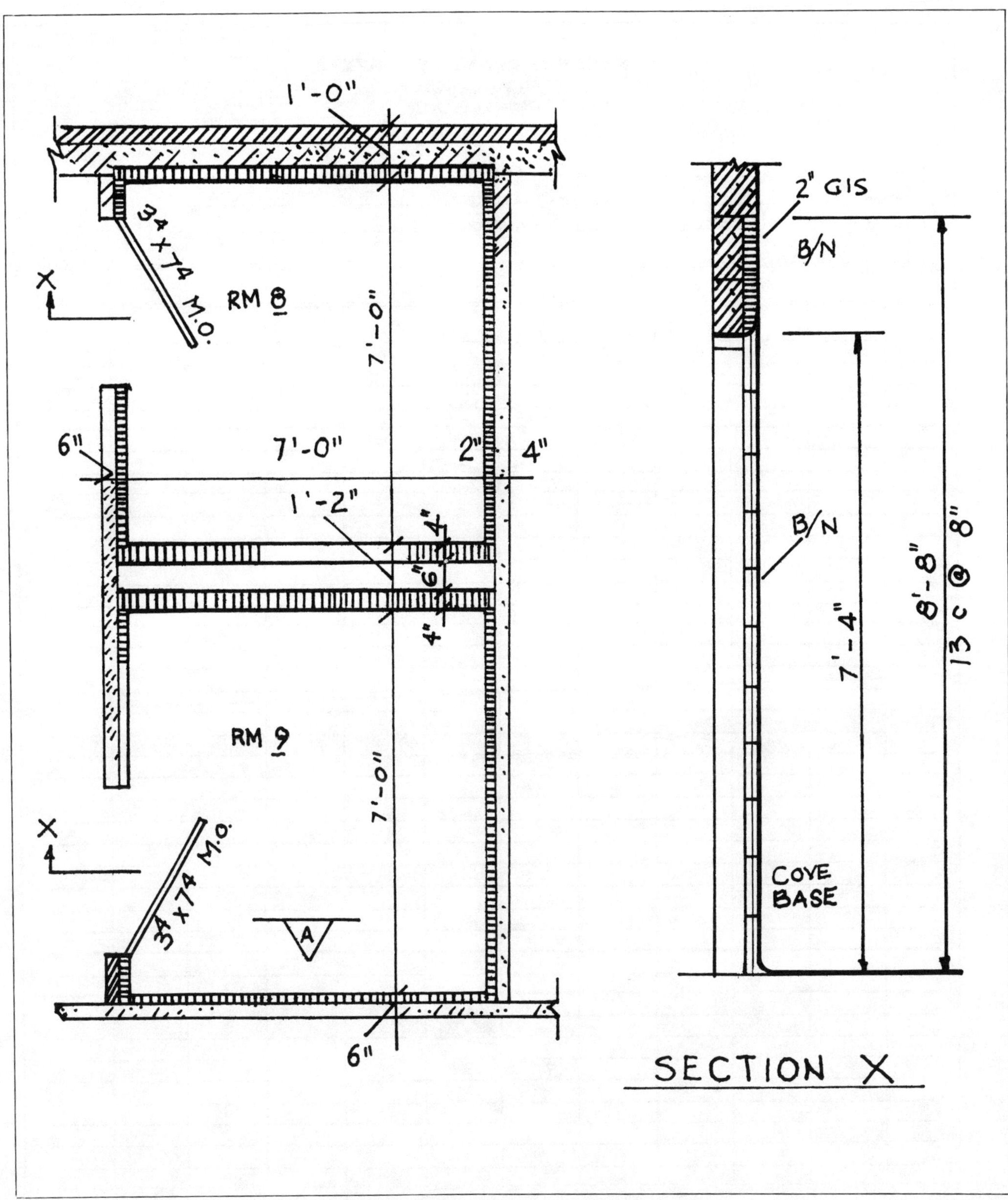

Plan showing layout of structural glazed tile
Figure 2-20

MASONRY QUANTITY SURVEYS

123 Beech Drive
Cincinnati, OH 45123

DATE

SHEET   OF

EST. BY

BID DUE

BLDG. ___________________________   OWNER ___________________________

LOCATION ___________________________   ARCHITECT ___________________________

PLAN NOS. ___________ DATE ___________   GEN. CONTR. ___________________________

				COVE BASE D.O.	2" G1S.	4" G1S.	B/N CORNS D.O.				
				LF	SF	SF	LF				
					$8\frac{8}{8}$	$8\frac{8}{8}$					
				$58\frac{8}{8}$	$44\frac{0}{}$	$14\frac{8}{8}$					
					(382)	(128)					
		DOOR	$3\frac{4}{}$ x $7\frac{4}{}$		② 48		② 48				
					.334						
				59	334	128	48				
					x 1.125	x 1.125					
					376 PCS.	144 PCS.					

Structural glazed tile take-off sheet
Figure 2-21

The accumulated length of the walls lined with 2'' G1S (glazed one side) tile is 44'0'' (6 x 7'4''). Note that we've added 4'' to each 7'0'' wall for overlap. The accumulated length of the 4'' G1S walls is 14'8'' (2 x 7'4''). Section X shows that the first course is a cove base unit. For simplicity, we'll include this special unit with the field units, and account for the extra cost of the cove base by adding another item to our take-off: cove base D.O.

Now let's make some refinements. First, deduct the outs. Use the outs dimensions to pick up the special shapes (bullnose corners) around the doors. Look back to Figure 2-13. The field pieces are called stretchers and the special shapes are grouped by how expensive they are to make. The jamb units are in group I. The cove base and head units are in group II. The base specials and miter units are in group IV.

You can avoid writing down all the special shapes by converting them all to one shape, bullnose corners. (That's *B/N corns, D.O.* on the take-off sheet.) Here's how to do it. At the end of a run of bullnose corners (in lineal feet), add one extra foot. Add 2'0'' at each jamb and 2'0'' at the head. The door measures 3'4'' x 7'4''. So the lineal feet of bullnose corners is 24'0'' (adding 9'4'', 9'4'' and 5'4'').

Here's something to keep in mind. Measuring interior glazed tile walls can be very tricky. Although the walls in the sample plan were 7'0'', we allowed 7'4'' for lap at the corners. That seems like a generous allowance.

According to the lineal coursing table in Figure 2-22, our estimate allowed 11 pieces for every two courses, or 5½ pieces per course. Now look at elevation A in Figure 2-23. You can see that we need nine whole pieces, a 6'' cut, a 10'' cut and a 12'' cut for every two corners. If the mason is skilled, he can cut a 16'' piece into a 6'' and 10'', so 11 pieces will supply the job.

Pieces	Structural glazed tile 6T	Concrete block & structural glazed tile - 8W
1	1' - 0''	1' - 4''
2	2' - 0''	2' - 8''
3	3' - 0''	4' - 0''
4	4' - 0''	5' - 4''
5	5' - 0''	6' - 8''
6	6' - 0''	8' - 0''
7	7' - 0''	9' - 4''
8	8' - 0''	10' - 8''
9	9' - 0''	12' - 0''
10	10' - 0''	13' - 4''
11	11' - 0''	14' - 8''
12	12' - 0''	16' - 0''
13	13' - 0''	17' - 4''
14	14' - 0''	18' - 8''
15	15' - 0''	20' - 0''
16	16' - 0''	21' - 4''
17	17' - 0''	22' - 8''
18	18' - 0''	24' - 0''

Lineal coursing table
Figure 2-22

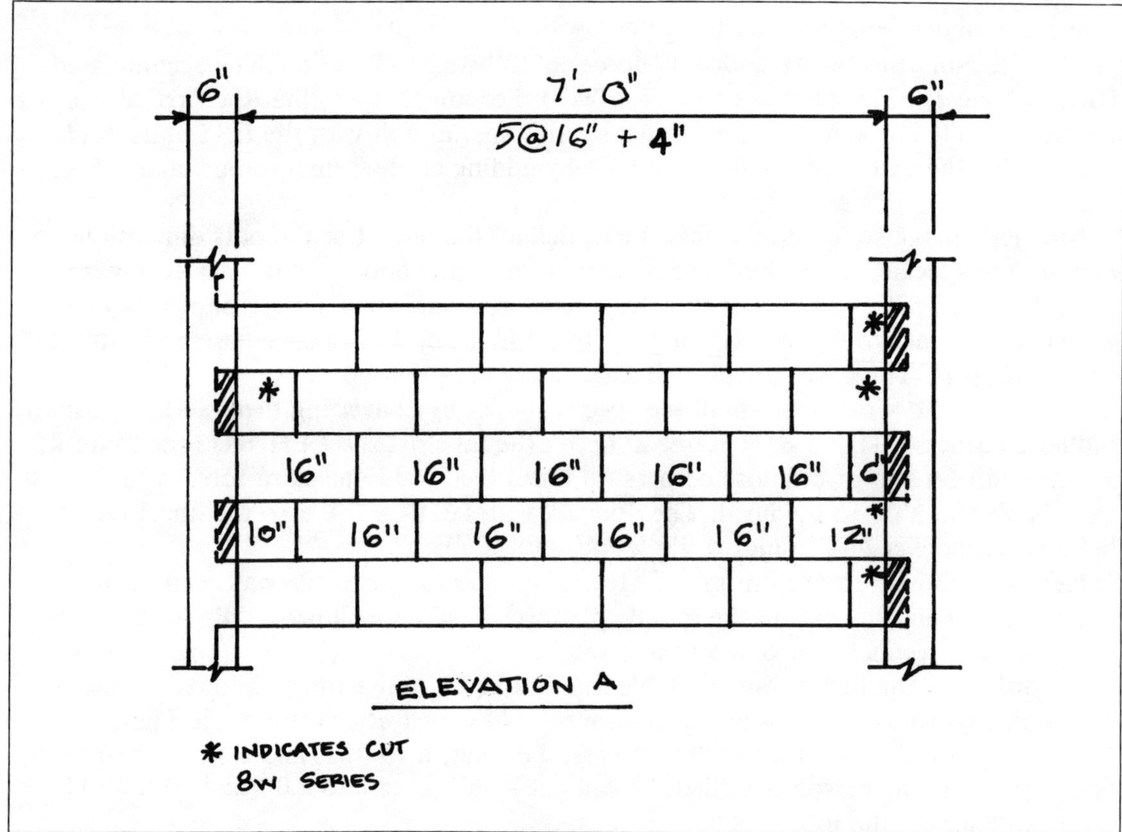

Elevation A
Figure 2-23

But if even one piece is broken, it could cause an expensive delay. Worse still, the color of the replacement block may not match the rest of the job. Figure 2-24 shows the measurement allowance to use for scaling structural glazed tile. It includes a safety allowance to cover those broken tiles.

If your estimate wins the job, make a detailed drawing of the glazed tile and count every piece. An accurate count can save many dollars.

Glazed Concrete Masonry Units

Spectra-Glaze is a popular concrete masonry unit made with a 1/8'' glazed facing. Spectra-Glaze is the registered trademark of The Burns & Russell Company. It's available in several textures and a wide range of colors. The glaze is applied after the block have been manufactured. The product is sold throughout the United States and Canada. Your local distributor can provide more information about this product. Figure 2-25 shows some of its physical properties.

	Scaled dimension	Lap at corners	Total dimension	Use
6T series				
	6' - 9"	4"	7' - 1"	8' - 0"
	7' - 0"	4"	7' - 4"	8' - 0"
	8' - 7"	4"	8' - 11"	9' - 0"
	9' - 2"	4"	9' - 6"	10' - 0"
8W series				
	6' - 9"	4"	7' - 1"	8' - 0"
	7' - 0"	4"	7' - 4"	8' - 0"
	8' - 7"	4"	8' - 11"	9' - 4"
	9' - 2"	4"	9' - 6"	10' - 8"

Sample showing measurement allowance when scaling structural glazed tile
Figure 2-24

Abbreviations

FR . . . . .Fire rating

W . . . . .Weight per square foot of wall surface

STC . . .Sound transmission class (average decibel loss of sound passing through the wall)

R . . . . .Thermal resistance (SF x HRS x F/BTU)

U . . . . . .Thermal transfer coefficient (BTU/SF x HRS x F)

M . . . . .Mass coefficient for correcting "U" value based on thermal cycling

MU . . . . .M x U

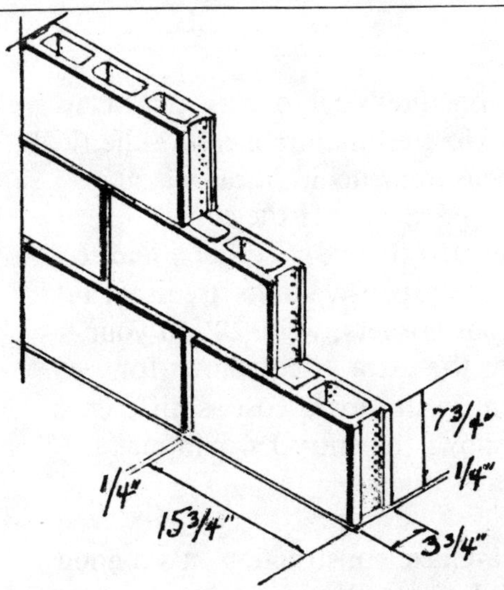

Description
4" Glazed concrete masonry units . . . . .8 x 16
8" Glazed concrete masonry units . . . . .8 x 16

Properties	4"	8"
FR	1	4 (with 75% solids)
W	37	53
STC Paint	44	59
STC No Paint	45	52
R	1.57	2.13
U	0.64	0.47
MU	0.61	0.44

Glazed concrete masonry units — physical properties
Figure 2-25

Size
Spectra-Glaze has the same (nominal) face dimensions as concrete block, namely 8'' x 16'', 8'' x 8'' and 4'' x 16''. They're made in thicknesses of 1'', 2'', 4'', 6'', 8'', 10'' and 12''.

Nomenclature
Special blocks are made for cove base and bullnose or square corners, much the same as structural glazed tile. Note Figure 2-26.

Here's how to read the identification numbers for Spectra-Glaze units:

1)   The first number is the thickness of the block.

2)   The second number is the height if it's less than the standard 8''.

3)   The letter or letters following the numbers mean:

> S - Stretcher
> C - Cap or sill
> O - Bullnose (1'' radius corners)
> G - Cove base
> CC - Wing wall cap
> J - Jamb
> P - Square corners
> T - Double face
> X - 13'' face
> U - Lintel block
> M - Miter
> R - Right
> L - Left
> V - Vertical

Estimating
Estimating Spectra-Glaze is a little more difficult than concrete block or structural clay tile. But the process is similar to estimating glazed tile. Most estimators measure the field in square feet and convert to pieces. Take additional measurements in lineal feet at corners, angles, sills, jambs, heads, coves, caps, and so on. Scale off the actual dimension from the plan, add together the individual lengths (between corners) and to this total add 1 foot for each corner, or 2 feet where more expensive units are used. For example, if the accumulated total is 24' and there are four corners, write 28' on your take-off sheet. You won't need 28 linear feet of tile, but the extra 4 feet allows for the higher cost of special shapes needed at corners. Identify this extra cost as difference only (D.O.) in the take-off and summary. Figure 2-27 shows the entry I would make.

Detail Drawings
Because of the many special shapes required for Spectra-Glaze construction, it's a good idea to prepare detailed drawings that show every block before ordering materials.

STANDARD SHAPES SERIES

Unit details shown are representative. Consult your nearest Manufacturer for precise sizes, shapes, and block configurations available.

Units supplied will be 2 or 3 core, open or closed end, depending upon local block manufacturing practices.

Double-glazed units provide the economy of two-face walls in a single operation, where precise bed-depth tolerances are not mandatory. For double-glazed units, bed-depth tolerances conform to ASTM C-90.

Cove Base

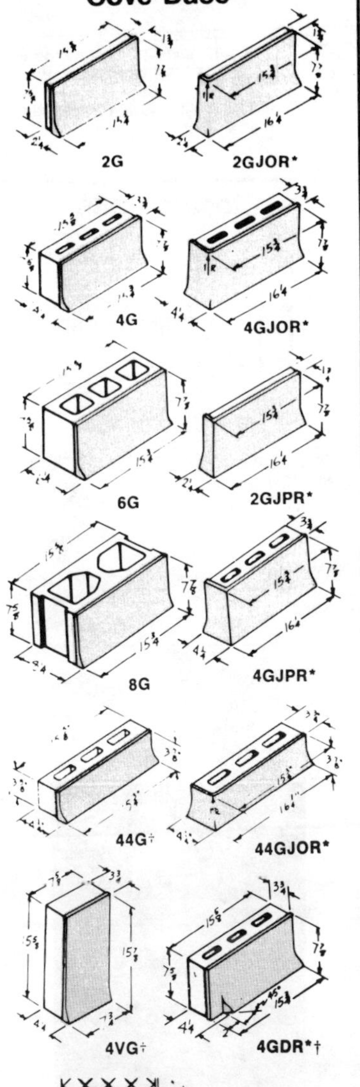

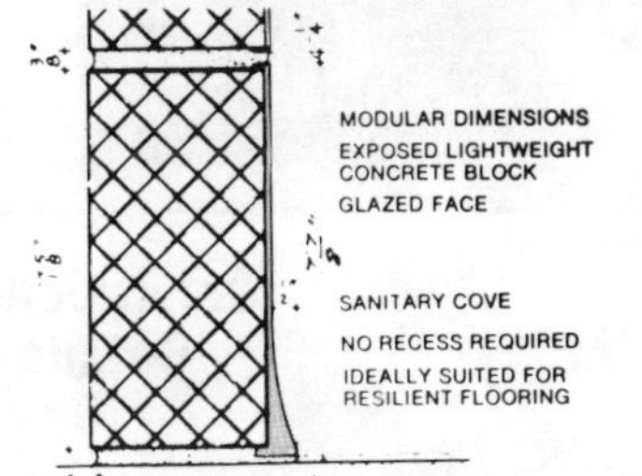

The Cove Base provides a modularly dimensioned sanitary base unit installed without a floor recess. Meets OSHA requirements.

Jamb

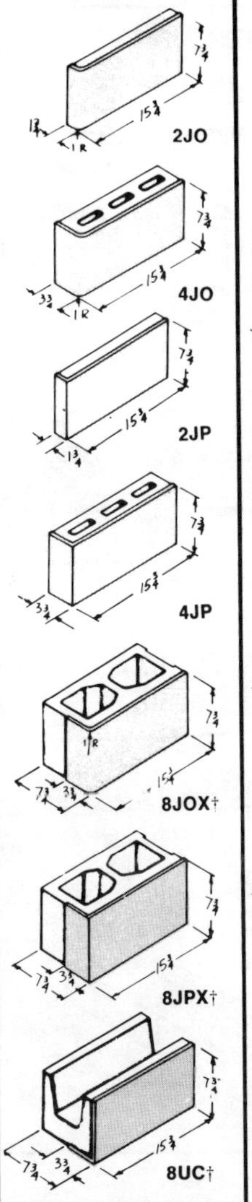

Field

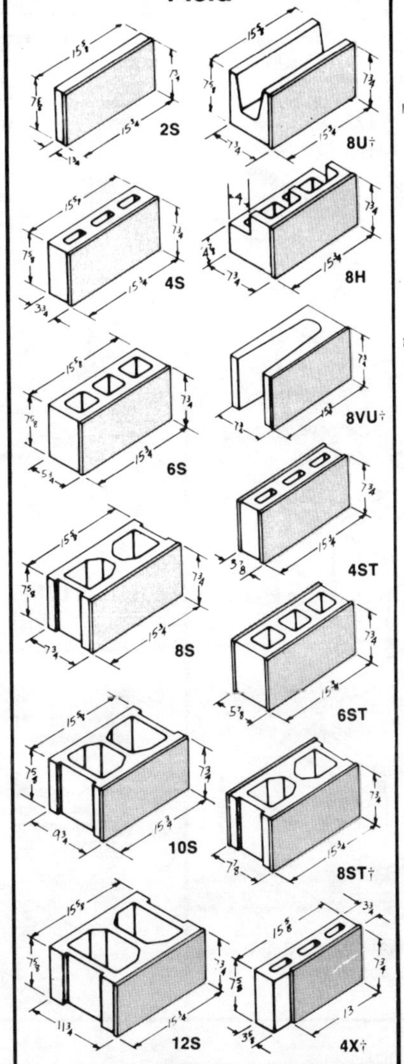

Cap

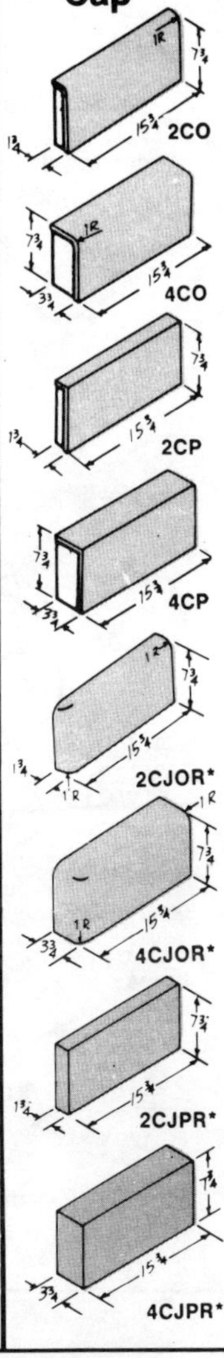

Straight Base

(4" high, glazed 2 sides)

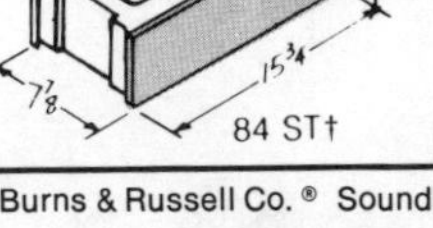

*Specify right or left (right shown).
†Also in other standard thicknesses.

Spectra-Glaze®/ Soundblox®

Pre-faced Acoustical Unit

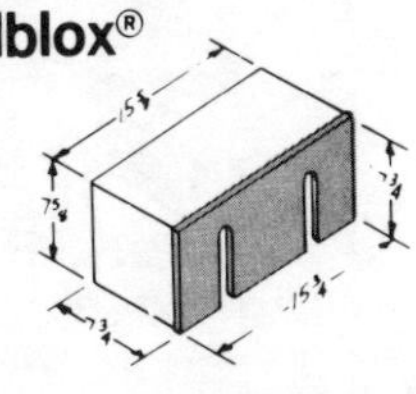

® Spectra-Glaze trademark exclusive property of the Burns & Russell Co. ® Soundbox trademark licensed in US exclusively by Proudfoot Co., Inc.

Courtesy: The Burns & Russell Co.

Standard shapes of glazed concrete masonry units
Figure 2-26

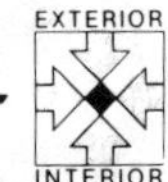

New SPECTRA-GLAZE/TRYM-SAVER™ Units

The SPECTRA-GLAZE/TRYM-SAVER™ System uses a unique, integrally bonded corrosion resistant wire mesh which acts as a permanent fastener to securely lock the unit into the wall structure. The mesh extends beyond the back of the molded unit and is easily pushed into the mortar bed. It also provides for easy application of mortar to the back of the unit. This integrally bonded mesh allows for the standard ¼" mortar joint.

Construction Details

for Standard Shapes Series (See other side)

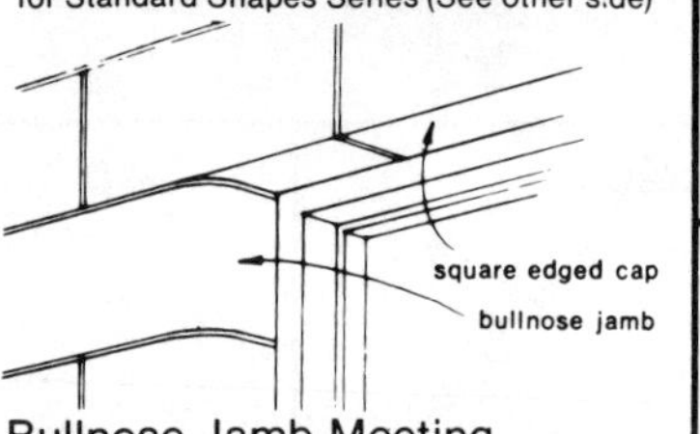

Bullnose Jamb Meeting Square edged Head or Sill

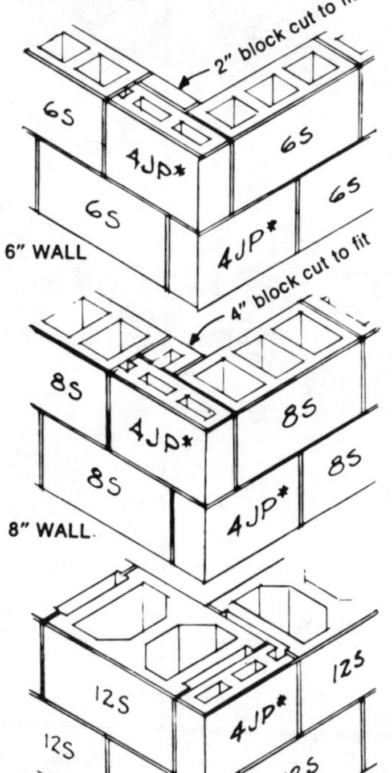

Typical External Corners

(4JO units may be substituted if bullnose corners are desired)

Corner Units

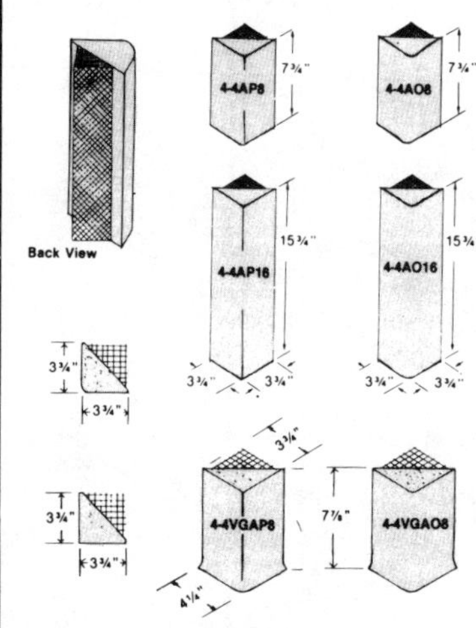

Head, Jamb & Sill Detail

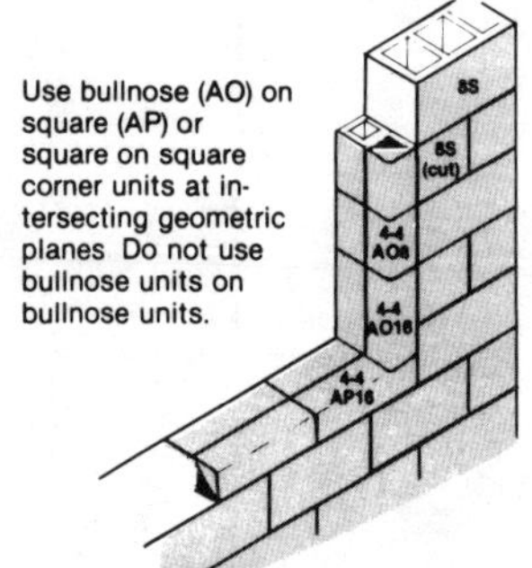
Use bullnose (AO) on square (AP) or square on square corner units at intersecting geometric planes. Do not use bullnose units on bullnose units.

Closure Units

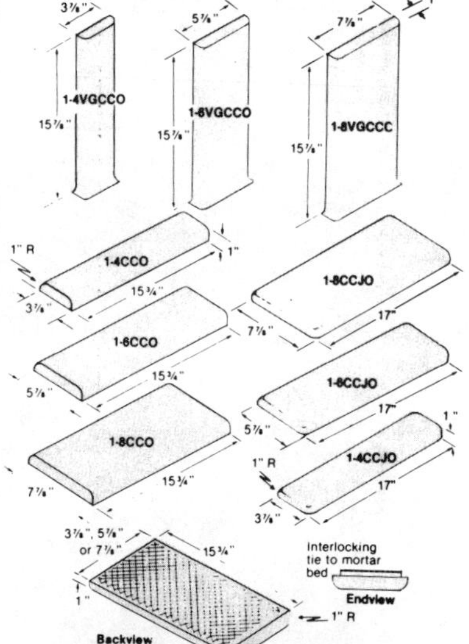

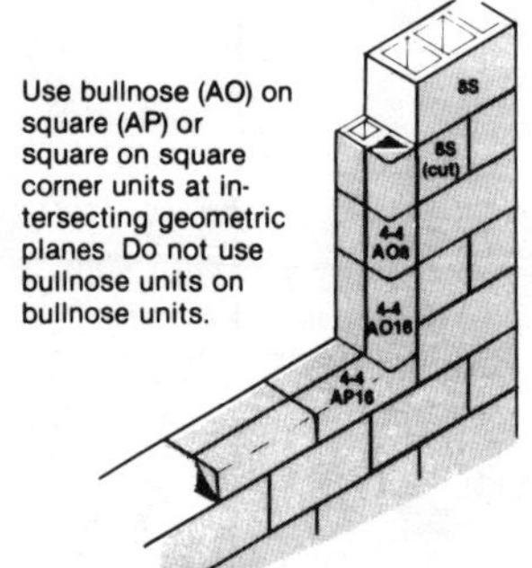

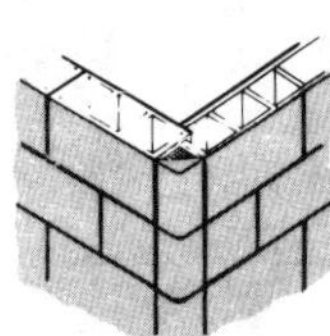

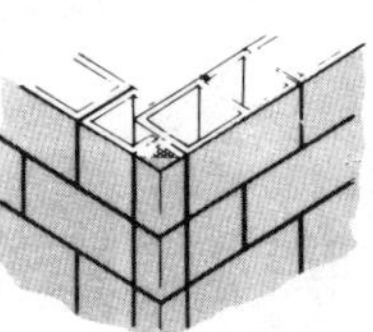

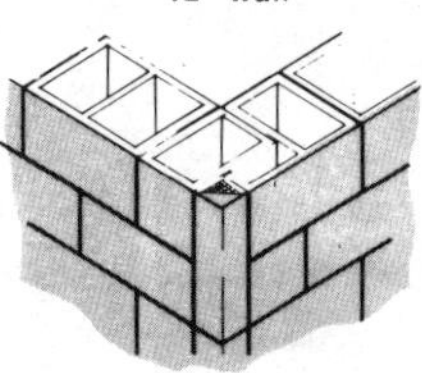

Construction Details

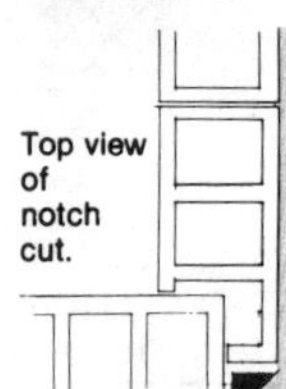

® Reg. US Pat. Off. Canada and foreign countries by The Burns & Russell Co.

Courtesy: The Burns & Russell Co.

**Standard shapes of glazed concrete masonry units
Figure 2-26 (continued)**

MASONRY QUANTITY SURVEYS

123 Beech Drive
Cincinnati, OH 45123

DATE

SHEET   OF

EST. BY

BID DUE

BLDG. ________________________________   OWNER________________________________

LOCATION ______________________________   ARCHITECT______________________________

PLAN NOS. ______________DATE ____________   GEN. CONTR. ____________________________

ITEM	UNIT	QUANTITY	MATERIAL		LABOR		WORK	TOTAL
			Unit	Amount	Unit	Amount		
BN CAP 4X8X16 GCMU D.O.	PCS.							

Additional cost identified as "D.O."
Figure 2-27

Glass Block

Glass block is usually made from clear, colorless glass. The units are hollow and air pressure in the cavity is usually somewhat below normal air pressures. Three sizes are popular: 6" x 6", 8" x 8" and 12" x 12". All are approximately 4" thick. Faces are smooth but slightly uneven, or ribbed in one or two directions.

Advantages of Glass Block

Architects like glass block for several reasons. First, they admit natural light like a window, but exclude sound better. They also provide more insulation than a window. The partial vacuum in each block increases the wall's insulating value. The U-value is usually about 0.55. Sound transmission loss will be about 37 decibels. Glass block walls resist wind, collision, fire, and vandals. They are air-tight, dust-proof and condensation-free. Maintenance is minimal. An occasional water rinse is all that's needed unless there's unusual exposure.

Before estimating a glass block wall, get the manufacturer's catalog and current price list. Most manufacturers will also provide a brochure with installation details and other technical information. Figure 2-28 shows descriptions and physical properties of glass block.

Panels

Generally glass block panels will be no more than 25 feet long or 20 feet high and won't exceed 144 square feet unless extra bracing is used. With extra bracing, the limit is extended to 250 square feet.

Abbreviations

FR . . . . Fire rating

W . . . . Weight per square foot of wall surface

STC . . . Sound transmission class (average decibel loss of sound passing through the wall)

R . . . . Thermal resistance (SF x HRS x F/BTU)

U . . . . . . Thermal transfer coefficient (BTU/SF x HRS x F)

M . . . . Mass coefficient for correcting "U" value based on thermal cycling

MU . . . . M x U

Description

Glass block	6 x 6
Glass block	8 x 8
Glass block	12 x 12

Properties	6 x 6	8 x 8	12 x 12
FR	0 - 1	0 - 1	0 - 1
W	20	20	20
STC Paint			
STC No Paint	38	38	38
R	2.52	2.64	2.74
U	0.397	0.379	0.365
MU	0.388	0.371	0.35

Glass block — physical properties
Figure 2-28

Figure 2-29 shows installation details and maximum panel size for exterior panels. The purpose of this book isn't to help you design masonry walls. I'm just supplying enough information so you'll be familiar with the materials involved and recognize the more common details in architectural drawings.

The Sample Estimate

Glass block is laid up in panels by masons. The sill of the opening should receive a troweling of asphalt. The jambs and head need expansion strips. The plans and specs will usually require panel anchors at jambs, and panel reinforcing in the horizontal joints. Some specifications require the mason contractor to furnish the aluminum chase.

The glass block in panels can easily be counted and priced by the piece. The asphalt coating, expansion strip material, joint reinforcing, caulking and the aluminum chase can be measured in lineal feet.

For our sample take-off, look at the panel shown in Figure 2-30. Figure 2-31 is the take-off sheet for that panel. Figure 2-32 is the summary with the quantities of each component, ready for pricing.

If an entire wall will be made of glass block, it may be easier to calculate the square foot area and convert to pieces. Keep any curved block areas separate and price them accordingly.

Exterior Panels

Maximum 144 Square Feet
General

PC GlassBlock™ panels may be a maximum of 25 feet long or 20 feet high, but may not exceed a total of 144 square feet. PC GlassBlock panels are designed to be mortared to the sill, with jamb and head providing for movement or settling.

Structural members shown are to indicate principles of construction. Sizes must be calculated for loads applied, information shown on these pages is not intended to conflict with any local building code requirements.

All details shown are for Standard (3⅞" thick) PC Glassblock™ units. Modify as necessary for THINLINE SERIES PC GlassBlock™ units (3⅛" thick) and VISTABRIK® solid glass block (3" thick).

The use of THINLINE SERIES PC GlassBlock™ units in exterior applications should be limited to light commercial and residential applications.

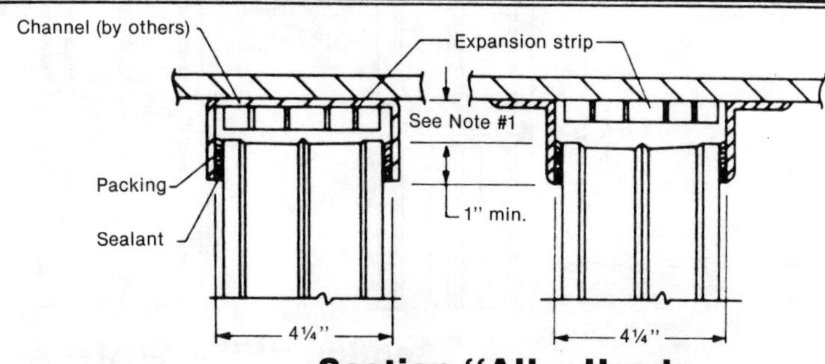

Section "A" — Heads

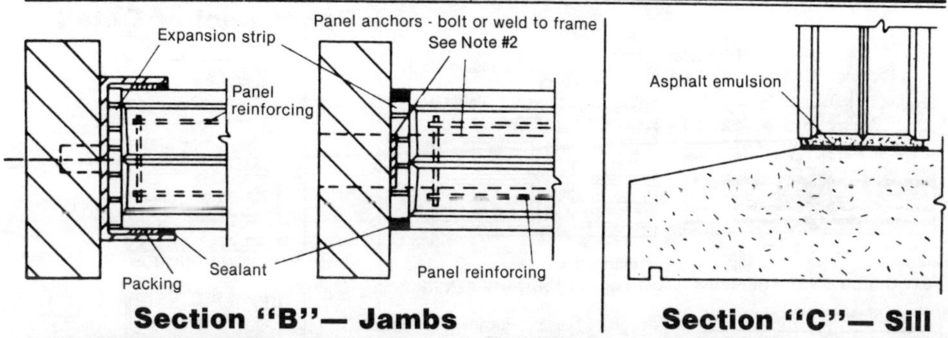

Section "B" — Jambs   Section "C" — Sill

Maximum 250 Square Feet

PC GlassBlock™ panels may exceed 144 square feet in area (but may not be more than 250 square feet) only if the panel is braced by a mortared stiffener.

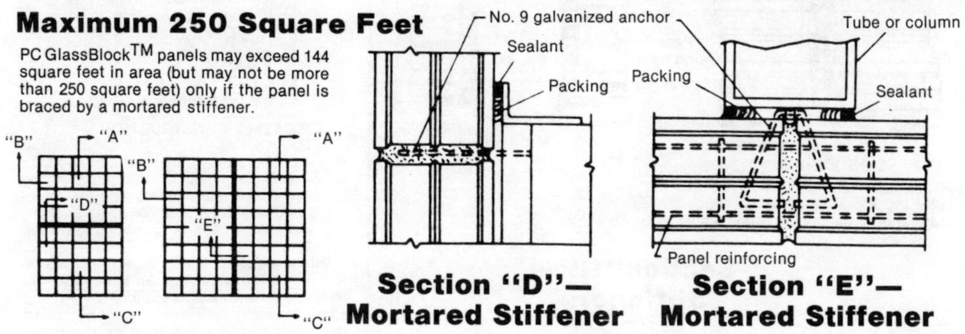

Section "D" — Mortared Stiffener   Section "E" — Mortared Stiffener

NOTES:
1. This dimension is determined by the deflection of the structural member above the glass block.
2. Limit panel to 10' height.

Courtesy: Pittsburgh Corning Corporation

Glass block — installation details
Figure 2-29

Large Continuous Exterior Panels

General   PC Glassbrick^{TM} panels may be a maximum of 25 feet long or 20 feet high, but not more than 144 square feet in total area. See Section A, B, C, for head, jamb, and sill details.

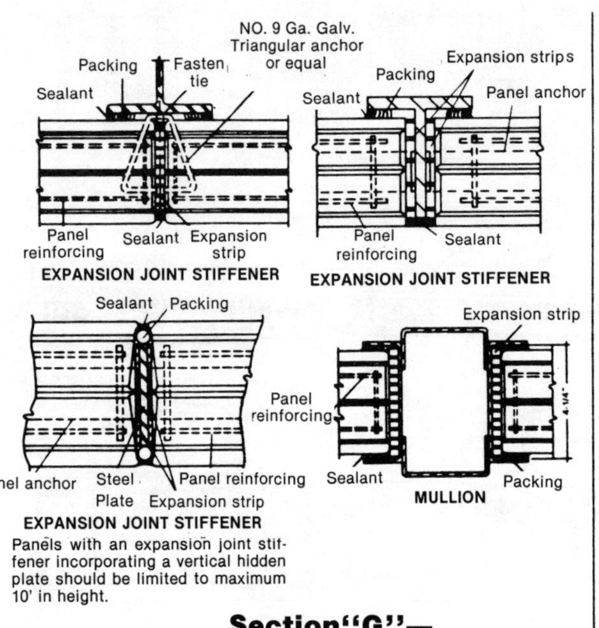

Section "F"— Shelves

Section "G"— Stiffeners

Panels with an expansion joint stiffener incorporating a vertical hidden plate should be limited to maximum 10' in height.

Panel Anchor Detail

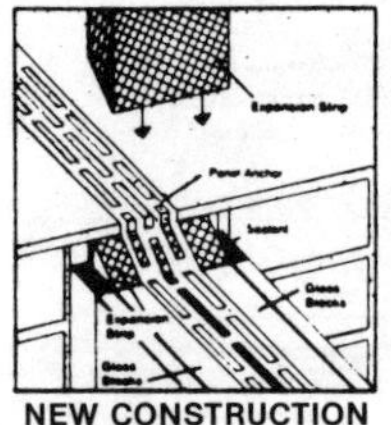

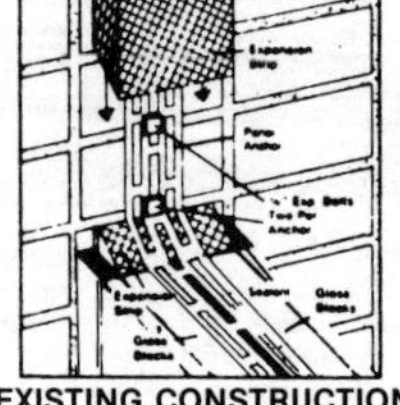

Panel anchors providing lateral support for PC GlassBlock panels are restricted only by building code requirements and the directions of the architect. Where panel anchors are forbidden, channel construction shall be used.

When required, install Panel Anchors as shown on the drawings. All panel anchors must be bent within the expansion joint and shall generally be placed 24" or 16" apart occurring in the same joint as the panel reinforcing and must be completely embedded in mortar joint of the glass block panels extending 12" into the joint.

Courtesy: Pittsburgh Corning Corporation

Glass block — installation details
Figure 2-29 (continued)

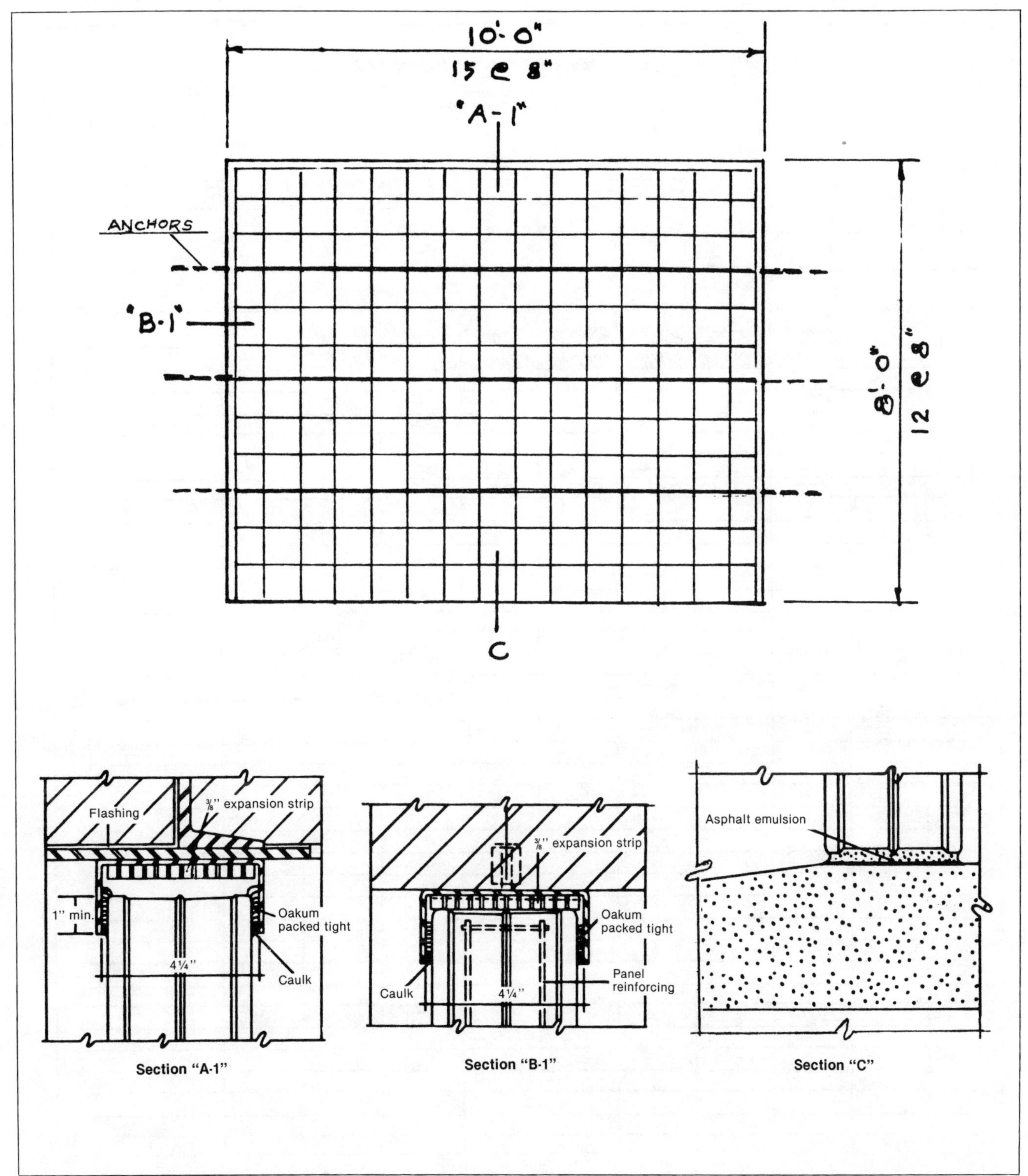

8 x 8 glass block panel
Figure 2-30

MASONRY QUANTITY SURVEYS

123 Beech Drive
Cincinnati, OH 45123

DATE
SHEET   OF
EST. BY
BID DUE

BLDG. _______________________   OWNER_______________________

LOCATION _______________________   ARCHITECT_______________________

PLAN NOS. ___________DATE ___________   GEN. CONTR. _______________________

		GLASS BLOCK 8x8	PANEL ANCHORS	EXP. STRIP	ASPHALT COATING	JOINT REINF.	CAULK	ALUM. CHASE			
		PCS	PCS	LF	LF	LF	LF	LF			
		12	3	8⁰	10⁰	10⁰	8⁰	8⁰			
		15	2	2	1	3	4	2			
		(180)	(6)	(16)	(10)	(30)	(32)	(16)			
				10⁰			10⁰	10⁴			
				1			2	1			
				(10)			(20)	(11)			
				26			52	27			
		180	6	26	10	30	52	27			

Glass block take-off sheet
Figure 2-31

MASONRY QUANTITY SURVEYS

123 Beech Drive
Cincinnati, OH 45123

DATE

SHEET   OF

EST. BY

BID DUE

BLDG. ______________________   OWNER______________________

LOCATION ______________________   ARCHITECT______________________

PLAN NOS. ____________DATE ____________   GEN. CONTR. ______________________

SUMMARY

ITEM	UNIT	QUANTITY	MATERIAL		LABOR		WORK	TOTAL
			Unit	Amount	Unit	Amount		
GLASS BLOCK, 8x8	PCS.	180						
ANCHORS	✓	6						
EXP. STRIP	LF	26						
ASPHALT COATING	✓	10						
JOINT REINF.	✓	30						
CAULKING	✓	52						
ALUMINUM	✓	27						

Summary sheet for glass block take-off
Figure 2-32

Gypsum Block

Gypsum blocks are made of gypsum, the common name for hydrous sulphate of calcium. These blocks are lightweight, highly fire-resistant, nonbearing masonry units, used for partitions and furring. They don't withstand moisture very well. That's why concrete block or brick will be used in the first course. The face dimensions for gypsum block are 12" x 30" and they're made in 3" (solid), 3", 4", 6" and 8" (hollow) thicknesses.

Unlike hollow tile, gypsum block is cast, and not burned. That's why gypsum block has a more regular shape and isn't subject to shrinkage and warping. The regular shape makes it easier to lay.

Fire Resistance Rating

Gypsum block, even with its excellent fire resistance rating, is seldom used today. If you have to estimate gypsum block, contact the manufacturer for current information and prices.

Size	Weight per/SF	Mortar ½" jts. CY/MSF	Production SF/day
2 x 12 x 30 S	9	.547	267
3 x 12 x 30 H	10	.729	267
3 x 12 x 30 S	13	.729	229
4 x 12 x 30 H	13	.860	229
5 x 12 x 30 H	16	.991	200
6 x 12 x 30 H	18	1.121	178
8 x 12 x 30 H	24	1.383	145

Gypsum block — general information
Figure 2-33

The American Insurance Association lists the following fire resistance ratings for gypsum nonbearing walls and partitions:

> 2" solid blocks, unplastered: 1 hour
> 3" solid blocks, unplastered: 3 hours

Any plaster added to these walls will improve the fire resistance rating. And while we're on the subject of fire resistance, I suggest that you get a copy of the American Insurance Association's fire resistance ratings of other masonry materials, also. The cost is about $15. Write to:

> Fire Resistance Ratings
> American Insurance Services Group, Inc.
> 85 John St.
> New York, NY 10038

Because of its excellent fire resistance rating, 3" gypsum plank is used in many apartments to form the roof.

Estimating Gypsum Block

Because gypsum is light, it can be cast into larger sizes (such as 12" x 30") that are still light enough to handle. Be aware that this improves production but makes it necessary to move scaffolding more often.

Measure the area for gypsum block in square feet and then convert to pieces when pricing materials in the summary. Figure 2-33 shows weights, mortar requirements and production rates for gypsum block.

CHAPTER THREE

Brick

here are two categories of face brick: burned brick and composition brick. Burned brick are made from clay or shale, in many sizes, shapes, colors and textures. Composition brick are made from cement, lime, sand and stone aggregates. They're pressure molded instead of burned.

Face Brick Sizes

There's very little uniformity in brick sizes. Standard size concrete block is 8'' x 16''. There's no similar standard for brick. Face brick are manufactured in many sizes. Here are some of the common sizes:

D		H		L	
3-5/8''	x	2-1/4''	x	7-5/8''	(Modular)
3-5/8''	x	2-1/4''	x	8''	(Standard)
3-5/8''	x	2-3/4''	x	8''	(Jumbo)
4''	x	2-3/4''	x	8-1/2''	(Oversize)
3-5/8''	x	2-1/4''	x	11-5/8''	(Norman)
3-5/8''	x	2-3/4''	x	11-5/8''	(Jumbo Norman)

3-5/8"	x	3-5/8"	x	11-5/8"	(Utility)
3-5/8"	x	7-5/8"	x	7-5/8"	(Quad)
3-5/8"	x	11-5/8"	x	11-5/8"	(Panel)
5-5/8"	x	3-5/8"	x	11-5/8"	(Thruwall utility)
7-5/8"	x	3-5/8"	x	11-5/8"	(Thruwall utility)

Architects now commonly identify brick by actual dimensions rather than a name (such as Roman or Norman). The dimensions are always written in the same order: depth x height x length.

Shapes, Colors and Textures

Brick are available in many shapes, including special corners, sills, lintel brick, coping brick, and radial brick. Watch out for these shapes when you're doing your quantity take-off. Special shapes cost more, both for material and labor.

The color of brick depends on the chemical composition of the clays and the method of burning.

The texture of brick — whether it's rough, smooth or matte — can have an effect on bricklaying production. Mortar on a smooth surface brick can be wiped off easily with a piece of burlap. It's harder to clean mortar off the face of rough textured brick. They have to be laid with more care so mortar doesn't touch the exposed face. Any mortar on the face will probably have to be brushed off. Laying rough surface brick takes more time, adds an extra step to the process, and decreases mason productivity.

Figure 3-1 suggests how you might modify estimated production rates for matte finish and rough finish brick. These are the figures I use for my estimates. They may apply on your jobs too. But the only accurate estimate for your work will have to be based on work done by your crews. Use your experience and job records to set up a table similar to Figure 3-1.

Special brick	Size (inches)	Weight (pounds)	Production factor	Production per bricklayer per day
Smooth finish	2¼ x 7⅝	5.3	1.00	560
Matte finish	2¼ x 7⅝	5.3	.95	532
Rough finish	2¼ x 7⅝	5.3	.90	504

Special brick production
Figure 3-1

Classification

Brick are classified by their use. Face brick are used in finished walls. Common brick are used where quality and appearance aren't as important. Glazed brick are used where a durable, sanitary surface is required. Fire brick are used in chimneys and incinerators where high temperatures would destroy other brick. Paving brick is laid flat on a base in applications such as walkways, driveways and patios.

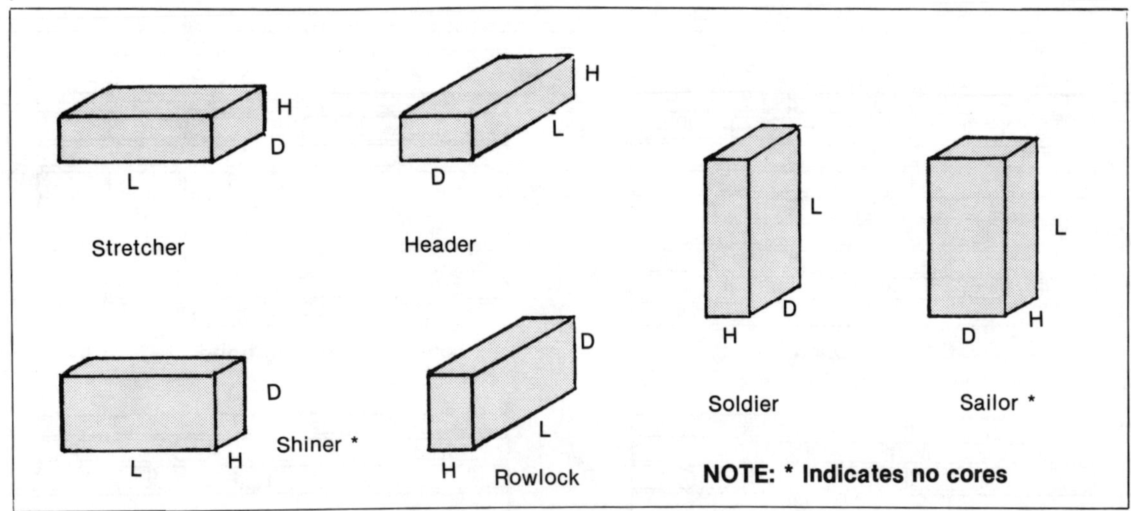

Six different brick positions
Figure 3-2

Specifications

These are the ASTM specifications for brick you'll see most often:

ASTM C 55 Concrete building brick: Does not specify aggregate; 2 grades, N 3500 PSI, S 2500 PSI; average gross area.

ASTM C 216: Refers to specifications for face brick which are solid masonry units (75% solid or more). If brick are to be 100% solid, this should be noted in the specifications.

Grade SW: Severe weather rating

Grade MW: Moderate weather rating

Type FBS Rough: Wide color range

Type FBS Smooth: Wide color range

Type FBX: Very close color and tolerances

Type FBA: Covers specifications that are determined by the architect and differ from the standards given above.

Patterns and Bond

Although brick are usually laid in the wall with the 2¼" x 8" face showing, they can be laid other ways. When brick are laid in the usual position, they're called stretchers. When they're laid other ways, they're called headers, rowlocks, soldiers, sailors and shiners. Figure 3-2 shows these positions.

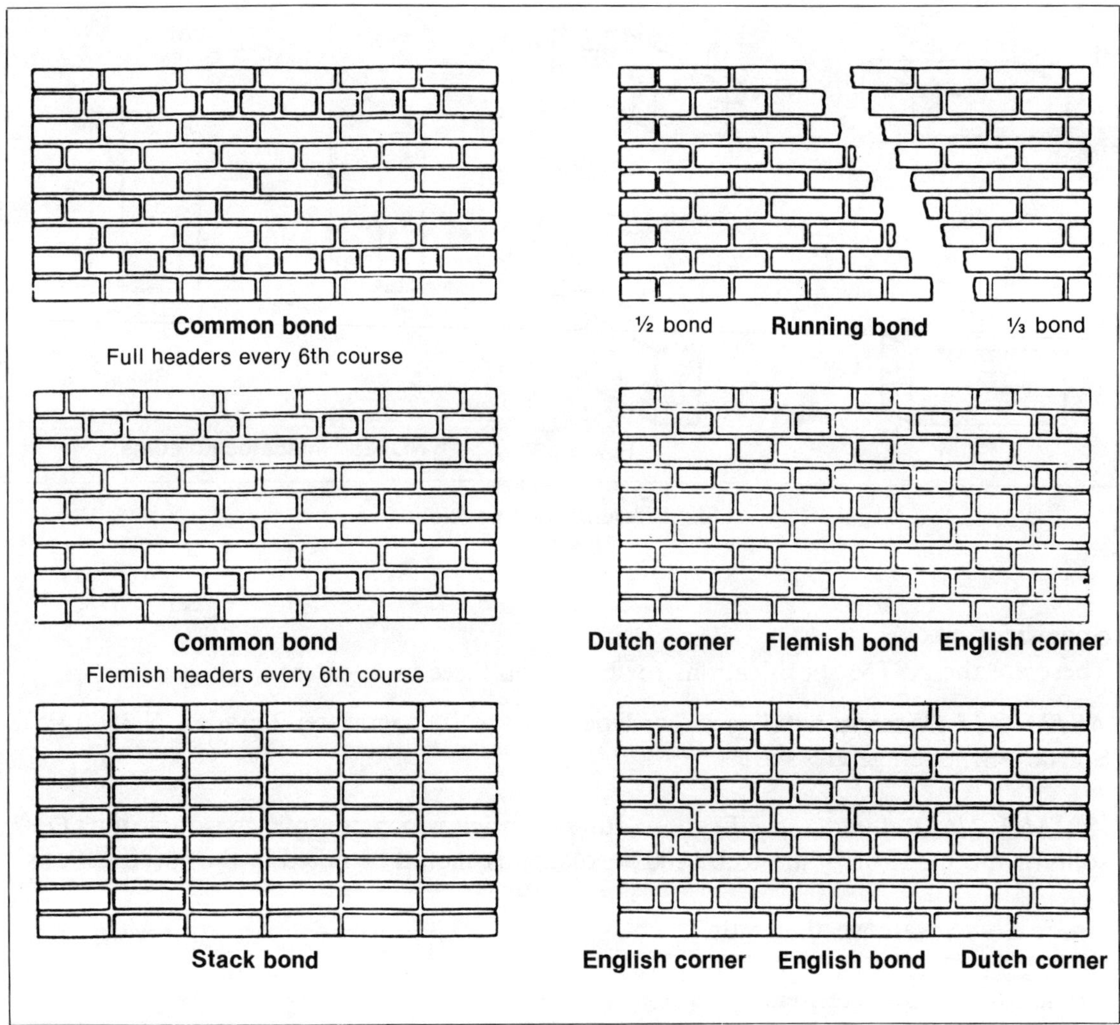

Brick bonds
Figure 3-3

Variations in the way brick are laid creates attractive patterns in the wall. This pattern is called the *bond.* There are five basic structural bonds used today. They are: running bond, common or American bond, Flemish bond, English bond and stack bond. All are shown in Figure 3-3.

Estimating

The bond used affects the labor cost of brick work because complex bonds require more time to lay. Stack bond, although a simple bond, is more expensive to lay than running bond.

Pay particular attention to whether the brick specified are *standard* or *modular* size. Figure 3-4 shows the differences. Note that it takes more modular brick than standard brick to cover one square foot of wall.

Item	Modular brick 2¼" x 7⅝"	Standard brick 2¼" x 8"
Running bond	6.750	6.550
Common bond		
Full headers every 6th course	7.875	7.642
Full headers every 7th course	7.715	7.486
Flemish headers every 6th course	7.125	6.914
Flemish bond every course	9.000	8.734
Old English bond	10.125	9.825
English cross bond	10.125	9.825

Number of brick per square foot
Figure 3-4

Figure 3-5 shows dimensions, weights, number of units per square foot, daily production rates, and mortar requirements for most of the brick you'll be estimating. The production rates are based on the number of masonry units one bricklayer can lay in one day under normal working conditions. Figure 3-6 shows the descriptions and properties of some typical walls built of face brick or brick and block.

Face brick quantities are usually taken off in square feet and converted to pieces for pricing. But quantities of materials can also be taken off in lineal feet, cubic feet, cubic yards or square yards. To find the number of square feet in a face brick area, you need two dimensions — the height and the length in feet. If this sounds familiar, it's because the process is similar to the concrete block take-off we did in Chapter 2.

Let's look at an example. The area of a masonry wall is 8'8" high and 21'4" long. Convert feet and inches to decimal feet, then find the square foot area of the wall:

$$8.667' \times 21.334' = 185 \text{ SF}$$

Record it on the take-off sheet like this:

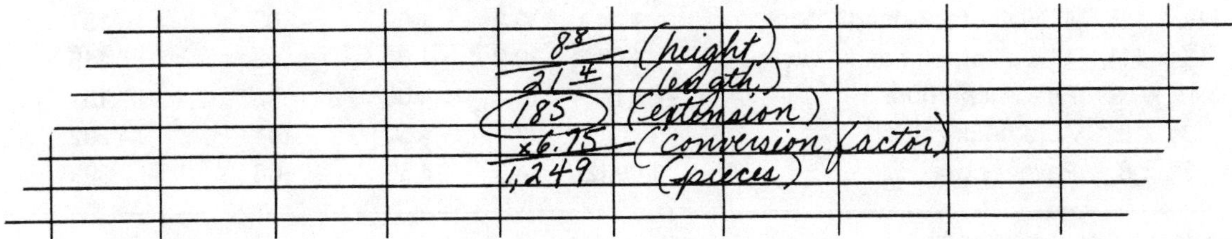

Remember, the circle around the number 185 means it's an extension. The conversion factor is for modular brick, running bond. You can look it up in Figure 3-4, or figure it out yourself, like this:

$$\frac{144}{2\text{-}2/3 \times 8} = 6.75$$

Dimension of face size exposed to view	Type of wall	Mortar CY/M	Weight (lbs.)	Pieces per SF	Production factor	Production per bricklayer per day
$2\frac{1}{4}$ x $7\frac{5}{8}$	8" wall (F2S) running bond	1.23	5.3	13.50	1.02	571
$2\frac{1}{4}$ x $7\frac{5}{8}$	4" wall running bond	.52	5.3	6.75	1.00	560
$2\frac{1}{4}$ x $7\frac{5}{8}$	4" wall running bond - cavity	.52	5.3	6.75	.95	532
$2\frac{1}{4}$ x $7\frac{5}{8}$	4" wall Flemish header - 6th	.52	5.3	7.13	.96	538
$2\frac{1}{4}$ x $7\frac{5}{8}$	4" wall full header - 7th	.54	5.3	7.72	.94	526
$2\frac{1}{4}$ x $7\frac{5}{8}$	4" wall stack bond	.52	5.3	6.75	.95	532
$2\frac{1}{4}$ x $7\frac{5}{8}$	4" wall stack bond - cavity	.52	5.3	6.75	.92	515
$2\frac{1}{4}$ x $7\frac{5}{8}$	4" Flemish bond	.56	5.3	9.00	.90	504
$2\frac{1}{4}$ x $7\frac{5}{8}$	4" English bond	.57	5.3	10.13	.85	476
$2\frac{1}{4}$ x $3\frac{5}{8}$	Header	.59	5.3	13.50	.90	504
$3\frac{5}{8}$ x $2\frac{1}{4}$	Rowlock	.59	5.3	13.50	.85	476
$7\frac{5}{8}$ x $2\frac{1}{4}$	Soldier	.52	5.3	6.75	.80	448
$3\frac{5}{8}$ x $7\frac{5}{8}$	Shiner - no cores	.66	5.3	4.50	.75	420
$7\frac{5}{8}$ x $3\frac{5}{8}$	Sailor - no cores	.66	5.3	4.50	.70	392
$2\frac{1}{4}$ x $11\frac{5}{8}$	4" wall running bond	.72	7.8	4.50	1.00	459
$2\frac{1}{4}$ x $11\frac{5}{8}$	4" wall running bond - cavity	.72	7.8	4.50	.95	437
$2\frac{1}{4}$ x $11\frac{5}{8}$	4" wall stack bond	.72	7.8	4.50	.95	437
$2\frac{1}{4}$ x $11\frac{5}{8}$	4" wall stack bond - cavity	.72	7.8	4.50	.93	426
$3\frac{5}{8}$ x $11\frac{5}{8}$	4" wall running bond	.79	12.5	3.00	1.00	291
$3\frac{5}{8}$ x $11\frac{5}{8}$	4" wall running bond - cavity	.79	12.5	3.00	.94	274
$3\frac{5}{8}$ x $11\frac{5}{8}$	4" wall stack bond	.79	12.5	3.00	.94	274
$3\frac{5}{8}$ x $11\frac{5}{8}$	4" wall stack bond - cavity	.79	12.5	3.00	.92	269
$7\frac{5}{8}$ x $7\frac{5}{8}$	4" wall stack bond	.70	14.0	2.25	1.00	238
$7\frac{5}{8}$ x $7\frac{5}{8}$	4" wall stack bond - cavity	.70	14.0	2.25	.94	223
$11\frac{5}{8}$ x $11\frac{5}{8}$	4" wall stack bond	1.04	30.2	1.00	1.00	157
$11\frac{5}{8}$ x $11\frac{5}{8}$	4" wall stack bond - cavity	1.04	30.2	1.00	.93	146
$4\frac{1}{2}$ x 9	Fire brick - floor	(1)	15.3	4.00	.72	151
$3\frac{3}{4}$ x 8	Acid brick - floor		7.1	4.50	.41	202
$3\frac{5}{8}$ x 8	Paver - floor	1.09 (2)	4.7	4.50	.66	398

(1) Use 250 pieces per 100 pounds.
(2) For pavers $1\frac{1}{2}$" thick, $\frac{3}{8}$" joints, 1" setting bed.

Face brick data
Figure 3-5

Abbreviations

FR . . . . .Fire Rating

W. . . . . .Weight per SF of wall surface

STC . . . . . .Sound Transmission Class (average decibel loss of sound passing through the wall)

R . . . . .Thermal Resistance (SF x HRS x F/BTU)

U . . . . .Thermal Transfer Coefficient (BTU/SF x HRS xF)

M . . . .Mass Coefficient for correcting "U" valve based on thermal cycling.

MU . . . . .M x U

Description
4" Solid face brick . . . . .2 2/3 x 8
4" Solid face brick . . . . .2 2/3 x 12
4" Solid face brick . . . . .3 1/8 x 12
4" Solid face brick . . . . .4 x 12

Properties (brick only)
FR 1
W 39
STC Paint . . . .
STC No paint 45
R 1.29
U 0.78
MU 0.74

Description
4" Hollow face brick . . . . .8 x 8
4" Hollow face brick .12 x 12

Properties
FR . . . .
W 24
STC Paint 41
STC No paint 39
R 1.59
U 0.63
MU 0.61

Properties of face brick walls
Figure 3-6

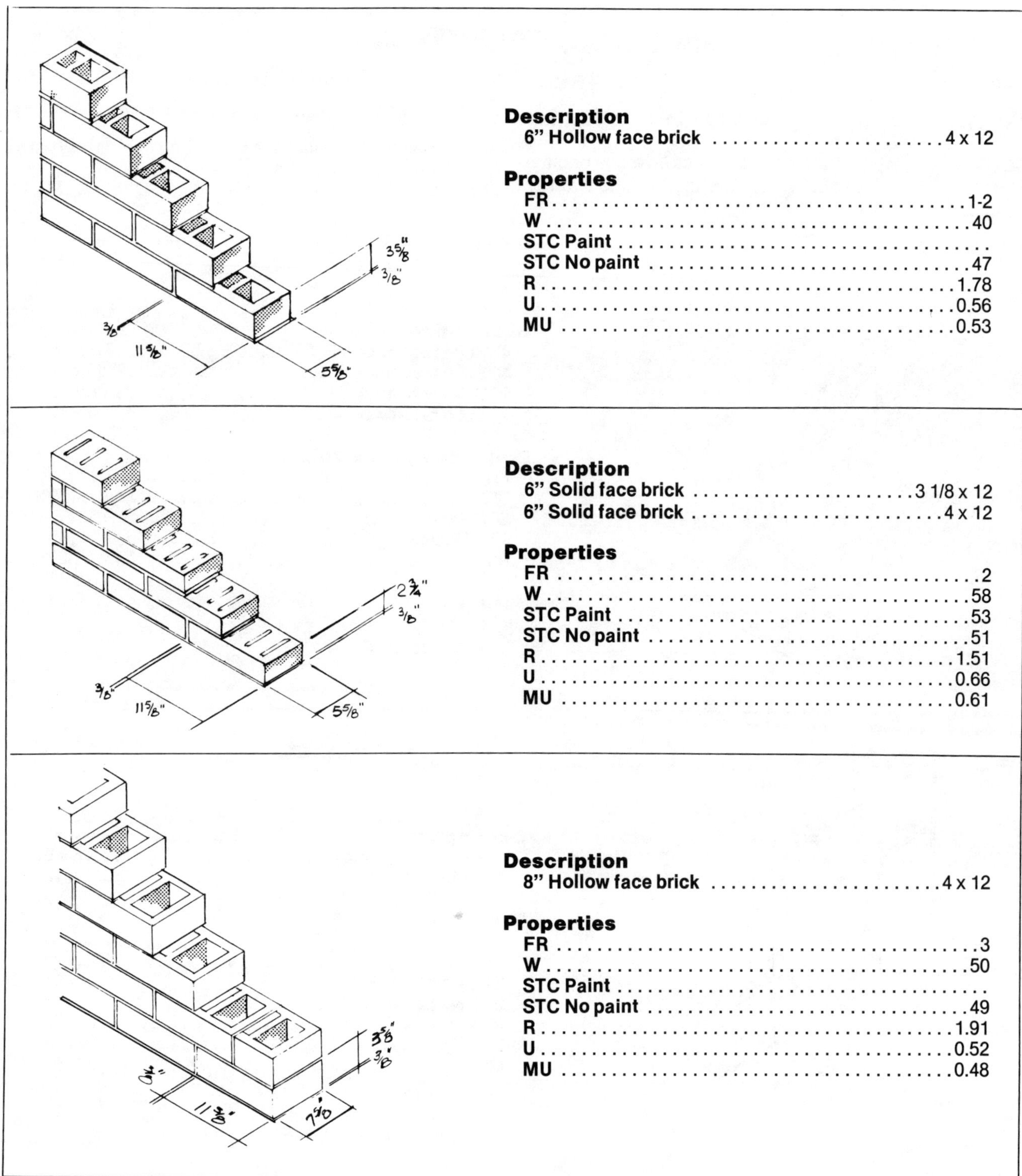

Description
6" Hollow face brick . . . . 4 x 12

Properties
FR 1-2
W 40
STC Paint . . . .
STC No paint 47
R 1.78
U 0.56
MU 0.53

Description
6" Solid face brick . . . . 3 1/8 x 12
6" Solid face brick . . . . 4 x 12

Properties
FR 2
W 58
STC Paint 53
STC No paint 51
R 1.51
U 0.66
MU 0.61

Description
8" Hollow face brick . . . . 4 x 12

Properties
FR 3
W 50
STC Paint . . . .
STC No paint 49
R 1.91
U 0.52
MU 0.48

Properties of face brick walls
Figure 3-6 (continued)

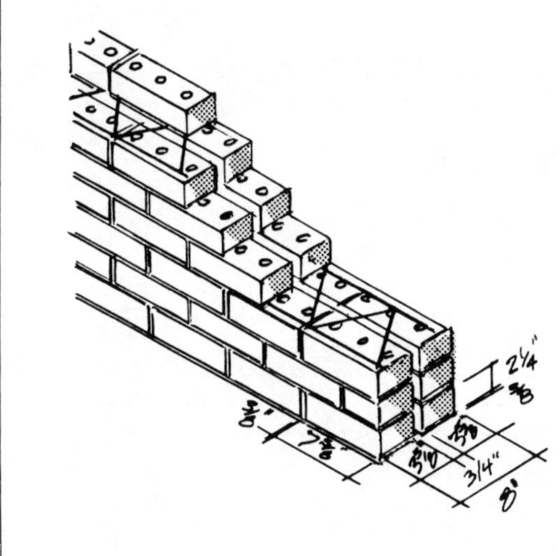

Description
8" Solid face brick, face two sides

Properties
FR 4
W 83
STC Paint 57
STC No paint 52
R 1.73
U 0.58
MU 0.52

Description
8" Solid face brick . . . . .4 x 12

Properties
FR 4
W 78
STC Paint . . . .
STC No paint . . . .
R 1.73
U 0.58
MU 0.52

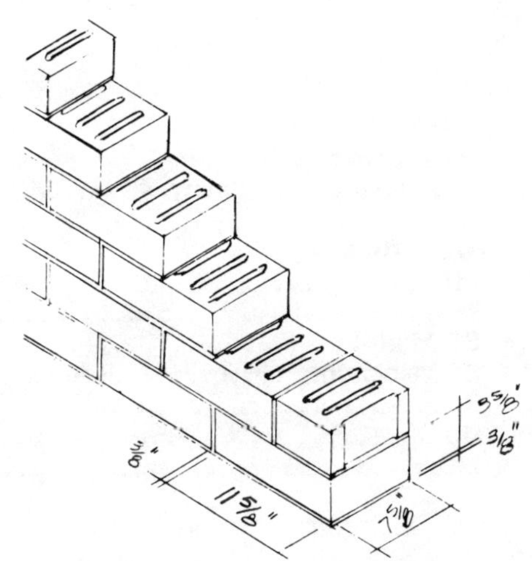

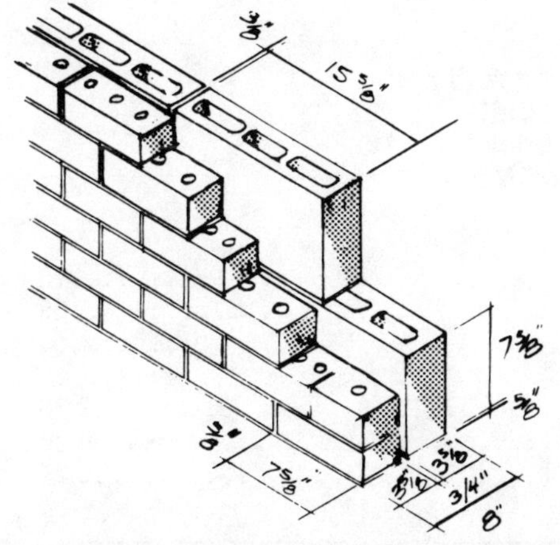

Description
4" Face brick, 4" LWCMU

Properties
FR 4
W 67
STC Paint . . . .
STC No paint 51
R 2.51
U 0.40
MU 0.37

Properties of face brick walls
Figure 3-6 (continued)

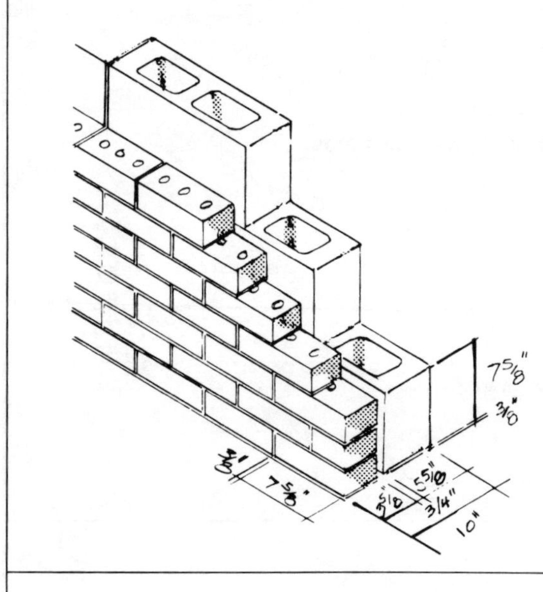

Description
4" Face brick, 6" LWCMU

Properties
FR 4
W 73
STC Paint . . . . .55 +
STC No paint . . . . .50 +
R 2.40
U 0.42
MU 0.38

Description
4" Face brick, 2" Cavity, 4" LWCMU

Properties
FR 4
W 64
STC Paint . . . .
STC No paint 54
R 3.48
U 0.29
MU 0.27

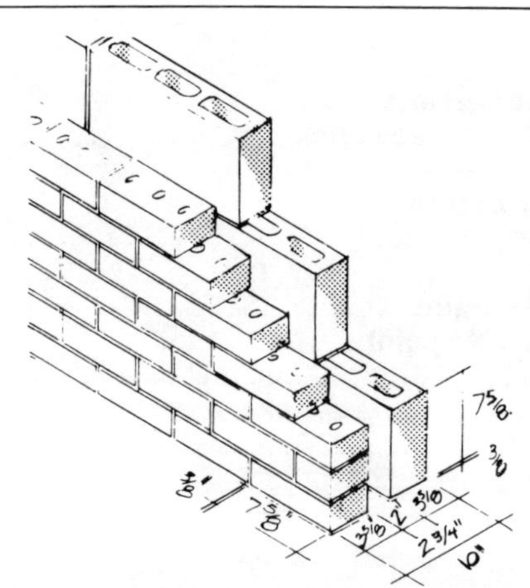

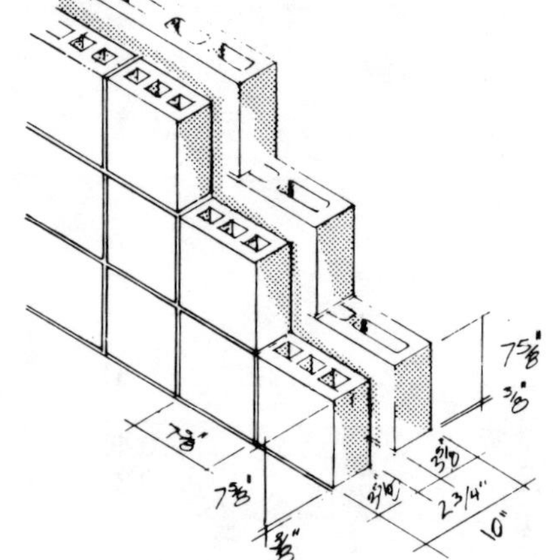

Description
4" Hollow face brick (8 x 8)
2" Cavity, 4" LWCMU
4" Hollow face brick (12 x 12)
2" Cavity, 4" LWCMU

Properties
FR 3
W 65
STC Paint . . . .
STC No Paint . . . .
R 3.78
U 0.26
MU 0.24

Properties of face brick walls
Figure 3-6 (continued)

The Sample Take-Off

Now we'll do a sample take-off for a simple face brick building. Look at the abstract of masonry specifications (Figure 3-7), a floor plan (Figure 3-8) and the wall section details (Figure 3-9). The wall sections show the face brick used and how they are built into the wall.

Step 1: Materials— As you look at wall section C, you'll note that the wall is made up of face brick tied to the wood stud backup. In sections A and B, you can see that the walls have the same brick as section C, except that some of the brick are laid as rowlocks and headers at doors and windows. This should give you a pretty good idea of the items you'll have to record on the take-off sheet:

		4" F.BRK w/ties	12"x8x16 Solid CB D.O.	12x8x16 CB	FLASH. @ FL.LINE				

Step 2: Finding the height— Wall heights are shown in section C: the height of the face brick is 11'4''. The height of the block is 3'4'', which includes the 12 x 8 x 16 solid concrete block. Add these heights to the take-off sheet:

		4" F.BRK w/ties	12x8x16 Solid CB D.O.	12x8x16 CB	FLASH. @ FL.LINE				
		11±		3±					

Step 3: Finding the length— Take the lengths needed to get the square foot area from the floor plan. Because this is a simple building and section C applies to the entire perimeter of the building, it's easy to arrive at a length. Just add up the four overall lengths of the building walls:

$$33'4'' + 51'4'' + 33'4'' + 51'4'' = 169'4''$$

Add the length to the take-off sheet:

		4" F.BRK w/ties	12x8x16 Solid CB D.O.	12x8x16 CB	FLASH. @ FL.LINE				
		11±		3±					
		169±	169±	169±	169±				

MASONRY QUANTITY SURVEYS
123 Beech Drive
Cincinnati, OH 45123

DATE

SHEET ___ OF ___

BLDG. ________________________ OWNER _______________________ EST. BY

LOCATION ______________________ ARCHITECT ____________________ BID DUE

PLAN NOS. ___________ DATE ___________ GEN. CONTR. ___________________

Specification Section ___*4*___ Date _______ Addenda _*NONE*_

Face Brick	Size *MODULAR, SMOOTH*	Allowance *$210.00 /M*	
Common Brick	Size	Material	
Glazed Tile	Size	Material	
Concrete Block	Size *12 x 8 x 16 STD* / *12 x 8 x 16 SOLID*	Material *HWCMU*	
Exp. Joints	Type	Material	
Control Joints	Type	Material	
Fill	Walls	Material	
Flashing	Furnished By *MASON*	Material { *.006" BLACK V/SQUEEN* *@ DR. & WO HEADS* *WD SILLS*	
Caulking	Furnished By	Material *1st FLOOR LINE*	
Parging	Thickness		
Anchors	Type Galv.	WT. Spacing H V	
*Ties	Type *DW 10* Galv. ✓	WT. *16 GA* Spacing *16"* H *24"* V	
Reinforcing *(12")*	Type *TRUSS* Galv. ✓	WT. *9 GA* Spacing *16"* V	
PC Concrete *(DOOR)*	(Sills) ✓ Copings	Lintels Facing	
FACE BRICK ~~Stone~~	(Sills) ✓ Copings Trim	Facing *HEADS OF OPNGS*	
Bond Beams	Fill Furn. By		
P.C. Lintels			
Cleaning	Materials		
Workmanship	Bond *RUNNING*	Joints *3/8" CONCAVE*	
Waterproofing			
Special			
Alternates			

Abstract of masonry specifications
Figure 3-7

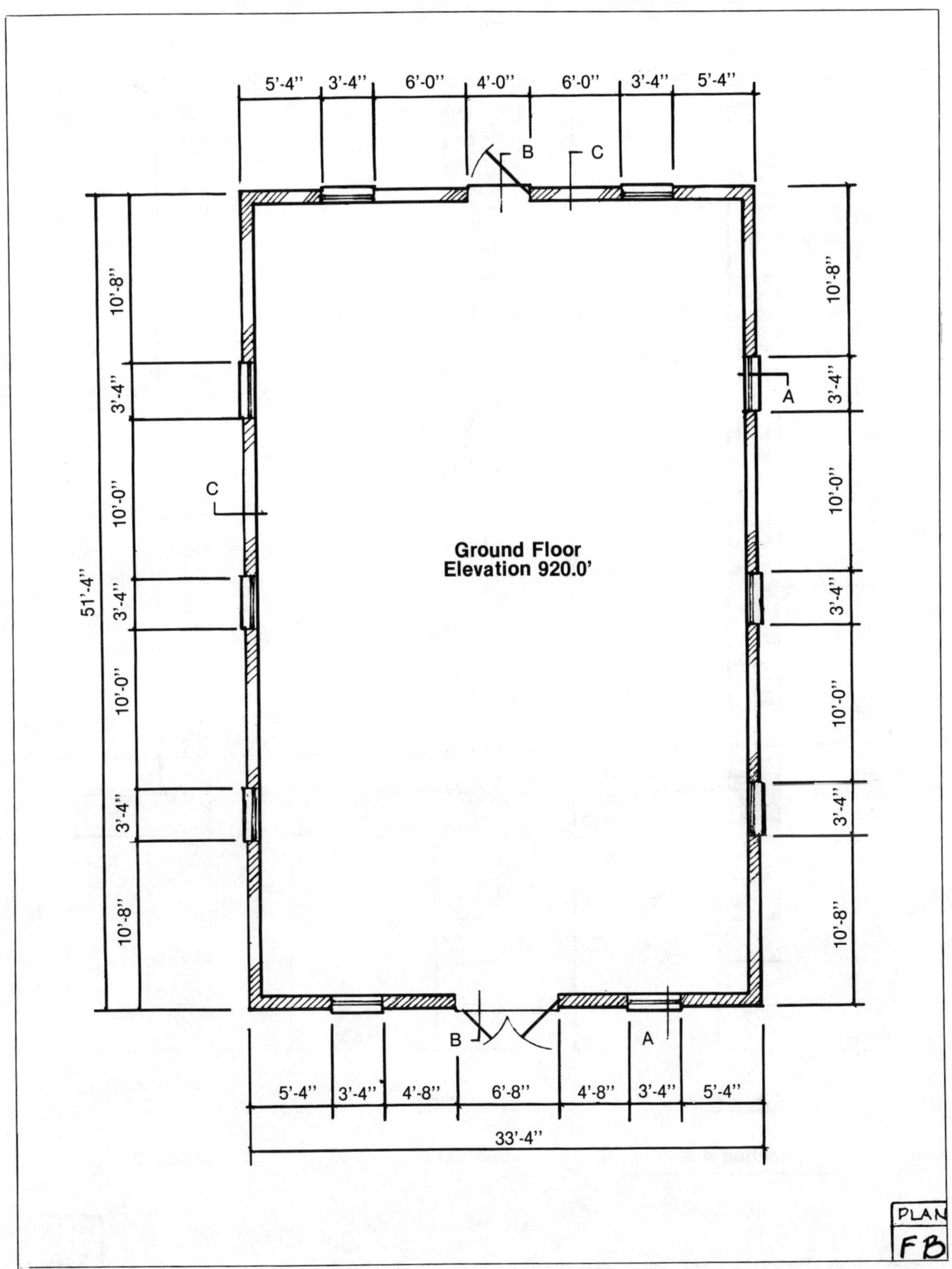

Floor plan for sample brick take-off
Figure 3-8

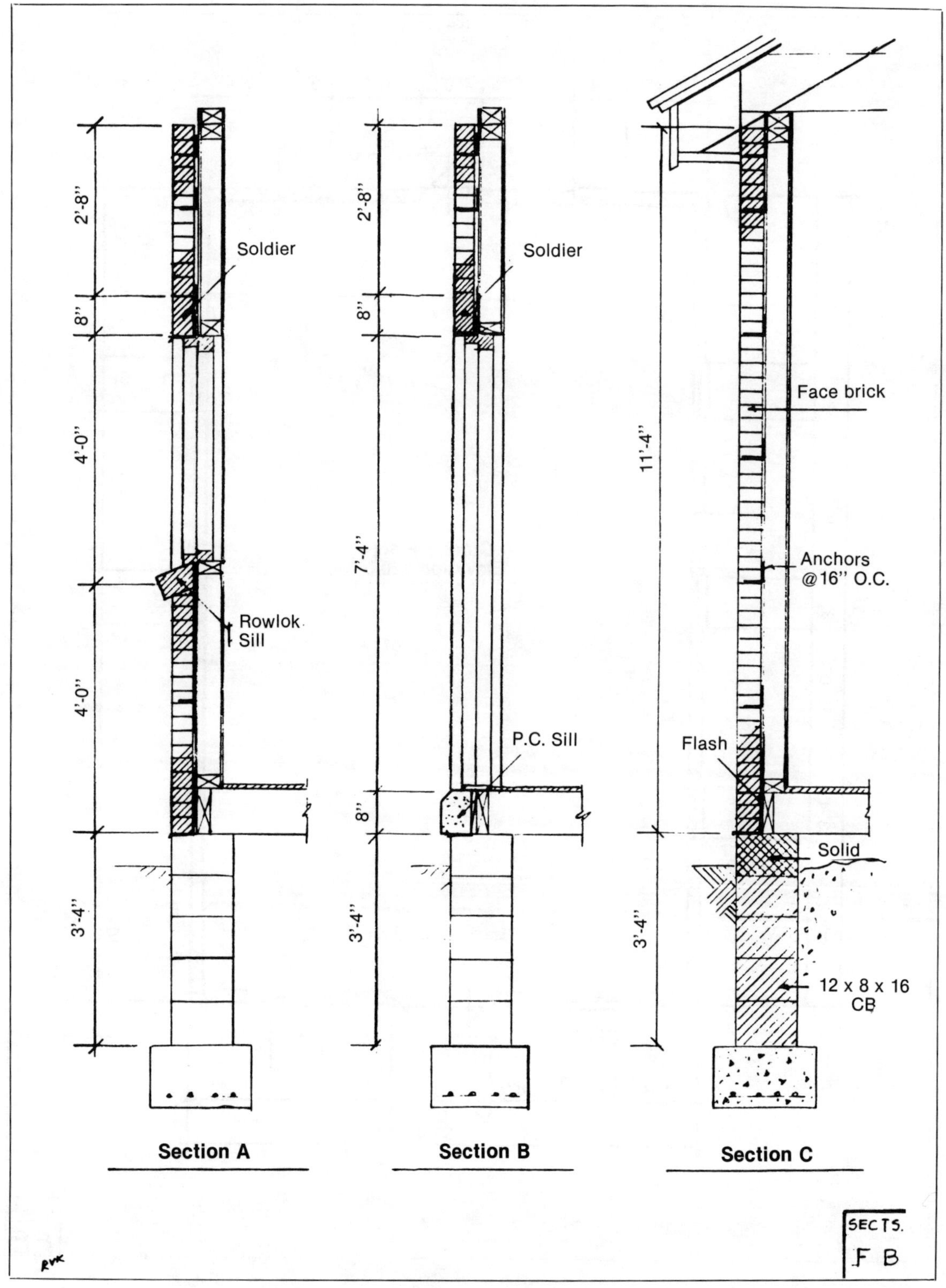

Wall section details
Figure 3-9

For larger floor plans, it's probably easier to measure (or scale) the lengths instead of adding together the dimensions. If you choose to scale the lengths on a floor plan, be sure to use the right measuring scale. And be alert for a plan that hasn't been reproduced in the correct scale. Add together one row of dimensions and compare that figure with the measured footage. If you're measuring hundreds of lineal feet at one time, it's a good idea to check the overall measurement with a wheel (map measure). It's easy to make a mistake and drop a few feet, or even a few hundred feet.

Extensions— The take-off sheet is now ready for extending. Multiply the height by the length and circle the product:

4"F.BRK w/ties	12x8x16 Solid CB D.O.	12x8x16 CB	FLASH @ FL.LINE			
11± 169± (1920)	170	3± 169± (565)	170			

Most of the masonry work is now on your take-off sheet and ready for the refinements. You can deduct all the openings on the same take-off sheet (Figure 3-10).

Recap and summary— Because this is a simple example, only one page was needed for the take-off. No summary is needed. You can transfer all the figures on the bottom line directly to the summary sheet for pricing. See Figure 3-11.

Estimating Fireplaces

Occasionally you'll have to estimate the cost of building a fireplace. Fireplaces are designed in many sizes, shapes and styles. Every fireplace estimate can be unique. But don't be intimidated by the complexity. And don't resort to guessing. Fireplace estimates can be both fast and accurate if you follow some logical steps.

Figure 3-12 is section and elevation drawings of a typical fireplace. Figure 3-13 shows dimensions for the fireplace parts identified in Figure 3-12: the hearth, the burning area, the throat, the smoke chamber and the flue. Figure 3-12 doesn't show the foundation, the chimney or the cap.

The dimensioning of a fireplace is very important. If the dimensions are out of proportion, the fireplace won't draw correctly. This table of dimensions can be useful in several ways:

- It provides you with information about what it takes to make a good working fireplace.

MASONRY QUANTITY SURVEYS

123 Beech Drive
Cincinnati, OH 45123

BLDG. *Sample Bldg.*   OWNER __________

LOCATION __________   ARCHITECT __________

PLAN NOS. *F. BRK* DATE __________   GEN. CONTR. __________

DATE
SHEET   OF
EST. BY *RVK*
BID DUE

		4" F. BRK w/TIES	12" Solid CB D.O. LF	12" CB	FLASH @FLOOR LINE LF	SOLDIER @HEAD D.O. LF	P.C. SILL 5x8 LF	FLASH @HEAD ⌐8"/4"	ROLOK @SILL LF	FLASH @SILL ⌐8"/4"
		11±		3±						
		169±	170°	169±	170°					
		(1920)		(565)						
DRS	6⅞×8⅞	① 57				① 8	① 7	① 9		① 9
"	4⁰×8⅞	① 34				① 6	① 4	① 6		① 6
WD	3±×4⁰	⑩ 155				⑩ 47		⑩ 54	⑩ 34	⑩ 54
		246								
		1674		565						
		× 6.75		×1.125						
		11,300	170	636	170	61	11	69	34	69
		✗	✗	✗	✗	✗	✗	✗	✗	✗
					+69 ·					
		WALL TIES		12" DUR	+69 ·					
		×.375		×.7						
		628		446	308					
		✗		✗	✗					

Sample brick take-off
Figure 3-10

MASONRY QUANTITY SURVEYS

123 Beech Drive
Cincinnati, OH 45123

DATE
SHEET   OF
EST. BY *RYK*
BID DUE

BLDG. *SAMPLE BLDG.*   OWNER

LOCATION   ARCHITECT

PLAN NOS. *F. BRK*   DATE   GEN. CONTR.

ITEM	UNIT	QUANTITY	MATERIAL		LABOR		WORK	TOTAL
			Unit	Amount	Unit	Amount		
4" F. BRK	PCS	11,300						
12 × 8 × 16 CB HW	✓	636						
MORTAR (N) F. BRK.	✓	11,300						
" (S) CB	✓	636						
CLEAN F. BRK	✓	11,300						
WALL TIES DW 10	✓	628						
REINF. 12" CB	LF	446						
12" CB SOLID D.O.	✓	170						
SOLDIER @ HEAD D.O.	✓	61						
ROWLOK @ SILL D.O.	✓	34						
P.C. SILL 5×8	✓	11						
FLASHING 12" W.	✓	308						

Summary sheet for sample brick take-off
Figure 3-11

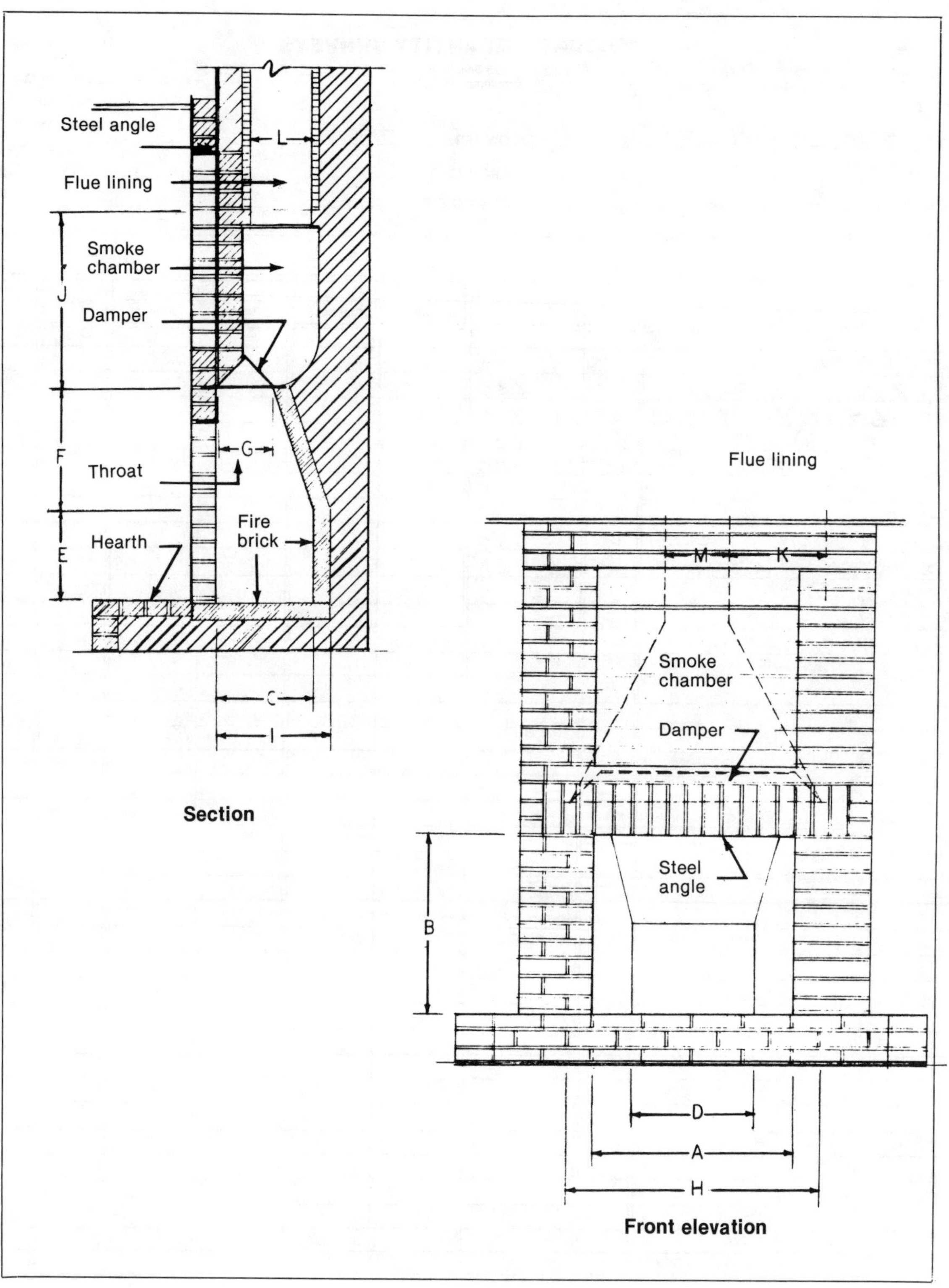

Typical fireplace details
Figure 3-12

Width (front)	Height	Depth	Width (back)	Back wall (vertical)	Back wall (sloped)	Throat	Width (rough opening)	Depth (rough opening)	Smoke chamber	Slope of smoke chamber	Standard rectangular flue lining (O.D.)		Standard round flue lining (I.D.)
A	B	C	D	E	F	G	H	I	J	K	L	M	O
26	24	16	13	14	14	8¾	39	20	24	15	8½ x	8½	10
28	28	16	15	14	18	8¾	42	20	25	14½	8½ x	13	10
30	30	16	17	14	20	8¾	42	20	25	14½	8½ x	13	10
32	28	16	19	14	20	8¾	44	20	26	15½	8½ x	13	10
34	30	16	21	14	20	8¾	46	20	28	16½	8½ x	13	12
36	30	16	23	14	20	8¾	46	20	28	16½	13 x	13	12
40	30	16	27	14	20	8¾	50	20	32	18½	13 x	13	12
42	30	16	29	14	20	8¾	54	20	35	20½	13 x	13	12
48	33	18	33	14	23	8¾	59	22	40	23	13 x	13	15
54	36	20	37	14	26	13	67	24	42	24½	13 x	18	15
60	39	22	42	14	29	13	71	26	45	26½	18 x	18	18
72	40	22	54	14	30	13	83	26	56	32½	18 x	18	18

Fireplace dimensions
Figure 3-13

- Plans seldom give the detail information that's shown in these tables.

- You can use it as a checklist of all the items that go into a fireplace.

Your job as an estimator is to account for all the materials involved, the accessories required and the labor to install them. It's almost impossible to set up a standard system to follow in making your take-off because of the variety of designs. Here are some general rules to follow, however.

The Fireplace Take-Off

You can make your take-off in three steps:

1) Study the plan and specifications carefully and list all the accessory items called for, including:

a) Damper: size
b) Ash dump: size
c) Ash pit door: size
d) Angles: size and number
e) Flue lining: size and lineal feet
f) Firebrick: square feet
g) Hearth facing material: square feet
h) Fireplace facing material: square feet
i) Chimney facing material: square feet
j) Chimney cap material: size, pieces
k) Miscellaneous items: screens, tools, etc.

2)   After studying the details, you can break the fireplace down into various geometric shapes — parallelepipeds, prisms, cylinders, spheres, and so on.

Make sure your measurements are out-to-out dimensions, including facing material and voids. Carefully calculate the volume of each of the geometric shapes in the fireplace, then add them together to find the total cubic feet of fireplace. Be sure to include the volume of the foundation, the hearth, the smoke chamber, the flue and the cap.

3)   The third step is to determine the volume of the facing materials of the hearth and fireplace wall, the volume of the facing materials exposed above the roof, and the volume of the cavities in the foundation, the fireplace area, the smoke chamber and the flue.

To find the net cubic feet of masonry fill, subtract the total volume of the outs from the total volume of fireplace. Finally, convert the net cubic feet to pieces of brick or block, and price them in the summary.

A Sample Take-Off

Suppose we had to make a quantity take-off of the fireplace in Figure 3-14. Figure 3-15 shows how I would compute quantities for this project. Notice that I've numbered each column of the take-off, from 1 through 10. Follow along on these numbered columns while I explain each step of the take-off.

Columns 1, 2 and 3: Hearth, fireplace and chimney— The first step is to determine the gross volume of the masonry mass. In this case, the fireplace is divided into three parts: the hearth, the fireplace and the chimney. Calculate the volume of the hearth using the dimensions on the plan in Figure 3-14. It's 8" high, 1'4" deep and 6'8" wide. That's a total of 6 cubic feet.

The volume of the fireplace is:

8'0"   high (0'8" + 6'10-5/8" + 0'5-3/8")
2'6½"   deep
5'4"   wide

Total volume: 108.5 CF

The volume of the chimney is:

11'0"   high (3'4" + 1'8" + 14'0" - 8'0")
2'6½"   deep
3'4"   wide

Total volume: 93.3 CF

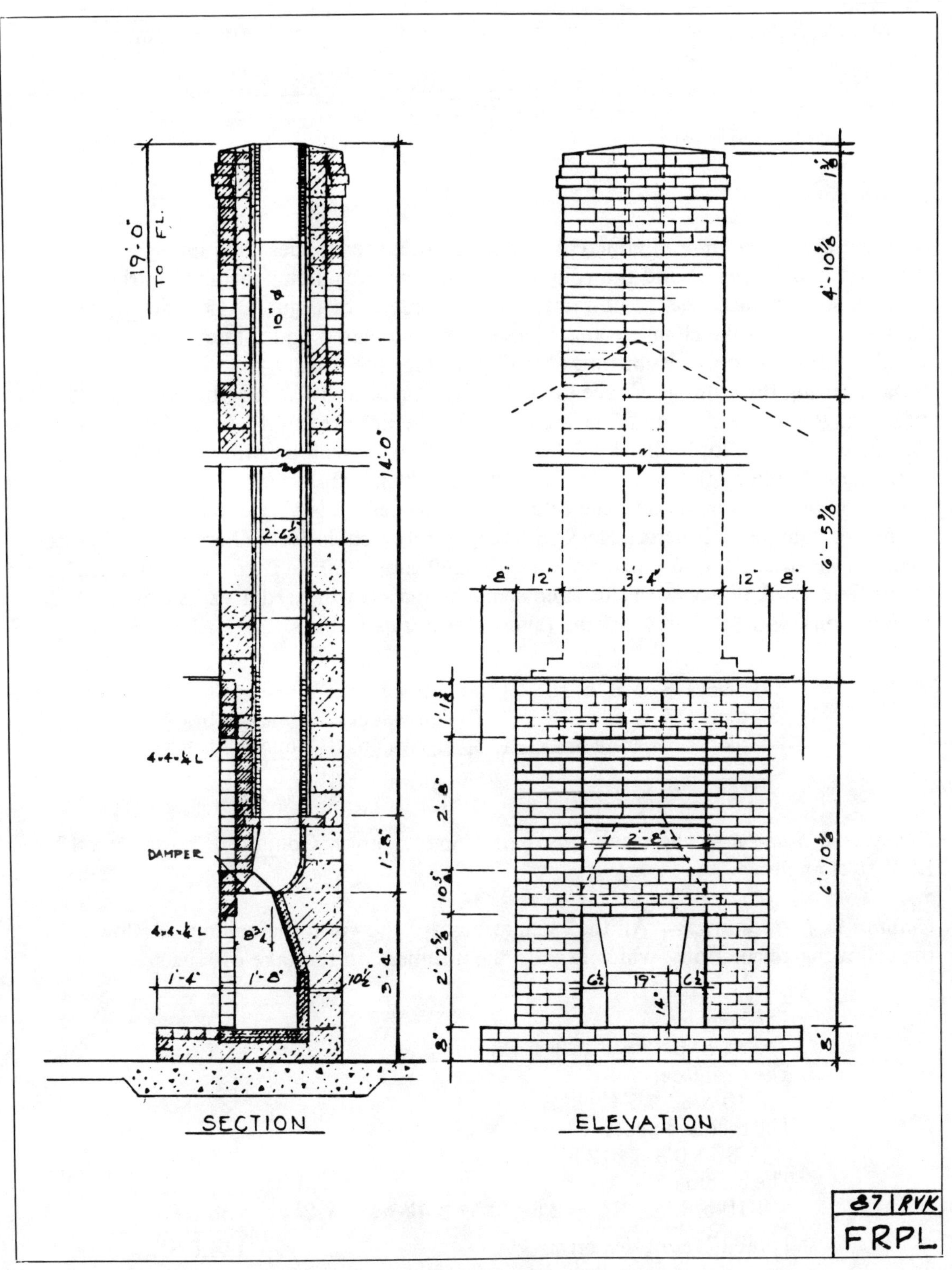

Fireplace details for sample take-off
Figure 3-14

Now add the gross volume of the three parts to find the total gross volume:

$$
\begin{array}{r}
6.0 \\
108.5 \\
\underline{93.3} \\
207.8 \ \ \text{CF}
\end{array}
$$

To get the net volume of concrete block, subtract the cavities (flue lining, smoke chamber, and fireplace) and the volume of other masonry items included in the gross volume, such as face brick. Look in the middle section of Figure 3-15. The volumes of the flue lining, smoke chamber and fireplace are calculated and totaled. They're easy to calculate. Just multiply height times the depth times the width.

But figuring the volume of face brick (4" face brick and flat face brick) is a little different. Read down column 7 in Figure 3-15. The net area of 4" face brick is shown as 102 square feet. Multiply that by 0.333' (4") to find the volume. It's shown as 34 cubic feet. The net area of flat face brick is 9 square feet. Multiply that by 0.222' (2⅔") to find a volume of 2 cubic feet. The total volume to deduct is 57.1 cubic feet.

The net volume of concrete block masonry is 150.7 cubic feet. There are 1.69 pieces in 1 cubic foot of 8 x 8 x 16 units. So multiply 1.69 times 150.7. There are about 255 pieces of concrete block masonry in this fireplace. The mason will need a variety of sizes of units to work with. I suggest pricing (and ordering) as follows:

150 pieces 8 x 8 x 16	(150 equivalent 8" concrete brick)
150 pieces 4 x 8 x 16	(75 equivalent 8" concrete brick)
360 pieces concrete brick	(30 equivalent 8" concrete brick)
	255 equivalent 8" concrete brick

Columns 4, 5 and 6— These columns are self-explanatory. Column 4 shows 4" x 4" x 1/4" steel angles.

Column 7: 4" face brick— All the calculations are shown in the column. Follow along in the following calculations, which explain the numbers on the take-off sheet.

The hearth:	
0'8" x (6'8" + 1'4" + 1'4")	7.0 SF
The fireplace:	
6'10-5/8" x 5'4"	37.0 SF
The recessed panel:	
(2'8" + 0'8") x (2'8" + 0'8")	12.0 SF
The chimney:	
4'10-5/8" x (3'4" + 2'6-1/2" + 3'4" + 2'6-1/2")	58.0 SF
Total 4" face brick area:	114.0 SF
Deduct the fireplace opening:	
2'2-5/8" x 2'8" = 5.92. Round down to	5.0 SF

MASONRY QUANTITY SURVEYS

123 Beech Drive
Cincinnati, OH 45123

DATE

SHEET   OF

EST. BY

BID DUE

BLDG. ___________________________   OWNER___________________________

LOCATION ___________________________   ARCHITECT___________________________

PLAN NOS. ___________ DATE ___________   GEN. CONTR. ___________________________

	①	②	③	④	⑤	⑥	⑦	⑧	⑨	⑩
	HEARTH CF	FIREPLC CF	CHIMNEY CF	LS 4×4×¼	DAMPER	FLUE LINING 10" Ø	4" F. BRK	F. BRK FLAT (NO CORES)	FIRE BRK. FLAT	CORBEL LF D.O.
	0^8	8^0	11^0	4^0		14^0	0^8	6^8		11^9
	14×6^8	$2\frac{6\frac{1}{2}}{2} \times 5^4$	$26\frac{1}{2} \times 3^4$	2	1	1	9^4	1^4	$1^{10}\frac{1}{2} \times 3\frac{1}{2}$	3
	(6.0)	(108.5)	(93.3)	(8)		(14)	(7)	(9)	(7)	(36)
							$6\frac{10\frac{5}{8}}{}$		3^0	
							5^4		6^0	
							(37)		(18)	
FLUE $12\emptyset \times 14^0$			(1) 11.0				3^4		25	
SK CHMB $1^0 \times 1^8 \times 1^{10}$			(1) 3.1				3^4			
FR PL $1\frac{5}{8} \times 2^{10}\frac{1}{2} \times 2\frac{1}{2}$			(1) 7.0				(12)			
F. BRK $0^4 \times 102^0$			(1) 34.0				$4^{10}\frac{5}{8}$			
							11^9			
F. BRK FL $03\frac{2}{3} \times 9^0$			(1) 2.0				(58)			
							114			
FR PL OPNG $2^8 \times 2^2 \frac{5}{8}$							(1) 5			
RECC'D PNL $2^8 \times 2^4$							(1) 7			
			93.3				114			
			57.1				12			
	60	108.5	36.2	8	1	14	102	9	25	36
	✗	✗	+6.0	✗	✗	✗	×6.8	×4.5	×3.6	
			+108.5				694	41	90	
			150.7				✗	✗	✗	✗
			×1.69							
			255							
			✗							

Order

	8 × 8 × 16	150	pcs
	4 × 8 × 16	150	"
	CONC BRK	360	"

Sample fireplace estimate take-off
Figure 3-15

Deduct the recessed panel:
2'8" x 2'8"   7.0 SF

Total deductions: 12.0 SF

Net 4" face brick area:
114 - 12   102.0 SF

Number of face brick units:
102 x 6.75 (use 6.8)   694 pieces

Column 8: Flat face brick— The flat face brick is calculated just like the 4" face brick. There are 9 square feet of face brick without cores. That's 41 pieces (9 x 4.5).

Column 9: Fire brick— The dimensions of the most commonly used fire brick are 2" x 4½" x 9". The first step is to increase the actual dimensions on the plans to multiples of 4½". That way the floor and walls can be built of whole and half units (laid flat). For example:

Floor:
   Actual dimension   1'10-1/2" x 3'1"
   Figure   1'10-1/2" x 3'4-1/2"   7.0 SF
Side walls:
   Actual dimension   1'6-1/2" x 2'8"
   Figure   1'10-1/2" x 3'0"
Back wall:
   Actual dimension   2'0" x 2'8"
   Figure   2'3" x 3'0"
Total wall area:
   (1'10-1/2" + 1'10-1/2" + 2'3") x 3'0"   18.0 SF

Total fire brick area: 25.0 SF

25 x 3.6 (units per SF)   90 pieces

Column 10: Corbel— The total length of corbel is three times the perimeter of the chimney.

Paving Brick

Although brick paving deals with unit masonry, that's about all it has in common with normal bricklaying. Mortared brick paving is best done by experienced masons. It takes a mason's skill and judgment to get joint thickness and brick spacing right when mortar is involved. This skill isn't required for mortarless brick paving. Laying brick without mortar requires little skill. But it does require endurance — and some attention to detail in placing the pavers so they match.

Figuring quantities for brick paving is easy. Estimating production isn't. Base your estimates on your cost records and what you know about the skill and speed of your masons. Better yet, avoid paving work completely. Subcontract the work to a company that specializes in brick paving. But you'll still have to do a quantity take-off and make a rough labor estimate so you can evaluate the sub-bid.

Like face brick, paving brick are either burned or composition brick. Burned brick are made from clay or shale, in many sizes, shapes, colors and textures. Composition brick are pressure molded from cement, lime, sand and stone aggregate. They also come in many sizes, shapes and colors.

There are many brick paving patterns. Some of the typical ones are shown in Figure 3-16.

Burned Brick Pavers

Any burned brick used for outdoor paving should meet ASTM specification C 902 for pedestrian and light traffic paving brick. The type will be FBS and grade SW. Compressive strength should be 10,500 PSI and maximum average absorption rate should not exceed 4%. The rating for maximum freeze-thaw cycles should be 100.

Salvage brick (also known as *used* brick) are popular in ornamental brickwork but shouldn't be used for outdoor paving unless they meet the specifications I've just given.

Burned paving brick are manufactured in many sizes and shapes. Figure 3-17 shows some of the ones you'll see most often. They're also available in interlocking patterns. Your masonry dealer will have manufacturers' catalogs that show the pavers that are available in your community.

There are also many colors and textures available. Various shades of red are the most popular. Other colors include buff, gray and brown shades. Use textured units where you need a slip-resistant surface.

Composition Brick Pavers

Composition brick pavers are also manufactured in many sizes, shapes and interlocking patterns. Again, the best source of information on these products are manufacturers' catalogs. Get your dealer to quote current prices on these products.

Composition pavers are laid in a variety of patterns: herringbone, basket weave, running bond, interlocking, fish scale, stack, random, hexagon, and so on. Most of them are shown in Figure 3-16. Special edge stones are also available.

The UNI products shown in Figure 3-18 are manufactured throughout the United States and Canada. They're available in many pleasing earth-tone colors. UNI is a registered trade mark.

Waffle-type pavers are becoming more popular. They're designed so that grass can grow up through cores to give the paved area a grassy look. Some of the popular UNI grass pavers are shown in Figure 3-19.

The Base for Paving Brick

The base used to support brick paving can be rigid, semi-rigid or flexible. The most common *rigid* base is a reinforced concrete slab on grade. A *semi-rigid* base would be asphalt or bituminous paving. A *flexible* base will be either compacted gravel or sand.

Mortared brick paving is usually installed over a rigid base such as concrete. Look at section A of Figure 3-20. It is permanent, has excellent weathering properties and low maintenance needs, and can be laid in various attractive patterns.

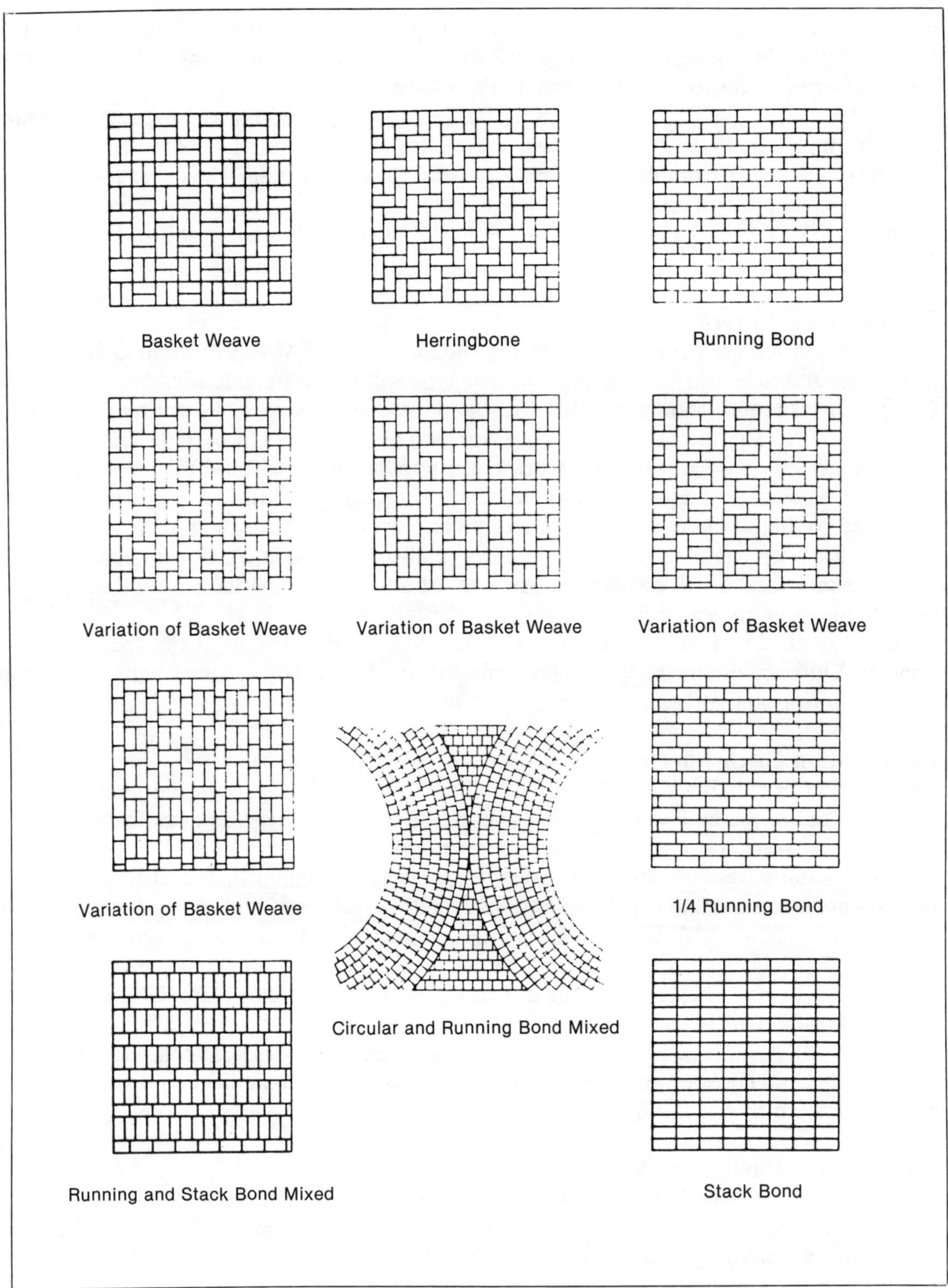

Brick paving patterns
Figure 3-16

Size & shape	Thickness (in inches)	Approximate weight (lbs.)	Units per square foot (with 3/8" joint)	Units per square foot (with no joints)
4" × 8"	3/4 1-5/8 2-1/4	1.8 4.0 5.5	3.93 3.93 3.93	4.50 4.50 4.50
3⅝" × 7⅝"	3/4 1-5/8 2-1/4	1.6 3.5 4.8	4.50 4.50 4.50	5.21 5.21 5.21
6"×6" 8"×8"	1-5/8 (6" size) 1-5/8 (8" size) 2-1/4 (6" size) 2-1/4 (8" size)	4.5 8.0 6.2 11.1	3.54 2.05 3.54 2.05	4.00 2.25 4.00 2.25
7⅝" × 7⅝"	1-5/8	7.3	2.25	2.48
8" × 3⅝"	2-1/4	4.2	----	6.00
6" or 8" (hexagon)	1-5/8 (6" size) 1-5/8 (8" size) 2-1/4 (6" size) 2-1/4 (8" size)	3.9 6.9 5.4 9.6	3.65 2.17 3.65 2.17	4.62 2.60 4.62 2.60

Burned brick pavers
Figure 3-17

Name	Size (in inches)	Weight (approx. lbs.)	Units per square foot
UNI—DECOR® ™	5 1/2 x 2 3/8 x 9 5 1/2 x 3 1/8 x 9	8.1 10.4	3.50 3.50
UNI—STONE® ™	4 1/2 x 2 3/8 x 9 4 1/2 x 3 1/8 x 9	7.9 10.6	3.65 3.65
CLASSICO® ™	4.52 x 2.375 x 6.77 4.52 x 2.375 x 4.52 4.52 x 2.375 x 2.24 4.52 x 2.375 x 4.40 3.38 x 2.375 x 4.40	5.7 3.8 2.7 1.4 1.8	4.71 7.05 14.23 9.68 7.24
MUNICH STONE	8 2/3 x 2 3/8 x 8 2/3 8 2/3 x 3 1/8 x 8 2/3	9.6 13.33	3.00 3.00
HOLLAND STONE	4 1/4 x 3 1/8 x 8 1/2	9.4	4.00
HOLLANDSETTS	4 1/4 x 3 1/8 x 8 1/2	9.3	4.00

Courtesy: Interpave Corp.

Interlocking concrete pavers
Figure 3-18

Name	Size	Weight (approx. lbs.)	Units per square foot
 **MONOSLAB**®	16 x 4 1/2 x 24	78.0	.375
 **TURFSTONE**	16 x 3 x 24	60.5	.375
 **UNI—GREEN**®	11 x 4 x 22	44.8	1.670

Courtesy: Interpave Corp.

Grass pavers
Figure 3-19

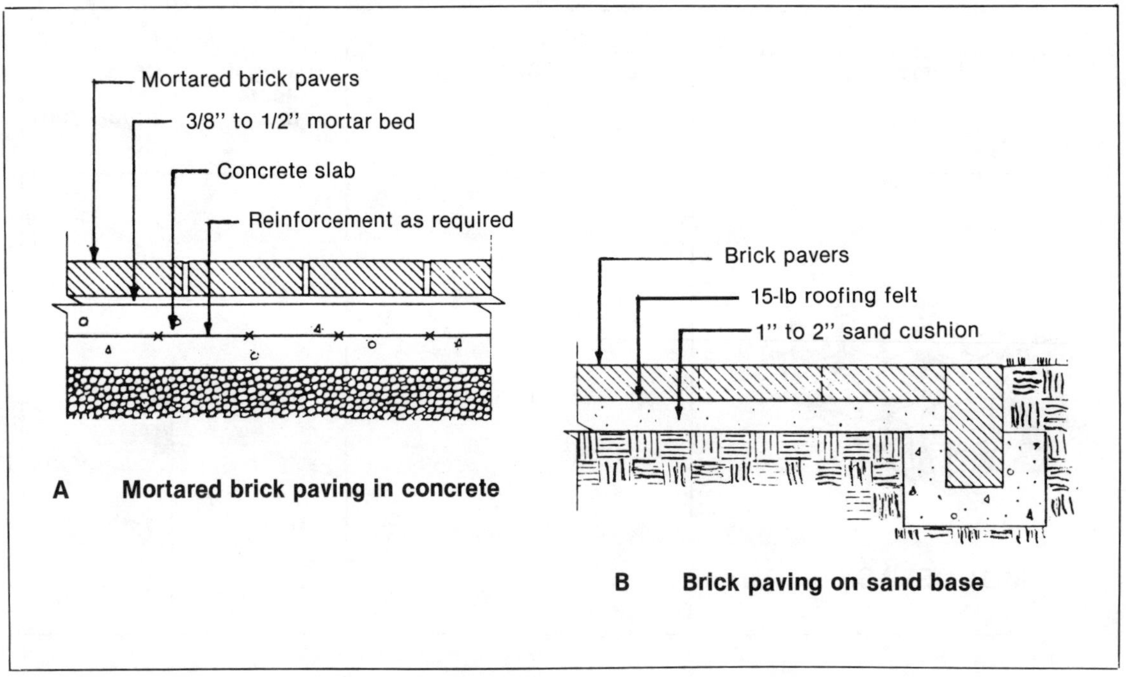

Two commonly-used brick paving bases
Figure 3-20

Mortarless brick can be installed over all three types of bases. It's popular because it's economical, gives good performance and is durable because the brick interlock. Section B of Figure 3-20 shows mortarless brick installed over a sand base.

The Take-Off

Each type of paving should be noted and measured separately. The size, shape, pattern and texture will affect the production and labor cost. Identify the type of material for the joints and bedding, whether it's sand or mortar, and measure the quantities carefully. Describe the type of edging and the expansion joint material and determine the quantities.

The take-off is simple: measure the area and determine the number of square feet. Use this square foot area to calculate the number of brick required, the amount of bedding and jointing material needed, and the area of cleaning and waxing. Measure the expansion joint material and special edging units in lineal feet. List and price all the paving items on the summary sheet.

Sometimes you have to include the cost of the paver base in your bid. Of course, brick masons are capable of doing this work, but I recommend excluding this work from your bid or getting sub-bids.

I won't go into any more detail about brick paving. It's a highly competitive specialty that doesn't require a brick mason's skills. Avoid it if you can. If it's included in the specs, get a sub-bid. I've just tried to acquaint you with this type of work so you can take off quantities and use them for checking the sub-bids of paving contractors.

Acid Brick

Acid brick, as the name implies, is used for special conditions, such as building chemical-resistant floors, bins, and troughs in refineries, breweries, dairies, laboratories, and chemical plants. This is masonry, of course, but it's not like most other brickwork. It's specialized work best left to experts.

Nearly all well-burned clay masonry units have a high degree of chemical resistance. For extreme exposures, however, chemical-resistant clay masonry units (ASTM C 279) are recommended. They're formulated from hard-burned shale for maximum chemical resistance. The standard size is 3⅞'' x 1⅜'' x 8''. Special shapes, cove base and corners are available. The brick colors are usually earth tones. The ends are ground to size for a perfect fit. They're available in a choice of surfaces.

The laying of acid brick begins with a smooth concrete surface which is coated with a special primer. Then 1/4'' membrane is laid in the primer. The brick are then set in a special acid-proof mortar, made up of acid-resisting powder and liquid resin.

Figure 3-21 is a sample specification provided by Atlas Minerals and Chemicals Inc., Mertztown, PA 19539. If you intend to handle any acid brick jobs, start a file of information on this product. The specifications will usually tell you the results that are expected, but the manufacturer's brochures will have more detailed information about the use and application of the products.

The Take-Off

Laying acid brick, like laying paving brick, is specialty work. You can bid on the job, but another contractor who specializes in this type of work will probably have lower costs and more skilled tradesmen. You may be better off excluding this work or getting a sub-bid from a contractor who handles a larger volume of acid brick masonry.

If you're going to take on an acid brick job, first go over the specifications thoroughly so you understand what's required. Then take time to examine the work site. The working conditions will have a definite effect on production. Here are some of the working conditions you'll be looking for:

1) Heat, cold, humidity, wind, or other weather factors

2) The location of the work. Is it high or low? Is there head room? Will the brick layer be working among pipes or other obstructions?

3) Contact with chemicals. Will special clothes be required, or gloves and goggles?

Measure the square feet of area to be paved. Multiplying this area by the brick factor (pieces per square foot) will give you the number of brick required. The area will also give you a basis for pricing the primer, membrane, control joints and cleaning. Take off cove base, bullnose caps and corners in lineal feet. Get a good quantity survey and a current list of prices and you'll have enough information to evaluate sub-bids.

Atlas Minerals & Chemicals Division
Mertztown, Pennsylvania 19539

Specification for Acid-Proof Brick Floors

Scope:

The work covered by this specification consists of furnishing all materials, equipment and labor to completely install the acid-proof brick floor in strict accordance with the applicable drawings and specifications.

General:

The concrete substrate upon which the acid-proof membrane and acid-proof brick floor is to be installed must be a neat, dense, homogenous finished concrete surface free of pits and honeycomb properly sloped to all drains and trenches. A minimum pitch of 3/16" per foot must be maintained to insure proper drainage. The concrete substrate is to be floated free from ridges and depressions. A maximum variation of 1/8" is allowable as measured under an 8' long straight-edge laid in any direction. All contours, elevations and slopes desired in the finished floor must be present in the substrate, less the thickness of the *Atlastic 31* membrane, and the acid-proof brick. The *Atlastic 31* membrane and the brick floor cannot be manipulated to make up for deficiencies in the concrete substrate. The finished concrete must have a tight, sand finish, free of laitance. The finished slab must be kept clean and dry, free of all dirt, oil, grease or similar contaminants under cover and protected from the elements.

All floor drains are to be set by the mechanical contractor prior to pouring of any concrete slabs. The tops of the drains shall be set above the concrete fill and 1/8" below the elevation of the finished acid-proof brick floor. All drains shall be set level.

During the installation of the acid-proof brick floor, the slab temperature shall not be below 65 degrees F. and not above 85 degrees F.

Material:

A. Primer
The primer shall be *Atlastic 31* Primer as manufactured by *Atlas Minerals and Chemicals Division,* Mertztown, Pennsylvania. After the concrete surface is inspected and found to be free from defects one coat of *Atlastic 31* Primer is applied by brush or spray and allowed to dry until tack-free. The drying time is a function of the ambient temperature, i.e., temperature above 70 degrees F., approximately 4 hours, below 70 degrees F. more than 4 hours. Care should be taken to insure that all surfaces are completely primed.

B. Atlastic 31

Atlastic 31, as manufactured by *Atlas Minerals and Chemicals Division,* Mertztown, Pennsylvania, is an oxidized asphalt, free from fillers or adulterants. It shall contain no coal tar, phenol or naval store products.

Courtesy: Atlas Minerals & Chemicals, Inc., Mertztown, PA

Sample specification for acid brick
Figure 3-21

Heat **Atlastic 31** until hot enough to flow like water. Pour three to four gallons at a time on the primed concrete. Quickly spread to a uniform thickness by means of a tempered Masonite squeegee. The first several layers of **Atlastic 31** should be thin so that all bubbles resulting from freeing of entrained air or moisture in the concrete will be broken. Apply additional **Atlastic 31** until a uniform 1/4" thick continuous film is obtained.

C. Acid-Proof Brick

Brick shall be standard 8 x 3¾ x 1⅜" floor brick. The brick shall be dark red in color and shall be hard burned Eastern shale for maximum chemical resistance. The brick and shapes, such as cove base and corners, shall not absorb more than 5% of its weight of water and shall conform to ASTM C279. All brick must be dry and free of dirt or dust when laid. They must be free from cracks, chips, warpage and must be uniform in color.

D. Acid-Proof Mortar Vertical Joints Only

Carbo-Alkor Mortar is room temperature curing chemical resistant mortar, prepared by mixing two parts by weight of an inert carbonaceous powder containing an acid setting agent, with one part by weight of a furfuryl alcohol based resin. Powder and resin are as manufactured by **Atlas Minerals and Chemicals Division**, Mertztown, Pennsylvania. **Carbo-Alkor** Mortar must contain sufficient reserve setting agent to withstand contamination by 2% by weight of Portland Cement Powder and still set hard at 75 degrees F.

Powder Other than the inorganic acid setting agent, the **Carbo-Alkor** Powder shall contain no water soluble or acid soluble ingredients and at least 90% of it shall consist of inert carbonaceous material properly graded to produce optimum workability of the mortar and minimum porosity in the finished cement. The powder shall be free from organic sulfonic acids, iron compounds and organic chlorides.

Liquid Resin The **Carbo-Alkor** Liquid Resin shall be substantially a furfuryl alcohol polymer reduced with monomeric furfuryl alcohol and shall contain a minimum of 90% polymerizable materials with no free furfuryl, phenol or formaldehyde present. The **Carbo-Alkor** Cement, when fully set, must be resistant to all concentrations of sodium hydroxide, hydrofluoric acid, hydrochloric acid, sodium chloride, acetone, ethyl alcohol, gasoline, benzene, detergents, vegetable and mineral oils and various food acids at temperatures up to 350 degrees F.

E. Expansion Joints

Thioment Expansion Joint Compound must be a two component system consisting of a base compound and accelerator which, when mixed together following the manufacturer's instructions, form a pourable product of high viscosity and capable of conversion at room temperature to a tough elastomeric solid. Both components are as manufactured by **Atlas Minerals and Chemicals Division,** Mertztown, Pennsylvania.

The base compound shall be composed of a fluid polysulfide polymer and a carbonaceous filler.

Courtesy: Atlas Minerals & Chemicals, Inc., Mertztown, PA

Sample specification for acid brick
Figure 3-21 (continued)

Expansion joints shall be provided in the brickwork immediately above my control joint in the substrate. Expansion joints shall be 1/4" minimum width and poured to the full depth of the joint. Under no circumstance should back-up fillers be used in lieu of **Thionent.**

In traffic areas if Expansion Joints are required, **Rezklad** Expansion Joint shall be used.

F. Installation of Acid-Proof Brick

Before laying any brick, membrane should have a final inspection to insure:

1. Minimum 1/4" thickness was obtained. 2. Proper grades and slopes to drain have been achieved. 3. Maximum variation under an 8' straight-edge laid in any direction does not exceed 1/16".

Application of *Carbe-Alkor* Cement to Brick

Carbo-Alkor Cement is buttered on acid-proof brick using the usual bricklayer's method. Brick should be clean and dry and at a moderate temperature before being laid. Temperature at the time of installation should be between 60 degrees F. and 85 degrees F. When it is not, the steps noted above should be taken. In addition when the temperature is below 60 degrees F., portable heaters, such as salamanders, should be used to bring the temperature up to the minimum. The brick may also be heated but care should be taken to be sure that they do not become too hot to handle with the bare hands.

During and after completion of the installation the area must be kept dry and free from foreign matter such as construction dirt, Portland Cement, plaster and other contaminants which would interfere with the setting of the cement.

Fully butter (2) vertical surfaces of brick. Set brick onto the membrane squeezing and tapping until true, then remove excess mortar with trowel. Lay bricks so that joints are broken and laid in even courses. Vertical joints shall not exceed 1/8" in width. Finished floor shall be uniformly level and/or shall pitch uniformly to drains, free from humps and depressions to assure complete drainage. Adjust high and low corners of floor brick or cut brick to produce a uniformly smooth floor.

All cutting of brick as required for fitting against walls, drains, columns, valleys and the like, shall be made with brick saw. Cut brick carefully and accurately and fit neatly around all adjoining work. Broken irregularities resulting from trowel cutting and large triangular areas filled with mortar will not be permitted.

Keep traffic off completed areas until joints have hardened.

Courtesy: Atlas Minerals & Chemicals, Inc., Mertztown, PA

Sample specifications for acid brick
Figure 3-21 (continued)

CHAPTER FOUR

Stonework

he term *cut stone* includes all stone cut or machined to size and shape. There are many types of stone, but the most popular is Indiana limestone. I'll mention other cut stone, but most of this chapter will concentrate on Indiana Limestone.

Indiana Limestone

Indiana limestone began forming eons ago when billions of minute marine animals died. Their bodies were compressed by many layers of earth into a stone known to geologists as "oolitic limestone." The deposits are located almost exclusively in three counties in Indiana.

The limestone is practically non-crystalline in character, usually having no cleavage plane. It's also remarkably uniform in composition, texture and structure. And it has a thermal expansion rate that's less than half that of many other building materials. That means the "moving joints" and wide cracks common to many other masonry materials aren't a problem with Indiana limestone.

This particular type of limestone has become famous throughout the United States for its building capabilities, durability, distinctive appearance and sheer beauty. There are three grades of Indiana limestone, based on the fineness of grain: select, standard and rustic. It's marketed in three colors, also: gray, buff and variegated.

Finishes

Indiana limestone is sold with a variety of standard machine and hand-tooled finishes. Here are some of the most commonly-used finishes:

Sand-sawn finish— The texture left on the stone as it comes from the gang saw. It's a moderately smooth, granular surface, varying with the texture and grade of the stone.

Rough shot-sawn or chat-sawn finish— A rough gang-saw finish produced by sawing with coarse chat or chilled steel shot.

Smooth machine finish— This is generally recognized as the standard finish.

Machine finish— A finish produced by the planers.

Wet rubbed finish— A smooth finish obtained by rubbing with sand and water or carborundum and water.

Honed finish— A superfine smooth finish.

Machine tooled finish— A grooved finish produced by four, six or eight parallel, concave grooves to the inch.

Carborundum finish— A very smooth finish, produced by a carborundum machine instead of a planer.

Plucked finish— A special finish obtained by rough planing the surface of the stone, breaking or plucking out small particles to give a rough texture.

Stone Anchors

Figure 4-1 shows typical anchors for anchoring stone to masonry. They're made from 1/8'' x 1'', 3/16'' x 1'', 3/16'' x 1¼'', 1/4'' x 1'' and 1/4'' x 1¼'' steel, in plain finish, electro-galvanized or hot dip galvanized, and stainless steel. You can get special sizes made to order. They're also available in brass, bronze and zinc alloy.

The Estimate

Ordinarily, stone requirements are measured in square feet, lineal feet and cubic feet, depending on the use. Panels and facing areas are measured in square feet of a specified thickness. Measure each thickness separately. Measure sills, copings, ledges, caps, and similar items in lineal feet of each profile. Measure cheek blocks, slabs and columns by the cubic feet of each item.

It's important to keep the quantities of each item separate for two reasons: The cost of the material for the various items will be different, of course. And the cost of the labor to install the different items will vary.

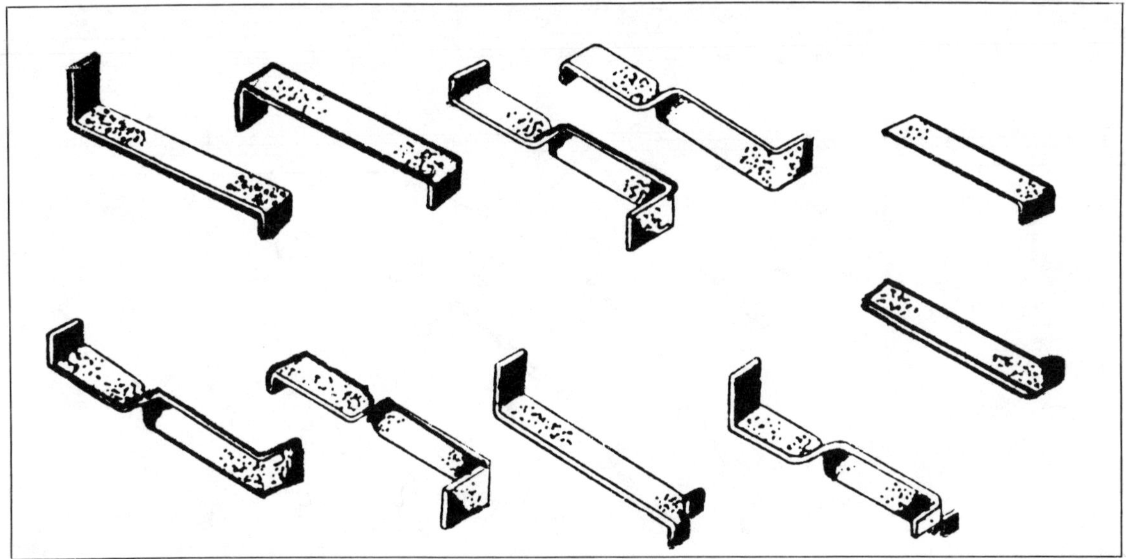

Stone anchors
Figure 4-1

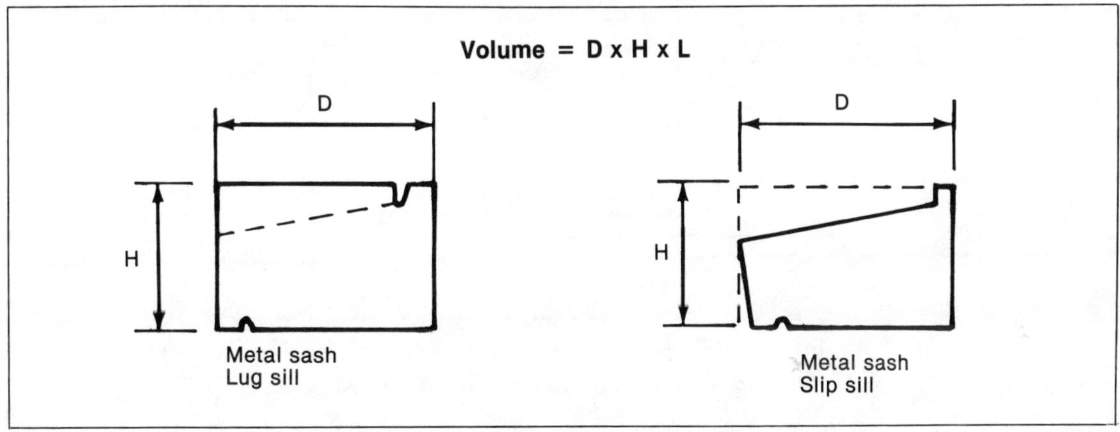

Finding the boxed-in dimensions of typical sills
Figure 4-2

On jobs where there's a considerable amount of stone, stone fabricators will make their own take-off and will usually be willing to tell you the quantities in cubic feet for each item. Keep a list of those fabricators who are willing to work with you. Using the fabricator's figures to check your estimate is helpful. But do your own take-off and convert the answer to cubic feet first. No prudent masonry estimator would submit a bid based only on a fabricator's take-off.

When figuring the cubic feet of irregular items such as sills, copings, caps, and so on, the volume should be based on overall or "boxed-in" dimensions, not the net dimensions. Figure 4-2 shows how to find the boxed-in dimensions of some typical sills. You'll also use the boxed-in measurement at arches and curved walls. Figure 4-3 shows how.

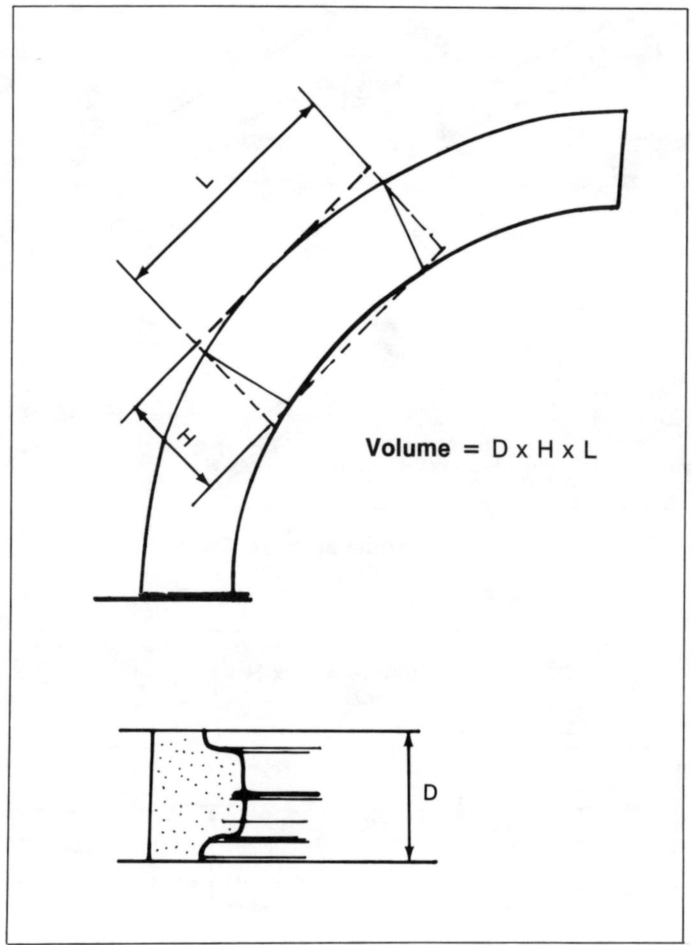

Finding the boxed-in dimensions of curved stone
Figure 4-3

Look at Figure 4-4 for some additional information on Indiana limestone, including the wind load design, thermal resistance and physical properties. Figure 4-5 gives typical production rates and mortar requirements for laying limestone and sandstone. The production rate is figured in square feet per bricklayer per day, based on average stone weight. But as with all production rates in this manual, these figures are only a general guide until you have more accurate rates based on your own cost records. Actual production rates will vary widely with working conditions and the crew you use.

Engineers usually assume the average weight of Indiana limestone is 165 pounds per cubic foot. That's a generous average and allows for mortar. The actual average weight of seasoned Indiana limestone will be about 144 pounds per cubic foot.

Now let's look at a sample limestone facing take-off.

LIMESTONE NOTES

COMPOSITION AND STRUCTURE

Indiana Limestone is a calcite-cemented calcareous stone formed of shells and shell fragments, practically non-crystalline in character. It is found in massive deposits located almost entirely in Lawrence, Monroe, and Owen counties in Indiana. This limestone is characteristically a freestone, without pronounced cleavage planes, possessing a remarkable uniformity of composition, texture, and structure. It has a high internal elasticity, adapting itself without damage to extreme temperature changes.

COLOR

Indiana Limestone is marketed in the following color-tones.
GRAY-The Gray is a silvery gray stone with a slightly bluish cast.
BUFF-The Buff varies from a very light creamy buff or buff-gray, to a distinct brownish-buff.
VARIEGATED -Consists of both buff and gray stone with some pieces containing both color-tones.

AVERAGE WEIGHT

The average weight of dry (seasoned) Indiana Limestone is 144 LBS. per cubic foot.

WIND LOAD DESIGN

Recommended thickness based on uniform windload of 20 LBS./SF safety factor 10 to 1 supported at top & bottom only

PANEL HEIGHT	THICK-NESS	WT. LB./SF. STONE ONLY	MAX. PANEL WIDTH
8'-0''	3''	36	6'-0''
8'-6''	3 1/4''	39	6'-0''
9'-0''	3 1/2''	42	5'-6''
9'-6''	3 5/8''	44	5'-0''
10'-0''	3 7/8''	47	4'-6''
10'-6''	4''	48	4'-6''
11'-0''	4 1/4''	51	4'-6''
11'-6''	4 1/2''	54	4'-6''
12'-0''	4 5/8''	56	4'-0''
12'-6''	4 7/8''	59	4'-0''
13'-0''	5''	60	4'-0''
13'-6''	5 1/4''	63	4'-0''

THERMAL CONDUCTANCE & RESISTANCE

Values based on conductivity (K) of 6.5 Btu/hr/SF/°F/in

Thickness	Conductance	Resistance	Thickness	Conductance	Resistance
2''	3.25	.31	06''	1.08	0.93
3''	2.23	.45	08''	0.81	1.25
4''	1.62	.62	10''	0.65	1.54
5''	1.30	.77	12''	0.54	1.85

PHYSICAL PROPERTIES AND RECOMMENDED VALUES

PROPERTY	VARIABLE RANGE	DESIGN CONSIDERATIONS	RECOMMENDED WORKING VALUE (Safety Factor = 10)	SOURCE
Weight (dry, seasoned)	140-150 per CF.			ASTM C97-47
Specific Gravity	2.1-2.75			ASTM C97-47
Absorption by weight	0.6-7.47	7 1/2% Max.		ASTM C97-47
Compressive Strength	4000-12000 PSI	Rec. min. 4000 PSI	400 PSI	ASTM CI70-50
Modulas of Rupture	700-1600 PSI	Rec. min. 700 PSI	70 PSI	ASTM C99-52
Tensile Strength	300-715 PSI	Rec. min.300 PSI	30 PSI	US Bur. Stds.
Modulus of Elasticity	3,300,000-5.8 PSI			ILI
Shear	900-1800 PSI	Rec. min. 900 PSI	90 PSI	US Bur. Stds.
Coefficient of Expansion*	0000024-30-in. F°			US Bur. Stds.
Abrasive Resistance	5.8-17.4			ASTM C241-51
Fire Resistance Rating (4'' stone)		1 hr. 39 min.		UL Pilot Test
Light Reflection Factor	50%-55%			ILI
Porosity (% pore space)	11.76-17.72			ILI

*Thermal expansion of most materials intimately associated with Indiana Limestone is approximately 3 times the rate of limestone:
Indiana Limestone .0000027. Concrete .0000080, Steel .0000067, Marble (ave.) .0000073, Granite (ave) .0000045, glass (ave.) .0000048.

Low expansion rate of Indiana Limestone thus has important dimension advantages. The well-know "moving joints" and wide cracks common to many other materials are almost entirely eliminated with the use of Indiana Limestone.

The moisture expansion of Indiana Limestone, due to moisture variation, is considered negligible.

Limestone notes
Figure 4-4

Production Per Bricklayer Per Day

Limestone 165 lb/CF
Sandstone 147 lb/CF
Precast concrete 144 lb/CF

Use	Description	Size	Production	CF Equivalent
Veneer	Sawn 4 sides	4″	54 SF	18.0
Veneer	Sand rubbed	4″	51 SF	17.0
Sawn ashlar	Random coursed	4″	50 SF	16.7
Split ashlar	Coursed	4″ x 2-¼″	54 SF	18.0
Split ashlar	Coursed	4″ x 5″	57 SF	19.0
Split ashlar	Coursed	4″ x 8″	63 SF	21.0
Paving	Random	1″ & 2″	60 SF	—
Plain trim	Sawn	5″ x 3″	143 LF	14.9
Plain trim	Sawn	10″ x 3″	77 LF	16.1
Plain trim	Sawn	14″ x 3″	58 LF	17.0
Molded sills	Sand rubbed	6″ x 3″	96 LF	12.0
Molded sills	Sand rubbed	6″ x 5″	72 LF	15.0
Steps	Sand rubbed	14″ x 6″	45 LF	26.3
Bevel coping	Sand rubbed	9″ x 4″	80 LF	20.0
Bevel coping	Sand rubbed	13″ x 4″	65 LF	23.5
Carved letters	Inset	8″	6 EA	—
Carved letters	Raised	8″	4 EA	—

Mortar
CF cut stone x (0.04 to 0.10) = CF mortar

Production rates and mortar requirements for limestone, sandstone and precast concrete
Figure 4-5

A Sample Stone Take-Off

This stone take-off is for the building shown in Figures 4-6 (floor plan) and 4-7 (wall sections). Figure 4-8 shows the specifications and Figure 4-9 is the completed take-off sheet. It's similar to the face brick take-off in Chapter 3. If you compare the two take-offs, you'll see that the headings on the take-off sheet are changed to relate to limestone instead of face brick. The first column is headed *4″ limestone veneer with ties* instead of *4″ face brick with ties.*

The opening sizes stay the same, so the *outs* or deductions are the same on both take-offs. Compare the two take-off sheets (Figure 3-10 and Figure 4-9). You'll see that most of the numbers are the same.

On the bottom line, the quantity of limestone is 1,674 square feet. Transfer it to the summary sheet as square feet. This makes for easier material pricing, and it's convenient for estimating other items such as production and cleaning, which are priced in square feet. There's more about this in Chapters 7 and 8.

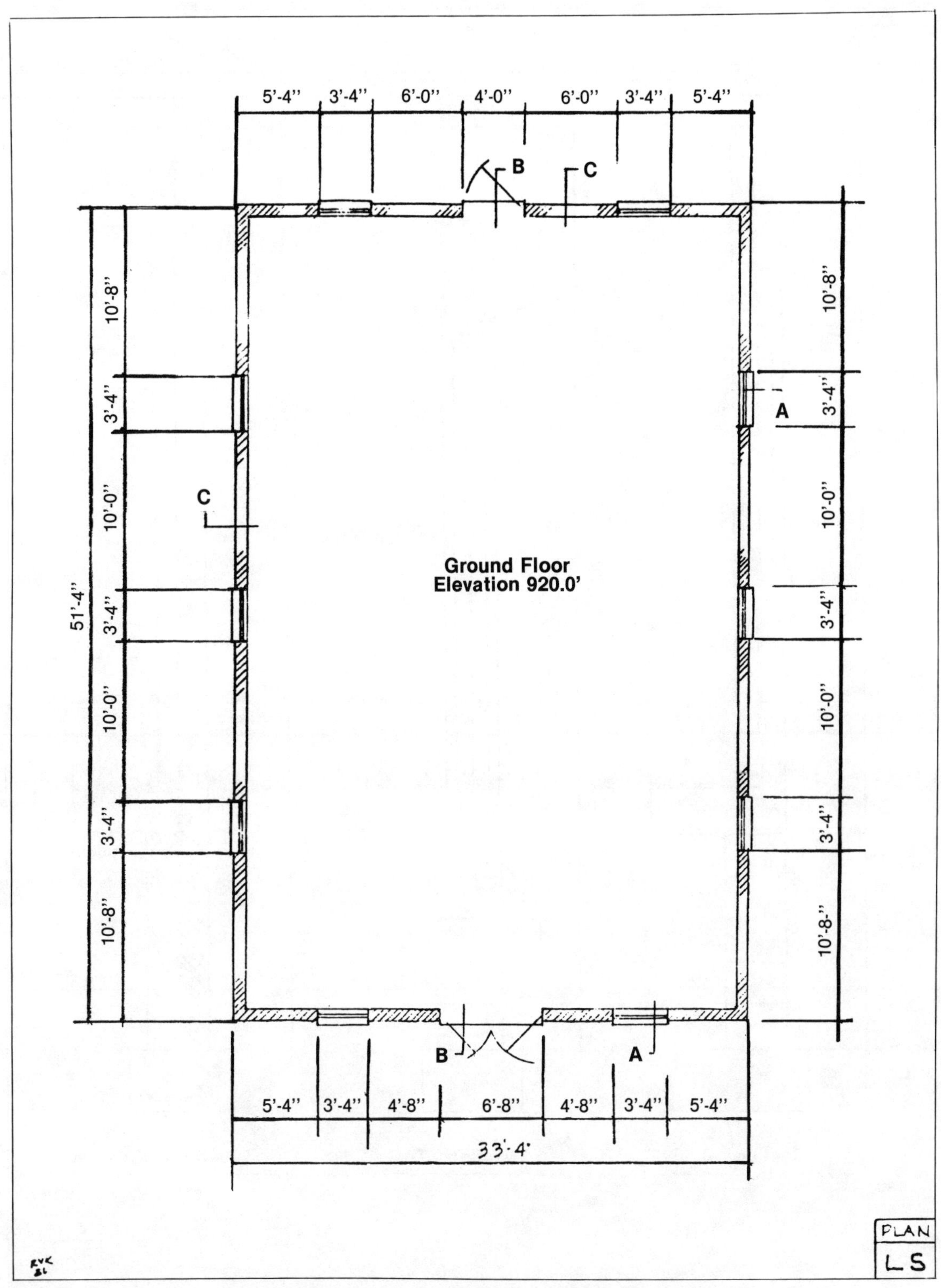

Floor plan for sample limestone take-off
Figure 4-6

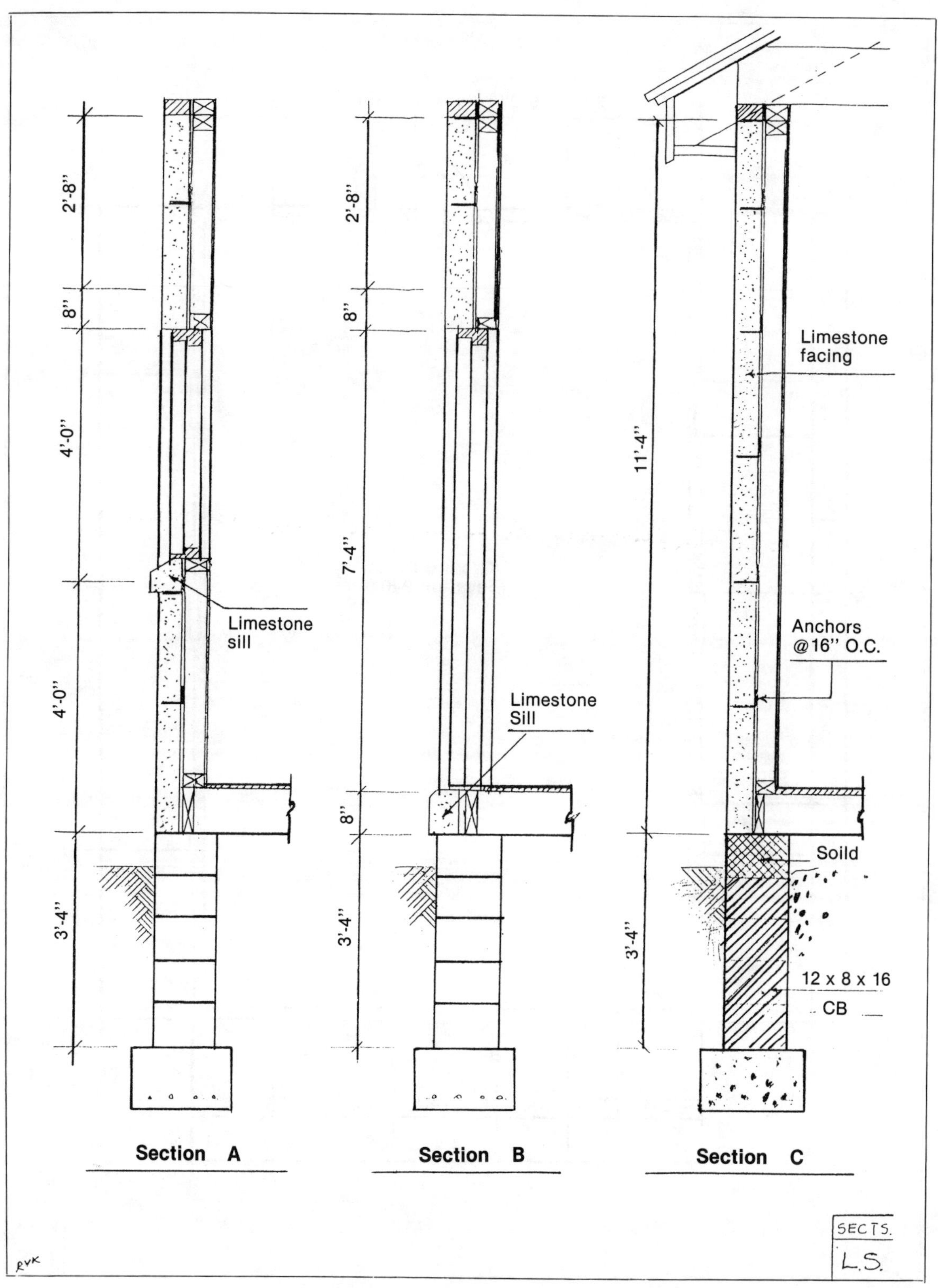

Wall sections for sample limestone take-off
Figure 4-7

MASONRY QUANTITY SURVEYS

123 Beech Drive
Cincinnati, OH 45123

DATE

SHEET   OF

EST. BY

BID DUE

BLDG. *SAMPLE BUILDING*   OWNER _______________

LOCATION _______________   ARCHITECT _______________

PLAN NOS. *L.S.*   DATE _______________   GEN. CONTR. _______________

Specification Section _______________ Date_______________ Addenda_______________

Face Brick	Size	Allowance				
Common Brick	Size *STD.*	Material				
Glazed Tile	Size	Material				
Concrete Block *(FDN.)*	Size *12 x 8 x 16*	Material				
Exp. Joints	Type	Material				
Control Joints	Type	Material				
Fill	Walls	Material				
Flashing	Furnished By	Material				
Caulking	Furnished By	Material				
Parging	Thickness					
Anchors	Type	Galv.	WT.	Spacing	H	V
Ties	Type *CRIMPED* Galv. ✓		WT. *24 GA*	Spacing	H *16"*	V *24"*
Reinforcing	Type	Galv.	WT.	Spacing		V
PC Concrete	Sills	Copings	Lintels	Facing		
Stone	(Sills)	Copings	Trim	(Facing) *4" SMOOTH LIMESTONE*		
Bond Beams	Fill Furn. By					
P.C. Lintels						
Cleaning	Materials *SOAP & WATER*					
Workmanship	Bond	Joints				
Waterproofing	*NONE*					
Special						
Alternates						

Specification sheet for sample limestone take-off
Figure 4-8

MASONRY QUANTITY SURVEYS

123 Beech Drive
Cincinnati, OH 45123

DATE

SHEET   OF

EST. BY   *RVK*

BID DUE

BLDG.   *SAMPLE BLDG*   OWNER

LOCATION   ARCHITECT

PLAN NOS.   *LS*   DATE   GEN. CONTR.

			4" LS Veneer w/ Ties SF	12" CB Solid D.O LF	12" CB SF	Flash @ Fl. Line	Soldier @ Head	LS Sill 5×8 @ DR LF	Flash @ Head	LS Sill 5×5 @ Wind LF	Flash @ Sill
			11⁻		3"						
			169⁴	170°	169⁻	NONE	NONE		NONE		NONE
			(1920)		(565)						
DR	6⁻ ×8⁻		① 57					① 7			
"	4° ×8⁻		① 34					① 4			
WD	3⁴ ×4°		⑩ 155							⑩ 34	
			246								
				170 ×.75	565 ×1.125						
			1674	128	636	—	—	11	—	34	—
			✓	✓	✓			✓		✓	
			WALL TIES ×.375 628 ✓	12" REINF ×.700 446 ✓							

Sample limestone take-off
Figure 4-9

Because the stone take-off is very similar to the face brick take-off, we can use the same forms and measurements. The same technique can be used for other facing materials, such as fieldstone, granite, marble, even precast concrete.

When you're estimating stonework, make sure you understand what is included in the stone fabricator's sub-bid. As mentioned above, many stone fabricators will give you sub-bids for all the quantities of stone in their take-off. Their quantities are usually in cubic feet, so you'll have to convert all your stone items from square feet to cubic feet to compare them. Figure 4-5 will help you do this.

Here's how we convert the limestone in our take-off:

$$\underline{1674 \text{ SF of } 4'' \text{ facing}}$$
$$1674 \times \frac{4}{12} = \qquad 558.0 \text{ CF}$$

$$\underline{11 \text{ LF of sill } 5 \times 8}$$
$$11 \times \left(\frac{5 \times 8}{144}\right) = \qquad 3.1 \text{ CF}$$

$$\underline{34 \text{ LF of sill } 5 \times 5}$$
$$34 \times \left(\frac{5 \times 5}{144}\right) = \qquad \underline{6.0} \text{ CF}$$
$$\text{Total} \qquad 567.1 \text{ CF}$$

The price the fabricator gives you is a lump sum figure based on the cubic feet in his take-off. If it checks with your cubic foot estimate, use his price, adding it to the bottom of your summary sheet as a sub-bid. Be sure it includes tax, trucking, loading and unloading.

Transfer all the items from your take-off sheet to the summary sheet. There won't be any numbers in the material column opposite the limestone veneer or sills because the sub-bid includes the material cost delivered to the job.

You will, however, have numbers in the labor column opposite these items. The sub-bid doesn't include labor costs. You'll fill in the labor costs according to the production rates for setting each item.

A complete limestone take-off and estimate is explained in Chapter 11, including how to handle sub-bids.

Some Tricks of the Trade

Stone is a challenging material to both masons and masonry estimators because it can be used in so many ways. The material cost for most bidders on a stone job will be about the same. But you'll have more decisions to make and skill to demonstrate when pricing the labor. Use your ingenuity when estimating stonework. Here are some examples that may help you get more jobs installing stone.

Example 1— An estimator had to decide how the limestone panels on a five-story office building would be hoisted into place. With the help of the masonry superintendent, he came up with a scheme. Outriggers were attached to the steel structure

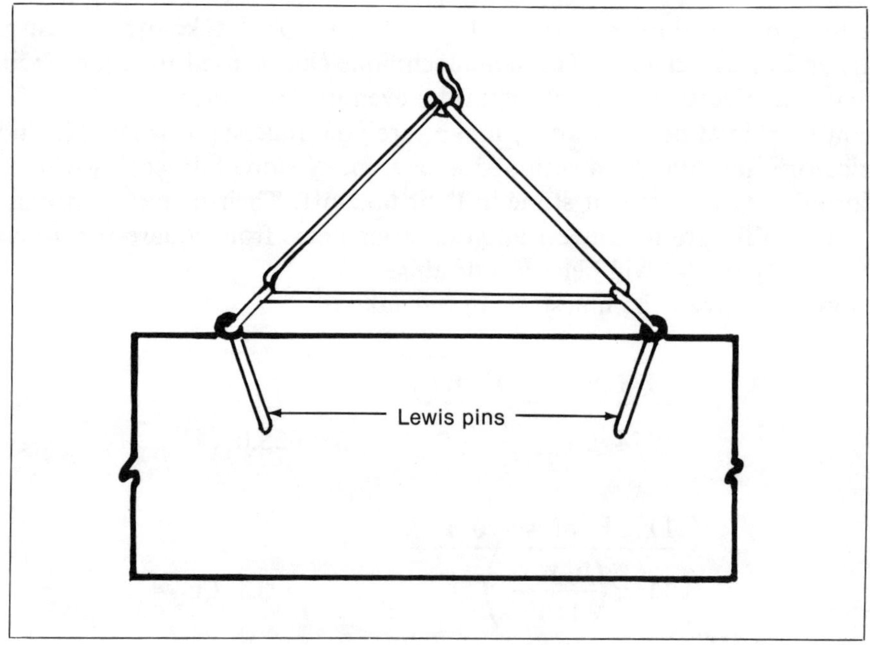

Lewis pins used for lifting stone
Figure 4-10

at the roof level, similar to those used for hanging scaffolding. These outriggers could be much lighter, however, because they had to hoist only the stone panels, one at a time. A monorail extending the full perimeter of the building was fastened to the outriggers. Then they suspended an electric motor with a lightweight, reel-type hoist from the monorail on a roller. With this arrangement they could move the hoist laterally around the building and raise and lower the hoist to the desired height from ground level with a remote control button.

The stone panels, with pre-drilled Lewis holes, were delivered to the job site at convenient locations around the building. Figure 4-10 shows the Lewis pins used for lifting the stone.

The panels were erected in record time, and the contractor made a good profit on a difficult job.

Example 2— The estimator and superintendent were even more ingenious on another job. It was an impressive hospital building entrance, with two huge slabs of stone cheek block on each side of the steps. The slabs were to be set on a concrete foundation faced with stone panels. Figure 4-11 shows the design.

The stones were approximately 4'0'' x 8'' x 8'0'', weighing about 3,400 pounds. The task at hand was to set, precisely, the huge stone atop the prepared foundation and stone facing without chipping the stones. That meant they couldn't resort to using crowbars for the final adjustment. Even though chipped stone can be patched with a simulated mortar, these patches aren't usually acceptable except in inconspicuous places.

After the stone facing was precisely set on a level foundation, they laid 1/4''-diameter stainless steel rods atop the stone and concrete to assure that the weight of the cheek

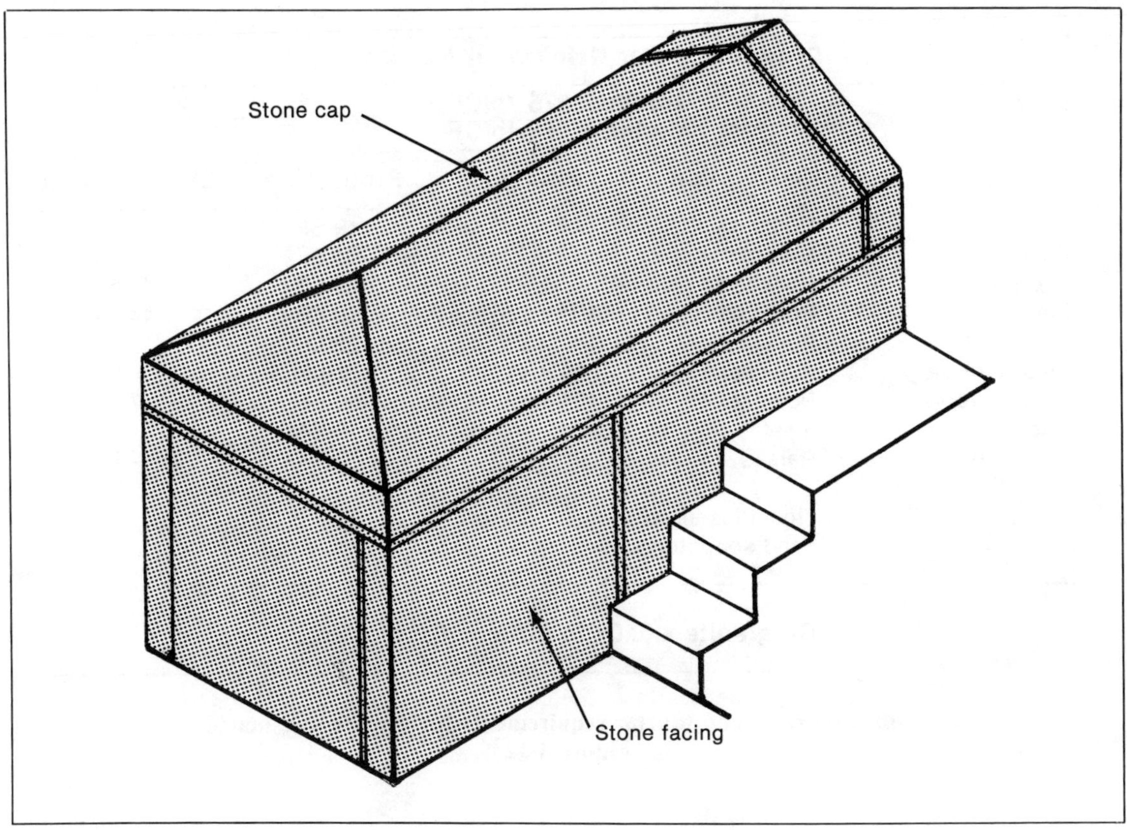

Cheek block at building entrance
Figure 4-11

blocks wouldn't squeeze the mortar beyond the 1/4'' thickness.

The hoist was readied, the slings were placed to carry the stone in a level position, and the mortar beds were prepared. Now here's where the experience of an astute superintendent was useful. He knew that after the huge stone was maneuvered into place and the slings removed, the chances of the stone falling into exactly the right position were slim. So he devised a scheme to let the huge stone down slowly. He covered the top of the foundation with ice cubes, arranged to evenly support the stone. The slings were removed and stone masons with blocks of wood guided the stone down slowly as the ice melted.

The cheek blocks were precisely set, with no chips, and the joints were exactly 1/4'' thick, ready for pointing.

Like a football coach, a good estimator must know what his men can do.

Granite

Granite is a fine stone used by architects to enhance the beauty of masonry work. Although it's not used as often as cut stone, you can find it on many public buildings, especially in entrances and steps.

Production Per Bricklayer Per Day

Granite	175 lb/CF
Marble	165 lb/CF

Use	Description	Size	Production	CF Equivalent
Veneer	Polished	4″	49 SF	16.4
Paving	Smooth	1″ & 2″	54 SF	—
Plain trim	Polished	5″ x 3″	129 LF	13.5
Plain trim	Polished	10″ x 3″	70 LF	14.6
Plain trim	Polished	14″ x 3″	53 LF	15.5
Sills & stools	Polished *	6″ x 1″	125 LF	5.3
Sills & stools	Polished *	10″ x 1″	100 LF	7.0
Carved letters	Inset	8″	5 EA	—
Carved letters	Raised	8″	2 EA	—

*Includes slate
and soapstone

Mortar
CF granite x (0.04 to 0.10) = CF mortar

Production rates and mortar requirements for granite and marble
Figure 4-12

Measure and price granite the same way you measure and price cut stone. Figure 4-12 gives typical production figures and mortar requirements for granite.

Marble, Slate

These materials are seldom included in the masonry section of the specifications. Occasionally, however, a masonry contractor is asked to include items such as sills and ledges in a bid. If this happens to you, there are two things to look out for. Note the exact thickness (3/4″, 1″, 1¼″, etc.) and check the number of polished faces when pricing. Take off quantities of materials in lineal feet of the various sizes and types.

The production rates for granite in Figure 4-12 also apply to marble and slate.

Precast Concrete

Precast concrete items such as sills, caps, copings, cornices and steps are often specified in the masonry section of the specifications. If so, you'll include them in your take-off and request sub-bids from local fabricators for competitive prices of the materials.

Here are some of the items you may be requesting sub-bids for: stone slabs, patio stones or stepping stones, splash blocks, posts, bollards, balusters, surveyor's monuments, copings, sills, steps, catch basins, curbs, driveway markers, benches, tables and planters.

The Estimate

The estimating procedure is the same as for cut stone. The production rates and mortar requirements in Figure 4-5 apply. Note that mortar quantities for all stonework vary with conditions. Some stones are neatly cut on the back side, while others are very rough. The voids caused by rough stones are filled with mortar. You'll have to use judgment and experience when making mortar estimates.

Fieldstone

Fieldstone (rubble and flagstone) is used in many communities to accent better quality buildings, park walls, walkways, entrances, patios, and landscaping. In many parts of the U.S. beautiful and durable stone is available at modest prices. It's no wonder that fieldstone is popular.

Kinds and Descriptions

Once you know the basics of fieldstone, you'll want to learn to recognize the various types of stone by name. Here's a list of some of the varieties of stone, with their colorful names and a brief description of each:

Snow Mountain Crystal— A white mountain stone with sections of pale quartz laced with veins of silver and green mica. Quarried from the Blue Ridge Mountains, this stone is a chunk-type rubble. Approximate coverage is 45 to 50 square feet per ton.

California Travertine— A rugged chunk-type rubble characterized by interesting textures combined with soft neutral colors of brown, tan, cream, and off-white shades. This travertine marble is quarried from the Feather River Canyon area of Northern California. Approximate coverage is 45 to 50 square feet per ton.

California Driftstone— A heavily eroded chunk rubble ranging in color from medium to earthy brown to nearly black. The eroding action of desert sand storms has produced a texture finish on the stone similar to that of driftwood. Approximate coverage is 35 to 40 square feet per ton.

Indian Creek Fieldstone— A natural strata-face sandstone for webwall construction, with an interesting range of weathered earthy color tones. Irregular shapes lend well to random fieldstone patterns. Approximate coverage is 50 to 55 square feet per ton.

Silver Green— A silvery green mountain stone with some flint and light orchid overtones. Quarried from the Blue Ridge Mountains, this stone is laid in a modified fieldstone pattern. Approximate coverage is 50 to 55 square feet per ton.

Victor Red Rock— A chunk-type rubble with a weathered surface of reddish brown to orange. When it's broken open, it reveals a bone-white, heavily fossilized rock. Approximate coverage is 35 to 40 square feet per ton.

V.O. Blue Frost Rubble— A light blue-gray chunk rubble with a few light tans and blacks for emphasis. Its wide variety of shapes and sizes offer an interesting interplay of light and shadow. Approximate coverage is 35 to 40 square feet per ton.

Ebony Stone— A jet black mountain stone with white veining and some overtones of green and gold. Quarried from the Blue Ridge Mountains, this stone is a chunk-type rubble. Approximate coverage is 50 to 55 square feet per ton.

V.O. Drift (Pink Thins)— A volcanic tuff formed 700,000 years ago in the rugged Sierra Nevada Mountains of Northern California. Has pinkish-gray background with highlights of rust-orange. Produced with sawn back and natural-weathered face, this stone weighs only 8 pounds per square foot and is affixed to the wall with mastic mortar. Approximate coverage is 250 square feet per ton.

Santa Fe Lava— A "heavy" lava from America's newest deposits in New Mexico (only 2,000 years old). Rust black in color, this deposit is much cleaner than older ones, which are often laden with silt, so it's better suited for building stone. Approximate coverage is 55 to 60 square feet per ton.

Mountain Orchid— A multi-colored stone with a basic orchid background and overtones of green, yellow, red and white has various colored flint pebbles. Quarried from the Blue Ridge Mountains, this stone is laid in a modified fieldstone pattern. Approximate coverage is 45 to 50 square feet per ton.

Victor Log— An extremely hard quartzite with honey-cream and pink to light gray and deep rust color. Quarried from the mountains of north Georgia, this stone is laid in a webwall pattern. Approximate coverage is 45 to 50 square feet per ton.

Victor Silver Gray— An extremely hard quartzite with sparkling light to dark silver-gray coloring. Quarried from the mountains of north Georgia, this stone is laid in a webwall pattern. Approximate coverage is 45 to 50 square feet per ton.

V.O. River Rounds— Stone is predominantly granite smoothed from eons of washing and tumbling in river beds. Colors are subdued reds, pinks, greens, black, and white, with sizes ranging from 4" to 9". Approximate coverage is 40 to 45 square feet per ton.

Glacier Quarry Fossil Stone— A glacier-tumbled smooth stone composed of small animal and plant particles compressed and crystallized. Rust-gold coloring within the fossil impressions complement the blue-gray color range of the stone. Approximate coverage is 45 to 50 square feet per ton.

The Estimate

Your estimate for fieldstone will be by the square foot of coverage for each thickness.

Production Per Bricklayer Per Day				
Rubble stone 150 lb/CF (Fieldstone)				
Use	**Description**	**Size**	**Production SF/Day**	**CF Equivalent**
Veneer	4″ F1S random size	One man	60	20.0
Wall	8″ F1S random size	One man	42	28.0
Wall	8″ F2S random size	One man	30	20.0.
Wall	12″ F1S random size	One man	36	36.0
Wall	12″ F2S random size	One man	26	26.0
Wall	16″ F1S random size	One man	33	14.0
Wall	16″ F2S random size	One man	21	28.0
Wall	20″ F1S random size	One man	31	51.7
Wall	20″ F2S random size	One man	20	33.3
Wall	24″ F1S random size	One man	30	60.0
Wall	24″ F2S random size	One man	18	36.0
Pointing			200	
Cleaning			240	

Mortar
CF stone x (.015 to 0.40) = CF mortar

Production rates and mortar requirements for fieldstone
Figure 4-13

Unfortunately, fieldstone is purchased by the ton. Ask your supplier for conversions from ton to square foot for each type of stone and each thickness they sell. Some old-timers may remember buying this stone by the "perch," which is approximately 25 CF.

Figure 4-13 shows typical production rates for fieldstone, based on square feet per bricklayer per day. Again, use these only as a guide until you have better production rates based on your own crews.

CHAPTER FIVE

Mortar

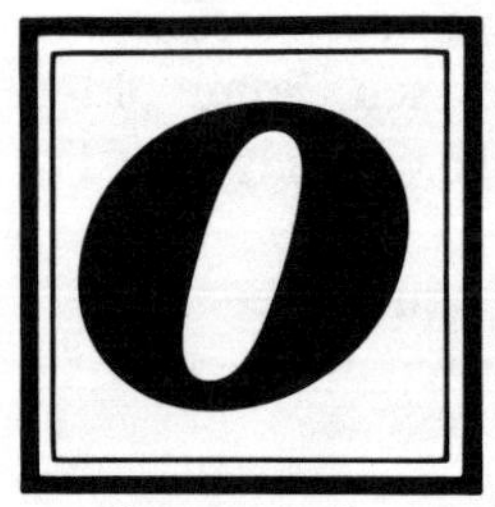

nce you've taken off the amount of unit masonry, the next step is estimating the mortar. But before you can do that, you must know what kind of mortar is appropriate for the job. This chapter begins with a short course in mortar — its history, its components, and the ASTM specifications.

All mortar is made with a cementing agent, a fine aggregate, and water. The cementing agent may be cement, lime, or a combination of cement and lime. The fine aggregate is usually sand.

Masonry mortars were used as far back as 2690 B.C. in the Great Pyramid of Giza in Egypt. The massive stone blocks of this monument were cemented together with a mortar made of burned gypsum and sand. Later, in ancient Greece and Rome, mortars were produced from materials such as burned lime, volcanic tuff and sand.

Mortar stayed about the same until early in the 20th century, when portland cement was first manufactured. This led to a greatly improved mortar made from portland cement and lime, and to a new product called masonry cement.

Mortar binds masonry units together, seals the joints against penetration by air and moisture, and bonds well with steel reinforcement, ties, and anchor bolts. Today, selecting the best mortar for a particular project means balancing the needs with the materials available. No single type of mortar is best for all purposes.

Material	ASTM Designation
Portland cement Types I, II, III	C 150
Air-entraining portland cement Types IA, IIA, IIIA	C 175
Blended cement Types IS, ISA, IP, IPA, S, SA	C 595
Masonry cement	C 91
Quicklime Hydrated lime	C 5 C 207
Aggregate	C 144

Note: A - Air entraining
     P - Pozzolan
     S - Slag

Reprinted with permission from Annual Book of ASTM Standards, Volume 4.05. Copyright ASTM, 1916 Race Street, Philadelphia, PA 19103

ASTM designations
Figure 5-1

ASTM Mortar Designations

The American Society for Testing and Materials has established standards for materials commonly used in mortars. Figure 5-1 shows the kinds of mortar and the ASTM designations. We'll look at them one at a time, beginning with portland cement.

Portland Cement (C 150)

Portland cement, the principal cementitious ingredient in masonry mortars, is a hydraulic cement. That means that it begins hardening when mixed with water. Portland cement comes in three types:

- Type I: For general purpose construction

- Type II: For resistance to sulphate action. It gives off less heat as hydration takes place

- Type III: For high early strength development

Air-Entraining Portland Cement (C 175)
Air-entraining portland cements are C 150, Types I, II, or III cement with a very small amount of an air-entraining additive. Three types are recommended by the ASTM: Type IA, Type IIA, and Type IIIA. An air-entraining agent makes the concrete more plastic when it's liquid and more durable when it's hardened. It also improves the bond of hardened mortar and reduces the amount of waste.

Blended Cement (C 595)
Blended cements include portland blast furnace slag cement, in these types: IS, ISA; portland pozzolan cement, types IP, IPA; and slag cement, types S, and SA.

Masonry Cement (C 91)
Masonry cement is a mixture of portland cement and finely ground inert limestone or hydrated lime. Gypsum is sometimes added to regulate the setting time. Other agents can be added to influence plasticity, water retentivity and durability.

Quicklime (C 5)
Quicklime is essentially calcium oxide (CaO). The disadvantage of quicklime is that it must be carefully mixed with water (slaked) and stored for as long as two weeks before using. Slaking the quicklime gives off heat from the chemical reaction. Take precautions when slaking quicklime. Wear gloves and protective glasses.

Hydrated Lime (C 207)
Hydrated lime is quicklime which has been slaked before packaging. It's much more convenient to use than quicklime because it can be mixed into the mortar right out of the bag.

Aggregate (C 144)
Natural and manufactured sand can be used in mortar. Natural sand comes right out of the ground. You'll often see it referred to as *bank-run sand*. Manufactured sand is made by crushing stone, gravel, or air-cooled blast furnace slag. It's characterized by sharp, angular particles.

Figure 5-2 gives recommended sand gradation limits. But architects and engineers don't always stick to the recommended gradations. When they do deviate, however, they make sure that compressive strength and water retention limits are exceeded. In certain areas of the country you can save quite a bit of money doing this.

Water
Water used for masonry mortars should be clean and free of acids, alkalies, and organic materials. Architects like to call it *potable* or *suitable for domestic consumption* in their specifications. Essentially, if you wouldn't drink it, don't use it for mortar.

Sieve size	Percent passing	
	Natural sand	Manufactured sand
No. 4	100	100
No. 8	95 - 100	95 - 100
No. 16	70 - 100	70 - 100
No. 30	40 - 75	40 - 75
No. 50	10 - 35	20 - 40
No. 100	2 - 15	10 - 25
No. 200	-	0 - 10

Reprinted with permission from Annual Book of ASTM Standards, Volume 4.05. Copyright ASTM, 1916 Race Street, Philadelphia, PA 19103

Standard specification for aggregate for masonry mortar (ASTM C 144)
Figure 5-2

Mortar Types

Of the cementing materials listed in Figure 5-1, masonry cement and a combination of portland cement and lime are used the most. Mortar is given a type designation by the ASTM based on the proportion of these materials. Figure 5-3 shows the types of mortar and the proportions of materials they must contain. Figure 5-4 shows the compressive strength of different types of mortar.

Mortar type	Parts by volume of portland cement* or portland blast furnace slag cement**	Parts by volume of masonry cement	Parts by volume of hydrated lime or lime putty	Aggregate measured in damp, loose condition
M	1	1 (Type II)	---	Not less than 2¼ and not more than 3 times the sum of the volumes of the cements and lime used.
	1	---	¼	
S	½	1 (Type II)	---	
	1	---	over ¼ to ½	
N	---	1 (Type II)	---	
	1	---	over ½ to 1¼	
O	---	1 (Type I or II)	---	
	1	---	over 1¼ to 2½	

*Types I, II, III, IA, IIA, IIIA	**Types IS, ISA

Reprinted with permission from Annual Book of ASTM Standards, Volume 4.05. Copyright ASTM, 1916 Race Street, Philadelphia, PA 19103

Mortar proportions by volume
Figure 5-3

**Compressive strength of cubes
for mortar types
(ASTM C 270)**

Mortar* type	Average compressive strength at 28 days, PSI
M	2,500
S	1,800
N	750
O	350

*Formerly A1, A2, B, and C

*Reprinted with permission from Annual Book of ASTM Standards, Volume 4.05.
Copyright ASTM, 1916 Race St., Philadelphia, PA 19103*

**Compressive strength of mortar according to type (ASTM C 270)
Figure 5-4**

Whether you use masonry cement or a portland cement and lime combination is largely a matter of economics and convenience. Either will produce acceptable mortar as long as the ASTM specifications are met.

Type M Mortar

Type M mortar is specifically recommended for unreinforced and reinforced masonry below grade and in contact with earth, such as foundations, retaining walls, walks, sewers and manholes. It has high compressive strength and excellent durability.

Type S Mortar

Type S mortar is recommended for use in reinforced masonry, for unreinforced masonry where maximum flexural strength is required, and for use where mortar is the only bonding agent between facing and backing. It has a reasonably high compressive strength and a high tensile bond strength.

Type N Mortar

Type N mortar is recommended for exterior walls wherever they're subject to severe exposure, for chimneys, and for parapet walls. It's a medium strength mortar suitable for general use in exposed masonry above grade.

Type O Mortar

Type O mortar may be used for load-bearing walls of solid masonry where compressive stresses do not exceed 100 PSI, provided that the exposure isn't severe. It has relatively low compressive strength but is suitable for limited exterior use and general interior use in load-bearing and non-bearing masonry. Check for the availability of prepackaged mortar.

Types A-1, A-2, B, C, and D Mortar

These type designations haven't been used since 1954. But you might come across them if you're dealing with specifications for an old building.

Estimating Mortar Quantities

Many masonry handbooks have tables that show the amount of mortar required to lay a given number of masonry units. Most of them agree on the amounts, but not all of them show how these quantities are determined.

Figure 5-5 shows how to find the quantity of mortar needed for two common masonry units:

1)   Section A shows how to find the cubic yards of mortar required to lay 1,000 modular (solid) face brick with 3/8'' mortar joints. A modular face brick is 7⅝'' long, 3⅝'' deep and 2¼'' high. To lay this unit, you would spread a layer of mortar L + H long, D deep and T thick.

2)   Section B shows the cubic yards of mortar required to lay 1,000 8 x 8 x 16 concrete block with 3/8'' mortar joints. To lay one of these, you'd spread mortar L + H long, *2D* deep and T thick.

Waste is included in these calculations. You'll notice that there's a 1/2'' allowance beyond the face of the unit. Some of this will be used for tooling. And note that the thickness of the joint is figured as 1/2'' instead of 3/8''. Some of this additional mortar will bond into the pores of the material.

Use these calculations as a guide until you have better figures based on the experience of your crews.

Figure 5-6 shows quantities of mortar required to lay 1,000 units of other masonry items.

Estimating Mortar Cost

To calculate the cost of mortar, you need to consider three variables: the materials, the proportions, and the additives. Figure 5-7 has several samples that show you how to calculate the cost of a cubic yard of mortar. Of course, you'll have to substitute your own costs for cement, lime and sand. Follow these examples when making your own calculations.

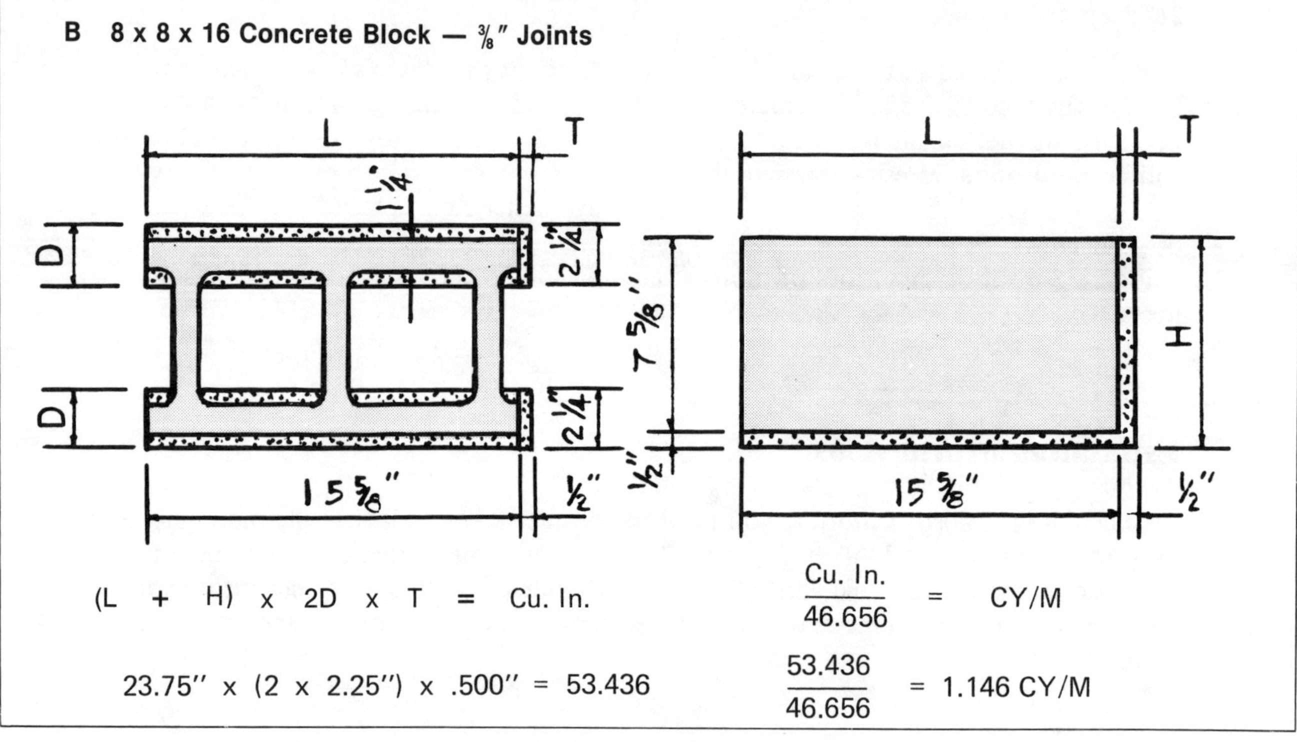

Mortar quantities needed for two common masonry units
Figure 5-5

Mortar Requirements

Concrete block
⅜″ joints

	CY/M
4 x 8 x 16 H	1.019
4 x 8 x 16 S	1.178
6 x 8 x 16 H	**1.146**
6 x 8 x 16 S	1.687
8 x 8 x 16 H	1.146
8 x 8 x 16 S	**2.196**
10 x 8 x 16 H	1.273
10 x 8 x 16 S	2.705
12 x 8 x 16 H	1.273
12 x 8 x 16 S	3.214
4 x 2¼ x 16 S	.911
4 x 4 x 16 H	.847
4 x 4 x 16 S	.979
8 x 4 x 16 H	.953
8 x 4 x 16 S	1.823
12 x 4 x 16 H	1.059
12 x 4 x 16 S	2.673

Structural clay tile
½″ joints

	CY/M
4 x 5 x 12 HC	.798
8 x 5 x 12 SP	1.099
4 x 8 x 12 HC	.887
8 x 8 x 12 HC	1.423
12 x 8 x 12 SP	1.188
4 x 10 x 12 HC	.975
1½ x 12 x 12 VC	.661
2 x 12 x 12 VC	.788
3 x 12 x 12 VC	.917
4 x 12 x 12 VC	1.023
5 x 12 x 12 VC	1.174
6 x 12 x 12 VC	1.303
8 x 12 x 12 VC	1.464
10 x 12 x 12 VC	1.817
12 x 12 x 12 VC	2.074

Spectra-Glaze
¼″ joints

Use mortar quantities as listed for concrete block.
Pointing should be considered.

Glass block
¼″ joints

4 x 6 x 6	.376
4 x 8 x 8	.498
4 x 12 x 12	.743

Facing brick
⅜″ joints

	CY/M
4 x 2¼ x 8 S	.515
4 x 2¼ x 12 S	.713
4 x 2¾ x 12 S	.738
4 x 4 x 8 S	.580
4 x 4 x 12 S	.781
4 x 8 x 8 H	.692
4 x 12 x 12 H	1.036
6 x 2¾ x 12 S	1.057
6 x 4 x 12 S	1.119
6 x 4 x 12 H	.676
8 x 4 x 12 H	.676
8 x 4 x 12 S	1.456

Structural glazed tile
¼″ joints

	CY/M
2 x 5 x 12 HC	.331
4 x 5 x 12 HC	.467
6 x 5 x 12 HC	.622
8 x 5 x 12 HC	.776
2 x 8 x 16 HC	.408
4 x 8 x 16 HC	.589
8 x 8 x 16 HC	1.002

Paving brick
⅜″ joints

4 x 1½ x 8 S	.268
1″ mortar bed	.820
8 x 1½ x 8 S	.354
1″ mortar bed	1.549
8 x 1½ x 8 S (Hex.)	.316
1″ mortar bed	1.347

H - Hollow   HC - Horizontal core   SP - Speed
S - Solid   VC - Vertical core

Mortar requirements for masonry units
Figure 5-6

<table>
<tr><td colspan="2">

Gypsum block
½″ joints

	CY/MSF
2 x 12 x 30 S	.547
3 x 12 x 30 H	.729
3 x 12 x 30 S	.729
4 x 12 x 30 H	.860
5 x 12 x 30 H	.991
6 x 12 x 30 H	1.121
8 x 12 x 30 H	1.383

Cut stone

.04 to .10 CF mortar per CF stone

</td><td colspan="2">

Precast concrete
.04 to .10 CF mortar per CF precast concrete

Fieldstone
.15 to .40 CF mortar per CF stone

Parging

	CY/MSF
⅜″	1.274
½″	1.698

Gypsum mortar

900 pounds gypsum cement
1 CY sand

</td></tr>
</table>

Mortar requirements for masonry units
Figure 5-6 (continued)

Standard   1:3   **Types**

		N	S	M
9 sacks masonry cement	@ $3.74 (N)	$33.66		
9 sacks masonry cement	4.12 (S)		$37.08	
9 sacks masonry cement	4.45 (M)			$40.05
1.5 tons sand	8.80	13.20	13.20	13.20
Per CY		$46.86	$50.28	$53.25

Standard   1:1:6

4.5 sacks portland cement	@ $4.68	$21.06
4.5 sacks lime	3.00	13.50
1.5 tons sand	8.80	13.20
Per Cy		$47.76

White   1:1:6   (With white sand)

4.5 sacks white portland cement	@ $12.12	$54.54
4.5 sacks lime	3.00	13.50
1.5 tons white sand	74.80	112.20
Per CY		$180.24

White   1:1:6   (With regular sand)

4.5 sacks white portland cement	@ $12.12	$54.54
4.5 sacks lime	3.00	13.50
1.5 tons sand	8.80	13.20
Per CY		$81.24

Color mortar   1:3

		N	S	M
9 sacks color masonry cement	@ $8.97 (S)		$80.73	
1.5 tons sand	8.80		13.20	
Per CY			$93.93	

Note: Use this table only as an example. Check current prices.

Calculating mortar costs
Figure 5-7

Finding the Mortar Cost per Unit

When you know the cost per cubic yard, it's a simple matter to find the cost of mortar per unit laid. For example, let's find the cost of standard type S mortar to lay modular (solid) face brick. Looking at Figure 5-6, we find it takes 0.515 cubic yards of mortar per 1,000 brick. In our example in Figure 5-7, a cubic yard of standard type S mortar costs $50.28. We can multiply that by 0.515 to find a total mortar cost per thousand brick of $25.89. Dividing that by 1,000, we come up with a per unit mortar cost of $0.02589, which we'll round to $0.026.

Let's try one more example. We're looking for the unit cost of standard type S mortar to lay 8 x 8 x 16 concrete block. In Figure 5-6 we find it takes 1.146 cubic yards of mortar per 1,000 block. We'll use the same mortar cost, $50.28. We multiply 1.146 by $50.28 to find the cost per 1,000, $57.62. Dividing by 1,000, we find a unit cost of $0.0576, or $0.058.

When we have the unit price, we're ready to fill in the prices on the summary sheet. Just multiply the unit cost by the number of units. Figure 5-8 shows a typical entry, based on the examples we've just done.

MASONRY QUANTITY SURVEYS

123 Beech Drive
Cincinnati, OH 45123

DATE

SHEET   OF

EST. BY

BLDG. ______________________   OWNER______________________   BID DUE

LOCATION ______________________   ARCHITECT______________________

PLAN NOS. __________ DATE __________   GEN. CONTR. ______________________

ITEM	UNIT	QUANTITY	MATERIAL		LABOR		WORK	TOTAL
			Unit	Amount	Unit	Amount		
MORTAR F. BRICK	PCS	30,000	.026	780 —				
" 8X8X16 CB	"	1,000	.058	58				
" 4X8X16 CB	"	900	.051	46				

Mortar calculations
Figure 5-8

CHAPTER SIX

Masonry Accessories

In this chapter we'll look at the miscellaneous materials you'll need. Very few projects use just mortar and block or brick. Nearly every estimate will include reinforcement, control or expansion joints, flashing, fill, insulation, flue lining, or clay coping. These are significant cost items and have to be considered carefully. Let's begin with wall reinforcement.

Wall Reinforcement

Wall reinforcing increases the strength of masonry walls. It's used for bonding and reinforcing composite and cavity walls for crack control, for anchoring masonry veneers, for increasing the strength of walls (flexural, axial and tensile strength) and to control temperature cracking. In areas where earthquakes are a structural hazard, reinforcing steel is essential in most walls.

Engineering design terms like flexural, axial, and tensile strength are beyond the scope of this book. If you're interested in learning more, however, I recommend *Concrete*

Masonry Handbook for Architects, Engineers, Builders by Frank A. Randall, Jr. and William C. Panarese. You can get a copy from the Portland Cement Association, 5420 Old Orchard Road, Skokie, IL 60076.

Dimensions

Reinforcing comes in many dimensions, patterns, and coatings. Figure 6-1 shows some of the reinforcing available for composite walls. Figure 6-2 shows reinforcing for cavity walls. The yard where you buy masonry supplies will probably have free literature on the reinforcing materials they sell.

Reinforcing is fabricated to accommodate composite walls, cavity walls and single wythe walls of thicknesses ranging from 3" to 18". It's manufactured in 10-foot lengths, and in several weights or sizes. Wire used in reinforcing must conform to ASTM A 82 for cold drawn steel wire for concrete reinforcement, and Federal Specification QQ-W-461f for hard tempered wire. Specifications usually call for the reinforcing to be laid in the wall at 16" o.c. measured vertically, with a 6" lap for bonding. Special prefabricated corners and ties are available.

Patterns

Many reinforcement patterns are available. They include *truss, ladder, tab-tie, 3-wire, 4-wire, drip,* and a variety of adjustable designs for cavity and veneer walls. The diagonal cross rods in the truss pattern help resist longitudinal tensile stresses. The cross rods in the ladder pattern give direct anchorage at 15" intervals along the reinforcement.

Read the specs carefully. Several patterns may be specified on a single job. Each pattern has its purpose. Look for different patterns when you're taking off wall reinforcing and list each pattern separately on your take-off sheet.

Finishes and Coatings

Reinforcing is available with a bright basic finish (uncoated) or with one of several zinc coatings. Coatings add corrosion protection at little additional cost. A stainless steel finish is also available. Zinc, the most widely used coating, is available in several coating weights. Reinforcement finishes and coatings usually are specified in accordance with ASTM standards. Make sure to provide reinforcement with the specified level of corrosion protection.

How to Estimate Wall Reinforcing

You don't have to measure reinforcing as a separate item. You can find the feet of reinforcing you'll need from the quantity of concrete block or brick measured. Here's an example: Assume you're estimating reinforcing for an 8 x 16 concrete block wall that's 14 courses high. The calculations would be:

$$\underset{[2]}{\overset{[1]}{\frac{1.333}{2}}} \times \underset{[4]}{\overset{[3]}{\frac{10.5}{10.0}}} \times \underset{[6]}{\overset{[5]}{\frac{6}{7}}} = \overset{[7]}{.60}$$

Design Types	Class	Side Rods	Cross Rods	Overall Wall Width	Backup Wall Width
Truss-2 wire*	Standard	No. 9	No. 9	8, 10, 12, 13, 14 or 16″	3, 4, 6, 8, or 10″
	Extra heavy	3/16″	No. 9		
Truss-3 wire	Standard	No. 9	No. 9	8, 10, 12, 13 14 or 16″	3, 4, 6, 8, or 10″
	Extra heavy	3/16″	No. 9		
Truss-4 wire	Standard	No. 9	No. 9	10, 12, 13, 14 or 16″	3, 4, 6, 8 or 10″
	Extra heavy	3/16″	No. 9		
Ladder-2 wire*	Standard	No. 9	No. 9	8, 10, 12, 13, 14 or 16″	3, 4, 6, 8 or 10″
	Medium	No. 8	No. 9		
	Extra heavy	3/16″	No. 9		
Ladder-3 wire	Standard	No. 9	No. 9	8, 10, 12, 14 or 16″	3,4, 6, 8 or 10″
	Medium	No. 8	No. 9		
	Extra heavy	3/16″	No. 9		
Ladder-4 wire	Standard	No. 9	No. 9	10, 12, 14 or 16″	3, 4, 6, or 10″
	Medium	No. 8	No. 9		
	Extra heavy	3/16″	No. 9		
Tab-Tie	Standard	No. 9	No. 9	8, 10, 12, 13, 14 or 16″	4, 6, 8, 10 or 12″
	Medium	No. 8	No. 8		
	Standard heavy	No. 9	3/16″		
	Heavy standard	3/16″	No. 9		
	Extra heavy	3/16″	3/16″		

* Also for single wythe walls

Reinforcing for composite walls
Figure 6-1

Design Types	Class	Side Rods	Cross Rods	Overall Wall Width	Backup Wall Width
Truss-2 wire*	Standard	No. 9	No. 9	8, 10, 12, 13, 14 or 16″	3, 4, 6, 8, or 10″
	Extra heavy	3/16″	No. 9		
Truss-3 wire	Standard	No. 9	No. 9	8, 10, 12, 13 14 or 16″	3, 4, 6, 8, or 10″
	Extra heavy	3/16″	No. 9		
Truss-4 wire	Standard	No. 9	No. 9	10, 12, 13, 14 or 16″	3, 4, 6, 8 or 10″
	Extra heavy	3/16″	No. 9		
Ladder-2 wire*	Standard	No. 9	No. 9	8, 10, 12, 13, 14 or 16″	3, 4, 6, 8 or 10″
	Medium	No. 8	No. 9		
	Extra heavy	3/16″	No. 9		
Ladder-3 wire	Standard	No. 9	No. 9	8, 10, 12, 13, 14 or 16″	3,4, 6, 8 or 10″
	Medium	No. 8	No. 9		
	Extra heavy	3/16″	No. 9		
Ladder-4 wire	Standard	No. 9	No. 9	10, 12, 14 or 16″	3, 4, 6, or 10″
	Medium	No. 8	No. 9		
	Extra heavy	3/16″	No. 9		
Tab-Tie	Standard	No. 9	No. 9	8, 10, 12, 14 or 18″	4, 6, 8, 10 or 12″
	Medium	No. 8	No. 8		
	Standard heavy	No. 9	3/16″		
	Heavy standard	3/16″	No. 9		
	Extra heavy	3/16″	3/16″		

* Also for single wythe walls

Reinforcing for cavity walls
Figure 6-2

Here are the steps you use to find the factor. The numbers of the steps that follow correspond with the numbers in brackets in the calculation.

[1]   Begin with the length of one 8 x 16 block (in feet).

[2]   Divide by 2 because the reinforcing is spaced 16'' o.c. (every other course).

[3]   Then multiply by the length of reinforcing plus a 6'' lap allowance.

[4]   Divide by the length of one piece of reinforcing (in feet).

[5]   Multiply again by the number of courses reinforced,

[6]   Divide by half of the total number of courses.

[7]   The result is the factor you use to find the linear feet of reinforcement per piece.

Now you can multiply the factor (0.60 in this case) by the number of block to find the linear feet of reinforcing required. If the wall requires 4,864 block, then the reinforcing required is:

$$4,864 \quad x \quad .60 \quad = \quad 2,919 \text{ LF}$$

Don't forget that this material is ordered by the bundle. Each bundle is 500 linear feet of reinforcing. To find how many bundles to order, divide the total by 500:

$$\frac{2,919}{500} = 5.8 \text{ or } 6 \text{ bundles}$$

Order six bundles of reinforcement. Figure 6-4 shows a sample take-off summary sheet that includes 4,864 block and the six bundles (3,000 LF) of reinforcing. Figure 6-5 shows the calculations that go on the back of the summary sheet. In each case, the first calculation finds the factor to use. The second calculation uses that factor to find the linear feet of reinforcing. The final calculation converts linear feet to the number of bundles to order.

Anchors and Ties

Anchors are used to attach masonry to its support, to other masonry, to a floor slab, a spandrel beam, or a column. Ties hold masonry together. Fasteners attach other building elements to masonry.

There are two basic types of anchors: rigid and flexible.

Rigid Anchors

Ridgid anchors resist tension, compression and shear, but not flexure. They're usually used in composite masonry construction. Anchor bolts embedded in masonry walls are used to hold sill plates firmly. Strip anchors tie intersecting walls together, and crimped anchors welded to door frames secure them in place. See Figure 6-6.

Flexible Anchors

Flexible anchors resist tension and compression, but not flexure or shear. They're most commonly used in cavity walls and for attaching masonry veneer walls to steel, concrete or other unit masonry. Some of these anchors are shown in Figure 6-7.

Some anchors, usually referred to as wall ties, are used in either rigid *or* flexible construction. See Figure 6-8. Figure 6-9 shows wire mesh ties used to bond intersecting walls at control joints.

The Estimate

Anchors and ties are usually made of galvanized rods, wire or sheet metal, or less frequently of stainless steel or bronze. The cost of anchors and ties is normally a small part of the overall bid price. But the cost will be much higher if the anchors specified have to be custom fabricated from special materials. Where anchors are welded to steel, the specifications will usually call for special painting to reduce corrosion at spots where the galvanizing is burned off.

To calculate the number of anchors or ties, you must know the spacing. It's usually 24" o.c. horizontally and 16" o.c. vertically, or one anchor every 2⅔ square feet. Your job specifications will identify the correct spacing.

MASONRY QUANTITY SURVEYS

123 Beech Drive
Cincinnati, OH 45123

DATE

SHEET   OF

EST. BY

BID DUE

BLDG. ______________________   OWNER______________________

LOCATION ____________________   ARCHITECT____________________

PLAN NOS. ____________ DATE __________   GEN. CONTR. ________________

EXAMPLE   SUMMARY   —   REINFORCING

ITEM	UNIT	QUANTITY	MATERIAL		LABOR		WORK	TOTAL
			Unit	Amount	Unit	Amount		
8" HWCB BRK B/U	PCS	4864						
6" LWCB CAV. B/U	✓	2431						
4" LWCB PART.	✓	5840						
— — — —								
— — — —								
— — — —								
— — — —								
— — — —								
— — — —								
8" STD-TR-REINF GALV	LF	3000					ⓐ	✳
6" EH-TABTIE " "	✓	1750					ⓑ	✳
4" STD-LADDER " BB	✓	3500					ⓒ	✳
✳SEE CALCULATIONS BACK OF THIS SHEET								

Summary sheet for sample reinforcing take-off
Figure 6-4

*** SUMMARY SHEET CALCULATIONS**

(a) 8" - STD - TR - GALV CL 1 - NO REINF. @ SLAB

$$\frac{1.333}{2} \times \frac{10.5}{10.0} \times \frac{6}{7} = .60$$

$$4864 \times .60 = 2919 \text{ LF}$$

$$\frac{2919}{500} = 6 \text{ BUNDLES}$$

(b) 6" - EH - TAB-TIE GALV. CL 3

$$\frac{1.333}{2} \times \frac{10.5}{10.0} \times \frac{7}{7} = .70$$

$$2431 \times .70 = 1702 \text{ LF}$$

$$\frac{1702}{250} = 7 \text{ BUNDLES } (1750')$$

(c) 4" - STD - LADDER GALV CL 1 - NO REIN TOP COURSE

$$\frac{1.333}{2} \times \frac{10.5}{10.0} \times \frac{6}{7} = .60$$

$$5840 \times .60 = 3504 \text{ LF}$$

$$\frac{3504}{500} = 7 \text{ BUNDLES } (3500')$$

Calculations for reinforcing take-off
(back of summary sheet)
Figure 6-5

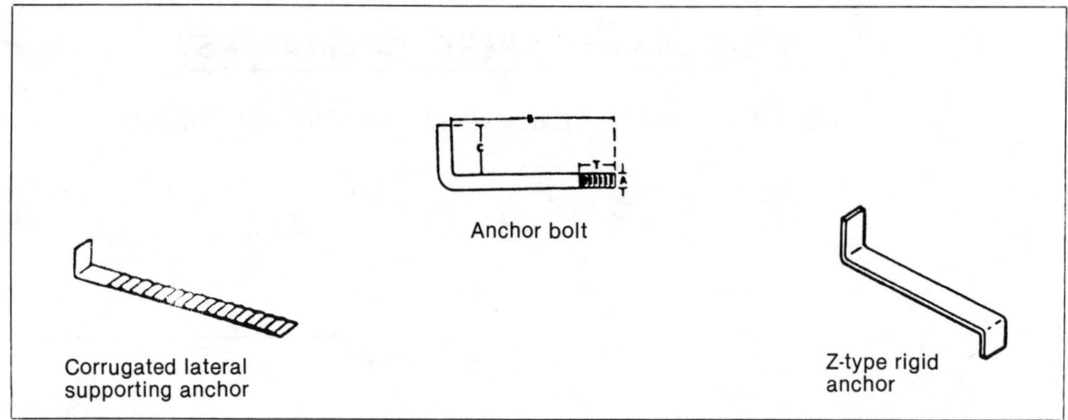

Rigid anchors
Figure 6-6

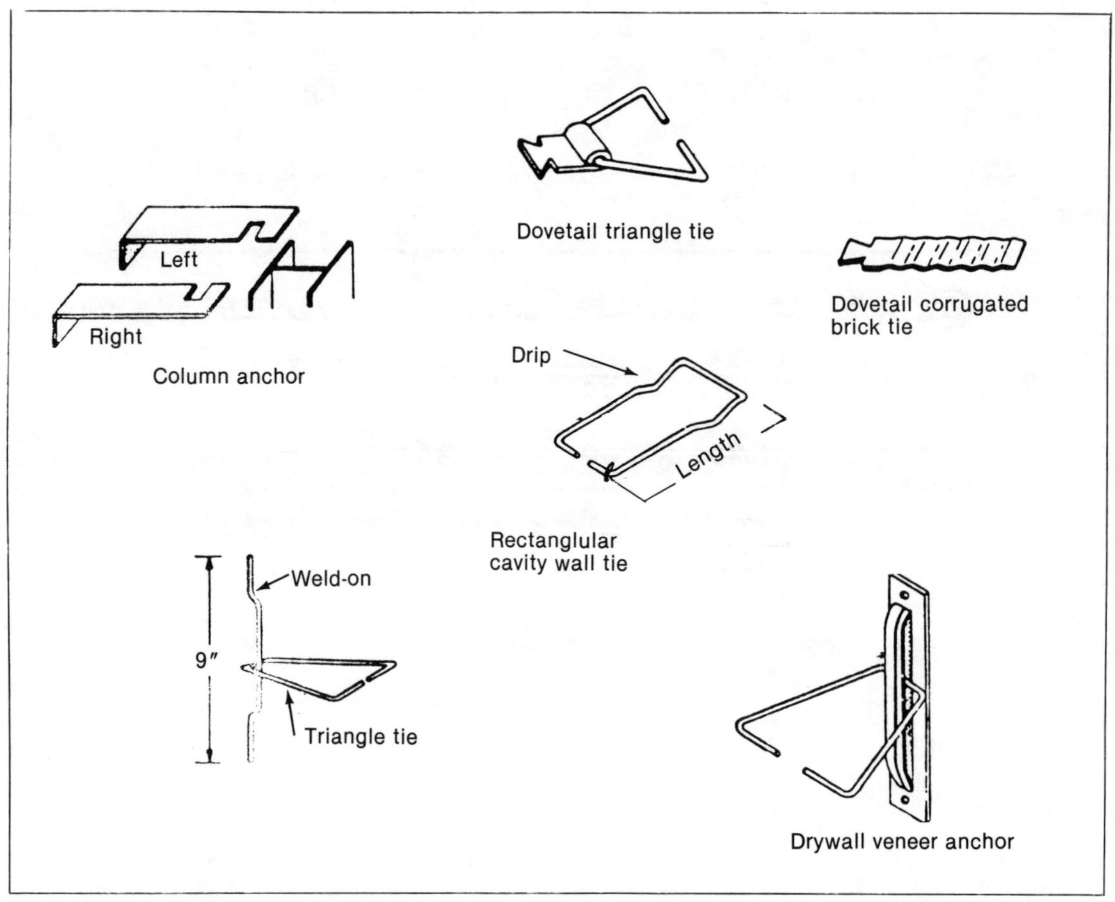

Flexible anchors
Figure 6-7

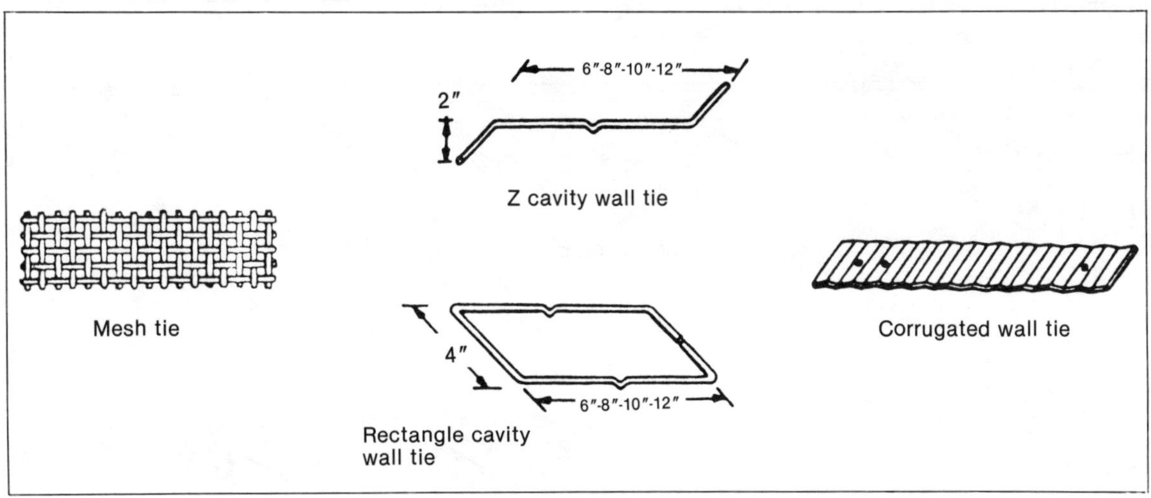

Wall ties
Figure 6-8

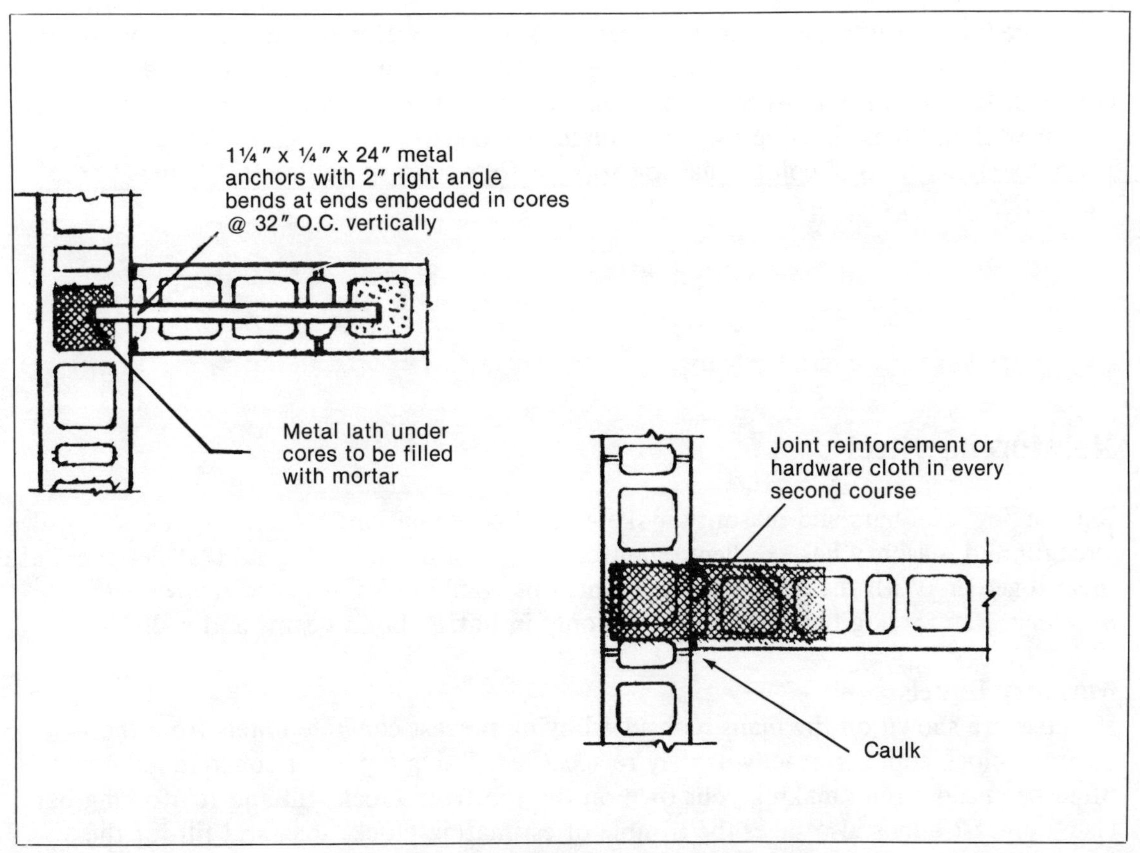

Wire mesh ties used to bond bearing walls
Figure 6-9

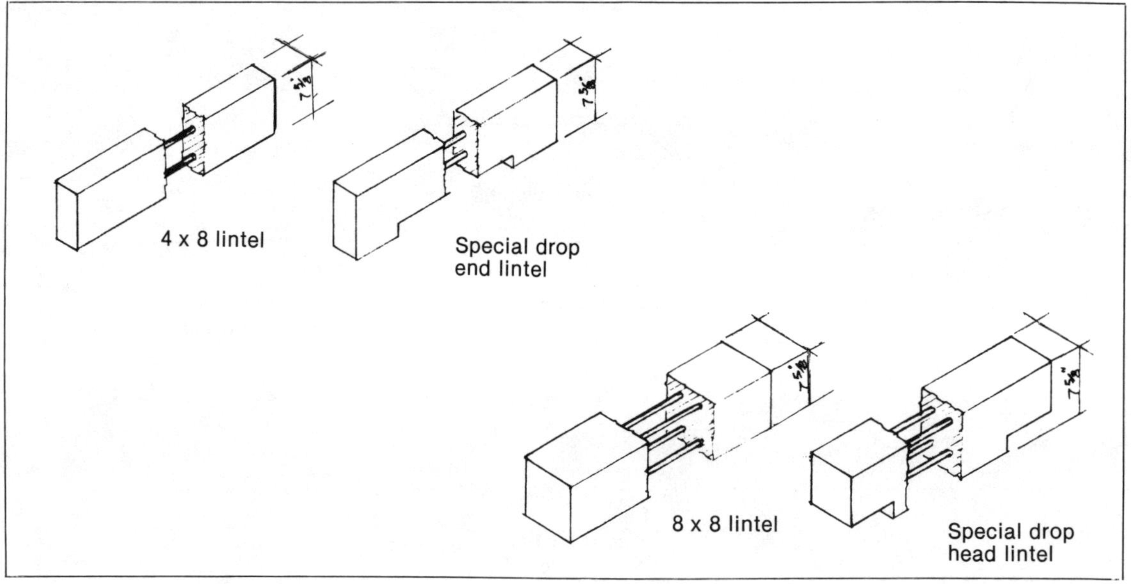

Typical precast lintels
Figure 6-10

Do the take-off in square feet (or linear feet) of each different anchor type or spacing, then convert to pieces so you can price them in the summary. For anchors used at columns, jambs and other specific locations, it's a simple matter of calculating the linear feet of wall and then dividing by the required spacing.

For example, if an 8' column has anchors on four sides spaced at 16'', your calculation would be:

$$\frac{4 \times 8'}{1.333} = 24 \text{ anchors}$$

Reinforcing Steel

Reinforcing steel bars and masonry make a good combination. Steel has excellent tensile strength and masonry has excellent compressive strength. So it's logical that designers use them together. With the help of some grout, this combination is called *reinforced masonry*. Reinforcing bars are used commonly in lintels, bond beams and walls.

Masonry Lintels

If lintels are shown on the plans, consider buying precast concrete lintels from the concrete block supplier exactly as they're specified. Using a precast concrete lintel will often be cheaper than making your own on the job from block, fill and reinforcing bars. Using precast lintels also saves the trouble of estimating block, steel and fill for the lintel. You will, however, have to take off the linear feet of lintel for each type of lintel required. Some of the more common designs are shown in Figure 6-10.

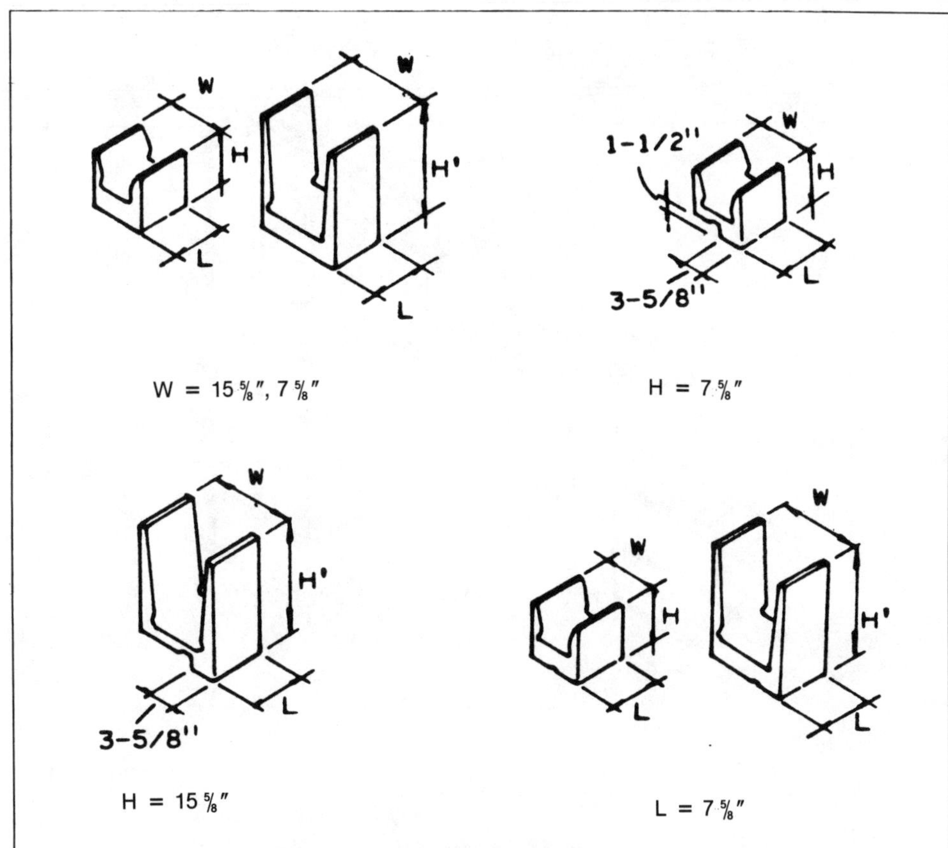

Concrete masonry lintel units
Figure 6-11

There are several advantages to precast concrete lintels: They can be delivered to the job ready for use. They don't require shoring. And they can carry a load as soon as they're set in place.

If you decide to assemble the lintels on site, you'll need specially formed lintel block. Some of these units are shown in Figure 6-11. The lintel units are laid end to end to form a channel in which reinforcing steel and concrete fill are placed. Until the fill has hardened, you'll need a temporary support for block placed above the opening. Another option is to fabricate the lintel on the floor then hoist it into place when the concrete has hardened. Figure 6-12 shows lintel block over an opening.

Bond Beams

Concrete bond beams are an important part of masonry walls. The difference between bond beams and lintels is that lintels always span openings. Bond beams are used to add strength around the perimeter of a building. You can expect to find bond beams at the top of masonry walls and sometimes at intermediate levels or under window sills. Bond beams can also serve as lintels over openings. They are constructed with special-shaped units that are filled with concrete and steel reinforcing. Figure 6-13 shows some of these units.

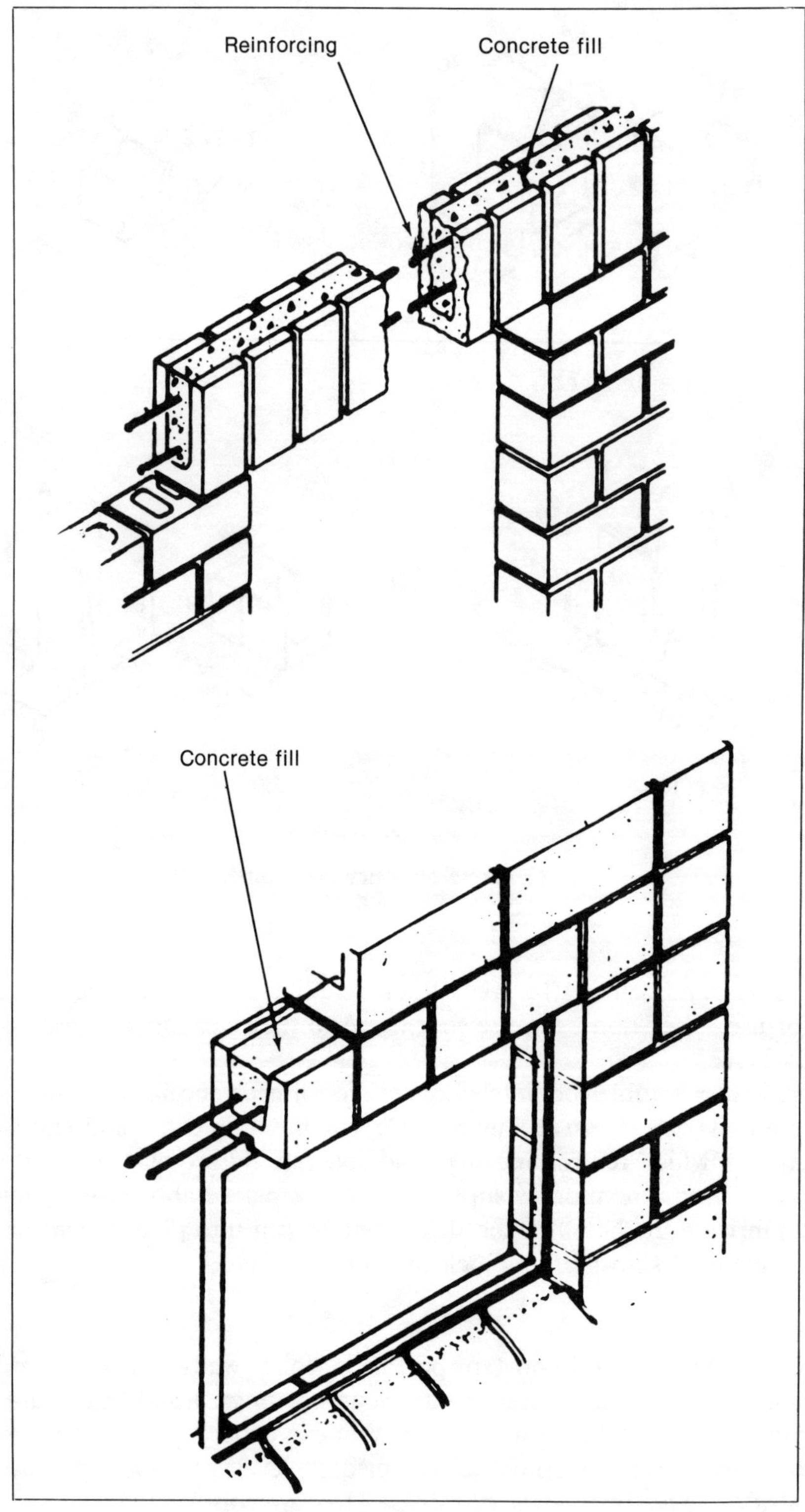

Typical lintel units
Figure 6-12

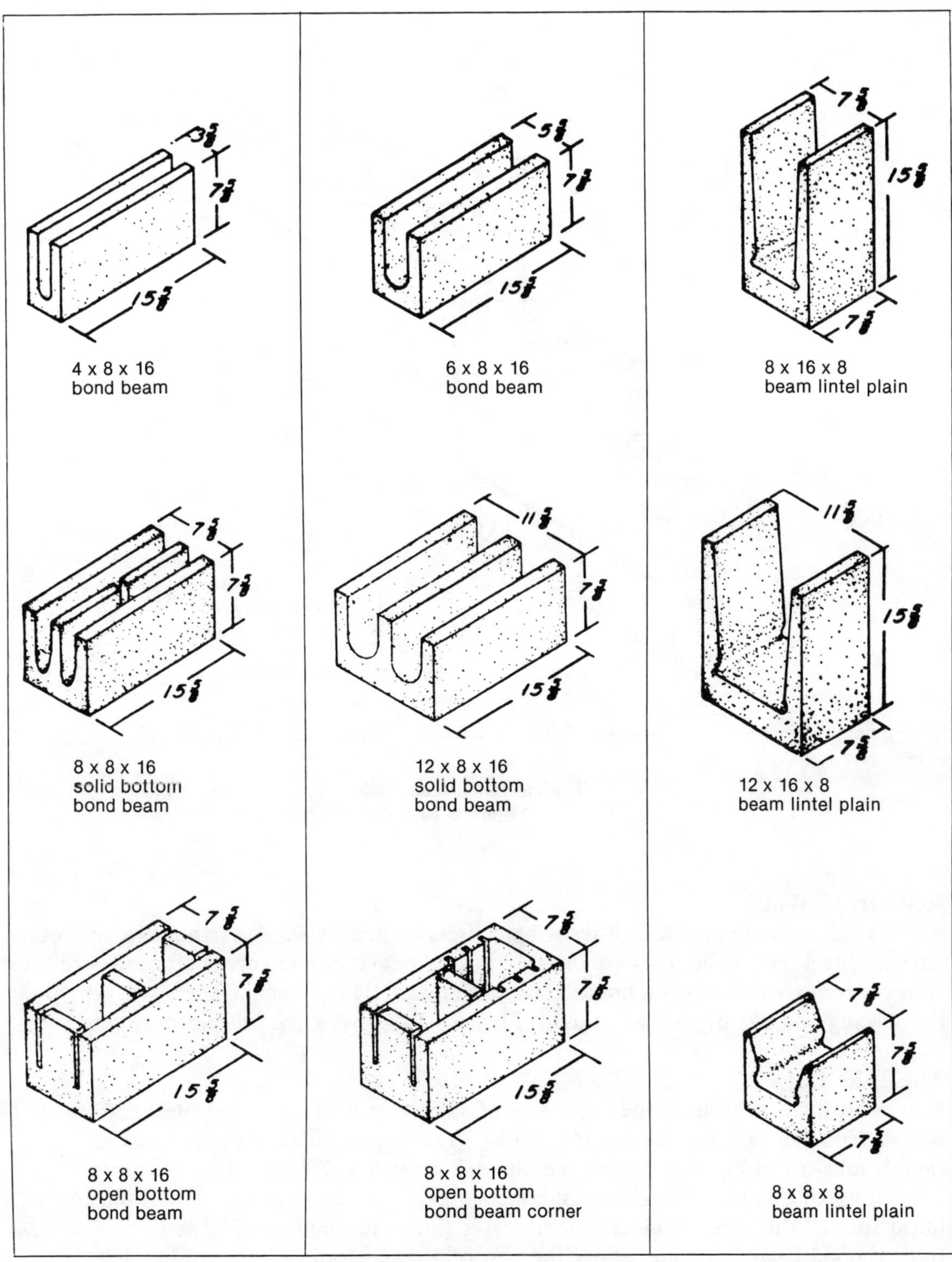

Typical concrete bond beam units
Figure 6-13

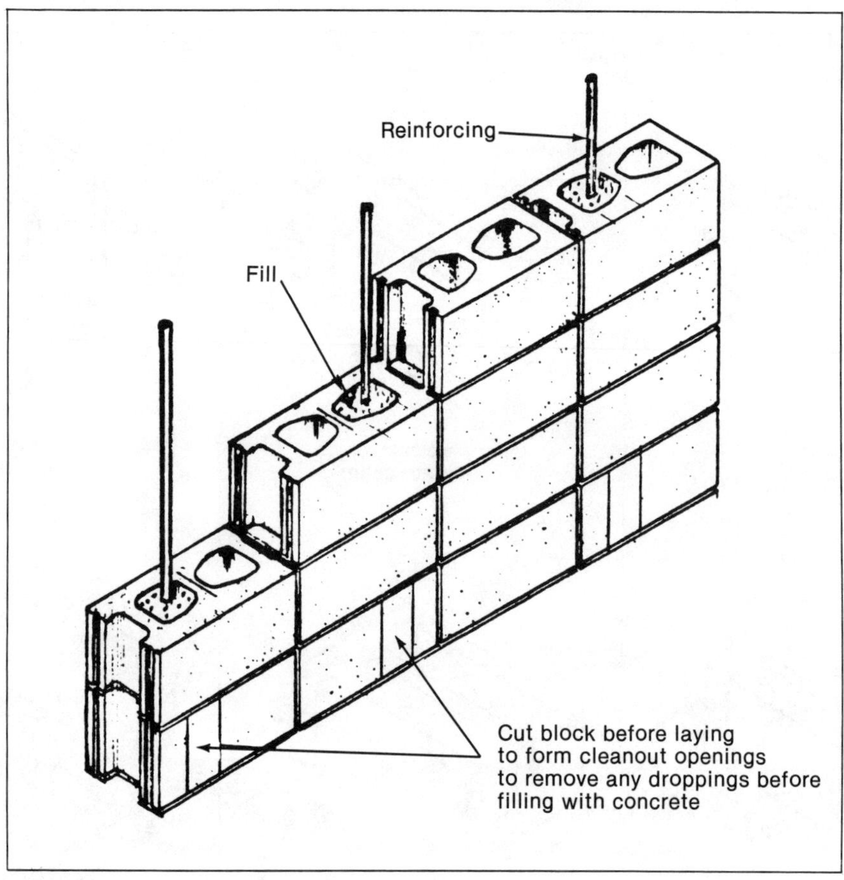

Typical reinforced wall
Figure 6-14

Reinforced Walls

Reinforced walls are designed to resist high stress caused by wind, earthquake, and other stresses. Steel reinforcing bars are inserted in block cavities and cores before they're filled with concrete. The result is a bonded composite wall. The plans and specs will tell you the spacing and size of steel to be used. Figure 6-14 shows a typical reinforced wall.

The Take-Off

You don't have to measure the linear feet of steel in precast concrete lintels and bond beams. You can calculate it from the "outs." I'll explain how it's done. Look at the sample take-off in Figure 6-15 and the take-off summary, Figure 6-16.

The cost of a linear foot of precast concrete lintel, over and above (D.O.) the cost of a linear foot of the concrete block it replaces, is shown in Figure 6-17. The cost of a linear foot of bond beam, over and above the cost of a linear foot of concrete block it replaces, is shown in Figure 6-18. These prices won't be accurate for your jobs, of course. But use the table as a model to produce a similar table that reflects *your* labor and material costs.

MASONRY QUANTITY SURVEYS

123 Beech Drive
Cincinnati, OH 45123

DATE ________

SHEET ____ OF ____

EST. BY *RVK*

BID DUE ________

BLDG. ________________________

LOCATION ________________________

PLAN NOS. ____________ DATE ____________

OWNER ________________________

ARCHITECT ________________________

GEN. CONTR. ________________________

EXAMPLE TAKE-OFF   *REINF. STEEL*

		8" LWCB		P.C. LINT 8×8	BOND BM 8×8	REINF. STEEL #4 W/ FILL	
		9^{4}		D.O.	D.O.	9^{4}	Wall height
		500			500	2^{4}	
		(4667)				(224)	no. of locations
	"OUTS"						
DR	$3^{4} \times 7^{4}$	(3) 73		(3) 14			$3 \times (3^{4} + 0^{8} + 0^{8}) = 14$
WD	$4^{0} \times 3^{4}$	(6) 80		(6) 32			$6(4^{0} + 0^{8} + 0^{8}) = 32$
		153					
		4514		46	500	224 VLF	
		×1.125				×1.20	lap allowance
		5079 pcs				267 LF	
		✓		✓	✓	✓	
						FILL 8"CB ×.33	
						75 pcs	equivalent 8" CB units

Sample lintel and bond beam take-off
Figure 6-15

MASONRY QUANTITY SURVEYS

123 Beech Drive
Cincinnati, OH 45123

DATE

SHEET   OF

EST. BY

BID DUE

BLDG. _______________________   OWNER_______________________

LOCATION _______________________   ARCHITECT_______________________

PLAN NOS. ____________DATE ____________   GEN. CONTR. _______________________

EXAMPLE SUMMARY   —   P.C. LINTS

ITEM	UNIT	QUANTITY	MATERIAL		LABOR		WORK	TOTAL
			Unit	Amount	Unit	Amount		
8" LWCB	PCS	5079						
P.C. LINTS 8×8 D.O.	LF	46						
BOND BM 8×8 D.O.	LF	500						
REINF. #4	LF	267						
FILL 8" CB	PCS	75						

Summary sheet for sample bond beam take-off
Figure 6-16

	4 x 8	4 x 8	6 x 8	6 x 8	8 x 8	8 x 8
D.O. (Cost of wall replaced, deducted)						
	2-#4	2-#5	2-#5	4-#4	4-#4	4-#5
Material						
Precast lintel/LF	1.792	1.970	2.897	3.020	3.972	4.190
Deduct block material	-.261	-.261	-.334	-.334	-.376	-.376
Total	1.531	1.709	2.563	2.686	3.596	3.814
Material/LF D.O.	$1.54	$1.71	$2.57	$2.69	$3.60	$3.82
Labor						
Precast lintel/LF	1.776	1.794	2.667	2.694	3.556	3.592
Deduct block labor	-.914	-.914	-1.013	-1.013	-1.515	-1.515
Total	.862	.880	1.654	1.681	2.041	2.077
Labor/LF D.O.	$0.87	$0.88	$1.66	$1.69	$2.05	$2.08

Note: No sales tax, fringes, tools and equipment, overhead or profit are included.

Sample unit prices — precast lintels
Figure 6-17

Begin the wall reinforcing take-off by searching the plans for every point where reinforcing will be used. Be especially thorough in the structural drawings. And here's a tip. When your reinforcing take-off is complete, call a steel fabricator who's estimating the job. They probably prepared a take-off of reinforcing steel in the masonry and may be willing to compare quantities with you.

Measure the vertical linear feet (VLF) for each type of reinforcing and each size. Count the number of locations and multiply by the VLF (including the lap). Look again at Figures 6-15 and 6-16. Figure 6-19 shows the size and weight of common grade 40 reinforcing bars. Most bar reinforcing is sold by the pound or ton, so you'll have to convert linear feet to weight.

Miscellaneous Steel

Your take-off has to include all the miscellaneous steel specified in the masonry section of the specifications. Here are some of the items to look for: lintel angles, corner guards, fireplace angles, fireplace dampers, ash-pit doors, cleanout doors, access doors, brick vents, scuppers, and anchor bolts. It's always a nice feeling to be able to say, "It's included in our bid." But even more, it gives you a feeling of confidence knowing that *everything* is included when you're preparing a close bid.

D.O. (Cost of wall replaced, deducted)

	4 x 8	6 x 8	8 x 8	10 x 8	12 x 8	8 x 16	12 x 16
	1-#4	1-#4	2-#4	2-#5	2-#5	2-#4 2-#4	2-#5 2-#5
Material							
Block (1 unit-16″) D.O.	.105	.113	.170	.331	.234	.842	1.210
Fill @ $2.00/CF	.140	.330	.500	.640	.830	1.000	1.660
Steel @ $0.23/#	.214	.214	.427	.640	.640	.854	1.280
Total	.459	.657	1.097	1.611	1.704	2.696	4.150
x .75	.345	.493	.823	1.209	1.278	2.022	3.113
Material/LF D.O.	$0.35	$0.50	$0.83	$1.21	$1.28	$2.03	$3.12
Labor							
Block (1 unit-16″) D.O.	.132	.152	.201	.230	.253	.402	.506
Fill @ $2.00/CF	.140	.330	.500	.640	.830	1.000	1.660
Steel @ .35/#	.320	.320	.640	.987	.987	1.280	1.973
Total	.592	.802	1.341	1.857	2.070	2.682	4.139
x .75	.444	.602	1.006	1.393	1.553	2.012	3.105
Labor/LF D.O.	$0.45	$0.61	1.01	$1.40	$1.56	$2.02	$3.11

Note: No sales tax, fringes, tools and equipment, overhead or profit are included.

Sample unit prices — bond beams
Figure 6-18

Bar No.	Size (in inches)	Pounds per LF	Material at —/lb	Labor at —/lb
2	1/4	.167		
3	3/8	.376		
4	1/2	.668		
5	5/8	1.040		
6	3/4	1.500		
7	7/8	2.040		
8	1	2.670		
9	1 1/8	3.380		
10	1 1/4	4.170		

Reinforcing rods (grade 40)
Figure 6-19

MASONRY QUANTITY SURVEYS
123 Beech Drive
Cincinnati, OH 45123

DATE

SHEET   OF

EST. BY

BID DUE

BLDG. _______________________________   OWNER_____________________________

LOCATION ____________________________   ARCHITECT__________________________

PLAN NOS. _______________DATE __________   GEN. CONTR. _______________________

EXAMPLE SUMMARY   —   MISC. IRON

ITEM	UNIT	QUANTITY	MATERIAL		LABOR		WORK	TOTAL
			Unit	Amount	Unit	Amount		
48" FIREPLACE DAMPER	*EA*	*1*						
12 x 12 ASH PIT	*"*	*1*						

Summary sheet for sample miscellaneous steel take-off
Figure 6-20

Sometimes the miscellaneous steel items will be furnished by others but installed by the masonry contractor. If that's the case, it should be spelled out in the specs.

On major buildings, especially public buildings, it's common for the architect to include a metal box and a date stone in the wall. You'll have to install this box and stone and may need to keep a mason standing by while the building is being dedicated. These dedication ceremonies can last for hours.

Miscellaneous steel items are usually counted by the unit and listed in the summary as shown in Figure 6-20.

Control Joints and Expansion Joints

Cracking in buildings and building materials is caused by restrained movement. Some of the more common movements that affect concrete masonry are caused by:

- Temperature changes, causing expansion and contraction cracks.

- Changes in moisture content, causing shrinkage and expansion cracking.

- Overload on structures, causing deflection and distortion movement.

- Soil loads, causing settlement cracking.

Control joints and expansion joints help prevent cracking by allowing movement at critical locations.

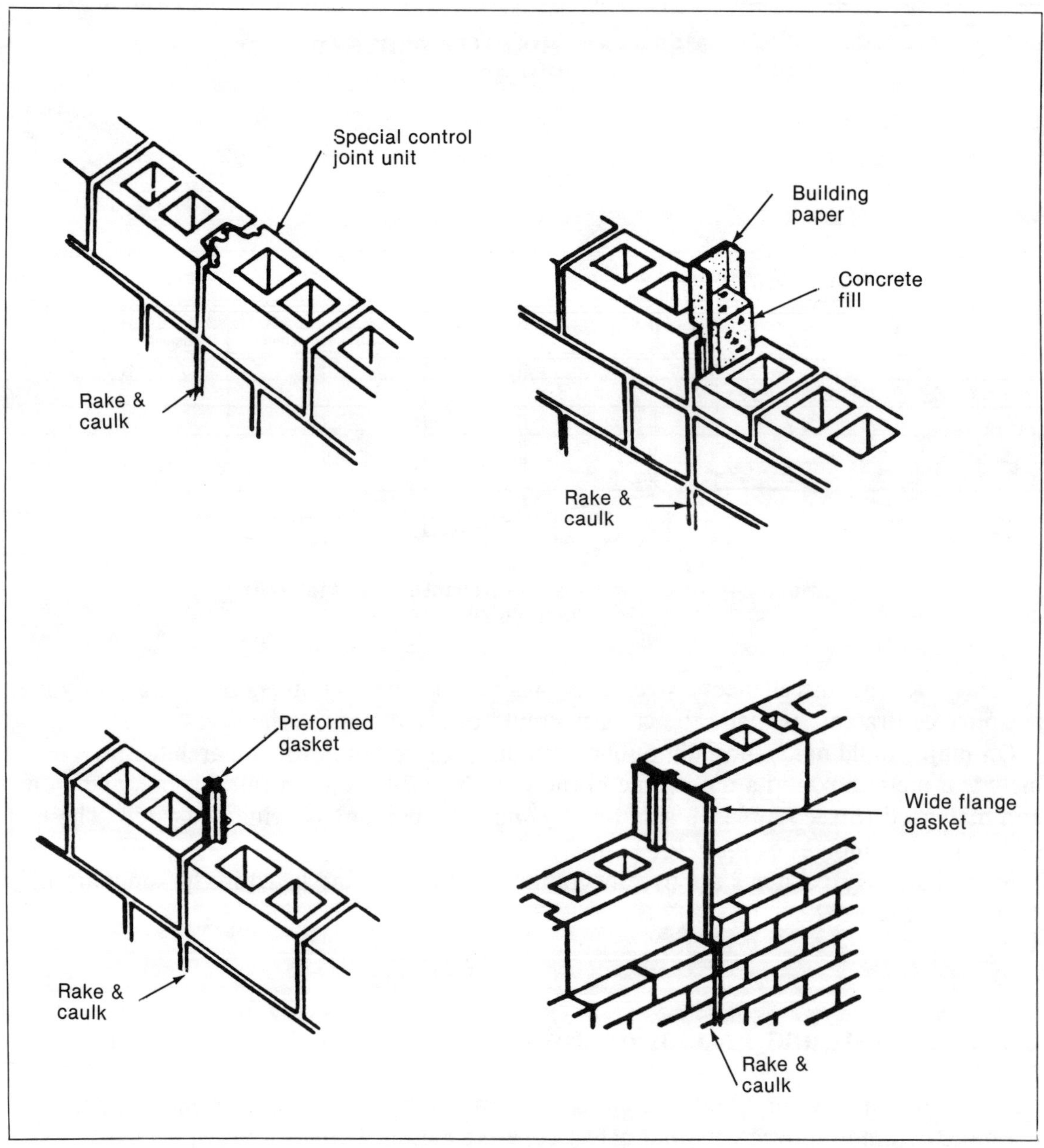

Typical control joint details
Figure 6-21

Control Joints

Control joints are vertical separations in a wall that are used to relieve horizontal tensile stress. They permit controlled movement at key points in a wall where stresses would otherwise concentrate. Figure 6-21 shows the most common types of control joints. Look for joints like these on the plans. Figure 6-22 shows the control joint spacing recommended by the Corps of Engineers.

Length of panels between control joints (in feet)

Wall height	With no reinforcing	With wall reinforcing at 16" O.C.	With wall reinforcing at 8" O.C.
Exterior Walls			
to 8'	15-20	20-25	20-30
8' to 12'	20-25	30-35	35-40
over 12'	25-30	30-35	35-40
Partition Walls			
to 8'	15-20	30-35	35-40
8' to 12'	20-25	35-40	40-45
over 12'	25-30	40-45	45-50
Veneer Walls			
to 8'	10-15	20-25	25-30
8' to 12'	15-20	25-30	30-35
over 12'	20-25	30-35	35-40

Dept of. the Army Corps of Engineers CE-206 011

Control joint spacing
Figure 6-22

Expansion Joints

Building materials expand and contract with changes in temperature. Laboratory tests have determined how much expansion and contraction to expect. This is called the *thermal coefficients of expansion* and is shown in Figure 6-23. These coefficients of expansion are used to calculate the amount of movement and thus the correct spacing of expansion joints.

Expansion joints can be very complicated because expansion and contraction will involve all parts of a building (roof, walls, floors and foundation). A few examples of expansion joint fillers are shown in Figure 6-24.

The Estimate

Check the plans and specifications for the location and details of all the control joints. These are usually marked on the drawings as "C.J." Your take-off should show the linear feet of joint, the number of locations for each type of joint, and a simple sketch to remind you of the type of joint you figured. This sketch will save time and trouble when pricing materials.

A common location for expansion joints is at ledge angles that support exterior masonry at floor levels. Measure this expansion joint horizontally and in linear feet. Expansion joints are usually identified on the plans as "E.J." Figure 6-25 is a diagram of a large building showing a typical expansion joint layout.

Material	Expansion in inches per degree F.
Metal	
Gray cast iron	.0000059
Steel hard	.0000073
Steel soft	.0000061
Stone masonry	
Ashlar masonry	.0000035
Brick masonry	.0000031
Concrete	.0000079
Granite	.0000047
Limestone	.0000044
Marble	.0000056
Sandstone	.0000061
Slate	.0000058
Wood, parallel to fiber	
Fir	.0000021
Oak	.0000027
Pine	.0000030

Coefficients of linear expansion
Figure 6-23

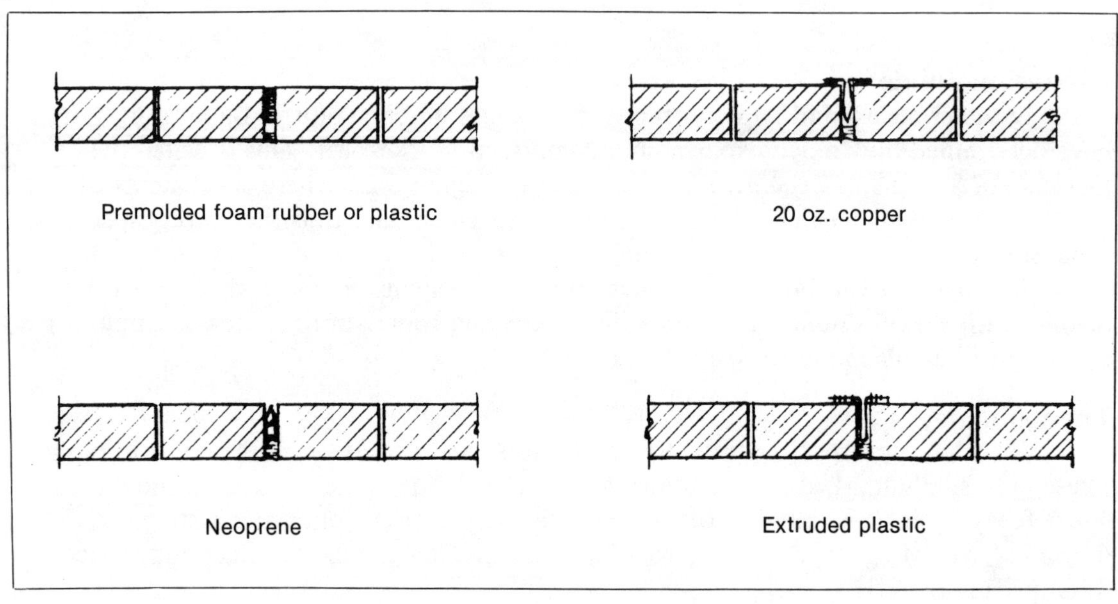

Expansion joint fillers
Figure 6-24

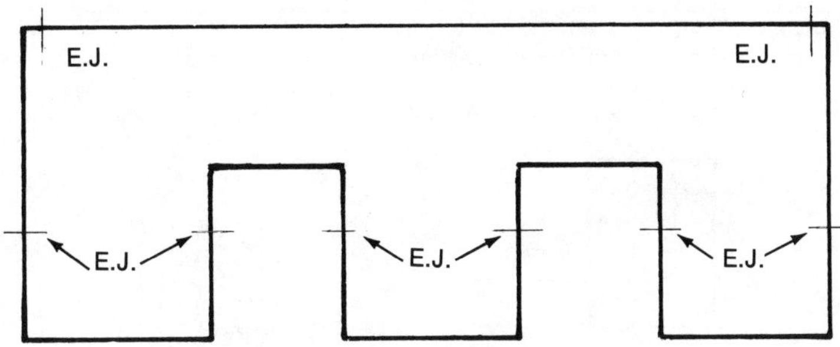

Typical expansion joint layout
Figure 6-25

MASONRY QUANTITY SURVEYS

123 Beech Drive
Cincinnati, OH 45123

DATE

SHEET   OF

EST. BY

BID DUE

BLDG. ___________________________   OWNER ___________________________

LOCATION ___________________________   ARCHITECT ___________________________

PLAN NOS. ___________ DATE ___________   GEN. CONTR. ___________________________

EXAMPLE   TAKE-OFF   —   CONTROL JOINTS

Sample control joint take-off
Figure 6-26

Your expansion joint take-off should show the vertical linear feet, the number of locations of each type, and a simple sketch. Figure 6-26 shows a sample take-off for control joints.

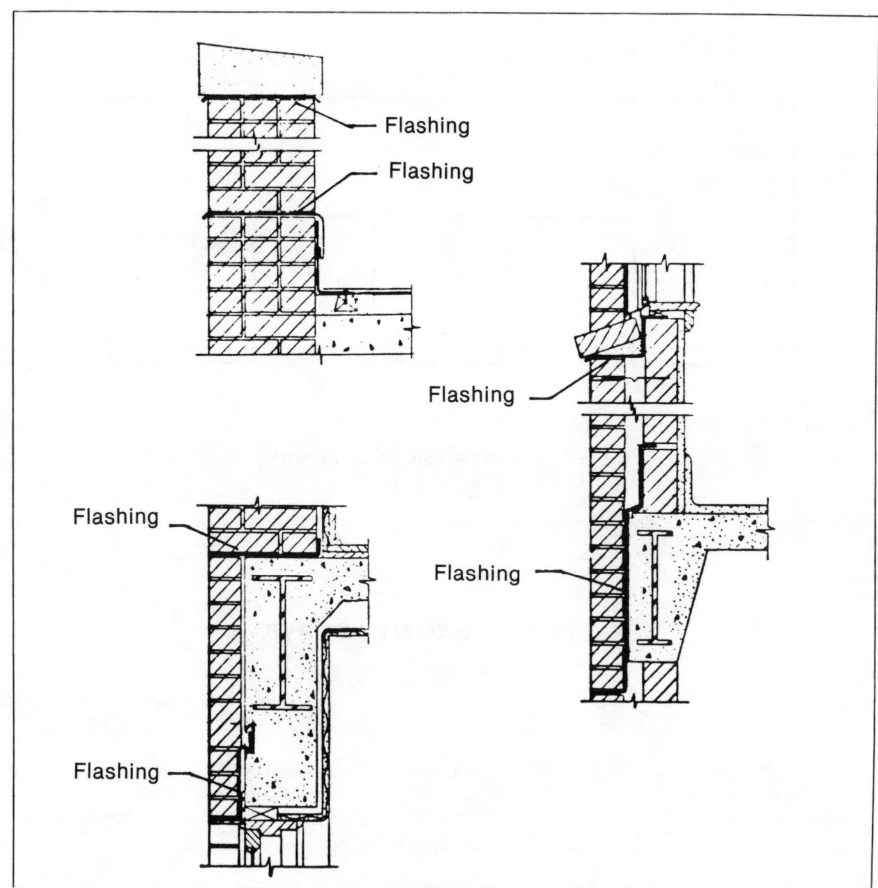

Typical flashing details
Figure 6-27

Flashing

As a masonry estimator, you'll be concerned only with the flashing described in the masonry specifications, commonly called *thru wall flashing*. Wall sections will show details and locations; the specs will describe the materials. Look for flashing at these locations:

> Foundations
> Spandrels
> Floor levels
> Window sills
> Heads of windows and doors
> Parapets and copings

Some typical flashing details are shown in Figure 6-27.

The Estimate

Flashing is usually installed horizontally and measured in linear feet. Measure each type separately and make a simple sketch showing the various bends. Flashing at copings, spandrels, and floor levels is usually continuous around the building perimeter. Record them on the take-off sheet along with the materials with which they are used. Flashing at window heads and window sills, doors and similar wall openings will not be continuous. Record this flashing on the take-off sheet where you calculate the "outs" for each window, door or other opening. See the sample take-off sheet, Figure 6-28.

Fill

Masonry specifications often call for concrete block to be filled with concrete, grout, sand, or granular insulation. Concrete fill is used to increase the wall strength at key locations, such as where a lintel or beam rests on a wall. Grout fill is usually used where reinforcing steel is placed in block cores. Sand fill is used to improve sound absorption and reduce sound transmission between rooms separated by block walls. Granular fill is used to improve the wall's insulation value.

The Estimate

Take off the quantity of filled block separately. Measure in square feet. Then convert wall area to the number of pieces for pricing. A table similar to Figure 6-29 can save you a lot of time when pricing block. Update it regularly so your material and labor prices are current.

Here's how you would use Figure 6-29 to find the cost of material needed to fill one 8" concrete block unit, if concrete costs $54.00 per cubic yard:

$$.248 \quad \text{x} \quad \$2.00 \quad = \quad \$.50$$
$$\text{(void CF)} \qquad \text{(cost/CF)} \qquad \text{(cost per block)}$$

Figure 6-30 shows how to list the fill on your take-off sheet.

Insulation

There are four major ways insulation is used in masonry walls.

1)   Loose fill in cores may be either vermiculite or perlite. To find the quantity of fill needed, look back at your concrete block take-off. Calculate the number of block that are to be filled. Then use Figure 6-29 to find the extra labor and material needed for that number of block.

2)   Cellular rigid insulation in cavities may be either polystyrene extruded foam board, polyurethane foam board, or foil backed polyisocyanurate foam board. The area to be covered is the same as the area of face brick at cavity walls. Transfer this square foot area to the summary sheet. Use a table like Figure 6-31 to price material and labor for cellular rigid insulation. Be sure the prices you use are current.

MASONRY QUANTITY SURVEYS

123 Beech Drive
Cincinnati, OH 45123

DATE
SHEET   OF
EST. BY
BID DUE

BLDG. _______________________________   OWNER _______________________________

LOCATION _______________________________   ARCHITECT _______________________________

PLAN NOS. _______________ DATE _______________   GEN. CONTR. _______________________________

EXAMPLE   TAKE-OFF   —   FLASHING

			4" F. BRK CB B/U	8" CB B/U		FLASH @ FND.		FLASH @ SILL	FLASH @ HEAD		
						⌐ 18		▢ 12"	⌐ 12"		
			10°	10°							
			142°	142°		142°					
			(1420)	(1420)							
WD	4°×4°		④ 64	④ 64				④ 22	④ 22		
DR	3°×7°		① 21	① 21		① −3		—	① 5		
			85	85		−3					
			1335	1335		139		22	27		

Sample flashing take-off
Figure 6-28

Item	Cells	Void CF	Concrete Material $54.00 /CY ($2.00 CF)	Concrete Labor $2.00 /CF	Sand Material $9.60 /ton ($.48/CF)	Sand Labor $1.50 /CF	LFV Vermiculite Material $4.60 /bag (4 CF)	LFV Vermiculite Labor $1.00 /CF	No. of bags per 1000 units	LFP Perlite Material $4.60 /bag (4 CF) ($1.15/CF)	LFP Perlite Labor $1.00 /CF	PSMI Mold. Inser. Material add-on	PSMI Mold. Inser. Labor add-on	FIP (foam in place) *sub-bid
4″ CB	3	.067	.14	.14	.03	.11	.08	.07	17	.08	.07	—	—	
6″ CB	2	.163	.33	.33	.08	.25	.19	.17	41	.19	.17	.58	.12	
8″ CB	2	.248	.50	.50	.12	.38	.29	.25	62	.29	.25	.58	.13	$1367.00
10″ CB	2	.320	.64	.64	.15	.48	.37	.32	80	.37	.32	.77	.13	
12″ CB	2	.412	.83	.83	.19	.62	.48	.42	103	.48	.42	.77	.13	
8″ CB	Ivany	.305	.61	.61	—	—	—	—	—	—	—	—	—	
12″ CB	Ivany	.529	1.06	1.06	—	—	—	—	—	—	—	—	—	
2″Cavity	SF	.167	.34	.34	.08	.26	.20	.17	42	.20	.17	—	—	
Hollow door frame	VLF	.084	.17	.17	—	—	—	—	—	—	—	—	—	

* See Figure 6-33

Sample unit prices for masonry fill
Figure 6-29

MASONRY QUANTITY SURVEYS

123 Beech Drive
Cincinnati, OH 45123

DATE

SHEET   OF

EST. BY

BID DUE

BLDG. ___________________________   OWNER___________________________

LOCATION _________________________   ARCHITECT_______________________

PLAN NOS. ____________ DATE __________   GEN. CONTR. ___________________

EXAMPLE SUMMARY — FILL

ITEM	UNIT	QUANTITY	MATERIAL Unit	MATERIAL Amount	LABOR Unit	LABOR Amount	WORK	TOTAL
FILL 8″ CB w/ SAND	PCS	320	.12	39–	.38	122.–		
″ 12″ CB w/ LFV	✓	4500	.48	2160–	.42	1890		

Summary sheet for sample masonry fill take-off
Figure 6-30

Product	U-value	Density	Material-$		Labor-$	
	1" @ 40°	(Lb/CF)	1"	2"	1"	2"
Polystyrene-extruded (PSE)	0.2	1.8-3.5				
Styrofoam (Dow) Foamular (US Gypsum)						
Polyurethane-expanded (PU)	0.16	1.5				
Thurane (Dow) Obsolete Elfoam (Elliot Co.)						
Polystyrene-expanded (PSB) (Beadboard)	0.26	1.0				
Dyfoam (Zonolite) Foam Master (FMI) Dur-O-Foam (Dur-O-Wall)						
Polyisocyanurate (PIC) Foil backed	0.139	2.0				
Thermax (Cellotex) 4' x 8' (16" w available)						
Polystyrene molded inserts (PSMI)	0.26	1.0				
Perlite-expanded granular fill (LFP)	0.37	5.0-8.0				
Vermiculite-exfoliated granular fill (LFV)	0.47	7.0-8.2				
Urea formaldehyde-foam in place (FIP)	0.20	0.6-1.0				
Air space	1.03	—				

Common types of insulation
Figure 6-31

3)   Cellular foam-in-place in cores will be filled with urea formaldehyde. The number of block to be filled should be kept separate from your concrete block take-off. Because this is special work, you'll have to get sub-bids from subcontractors who handle it. Their price will include taxes and fringe benefits. But don't forget to add overhead and a fair profit when you include the sub-bid in your bid.

4)   Cellular rigid inserts in cores will be made from molded polystyrene foam. This is a type of insulation made to fit into the cores of concrete block. Your supplier will quote the material cost, but you'll have to add the cost of installation. Again, use your concrete block take-off to figure the quantity needed.

The plans and specs should explain what insulation will be used and where it will be placed.

Insulation Terminology

Masonry estimators need to be familiar with the types of insulation available and the properties of each. Figure 6-31 describes the more common types of insulation and shows the density and thermal conductivity of each.

For more information on insulation, see Figure 6-32.

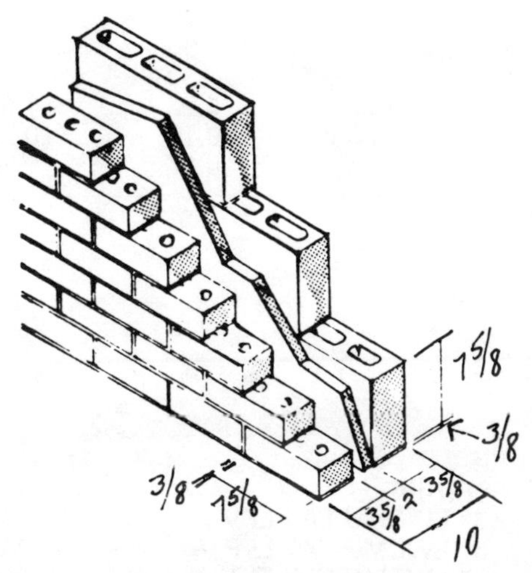

Abbreviations

LFV . . . . Loose Fill, Vermiculite
LFP . . . . Loose Fill, Perlite
FIP . . . . Foam in Place
PSMI . . . . Polystyrene Molded Inserts
PSB . . . . Polystyrene Board
PSE . . . . Polystyrene Extruded Board
PU . . . . Polyurethane Board
PIC . . . . Polyisocyanurate Board, Backed

Description

4″ face brick, 2″ cavity with 2″ PSB, 4″ LWCMU
4″ face brick, 2″ cavity with 2″ PSE, 4″ LWCMU
4″ face brick, 2″ cavity with 2″ PU, 4″ LWCMU
4″ face brick, 2″ cavity with 2″ PIC, 4″ LWCMU
4″ face brick, 2″ cavity with 2″ LFV, 4″ LWCMU
4″ face brick, 2″ cavity with 2″ LFP, 4″ LWCMU
4″ face brick, 2″ cavity with 2″ FIP, 4″ LWCMU

Properties	2″ PSB	2″ PSE	2″ PU	2″ PIC	2″ LFV	2″ LFP	2″ FIP
FR	1	1	1	1	4	4	1
W	65	65	65	65	.65	65	65
STC Paint							
STC No Paint	54	54	54	54	54	54	54
R	10.64	14.29	15.98	20.60	7.87	8.63	13.70
U	0.099	0.070	0.063	0.049	0.13	0.12	0.073
MU	0.086	0.064	0.057	0.044	0.12	0.11	0.067

Insulation properties
Figure 6-32

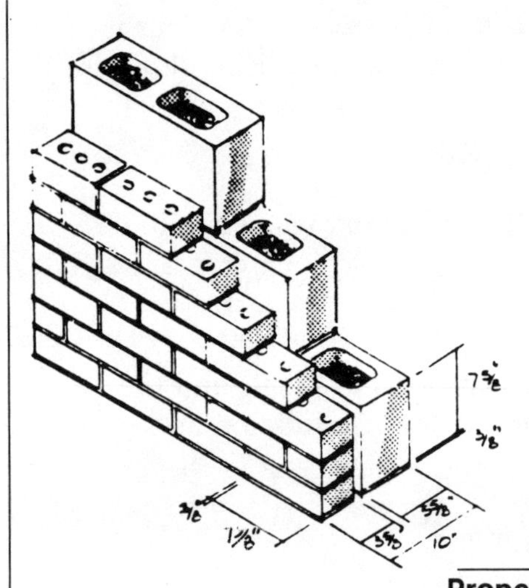

Description

4″ face brick, 6″ LWCMU F/W LFV
4″ face brick, 6″ LWCMU F/W LFP
4″ face brick, 6″ LWCMU F/W FIP
4″ face brick, 6″ LWCMU F/W PSMI

Properties	LFV	LFP	FIP	PSMI
FR	4	4	4	5
W	75	75	75	75
STC Paint	55 +	55 +	55 +	55 +
STC No Paint	50 +	50 +	50 +	50 +
R	4.57	4.88	5.20	4.61
U	0.22	0.20	0.19	0.22
MU	0.20	0.18	0.17	0.20

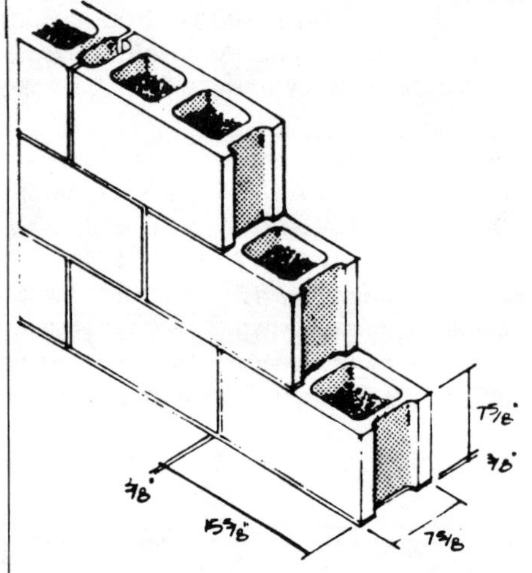

Description

8″ LWCMU F/W LFV
8″ LWCMU F/W LFP
8″ LWCMU F/W FIP
8″ LWCMU F/W PSMI

Properties	LFV		LFP		FIP		PSMI	
	LW	HW	LW	HW	LW	HW	LW	HW
FR	4	4	4	4	2	1-1½	2	1-1½
W	39.5	53	39.5	53	39.5	53	39.5	53
STC Paint	48		48		48		48	
STC No Paint		48		48		48		48
R	5.53	3.47	5.78	3.58	6.37	3.77	4.17	2.94
U	0.19	0.29	0.17	0.28	0.16	0.27	0.24	0.34
MU	0.17	0.27	0.16	0.26	0.15	0.25	0.23	0.32

Insulation properties
Figure 6-32   (continued)

MASONRY QUANTITY SURVEYS
123 Beech Drive
Cincinnati, OH 45123

DATE

SHEET   OF

EST. BY

BID DUE

BLDG. ______________________   OWNER ______________________

LOCATION ______________________   ARCHITECT ______________________

PLAN NOS. ___________ DATE ___________   GEN. CONTR. ______________________

EXAMPLE SUMMARY   — INSULATION

ITEM	UNIT	QUANTITY	MATERIAL		LABOR		WORK	TOTAL
			Unit	Amount	Unit	Amount		
				18,940		22779		
SALES TAX 5%				947		7517	FRINGS 33%	
				19,887		30296		
				✗		19887	MTL	
						50183		
						5018	T&E 10%	
						55201		
FOAM-IN-PLACE						1367	SUB-BID	
						56568		
						2263	OH 04%	
						58831		
BID $63,500 ⁰⁰						4706	P 08%	
						63537		

Sample summary sheet
Figure 6-33

The Estimate

Figure the area of cellular rigid insulation that will be placed in cavities. Write that number on your take-off sheet and transfer it to the summary sheet. You'll usually take off the other three kinds of insulation along with the block. Each type is figured separately, recorded in square feet on the take-off sheet, converted to pieces, and transferred to the summary sheet.

If the specifications call for urea formaldehyde (foam-in-place) insulation, get a bid from a subcontractor. Figure 6-33 shows a summary sheet showing the sub-bid for foam-in-place insulation.

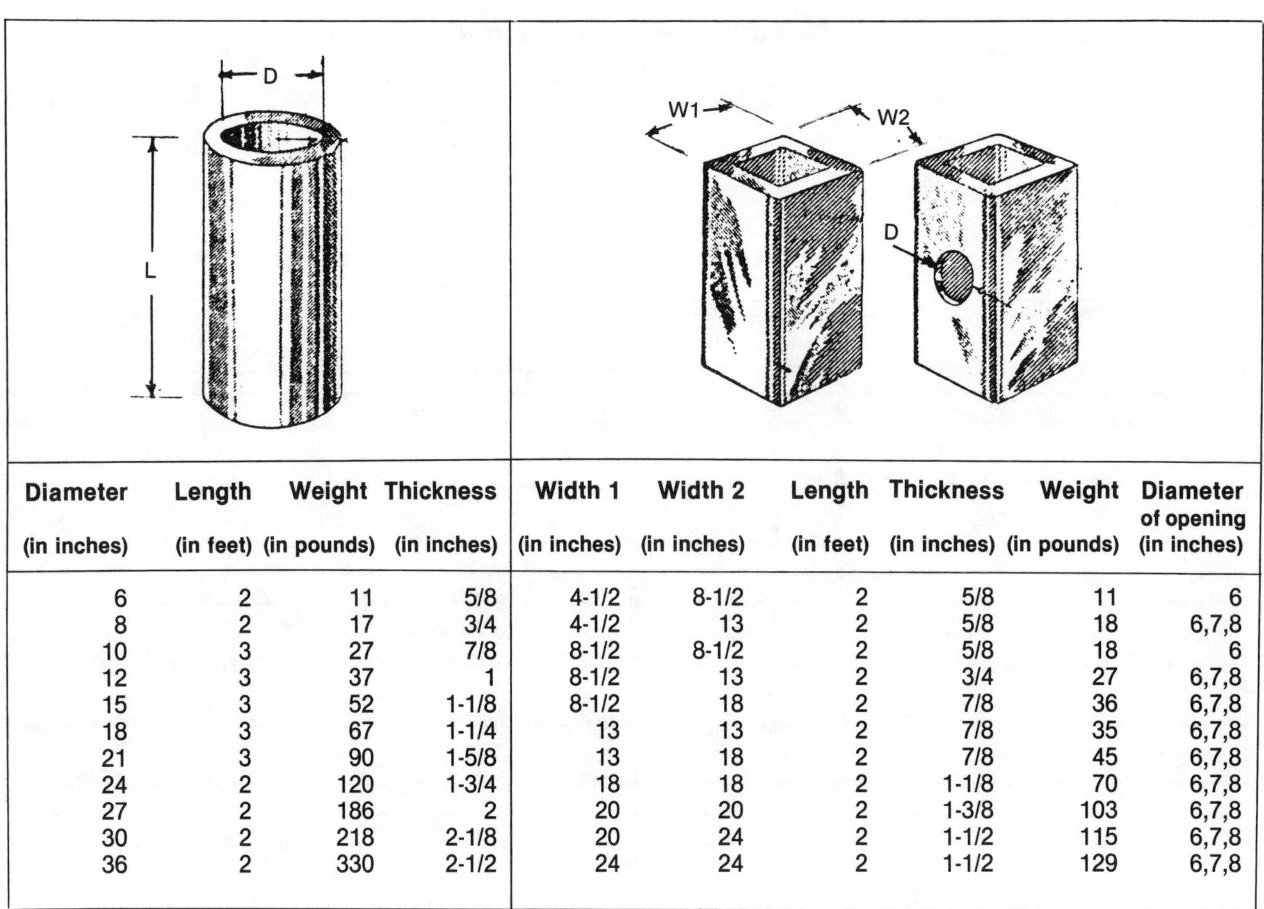

Diameter (in inches)	Length (in feet)	Weight (in pounds)	Thickness (in inches)	Width 1 (in inches)	Width 2 (in inches)	Length (in feet)	Thickness (in inches)	Weight (in pounds)	Diameter of opening (in inches)
6	2	11	5/8	4-1/2	8-1/2	2	5/8	11	6
8	2	17	3/4	4-1/2	13	2	5/8	18	6,7,8
10	3	27	7/8	8-1/2	8-1/2	2	5/8	18	6
12	3	37	1	8-1/2	13	2	3/4	27	6,7,8
15	3	52	1-1/8	8-1/2	18	2	7/8	36	6,7,8
18	3	67	1-1/4	13	13	2	7/8	35	6,7,8
21	3	90	1-5/8	13	18	2	7/8	45	6,7,8
24	2	120	1-3/4	18	18	2	1-1/8	70	6,7,8
27	2	186	2	20	20	2	1-3/8	103	6,7,8
30	2	218	2-1/8	20	24	2	1-1/2	115	6,7,8
36	2	330	2-1/2	24	24	2	1-1/2	129	6,7,8

Glazed and unglazed flue linings
Figure 6-34

Watch carefully for rigid insulation that's listed in the specs other than in division 4. The specs should state clearly which contractor is to furnish and install these items. If it's not clear, price the work separately and submit a separate bid.

Flue Lining

Flue lining (vitrified clay pipe commonly used in chimneys) is usually furnished and installed by the masonry contractor. Flue lining comes in square, rectangular and round shapes, usually in units 2 feet long. The square and rectangular shapes are made in many sizes, varying from 4" x 8" to 24" x 24" (outside dimensions) and with wall thicknesses from 5/8" to 1⅛". Round flue lining is made in sizes varying from 6" to 36" in diameter (inside dimensions) and with wall thicknesses from 5/8" to 2½". Figure 6-34 gives information on glazed and unglazed vitrified clay flue linings. Figure 6-35 describes vitrified clay stove pipe and flue thimbles.

Vitrified clay stove pipe, unglazed

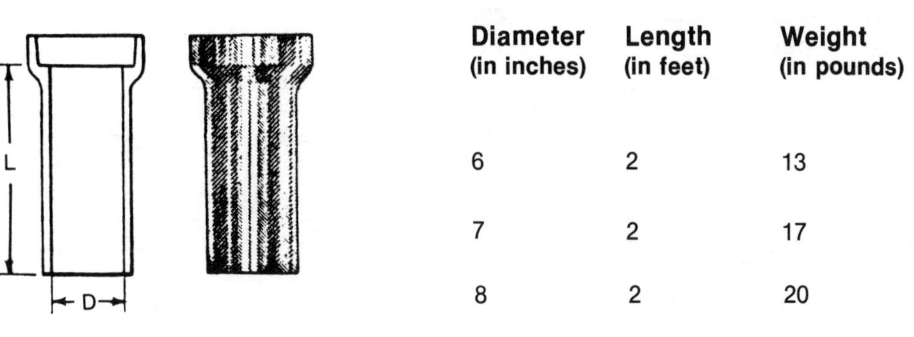

Diameter (in inches)	Length (in feet)	Weight (in pounds)
6	2	13
7	2	17
8	2	20

Vitrified clay flue thimbles, unglazed

Diameter (in inches)					Length (in inches)				Thickness (in inches)
4	4-1/2		6	9	12				1/2
5	''		''	''	''				5/8
6	''		''	''	''				5/8
7	''		''	''	''				11/16
8	''		''	''	''				3/4
9	''		''	''	''				13/16
10	''		''	''	''				7/8
12	''		''	''	''				1

Unglazed stove pipe and flue thimbles
Figure 6-35

MASONRY QUANTITY SURVEYS

123 Beech Drive
Cincinnati, OH 45123

DATE

SHEET OF

EST. BY

BID DUE

BLDG. ___________ OWNER___________

LOCATION ___________ ARCHITECT___________

PLAN NOS. ___________ DATE ___________ GEN. CONTR. ___________

EXAMPLE SUMMARY — FLUE LINING

ITEM	UNIT	QUANTITY	MATERIAL		LABOR		WORK	TOTAL
			Unit	Amount	Unit	Amount		
8" Ø FLUE LINING	VLF							
18 x 18 FLUE LINING	"							
6" Ø THIMBLE	EA							

Summary sheet for sample flue lining take-off
Figure 6-36

Flue lining is usually taken off in vertical linear feet. Figure 6-36 shows a typical take-off for flue lining.

Clay Coping

The masonry contractor usually furnishes and installs any clay coping or vitrified clay wall cap. These materials are made in several patterns. The most common are *single slant, double slant,* and *camel back.* Coping is made in three widths: 9'', 13'' and 18'', and in 24'' lengths. Figures 6-37 and 6-38 show typical salt-glazed double slant and camel back wall coping units.

Take off the coping in linear feet. Figure 6-39 shows a sample take-off.

Unit	Width (in inches)	Length (in inches)	Weight (in pounds)
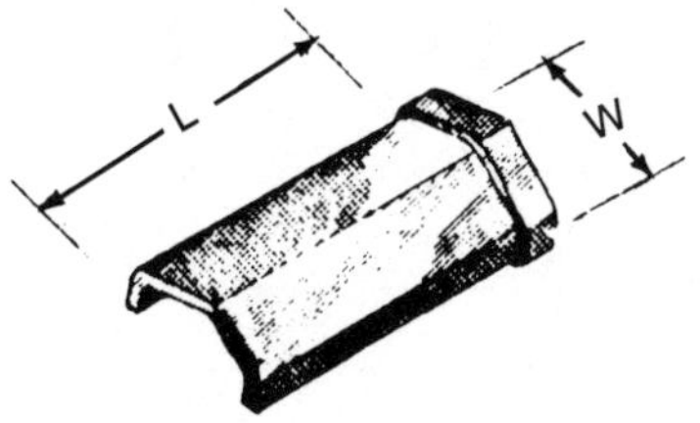	9	24	20
	13	24	30
	18	24	45
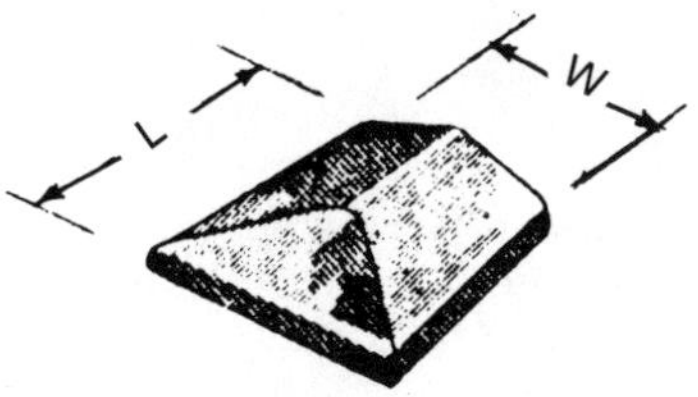	9	12	10
	13	12	15
	18	18	33
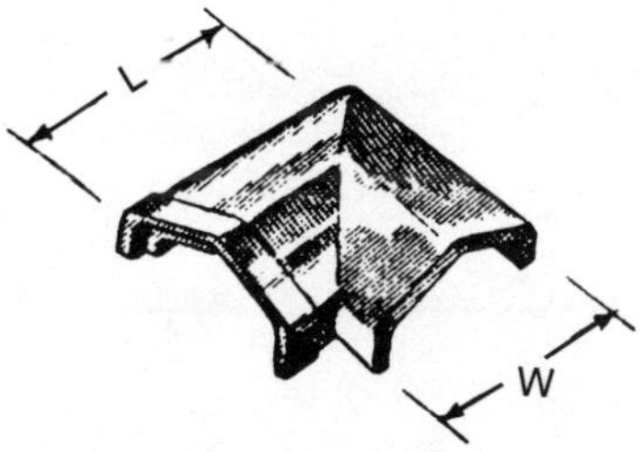	9	16¼	10
	13	17⅜	18
	18	22¼	40
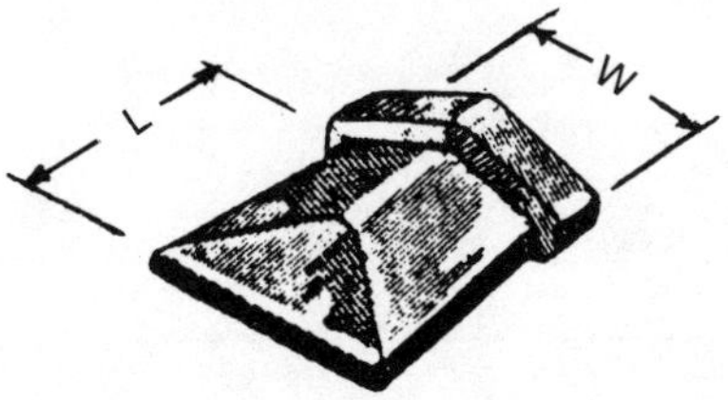	9	12	12
	13	12	18
	18	18	35

Salt glazed, double slant wall coping
Figure 6-37

Unit	Width (in inches)	Length (in inches)	Weight (in pounds)
	9	24	20
	13	24	30
	18	24	45
	9	12	8
	13	12	13
	18	18	33
	9	16¼	10
	13	17⅜	18
	18	22¼	40
	9	12	12
	13	12	18
	18	18	35

Salt glazed, camel back wall coping
Figure 6-38

MASONRY QUANTITY SURVEYS

123 Beech Drive
Cincinnati, OH 45123

DATE
SHEET   OF
EST. BY
BID DUE

BLDG. _______________________   OWNER_______________________

LOCATION _____________________   ARCHITECT____________________

PLAN NOS. ___________ DATE _________   GEN. CONTR. _______________

EXAMPLE SUMMARY   CLAY COPING

ITEM	UNIT	QUANTITY	MATERIAL		LABOR		WORK	TOTAL
			Unit	Amount	Unit	Amount		
13" CLAY COPING	LF							
· 18" " "								

Summary sheet for sample clay coping take-off
Figure 6-39

CHAPTER SEVEN

Masonry Wall Treatment

Most masons are ingenious craftsmen. They have to be. They have to do so many jobs besides laying brick and block. In this chapter, we'll look at some of the varied tasks masons are called on to complete. We'll start with caulking, then cover waterproofing and parging, jointing, pointing, tooling, tuck pointing, and cleaning.

Caulking

Architects often specify that caulking, especially caulking around masonry, be done by the masons. Assume that caulking will be part of your bid if any is specified in the masonry section.

Today, applying caulk isn't a simple matter of filling a joint with putty. Many new and improved caulking materials have been developed since the 1970s. Compared to the new caulks, the adhesion and service life of the old oil-based compounds isn't very good. Oil-based caulk still costs the least. But I recommend it only when joint movement will be small and the seal is protected from exposure to the sun.

The new compounds are a much better choice for most jobs. Let's look at some of these newer caulking materials.

One-Part Synthetic Rubber Structural Sealant

One-part structural sealant is made from polysulfide liquid polymers and sold under a trademark of the Thiokol Chemical Corporation. It's designed for application directly from the cartridge with a manual caulking gun and without mixing or preheating. It cures in air to produce a long-lasting weathertight seal in joints subject to normal movement. One-part sealant maintains an effective bond between practically all building materials, including metals, masonry, glass, and wood.

Two-Part Synthetic Rubber Structural Sealant

Two-part sealant is also made from Thiokol polysulfide liquid polymers. It's available in a non-sag consistency for mixing on the job before application. The compound is ideal for severe weather conditions or underwater applications. It will stand up under repeated joint movement throughout a wide temperature range. It provides superior adhesion, normally cures within 24 hours, and maintains an effective bond between practically all building materials, including metals, masonry, glass, and wood.

Solvent Acrylic Sealant

This is a one-part sealant that has good adhesive qualities and stays plastic for many years. No prime coat is needed when it's applied to most building materials, including glass, metal, masonry, porcelain, and wood. It's excellent for sealing around windows and doors and for sealing panel-to-panel joints, mullion and coping joints.

Acrylic Latex Caulk

This is a one-part, gun-grade compound suitable for both interior and exterior use. It doesn't cost much more than oil-base caulk, but can be expected to last from 8 to 12 years. It cures to a tough, rubbery seal that won't crack, dry out or lose adhesion. It usually stays bright and white for many years. Since it won't bleed, it's recommended for use with latex paints and can be painted with latex the same day it's applied.

Acrylic latex caulk withstands weathering, airborne fumes, and chemicals very well. But it's not suitable for use where the bead will be covered with standing water.

Butyl Caulk

Butyl caulk is a general-purpose caulking, sealing and glazing compound ready for application direct from the container. It's soft, flexible, adhesive and cohesive, virtually unaffected by freeze/thaw cycles, and highly resistant to ozone and ultraviolet exposure. It provides a durable, lasting seal between common construction materials. It's good for sealing glass in channel glazing and caulking joints in flashings.

Butyl caulk is a single-component material composed of pure butyl rubber with special antioxidants and synthetic resins, plus inert pigments and special fibers. It doesn't bleed or stain, and requires no priming. There are some limitations, however. Butyl caulk isn't as elastic as other caulking materials. It doesn't snap back completely after being stretched. Don't use it where there will be a lot of expansion. And don't use it in joints with asphalt or extruding type joint fillers.

MASONRY QUANTITY SURVEYS

123 Beech Drive
Cincinnati, OH 45123

DATE

SHEET   OF

EST. BY

BID DUE

BLDG. _______________________________   OWNER____

LOCATION _____________________________   ARCHITECT_____________________________________

PLAN NOS. ________________DATE ___________   GEN. CONTR. ________________________________

EXAMPLE SUMMARY   — CAULKING

ITEM	UNIT	QUANTITY	MATERIAL		LABOR		WORK	TOTAL
			Unit	Amount	Unit	Amount		
CAULK @ EXP JT	VLF							
CAULK @ STONE SILL	LF							

Sample take-off for caulking
Figure 7-1

The Estimate

Make your take-off in lineal feet. Usually the length of caulking needed is the same as
the length of some other material on the job. Combine the two take-offs. You'll usually
need caulking around control joints, framed openings, expansion joints at steel or stone,
knockout panels, and so on. List the materials on your summary sheet as shown in
Figure 7-1. If there's a lot of caulking on the job, or if exotic materials are needed, it
may be more economical and practical to get bids from a caulking subcontractor.

If you plan to do the work instead of subbing it out, Figures 7-2 through 7-4 can help
you estimate the costs. Figure 7-2 is a caulking coverage chart, showing lineal feet of
coverage per gallon of caulk. Figure 7-3 gives production rates for caulking in linear feet
per day and coverage figures for the most common sizes.

Backer rod is an extruded polyethylene foam which is highly flexible and compressible.
It's made in continuous lengths and in diameters ranging from 1/4'' to 1'', which are
sold by the reel. It's compressed in the joint to approximately 75% of its original
diameter with a blunt rounded tool.

Figure 7-4 shows production rates in linear feet per day for installing backer rod.
Backer rod has three purposes: It regulates the depth of the joint in relation to joint

Depth	Width			
	1/8″	1/4″	3/8″	1/2″
1/8″	1232 LF	616 LF	410 LF	308 LF
1/4″		308 LF	205 LF	154 LF
3/8″		136 LF	102 LF	
1/2″				77 LF

For estimating caulking use:
11 cartridges per gallon
231 cubic inches per gallon
21 cubic inches per cartridge

**Caulking coverage chart: LF per gallon
Figure 7-2**

Type	Production (LF/day)
Oil-base, gun grade	
1/4″ x 1/2″ (154 LF/gal)	260
1/2″ x 1/2″ (77 LF/gal)	240
Butyl caulk	
1/4″ x 1/2″ (154 LF/gal)	230
1/2″ x 1/2″ (77 LF/gal)	215
Acrylic latex caulk	
1/4″ x 1/2″ (154 LF/gal)	270
1/2″ x 1/2″ (77 LF/gal)	250

**Caulking prodution rates
Figure 7-3**

Rod Diameter	Joint Size	Production LF/day
1/4″	3/16″	465
1/2″	3/8″	460
3/4″	5/8″	455
1″	3/4″	450

Backer rod production rates
Figure 7-4

width. It provides a surface against which the sealant is compressed, improving adhesion to the side walls. Finally, it provides a nonadhering back surface, preventing a three-sided joint.

Waterproofing and Parging

Water is unwelcome in masonry walls. A wall that's saturated with water will freeze and thaw, causing cracking, crazing, spalling, and eventually disintegration. Excessive moisture can lower a wall's thermal insulating efficiency and cause paint, plaster and other finishes to deteriorate. Without water, efflorescence can't occur.

But you can't keep water off masonry walls. Rain and snow will fall. There's always water vapor in the air, from both natural evaporation and sources inside the building.

When moisture passes directly through clay masonry walls, it's always through the mortar joints. Under normal conditions, it's nearly impossible for any significant amount of water to pass directly through brick or tile. Highly absorbent brick or tile will absorb some water, but not enough to flow through the wall.

Dampproofing and waterproofing are often misused terms. *Damp*proofing refers to a reduction in moisture penetration by capillary action. *Water*proofing refers to treatments intended to *stop* the flow of water through a wall.

Many products are available that will help keep moisture out of masonry. Water repellants includes silicones, acrylics, penetrant sealers, epoxies, urethanes, vinyl ester and cementitious-type coatings. The architect will select a product appropriate for the conditions and exposure.

Item		Production SF/day
Silicone (100 - 200 SF/gal)	F. brick 1 coat	1000
Silicone (100 - 200 SF/gal)	F. brick 2 coat	600
Silicone (100 - 200 SF/gal)	C. block 1 coat	900
Silicone (100 - 200 SF/gal)	C. block 2 coat	600
Stearate (100 - 200 SF/gal	L.S. 1 coat	750
Stearate (100 - 200 SF/gal	L.S. 2 coat	550

Waterproofing coverage and production
Figure 7-5

The Estimate

Find the square feet of masonry wall to be treated from your take-off of the exterior walls. Figure 7-5 shows material and labor estimates for silicone and stearate waterproofing. List totals on your take-off summary as shown in Figure 7-6.

Some subcontractors specialize in this type of work. Get a quote from a specialty contractor on larger jobs or for a job with special requirements.

Parging

Parging is a cement-sand plaster coat applied to masonry walls. Quite often the specifications will call for parging the exterior of foundation walls. It's an effective barrier against water penetration, and should never be less than 3/8'' thick. Parging masonry walls made up of a face brick exterior with concrete block backup can be done two ways:

1)   By applying a cement-sand plaster coat to the back side of the brick

2)   By parging the concrete block backup on the side next to the brick

The layer of mortar between the two wythes is called the collar joint. The two wythes of masonry along with the collar joint are called a *composite wall.*

The Estimate

Parging areas are usually measured in square feet. Take off the area at the same time you estimate the facing material or the backup, depending on which area is to be parged. Figure 7-7 shows how to price it in the summary.

MASONRY QUANTITY SURVEYS

123 Beech Drive
Cincinnati, OH 45123

DATE

SHEET   OF

EST. BY

BID DUE

BLDG. ___________________________   OWNER_______________________________

LOCATION _______________________   ARCHITECT___________________________

PLAN NOS. ____________DATE _______   GEN. CONTR. _________________________

EXAMPLE   SUMMARY   —   WATERPROOFING

ITEM	UNIT	QUANTITY	MATERIAL		LABOR		WORK	TOTAL
			Unit	Amount	Unit	Amount		
WP SILICONE	SF							

Sample take-off for waterproofing
Figure 7-6

MASONRY QUANTITY SURVEYS

123 Beech Drive
Cincinnati, OH 45123

DATE

SHEET   OF

EST. BY

BID DUE

BLDG. ___________________________   OWNER_______________________________

LOCATION _______________________   ARCHITECT___________________________

PLAN NOS. ____________DATE _______   GEN. CONTR. _________________________

EXAMPLE   SUMMARY   —   PARGING

ITEM	UNIT	QUANTITY	MATERIAL		LABOR		WORK	TOTAL
			Unit	Amount	Unit	Amount		
PARGING 8" CB B/U	PCS							

Sample take-off for parging
Figure 7-7

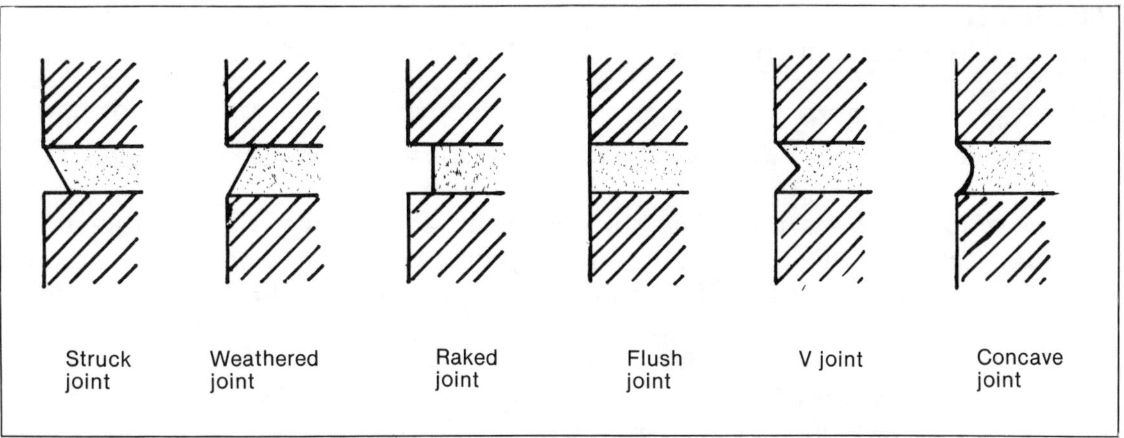

Mortar joints
Figure 7-8

Jointing, Pointing, Tooling and Tuck Pointing

Let's begin with definitions of these terms:

Jointing— This is the mortar spread between masonry units. It includes the bed joint, head joint, and collar joint. The cost of labor and material for this work is included with the cost of laying the brick or block.

Pointing— This is repair work done on mortar joints after the brick or block are laid. It includes filling nail holes, voids, and imperfections in the mortar joint. The cost for this work is treated the same as jointing.

Sometimes mortar joints are *raked* out after the brick or block are laid, so special mortar can be added. This is common with structural glazed tile. Inserting the new mortar is also called "pointing."

Tooling— This is work done on joints after the mortar has become thumbprint hard. Joints can be tooled in various patterns with a regular mason's trowel, a smaller trowel, or a special tool called a *jointer*. Figure 7-8 shows the different types of joints.

Tuck pointing— When masonry joints have deteriorated or need repair long after the brick or block have been laid, the work is called *tuck pointing*. This involves digging loose mortar out of the joint to a minimum depth of 1/2" and replacing it with new mortar. Working new mortar into the wall and making it look attractive is usually called *repointing*.

A special tuck-pointing jointer is used for this work. The size and shape of the tool used is important. Usually it should be a size that produces a joint matching the original. Special jointers are made for each type of joint: concave, recess, weather, beaded, and others. Using the right tool will reduce mortar smears on adjoining masonry and make washing down unnecessary.

The Joints
Now we'll look at the different types of joints. Look at Figure 7-8.

Struck joint— This is the easiest of all joints and is common on interior walls. It isn't recommended for exterior walls because it's less weather-resistant than other types.

Weathered joint— A water-shedding, low cost joint, far superior to the struck joint for exterior installations. It's formed as a plain cut joint, and finished with a trowel after the mortar has begun to stiffen. This leaves a shadow line which adds to the texture of the wall.

Raked joint— This type of joint produces a deep shadow line by depressing the mortar joint. It's often used on the finer types of face brick work. The raked joint is formed by raking the joint deep and clean.

Flush or plain cut joint— This joint is formed by cutting surplus mortar from the face of the wall. If a rough texture is desired, the joint must not be worked with the trowel.

V joint— This is a very watertight joint because of its shape and dense face. It's formed by pressing a V-shaped tool into the joint.

Concave joint— This is probably the most satisfactory joint for most work because it's both weather resistant and inexpensive. It's formed with a special tool or a bent iron rod.

The Mortar
Mortar used for tuck pointing should match the existing mortar joints. A bad match will be an obvious mistake. Mortar consisting of two parts fine screened sand and one part portland cement will make a durable, attractive joint.

The Take-Off
The cost of jointing is usually figured as part of the cost of laying brick or block. This was explained in Chapter 5. Pointing, tooling and tuck pointing should be figured and priced by the square foot. See the sample estimate in Figure 7-9.

Cleaning

When wall construction is completed, *cleaning, washing down* or *rubbing* can begin. As a masonry estimator, you should understand that cleaning exterior masonry walls is entirely different from cleaning interior masonry walls.

Cleaning Exterior Walls
The finished appearance of a masonry wall depends primarily on the skill of the mason. But a good cleaning will improve a wall's appearance and eliminate some of the mistakes before they become permanent. Cleaning by hand with a bucket and brush is the most

MASONRY QUANTITY SURVEYS
123 Beech Drive
Cincinnati, OH 45123

DATE
SHEET   OF
EST. BY
BID DUE

BLDG. _______________________________   OWNER_________________________________

LOCATION _____________________________   ARCHITECT______________________________

PLAN NOS. ______________DATE __________   GEN. CONTR. ____________________________

EXAMPLE SUMMARY   —   POINTING

| ITEM | UNIT | QUANTITY | MATERIAL | | LABOR | | WORK | TOTAL |
			Unit	Amount	Unit	Amount		
MORTAR BRK.	PCS.							
" BLK.	"							
RAKE JOINTS — F. BRK	SF							
POINT W/ WHITE MORTAR	"							

Sample take-off for pointing
Figure 7-9

common method. The specs will probably describe the cleaning agent, either detergent, soap, muriatic acid or a chemical cleaner.

Cleaning face brick requires special equipment and materials: hanging scaffold, hoses, barrels, brushes, scrapers, and plenty of water. The cleaning materials to use depend on the type of brick. Follow the manufacturer's recommendations and test your cleaning procedure on a small, inconspicuous area before beginning work on the entire wall.

Here are some recommended procedures for cleaning the more common face brick:

Red flashed face brick— Use muriatic acid or a commercial cleaning agent. Smooth texture brick is easier to clean than rough texture brick. Rough texture brick may require high pressure water cleaning or sandblasting.

Red sand finish brick— Clean with plain water and a scrub brush, or water, sparingly-applied, under high pressure. Heavy mortar stains may require use of cleaning solutions. Sandblasting is not recommended.

Light colored brick— Cleaning light brick — white, tan, buff, gray and pink brick, as well as brown and black brick — can cause problems. These brick should be cleaned only with plain water, detergents or the recommended cleaning compounds. Manganese colored brick units tend to react to muriatic acid solutions, and bleed. Light colored brick are more susceptible to "acid burn" than are darker units. Sandblasting is not recommended for sand finish brick.

MASONRY QUANTITY SURVEYS

123 Beech Drive
Cincinnati, OH 45123

DATE

SHEET   OF

EST. BY

BID DUE

BLDG. ___________________________   OWNER ___________________________

LOCATION ___________________________   ARCHITECT ___________________________

PLAN NOS. __________ DATE __________   GEN. CONTR. ___________________________

EXAMPLE SUMMARY — CLEANING

ITEM	UNIT	QUANTITY	MATERIAL		LABOR		WORK	TOTAL
			Unit	Amount	Unit	Amount		
CLEAN F. BRK. W/ SOAP + WATER	PCS	18,475	.004	74 –	.04	739 –		
CLEAN BLK.	✓	6,400	—	–	.03	192 –		

Sample take-off for cleaning
Figure 7-10

Stone— When cleaning stone, especially stone trim, plan to wash the stone with clean water and fiber brushes, followed by a liberal hosing down to remove dust and particles. Larger stone areas and rough finishes look better when washed down with a high pressure water blaster. Acids or chemicals aren't usually used to clean new stone.

Colored mortar— should be cleaned only with cleaning agents or mild detergents.

Cleaning Interior Walls

Concrete block, glazed tile and glazed concrete block require very little cleaning. After the joints have been tooled and set, cut off the mortar burrs with a trowel and then rub with burlap.

The Estimate

On exterior walls, the area to be cleaned will probably be the same as the total wall area. Estimate the cost of materials and labor needed for cleaning the entire surface. Be sure to include the cost of scaffolding (if required), brushes, hoses, cleaning agents, and manpower. Then divide the total labor and material costs by the number of brick or block in the job. Figure 7-10 shows how the cost of cleaning might appear on your summary sheet.

For interior walls of concrete block, glazed tile, or glass block, the area to be cleaned will be the same as the total wall area, unless both faces of the block or tile are exposed. For walls exposed on one face, the cost of cleaning is included with the cost of laying up the masonry. For interior walls exposed on two faces, the cost of cleaning the second face must be added separately.

Masonry cleaning will usually be described in the masonry section of the specifications. On a larger job, you may want to request subcontract bids from a contractor who specializes in this work. Sometimes the price quoted will be less than the cost of work done with your own crews.

CHAPTER EIGHT

Estimating Production

Estimating production rates is usually a masonry estimator's most difficult task. How long will it take your crew to finish the job? How many units will your bricklayers set per day? This chapter will help you answer these questions.

Understand first that it's impossible to predict productivity exactly. Masons are human beings and all humans are different. Each has strengths and weaknesses, special skills and deficiencies, likes and dislikes. And every mason has good days and bad days. That's why production rates vary, not only from job to job and crew to crew, but also from day to day. That's why estimating is an art as well as a science. There is no one production rate that fits all jobs.

But don't misunderstand me. Estimating production rates isn't a gamble. There are good estimates and bad estimates, just as there are good masonry estimators and bad masonry estimators. The good masonry estimators I know produce consistently reliable production estimates. Not perfect, of course, but good estimates for most jobs and for work under most conditions.

What does it take to make good production estimates? Let me answer this way. The good estimators I know tend to be very well organized. They work neatly and systematically through the plans and specs, following the same procedure each time, using either written or mental checklists, compiling figures and writing them in neat columns, showing all their calculations and extensions to make checking easier.

Good estimators also tend to be good information collectors. They never stop collecting reference tables, manhour data, manufacturers' catalogs, and cost information from completed jobs. I suspect that most of the experienced masonry estimators who buy this book will already have many of the tables I've included between the covers of this manual. But I know that most good masonry estimators will buy this book anyhow, just to be sure their estimating library is complete and current.

But it takes more than care, attention to detail and stacks of reference tables to make a good estimator. It takes knowledge, judgment, and skill. Good masonry estimators aren't born. They're made — through practice and experience. I don't think there's any substitute for learning by doing — even if it means making mistakes.

This chapter is intended to help you develop some judgment in estimating labor costs. I'll identify most of the major factors that affect production rates and suggest what to watch for when estimating manhour requirements.

Factors Affecting Productivity

The main influence on production rates is usually weight of materials. A bricklayer who lifts a 20-pound concrete block to a height of 2 feet exerts 40 foot-pounds of work. For you to do the same work lifting a 0.04-pound pencil would require 2,000 lifts of 6 inches each! If you've worked as a mason you know that the weight lifted and the height of the lift have a major effect on productivity. There are limits to how much work any human being can handle day after day. Every masonry estimator should understand that heavier brick or block lifted to greater heights will reduce production.

By production I mean the number of units a bricklayer can lay in one day under normal conditions. The curve shown in Figure 8-1 shows how the production rate varies with weight. The curve was compiled from actual field reports. It shows there's a direct relationship: more weight, less production; less weight, more production — but it's not necessarily on a straight line.

But estimating production rates is more complex than just calculating work in foot-pounds. There are many other factors to consider:

1) *Working conditions:* heat, cold, humidity, wind

2) *Access to the work:* high, low, among pipes

3) *The working handle the unit provides:* solid, cored, horizontal cell

4) *The shape of the unit:* fluted, split, vertical cell, horizontal cell

5) *The type of workmanship required:* tooling of joints, bonding pattern

6) *The material involved:* textured brick, select glazed tile, scored block

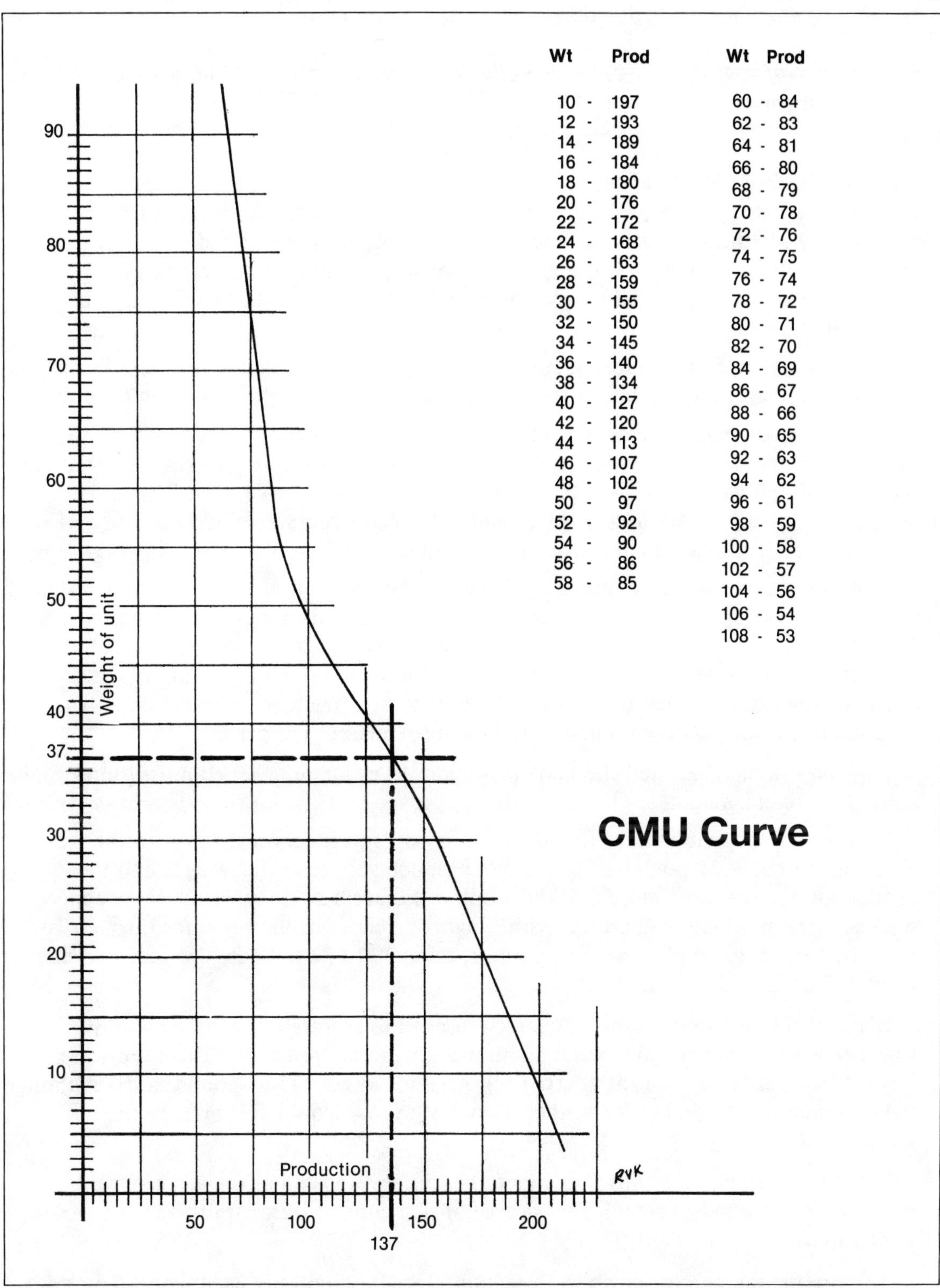

Basic production curve (running bond, exposed)
Figure 8-1

7) *The type of mortar:* high-strength cement, colored mortar

8) *Amount of mortar used per unit:* solid brick, vertical cell clay tile, glass block, stone, thickness of joints

How to Estimate Production

The best estimate of crew productivity on the next job will always be based on productivity for the same crew on the last similar job. That's why old estimates and records of completed jobs are so important. Most good masonry estimators are good record keepers. They consider records of completed jobs to be as valuable (and as confidential) as the combination to the company safe.

If you don't have them already, start building your file of production reports. Begin with the common masonry units. Then accumulate figures on the less common units.

Sometimes you can make an educated guess about production rates based on the weight of materials. For instance, assume that on most jobs your bricklayers lay about 160 units of lightweight concrete block (weighing 27 pounds) each day. The same bricklayers lay about 180 units of 18-pound lightweight concrete block each day. Using this data, you can make a chart like the one in Figure 8-2.

Using this curve, you can estimate production for any unit weighing between 18 and 27 pounds. For example, estimate production for a similar unit weighing 22½ pounds. Since 22½ pounds is midway between 18 and 27 pounds, it's reasonable to assume that production will fall about halfway between the rates for 18 and 27 pound block on the chart. In our example, that point is at 170 units a day. You can safely assume that production for the 22½-pound units will be approximately 170 per day.

You can use the chart and the same procedure to estimate production for other similar units of different weights.

Experienced estimators have found that a mason's production varies with the weight of a unit up to about 37 pounds. Fatigue sets in much sooner at this weight and the production rate falls off more quickly. Look at Figure 8-3. It shows the same concrete masonry unit production chart but with weights extended from 9 pounds through 107 pounds. Notice that adding only 15 pounds, from 37 to 52 pounds, decreases production from 137 units to 92 units.

It's probably for this reason that some union rules require two masons working together when masonry units weigh 37 pounds or more. Notice that these units are labeled "2-man block" on the chart. Each mason can lay 137 37-pound units. Although the two masons lift the block together, they both use a trowel and prepare the mortar for setting.

But don't assume that units that weigh the same will install at the same rates. Some units and some bonds have a higher degree of difficulty. I'll explain this in the next few paragraphs.

The production curves shown in this chapter are based on my experience. Yours won't necessarily be the same. Use my charts as a guide until you have your own data. Then make up charts of your own that fit your experience.

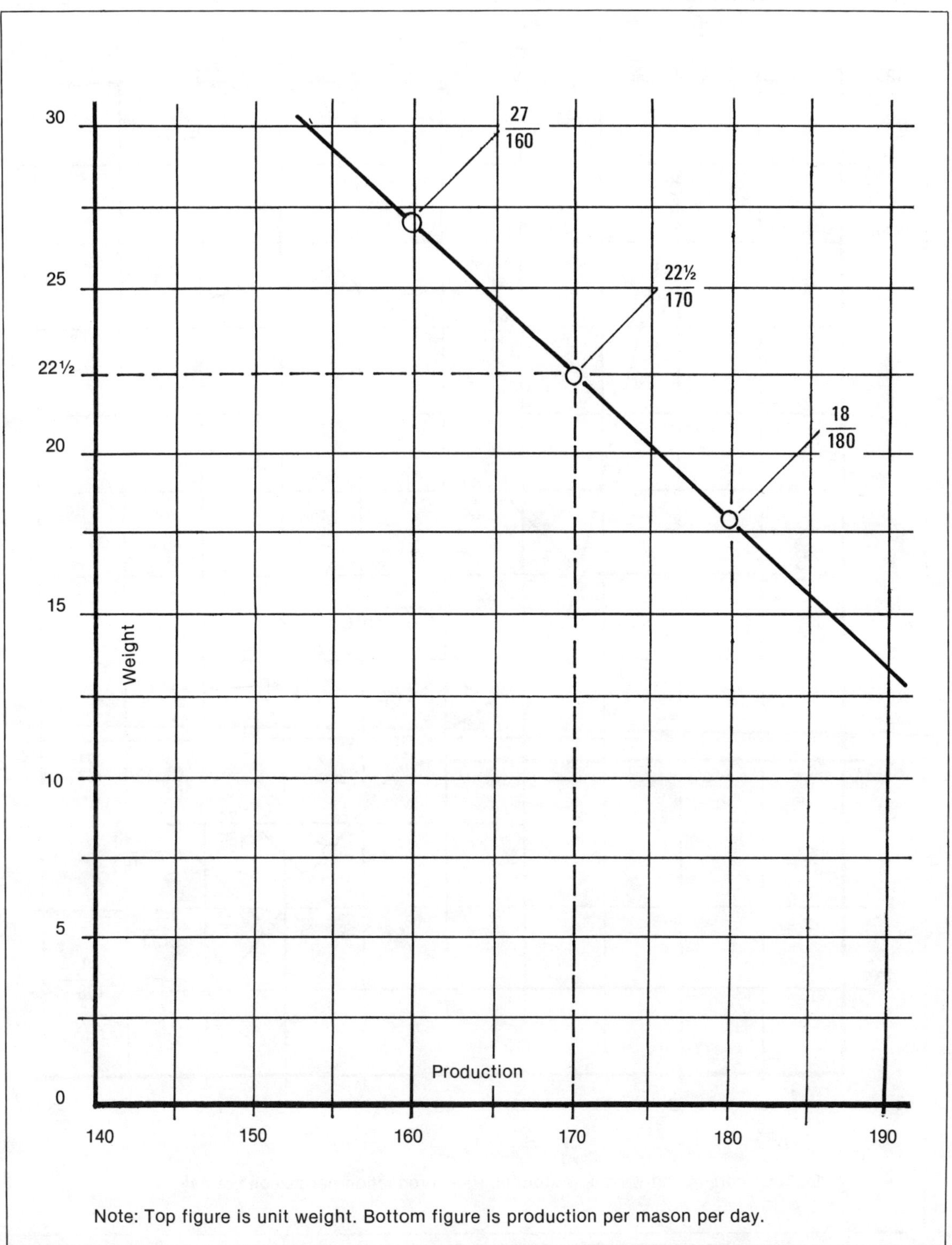

CMU curve
Figure 8-2

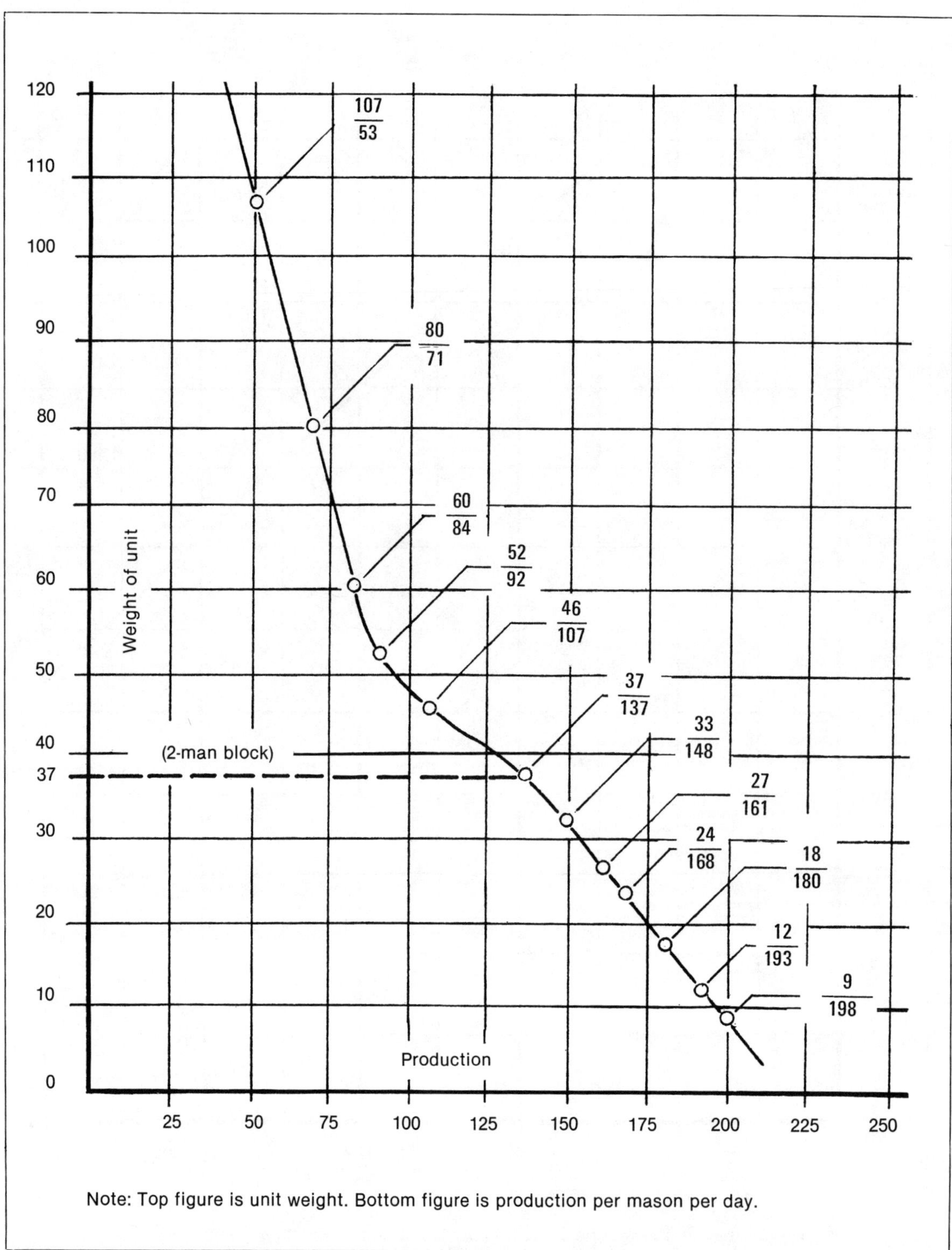

CMU curve
Figure 8-3

Using a Production Factor

Figure 8-4 shows a sample face brick production curve. Say your production rate chart shows that a mason can be expected to lay 560 units of this face brick each day under normal conditions. But what if conditions aren't normal? What if you're using a more complex bond or different block? What then?

You can assume that laying the same units under more difficult conditions will reduce the rate of production. This difference can be expressed as a percentage and is called a *degree of difficulty production factor.*

Figure 8-5 shows how these degree of difficulty factors can help you determine other production rates. In this case, we've found that laying face brick in Flemish bond reduces production to 90% of the production rate for running bond. We would multiply the 560 units per day for running bond by 0.90 to find the production rate for Flemish bond. You can estimate that the production rate for face brick, 4'' Flemish bond, will be 504 units per mason per day.

For information about production of other masonry materials, see Figures 8-6 and 8-7. Figure 8-6 shows my production factors for other bonds. I've multiplied the standard production rate from Figure 8-1 by the production factor to find the production rate for other bonds. In my experience, production for stack bond will be about 92% of production for basic running bond, exposed. Multiplying 0.92 by 166 (the normal production for 25-pound units) gives us a production rate of 153 units per mason per day.

Figure 8-7 shows production factors for special block, including scored, slump, striated, split face, 4-flute, 8-flute, embossed, hex and sound block.

I've based all of these production factors on my experience and observations in the field. Again, yours might be different. Check these production factors against your experience before using them to make estimates. Make up a complete set of charts for the type of work you do and for your crews. Tables like this will help you make fast, accurate estimates.

Labor and Material

Labor is usually about 60% of the cost in most masonry jobs. That's why it's so important to estimate labor accurately. When making your take-off, try to picture in your mind how the materials will be assembled. Try to judge the ideal size and make-up of the crew that will do the work.

Calculating Unit Costs for Labor

Masonry crews include both bricklayers and helpers, usually hod carriers. But some jobs may require operating engineers, welders, iron workers, or carpenters.

The generally accepted ratio of bricklayers to hod carriers, for a medium size job with good working conditions, is about two to one. Job conditions will dictate the size of the crew. Most jobs will be most efficient with small crews. Others require a larger crew. If working space is available, a large crew may be more efficient than a small crew. Jobs with difficult scaffolding conditions, hoisting problems, lack of working or storage space, or crowded areas around pipes and beams may require more support personnel.

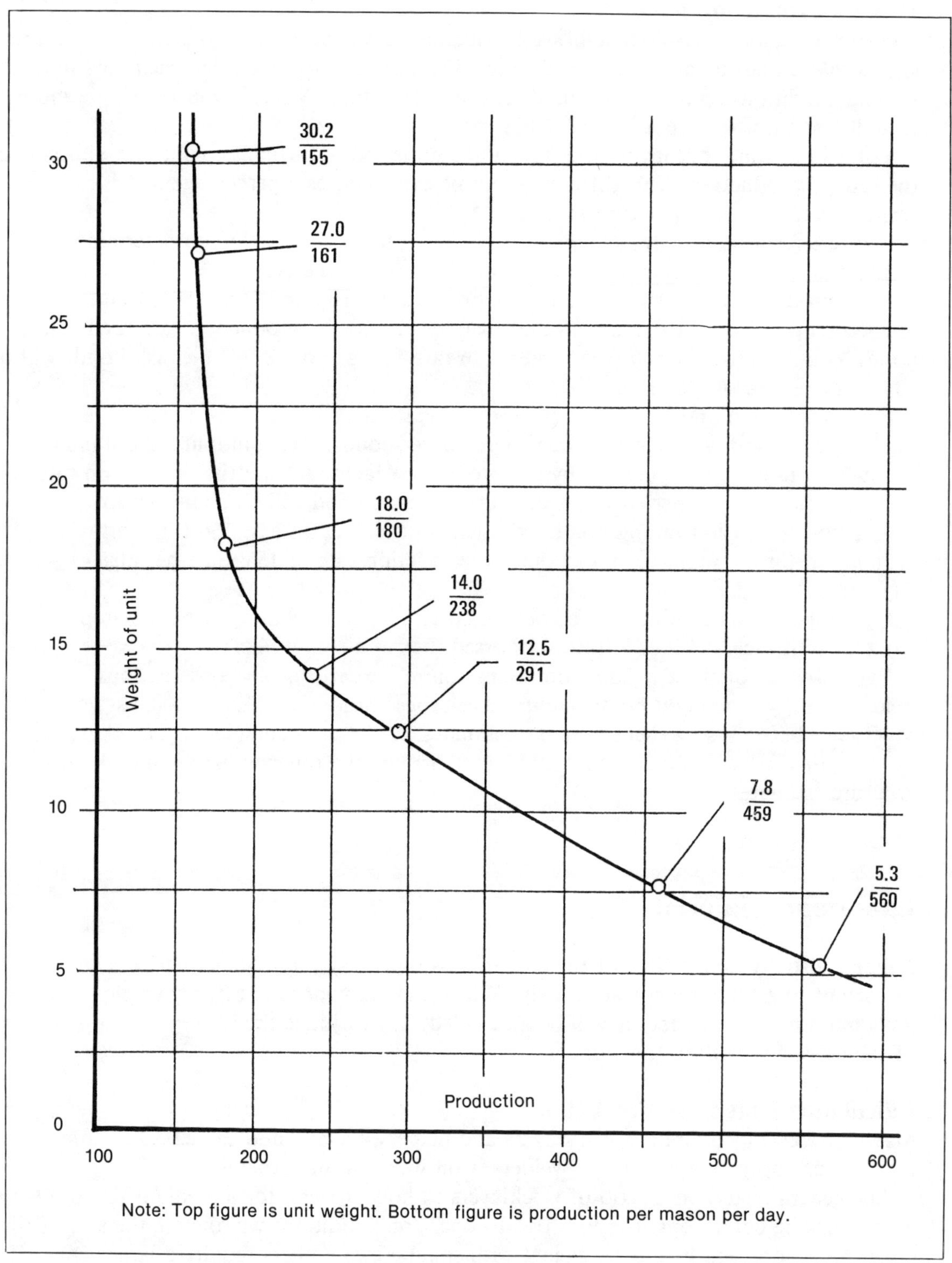

Face brick curve
Figure 8-4

Material	Production factor	Production special work
Face brick		
4 x 2⅔ x 8 4″ running bond	1.00 x (560)	560
4 x 2⅔ x 8 4″ Flemish bond	.90 x (560)	504
4 x 2⅔ x 8 headers	.90 x (560)	504
4 x 2⅔ x 8 soldiers	.80 x (560)	448
Concrete block		
8 x 8 x 16 LWCB 2-cell	1.00 x (163)	163
8 x 8 x 16 HWCB split face	.89 x (107)	96
8 x 4 x 16 LWCB half high	1.00 x (255)	255

Degree of difficulty production factors
Figure 8-5

HWCMU

Work condition	Production factor	4″ 25#	6″ 33#	8″ 37#	10″ 46#	12″ 52#
Basic running bond, exp.	1.00	166	148	137	107	92
Half high, running bond, exp.	1.00	192	183	179	170	163
Foundation, running bond, exp.	1.12	186	166	153	120	103
Backup, running bond, exp.	1.06	176	157	145	113	98
Cav. B/U, running bond, exp.	1.00	166	148	137	107	92
Parts., running bond, exp. (S2S)	.88	146	130	121	94	81
Stack bond	.92	153	136	126	98	85
Not exposed	1.05	174	155	144	112	97

LWCMU

Work condition	Production factor	4″ 18#	6″ 24#	8″ 27#	10″ 33#	12″ 37#
Basic running bond, exp.	1.00	180	168	161	148	137
Half high, running bond, exp.	1.00	199	193	190	183	179
Foundation, running bond, exp.	1.12	202	188	180	166	153
Backup, running bond, exp.	1.06	191	178	171	157	145
Cav. B/U, running bond, exp.	1.00	180	168	161	148	137
Parts., running bond, exp. (S2S)	.88	158	148	142	130	121
Stack bond	.92	166	155	148	136	126
Not exposed	1.05	189	176	169	155	144

Special work production
Figure 8-6

Special block	Size	Weight	Basic production	Production factor	Production special block
Scored	4 x 8 x 16	26	163	.95	155
	6 x 8 x 16	32	150	.95	143
	8 x 8 x 16	39	131	.95	125
	10 x 8 x 16	47	105	.95	100
	12 x 8 x 16	54	90	.95	86
Slump	4 x 4 x 16	13	191	.92	176
	8 x 4 x 16	20	176	.92	162
Striated	4 x 8 x 16	26	163	.91	149
	6 x 8 x 16	32	150	.91	137
	8 x 8 x 16	39	131	.91	120
	10 x 8 x 16	48	102	.91	93
	12 x 8 x 16	54	90	.91	82
Split face	4 x 2¼ x 16	10	197	.89	176
	4 x 4 x 16	16	184	.89	164
	4 x 8 x 16	33	148	.89	132
	8 x 4 x 16	23	170	.89	152
	8 x 8 x 16	46	107	.89	96
	10 x 8 x 16	55	88	.89	79
	12 x 4 x 16	31	153	.89	137
	12 x 8 x 16	61	84	.89	75
4-flute	4 x 8 x 16	33	148	.88	131
	8 x 8 x 16	39	131	.88	116
	10 x 8 x 16	55	88	.88	78
	12 x 8 x 16	61	84	.88	74
8-flute	4 x 8 x 16	35	143	.86	123
	8 x 8 x 16	41	124	.86	107
	12 x 8 x 16	56	86	.86	74
Embossed	4 x 8 x 16	26	163	.83	136
	6 x 8 x 16	32	150	.83	125
	8 x 8 x 16	39	131	.83	109
	12 x 8 x 16	54	90	.83	75
Hex	4 x 8 x 16	34	145	.85	124
Sound block	4 x 8 x 16	18	180	.80	144
	6 x 8 x 16	22	172	.80	138
	8 x 8 x 16	27	161	.80	129

Special block production
Figure 8-7

Your job is to determine what the labor cost will be per producing bricklayer. To do this, add together the labor costs for the bricklayers and support personnel. Then divide the total by the number of producing bricklayers. That's your crew cost per bricklayer per day. Base your labor cost on work days. But don't forget that hod carriers may have to start work a half hour before bricklayers.

Figure 8-8 shows the crew combinations and costs I use. The top part of the chart shows the crew makeup and the unit cost per bricklayer at typical crew wages. The bottom section shows the additional cost of adding one or two additional hod carriers for work above the first floor. Use this chart as a guide to make up a similar table, using your current labor rates.

I'll work through some examples to show you how to calculate the cost of various crews. Once you've established the labor unit for a particular crew, use the computed cost per bricklayer and the production rate per day to find your labor cost per unit laid.

Example A— Here's how to calculate the labor unit per day, per producing bricklayer, for a crew of five bricklayers (BL), three hod carriers (HC), and one foreman (WF) who's working 100% of the time laying brick:

1 WF	8 hours		@ $17.475	$139.80
5 BL	8 hours		@ $17.225	689.00
1 HC	½ hour (starting time)		@ $14.95	7.48
3 HC	8 hours		@ $14.95	358.80
				$1,195.08
Per producing BL, divide by 6				199.18
Round to				$200.00
With nonproducing foreman, labor unit is:				
Per producing BL, divide $1,195.08 by 5				$239.02
Round to				$239.00

In Example A, using the labor unit of $200.00 and a daily production rate of 154 8'' lightweight concrete block per man day, the unit price is:

$$\frac{\$200.00}{154} = \$1.30 \text{ per 8'' LWCB}$$

In Example A, using the alternate labor unit of $239.00 with a nonproducing foreman and a daily rate of 150 4'' structural glazed tile, the unit price is:

$$\frac{\$239.00}{150} = \$1.60 \text{ per 4'' SGT}$$

BL/HC ratio	BL foreman @ $17.475	BL @ $17.225	HC foreman @ $15.20	HC @ $14.95	Unit cost (working foreman) 100%	Unit cost (working foreman) 50%	Unit cost (nonworking foreman)
1-0	1	0	0	0	140	--	--
1-1 (1.00)	1	0	0	1	266	--	--
2-1 (.50)	1	1	0	1	203	--	--
4-2 (.50)	1	3	0	2	200	--	--
3-2 (.67)	1	2	0	2	221	--	--
6-3 (.50)	1	5	0	3	200	--	239
5-3 (.60)	1	4	0	3	212	--	--
4-3 (.75)	1	3	0	3	230	--	--
8-4 (.50)	1	7	0	4	199	213	--
7-4 (.57)	1	6	0	4	208	224	--
6-4 (.67)	1	5	0	4	220	240	--
10-5 (.50)	1	9	0	5	199	210	221
9-5 (.56)	1	8	0	5	206	218	231
8-5 (.63)	1	7	0	5	214	228	245
7-5 (.71)	1	6	0	5	225	242	263
12-6 (.50)	1	11	1	5	199	208	217
11-6 (.55)	1	10	1	5	205	214	225
10-6 (.60)	1	9	1	5	211	222	235
9-6 (.67)	1	8	1	5	219	232	247
8-6 (.75)	1	7	1	5	229	245	262

	2BL	4BL	6BL	8BL	10BL	12 or more BL
1st floor	203	200	200	213	221	217
2nd floor (1 add'l HC)	262	230	220	228	234	228
3rd floor (2 add'l HC)	322	260	240	244	248	239

Labor cost per day per bricklayer by crew size
Figure 8-8

Example B— Here's how to calculate the labor unit per day, per producing bricklayer, for a crew of seven bricklayers, five hod carriers, and one working foreman (50% production):

1 WF	8 hours	@ $17.475	$139.80
7 BL	8 hours	@ $17.225	964.60
1 HC	½ hour (starting time)	@ $14.95	7.48
5 HC	8 hours	@ $14.92	598.00
			$1,709.88
Per producing BL, divide by 7½			227.98
Round to			$228.00

In Example B, using the labor unit of $228.00 and a daily production rate of 560 brick, the unit price is:

$$\frac{\$228.00}{560} \ = \ \$0.41 \ \text{per brick}$$

Use this unit price in the labor column of the estimate summary. See Figure 8-9.

MASONRY QUANTITY SURVEYS

123 Beech Drive
Cincinnati, OH 45123

DATE
SHEET   OF
EST. BY
BID DUE

BLDG. ______________________   OWNER______________________

LOCATION ______________________   ARCHITECT______________________

PLAN NOS. __________DATE __________   GEN. CONTR. ______________________

ITEM	UNIT	QUANTITY	MATERIAL		LABOR		WORK	TOTAL
			Unit	Amount	Unit	Amount		
FACE BRICK	PCS	5000			.41	2050		
8" LWCB	✓	600			1.30	780		
4" SGT (6T)	✓	900			1.60	1440		

Sample take-off including labor units
Figure 8-9

Calculating Unit Costs for Material

Finding unit material costs is much easier because suppliers quote prices by the unit — the same way the materials are listed in the summary.

Face brick is usually quoted by the thousand (M) units. It's a simple matter to divide by 1,000 to get the unit price. But there is one complication. Every job has some waste. In this book I'm assuming 3% waste and adding this amount to the unit price. For example, assume the supplier's quote is $250.00 per thousand for face brick. The unit price, including a 3% waste allowance, is:

$$\frac{\$250.00}{1,000} \quad x \quad 1.03 \quad = \quad \$0.2575$$

$$\text{Round to} \qquad\qquad \$0.258 \text{ per unit}$$

Adding waste to the material price instead of increasing the quantity by 3% increases the cost of the material, but not the labor.

Getting Material Quotations

When you get a quotation for concrete masonry units, you may also receive the manufacturer's catalog. The catalog usually remains unchanged for several years, but the price list probably changes more often. Check with the block supplier to be sure you have the current price list and know about any discounts that may apply.

Quotations on structural glazed tile units and glazed concrete masonry units are furnished by the supplier.

You can usually get quotations on stone facing and stone trim from several stone fabricators. Their quote is usually a lump sum price in the form of a contract describing the material, how it is to be delivered, who will do the unloading, damage responsibility, applicable taxes, delivery sequence, and samples. Always ask the stone fabricators for their estimated quantities. They'll usually give them to you. It's a good way to check your own quantity estimate.

You shouldn't have any trouble getting plenty of competitive quotes on masonry accessories and wall treatment supplies.

Check to see if sales tax is applicable on the job you're figuring. Some states have a gross income tax and use tax. Taxes are usually added as a lump sum at the bottom of the estimate.

Fringe Benefits, Taxes and Insurance

These will be major expenses and may include:

1) Health and welfare
2) Pension
3) Apprentice training
4) Promotion
5) Construction advancement

6)   Social Security (FICA)
7)   Federal Unemployment Insurance Tax (FUI)
8)   State Unemployment Insurance Tax (SUI)
9)   Worker's Compensation Insurance (WC)
10) Public liability and property damage insurance

The costs for the first five items are negotiated between unions and management representatives. The amounts of these contributions will be a cost per hour and will vary with the number of hours worked.

The costs for items 6 through 9 are regulated by state and federal laws. Your accountant and insurance carrier will know the exact rates that apply. State Unemployment Insurance and Worker's Compensation Insurance rates vary, depending on the contractor's unemployment record. The amount of the contribution is a percentage of the labor cost.

The cost of public liability and property damage insurance is also a percentage of payroll.

Figure 8-10 shows a sample worksheet used to calculate fringe benefits, taxes and insurance. Make up a similar table using your labor rates, fringe benefits, taxes and insurance.

Overhead and Profit

Overhead is the expense of running a business — office salaries, office supplies, rent, utilities, small tools, office insurance, printing, auto and truck, advertising, postage,

	BL @ $17.225	BL foreman @ $17.474	HC @ $14.95	HC foreman @ $15.20
Health & Welfare	.970	.970	1.250	1.250
Pension	1.000	1.000	1.250	1.250
Apprentice training	--	--	.100	.100
Promotion	.150	.150	--	--
Construction advancement	.035	.035	.035	.035
Social Security (FICA) 6.7%	1.111	1.128	.982	.999
State & Fed. Unempl. 2.4%	.398	.404	.352	.358
Worker's Compensation 3.3%	.547	.556	.484	.492
Insurance 6.8%	1.128	1.145	.997	1.014
Total deductions	**$ 5.339**	**$ 5.388**	**$ 5.450**	**$ 5.498**
% of earnings	**31.00**	**30.83**	**36.45**	**36.17**

Use 33%

Typical costs of fringe benefits
Figure 8-10

interest on loans, legal and accounting fees, and countless other expenses that can't be charged to any particular job. These are very real costs and should be included in every bid you submit. The most common way is to add overhead as a percentage of the job cost. Here's how to calculate the overhead percentage.

Let's say that your business expenses (overhead) for the year can be expected to run about $50,000. You estimate gross volume for the year to be $500,000. That means your overhead percentage in every bid should be 10% of the bid price. Many small and medium-sized masonry contractors are able to keep overhead to between 4% and 6% of gross contract revenue. Larger contractors are seldom that economical. You can see that keeping overhead down makes your company more competitive.

Profit is the compensation allowed for the contractor's efforts, expertise, shrewdness and efficiency of operation, and the risk involved, tempered by his need for work. The profit percentage may be whatever the traffic will bear, usually about 10%.

Add overhead and profit in the summary just above the bottom line. Assuming your material take-off is accurate, labor and material prices are the same for all bidders, and overhead is about the same for all bidders, profit margin will be the major difference between your bid and the bids of other contractors.

Knowing that all the costs of the job are included in your bid, along with a fair profit, should give you added confidence in every bid you submit.

Finding the Right Bid Price

I went to a bid opening where the bidding general contractors and subcontractors had gathered to find out who won the job. But before opening the bids, each general contractor was handed a message from the architect in charge of the bid opening: "How much will you add to your bid to build a small cupola?"

The cupola was about 99% brickwork. Each general contractor asked his masonry sub for the add-on price. After some thought, one estimator for a masonry subcontractor wrote this on a piece of paper: "Add for one small cupola — deduct $500.00." He returned it to the general contractors he bid with. It won't surprise you to hear that our clever masonry estimator was the subcontractor for the winning general contractor. He had the low bid by $200.00.

This is a case where the successful estimator was very clever. He realized that the bidding would be very close, he knew exactly what his profit range was, and he suspected several masonry subs would use "no extra charge" for their add-on price. He preempted those no extra charge bids and got the job. And he made a fair profit. That's the spirit of successful bidding.

CHAPTER NINE

Tools and Equipment

If more than a few hand tools are going to be used on a job, your estimate should include an allowance for tool and equipment expense. This chapter will explain how tool and equipment expense should be estimated and included in your bid. I'll begin by explaining some broad principles that will apply no matter what tools and equipment are needed. Then we'll get down to studying some specific examples.

Good tools and equipment are expensive. They can be a major cost on a masonry job. Although you'll show tool and equipment expense as a lump sum on the bid, your estimate has to be based on an evaluation of the cost of each piece of equipment. You find those costs by developing a detailed list of the tools and equipment needed and the length of time they'll be required on the job. Then you'll price each item according to its expected useful life and maintenance cost.

Many small tools can be considered expendables — mortar hoes and boxes, buckets, extension cords, water hoses, mortar boards. They can't be expected to last beyond a single job and have little or no salvage value when the job is complete. Expendable tools can be charged to the job at 100% of the purchase price.

Equipment such as mortar mixers, forklifts, masonry saws, ladders, and wheelbarrows obviously aren't expendables. If they're rented for the job, the cost will be the rental expense plus any supplies they consume (such as gas and oil). If the equipment isn't rented for the job, computing the cost is much more difficult.

Some contractors make a rough estimate of the useful life of a piece of equipment. Then they charge the job with a proportionate share of that life for each day on the job. For example, if some scaffolding has a life expectancy of ten years and you're estimating a job that's expected to last one year, you would charge one-tenth of its cost to the job being bid. Using this method will produce unrealistically low equipment costs because it ignores the time value of money. At the end of ten years, if everything goes according to plan, you would have recovered only the cost of buying the scaffolding *ten years earlier!* By then equivalent scaffolding may cost several times more than the original scaffolding.

A better method is to charge each job for contractor-owned equipment at the fair rental value as if the equipment had been rented specifically for the job. Estimates using this method will be more accurate than estimates using the method described in the previous paragraph. And any errors will probably be on the high side rather than too low. After all, if the equipment really costs you as much as the rental rate, why did you buy it instead of renting it?

Figuring the exact owning and operating cost of each piece of equipment can be a complex problem and probably isn't worth the trouble in most masonry contracting companies. There are too many variables. Did you have to borrow money to buy the equipment? At what rate? If not, how much income was lost because you paid cash for the equipment instead of putting the money in a savings account? How many days a year will the equipment be in use? How much will it cost to service and maintain the equipment over its useful life? What's the salvage value when the equipment can no longer be used?

These are important questions for many excavation contractors because their investment in equipment is so heavy. But for most masonry estimators, approximate estimates will be plenty good enough.

I recommend that you estimate tool and equipment costs somewhere between the pro-rated daily cost of purchase (the lowest reasonable cost) and the fair rental rate (which is probably the highest reasonable cost). Develop a figure that seems appropriate for each piece of equipment and then make sure that figure is included in every estimate for jobs that will use the equipment.

After you've calculated the cost of all the tools and equipment for the job you're estimating, enter the lump sum into the summary at the bottom of the sheet.

Many experienced masonry estimators have found a fairly constant relationship between the total bid price and the cost of tools and equipment. For smaller jobs, the cost of tools and equipment is often about 10% of the total estimate. For larger jobs, the cost may dip to about 5%. For a typical masonry job, this rule of thumb is a quick and fairly accurate way to check your estimated tool and equipment costs.

Now let's take a closer look at some of the equipment used in masonry work, beginning with scaffolding.

Scaffolding Costs
We'll look at four kinds of scaffolding commonly used in masonry work: sectional, swinging and hanging scaffolding, and the Morgen system.

Sectional Scaffolding

Without scaffolding, Michelangelo would never have been able to do some of his most famous paintings. Without scaffolding, some of our most beautiful masonry would never have gotten off the ground. But masonry has been erected for centuries because masons found ways to get themselves, their tools and their equipment to where work had to be done.

Today, we can reach almost any building height with modern sectional scaffolding. This scaffolding — so simple, so versatile — can be put together almost without tools. Basically, the scaffold consists of end frames and cross braces. These cages provide various levels on which plank can be laid. Accessory items attached to the frames and braces, such as base plates for fixed frames and casters for rolling frames, make the scaffolding more useful. Screw jacks make leveling the frames easier.

Scaffolding can be purchased or rented. Assuming a lifetime use of 20,000 hours (about 10 years of use), you could find the cost per hour for each scaffold section. Charge this amount to each job, according to the estimated hours of use. You can calculate the number of hours the scaffolding will be needed based on the gross wall area. Scaffold area will probably be the same as the wall area computed in the take-off, with no deductions for doors, windows, or other openings.

Swinging Scaffolds

Swinging scaffolds are designed to provide a safe, adjustable platform for light duty work on masonry walls. Use them when pointing and washing down masonry, for setting stone and wall panels, and for other light operations when sectional scaffolding is impractical.

These scaffolds are suspended from 5/16'' galvanized steel wire rope for drops of 100, 150 and 200 feet. The machines have a dual mechanism: a direct ratchet for raising and a worm gear for lowering. The ratchet assures speed in raising, while the worm gear gives smooth operation and safety in lowering.

Platforms are made of carefully selected materials. They have steel reinforcements on the side members and are equipped with hinged toe-boards. The common lengths are 14, 16, 18, 20, 22, and 24 feet. Stirrups are 28'' wide.

A guard rail, mid-rail and center support stanchion are furnished with each complete scaffold. There's also a pair of roof hooks of ''S'' or ''L'' design. You may need a special anchoring system for unusual conditions. ''S'' hooks are available in several widths — 18 ", 24 ", or 30 ".

This scaffolding can be purchased or rented. Charge the rental cost or the owning and operating cost along with other tools and equipment.

Hanging Scaffolding

Hanging scaffolding is especially suited for high-rise buildings with structural steel or reinforced concrete frames. An 8'0'' wide wheeling scaffold is particularly adaptable for use where materials are hoisted and distributed in wheelbarrows directly from hoist to scaffold.

Each of these scaffolds is called a machine. One machine is required every 7 feet around the perimeter of the building. To figure the number of machines required to scaffold a building, first figure each wall separately. Divide the length of each wall by 7, then add one additional machine to find the number required for that wall. For continuous wheeling around corners, add one additional machine for each external corner.

Here's how to calculate the number of machines that will be required to completely scaffold a rectangular building that's 40 feet wide and 80 feet long.

$$\text{Length:} \quad \frac{80}{7} \quad + \quad 1 \quad = \quad 12 \text{ machines}$$

$$\text{Width:} \quad \frac{40}{7} \quad + \quad 1 \quad = \quad \frac{7}{19} \text{ machines}$$

$$\text{Total perimeter (19} \times \text{2)} \quad = \quad 38$$

Add for 4 external corners: 4

Total machines required: 42

The rental charge is usually based on a sliding scale, depending on how long the equipment will be used.

To compile a complete cost for this type of scaffolding, include the following costs:

- Machine rental
- Cable rental
- Anchors and ties for fastening to building frame
- Plank for floor and canopy
- Freight two ways
- Labor to erect and dismantle

The labor cost for erecting scaffold should be included with other labor costs associated with tools and equipment. It will appear as a lump sum at the bottom of the summary sheet.

Morgen Scaffolding

One of the most popular types of scaffolding is the Morgen system. It consists of lightweight triangular steel towers that support steel frames. The towers are 20'6'' high, spaced 7'6'' on centers. You can raise the tower to any height you need by adding 9' sections called inserts. The male end of the insert fits into a female sleeve. Each tower has a winch for raising the platform.

The steel frames support working platforms which hold the masons and laborers and their materials. The masons' platform is 21'' wide and 22'' below the laborers' platform, which is 40'' wide. See Figure 9-1.

There are several advantages of the Morgen system. First, the winches keep the mason working level at the most efficient position. The difference in height between the two levels make the handling of materials easier. Second, there's no interruption while planks, material, and men are being moved to a higher level. Third, the towers can be erected by two men and a gin pole, or a forklift. A forklift can move pairs of towers from wall to wall.

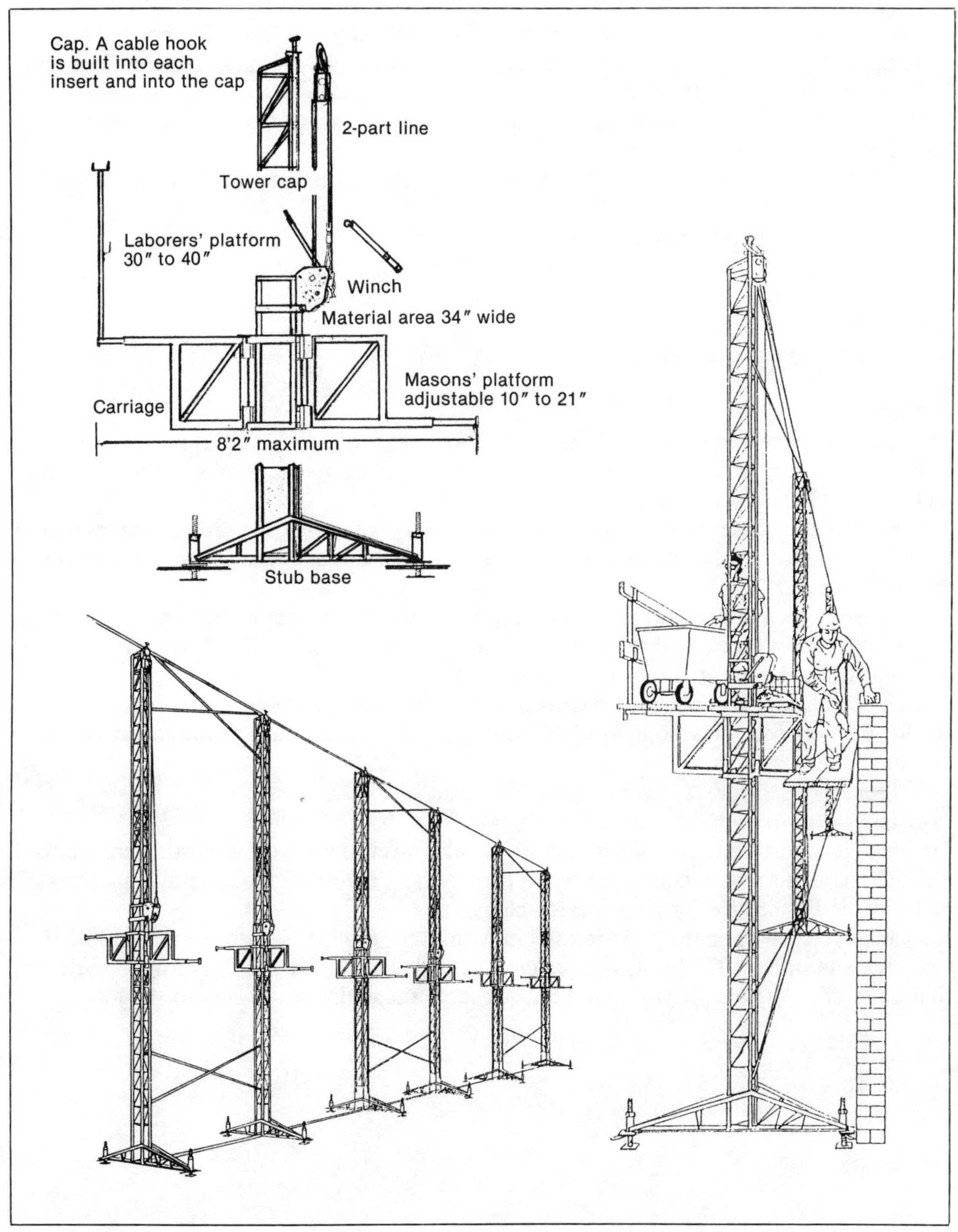

Courtesy: Morgen Manufacturing Co.

Morgen scaffolding
Figure 9-1

Many contractors like to have a supply of this scaffolding on hand. Except for an occasional lost part, it can be expected to last at least ten years. In many communities you can rent this type of scaffolding.

Regular 16'0" long scaffold plank is used with Morgen scaffolding and should be priced along with the scaffolding

To compile a complete cost for this type of scaffolding, include the following costs:

- Equipment (pro-rated charge or rental)
- Anchors and ties for fastening to the building
- Flooring plank
- Delivery charges
- Labor to erect and dismantle

Forklifts

This machine, when equipped with its many quick-change carriage attachments and accessories, is a very productive piece of equipment on most masonry jobs. Loading, lifting and material handling are just the beginning.

Forklifts can handle banded and palletized masonry anywhere the ground is reasonably level. Rubber-tired forklifts can hoist loads up to 4,000 pounds as much as 40 feet above ground level.

Brick and block are usually delivered on pallets that can accommodate the forks on the forklift. Most block dealers require a small deposit on each pallet delivered but make a refund when the pallet is returned to the yard.

Like other heavy equipment, forklifts are very expensive. Calculate the cost of keeping the lift on your job for as long as it's needed and add that amount to the bid as part of the lump sum for tools and equipment.

Hoists

On high-rise construction, you may need a tubular steel tower with a hoisting engine for hoisting materials and personnel to the upper floors. Very often the general contractor will provide this service for a contracted charge.

Include your cost for the hoist in the bid with other tool and equipment expenses. If you own and operate the hoist, then calculate the daily cost for job duration and add that amount to the bid. If you rent a hoist, charge the entire rental cost to the job.

Miscellaneous Costs

Besides the materials, labor, tools and equipment, every masonry job will include some miscellaneous costs. In this chapter we'll look at insurance coverage, the proposal and contract, bonds, fire ratings, testing, cold weather construction, utilities, and cleanup costs. Let's begin with insurance.

Insurance Costs

Every masonry contractor needs liability insurance. On significant projects your contract will always require it. But is the coverage you have the same as the coverage your contract requires? If you agree to provide some coverage that your policy excludes, you may be liable for a loss even though you have insurance. Only an expert can be sure that your coverage is adequate. Get the advice of your agent or broker. Fortunately, that's free.

The usual coverages include Worker's Compensation, comprehensive automobile liability, and comprehensive general liability. There's also contractual liability insurance for the benefit of the general contractor. It insures the general contractor for claims resulting from liabilities assumed by a subcontractor under the subcontract. The subcontractor buys and pays for all of this insurance.

The subcontract probably requires the subcontractor to place all his insurance coverage through a master policy bought by the general contractor. This arrangement is known as *wrap-up insurance.* While this type of insurance may have some advantages for the general contractor, there are disadvantages to the subcontractor. Here are some of the disadvantages:

• Increased clerical work because the subcontractor must have separate policies and audits for each job

• Loss of premium discounts, and therefore, higher insurance costs

• "Excess limits" charges on each separate wrap-up job instead of one single charge for public liability coverage

• If a lawsuit is settled without the consent of the subcontractor, the loss will be applied against the subcontractor's rating even when he has substantial proof that he wasn't liable.

I'm not a lawyer and won't offer any legal advice. I just want to identify some of the pitfalls in masonry contracting and suggest how they can affect your bid. And there's one final point: Don't overlook the cost of insurance when figuring the bid price.

The Proposal

Quite often you'll be asked to confirm your oral bid with a written proposal. This should alert you to spell out exactly what you've included and excluded in the bid. Don't hesitate to exclude anything that's questionable. Figure 10-1 is a sample proposal form that I've used.

The Contract

You won't use your own contract form on many jobs. The general contractor usually offers his own contract. But be familiar with contracts so you can understand what the general contractor requires.

Any bid or quotation can be made into a contract by adding at the bottom:

Gentlemen:

For the sum of $______________, we offer to furnish all labor, materials, tools, hoists, scaffolding and equipment necessary to erect in place **All Face Brick, Common Brick, Structural Glazed Tile and Concrete Block Walls and Partitions** required for the above building, in accordance with plan Sheets 1 to 48 and S1 to S23, all inclusive, dated November 1988, and specifications, together with Addenda Nos. 1 and 2, as prepared by John Smith, Architect.

The above figure is based on the following assumptions and conditions:

1. The following items are not included:

    a. Sewers, manholes, or other outside utilities.
    b. Waterproofing and/or dampproofing.
    c. Setting of flashing (except through-wall flashing built into our work).
    d. Caulking.
    e. Insulation (except cavity wall fill).

2. In general, internal corners of glazed tile are figured square, log cabin type, except in specific locations shown otherwise.

3. We will build in all necessary anchors, plugs, ties, mesh, reinforcing steel, incinerator iron and loose lintels weighing less than fifty pounds, occurring in our work; all such materials to be furnished by you, delivered on the several floors of the building where required, without charge to us. We include furnishing and placing of Duro-wall joint reinforcing in concrete block and hollow tile walls.

4. We include building in around doors and windows installed in line with the progress of our work. Pointing or slushing around doors and windows installed after our work is erected is not included.

5. Glazed tile and exposed concrete block walls will be cleaned down as the work progresses, room by room. Cleaning subsequent to completion and repair of damage by other trades is not included.

6. All necessary temporary roads, walkways, fences, barricades, electric current, temporary heat, sanitary conveniences, are assumed furnished and maintained by you, without charge to us.

In the event Alternate A is accepted, add the sum of $______________ to the above amount.

Terms of payment: 90% of the value of all materials delivered and work performed during any one month is due and payable on or before the tenth day of the succeeding month, until 50% of the work is completed. Thereafter, payments are to be 100% of the value. Final payment to be made within thirty days after the completion of all of our work.

Yours truly,

Doe Masonry Inc.
James Doe, President

Sample proposal
Figure 10-1

Accepted by:

Name:
Title:
Company:
Date:

Figure 10-2 shows a sample contract. Forms like this are sold at many office supply stores.

Bonds

There are several types of bonds that the masonry contractor may have to furnish. These bonds, known as surety bonds, are ordered by the contractor or subcontractor to guarantee that the owner receives all the benefits he's entitled to under the contract.

There are two types of contractors' bonds: performance bonds, and labor and material bonds. They may be combined into a single bond. A *performance bond* guarantees that the contractor will perform the contract. It usually provides that if the contractor fails to complete the contract, the surety company will complete the contract or pay damages up to the limit of the bond.

The *labor and material bond* guarantees the owner that all bills for labor and material contracted for and used by the contractor will be paid for by the surety company if the contractor defaults.

Get a Copy of the Bond

If the general contractor or owner-builder is required to furnish a labor and material payment bond, a copy of that bond should be delivered to the subcontractor. If you don't have a copy, the time you have to claim your rights under the bond may expire. Always get a copy of the general contractor's or owner's bond.

If the bond limits the obligation of the surety to the money received by the general contractor from the owner, the bond won't protect you against a general contractor who is unable to collect from an insolvent owner or an owner in default.

Getting bonded is like applying for a loan. The bonding company will want to know about your finances and the work you've done. Be prepared to answer questions on:

- Experience of key personnel
- Your finances (a current balance sheet and operating statement)
- Equipment and machinery owned and rented
- Projects completed

Include the cost of bond premiums as a separate item in your bid.

BUILDING CONTRACT

This Agreement, made and entered into on this _28_ day of _September_, 19 _87_ by and between _Sam Brown General Contractor_

of _Selby, Ohio_, and hereinafter designated as "First Party."

and _The Truss Masonry Company_

of _Noway, Ky._, hereinafter designated as "Second Party."

Witnesseth, That Said Second Party, for and in consideration of the sum of _$ 93,500.00_ _Ninety-Three Thousand Five Hundred dollars_ to be paid as hereinafter specified; hereby agrees to furnish unto said First Party all the labor and materials required

for the _the masonry work, per section 4200 of the specifications_

of a certain _Concrete Block warehouse_

to be erected for _John B. Sloan, Aspin, Ky._

on _his property @ 1400 N. 404th St._ _Roper, Ky. 44444_

in accordance with plans, drawings and specifications for the same as prepared and furnished by _Daryl & Daryl Architects, sheets 1 to 44 incl., dated 6-28-86_ which plans, drawings and specifications are hereby declared to be a part of this contract.

Said Second Party further agrees to furnish said materials and to do the said work promptly, in a workmanlike manner, without hinderance or delay to any other branch or class of work on said structure, and to work in harmony with and to render such assistance to said other branches of work as his connection therewith and the progress of said structure may require.

And Said First Party, for and in consideration of the true and faithful performance of said work and furnishing of said materials as aforesaid, hereby agrees to pay unto said Second Party said sum of $ _93,500.00_ in installments from time to time, upon the certificate of _acceptance by the architects_ as follows:

_90_ per cent _for all materials delivered and work performed each month, payable by the (10th) tenth of the following month_

and the remainder thereof when the aforesaid materials shall all have been furnished and said labor shall have been completed and accepted.

to be paid in full within 30 days

Signed in Duplicate in Presence of:

Margot Henry, Sec.

Herman Doolittle, Estimator

Signature of Parties:

Robert Truss, Pres.

Sam Brown, Pres.

_9-28-87_

Sample building contract
Figure 10-2

The Fire Rating

Every masonry estimator should understand how *fire ratings* affect masonry bids. Plans don't always show where various fire-rated materials are located. But you'll usually find that information in the specifications.

For example, the specifications may state that all concrete block will have a one-hour fire rating except that corridors and stairwells will have a two-hour fire rating. It's up to the estimator to separate the one-hour concrete block walls from the two-hour concrete block walls. In general, the higher the fire rating, the more it costs to build the wall.

The fire rating is the number of hours the construction will remain in place and prevent the temperature on the unexposed side from exceeding a certain temperature in a standard test fire. There are tables that show fire resistance ratings of 1/2, 3/4, 1, 1½, 2, 3 and 4 hours, as required by building codes. Laboratory tests show that fire resistance ratings for walls and partitions will vary with the materials and their equivalent thickness (E.T.).

Equivalent thickness is the average thickness of the solid material in the wall or partition. For example, the equivalent thickness for a concrete block wall that's nominal 8" thick (actually 7⅝" or 7.625") and 53% solid is:

$$.53 \times 7.625" = 4.04"$$

The equivalent thickness for a concrete block wall that's nominal 6" thick and 75% solid is:

$$.75 \times 5.625" = 4.22"$$

The graph shown in Figure 10-3 is made up from data taken from the American Insurance Association Fire Resistance Rating Tables. It shows the relationship between materials and equivalent thickness, and fire rating in hours. Use this graph as a guide only. It's not for design purposes. Where possible, use laboratory results rather than calculated results.

The examples shown are for 8" lightweight concrete block and 8" heavyweight concrete block, both 53% solid. The equivalent thickness for both types of block is 4.04, but the materials are different. So the 8" lightweight concrete block is rated two hours and the 8" heavyweight concrete block is rated one and one-half hours. If the specifications require that 8" heavyweight concrete block be used and that the fire rating be two hours, use 8" heavyweight concrete block with a higher equivalent thickness. An 8" heavyweight concrete block that's 58% solid will have an equivalent thickness of:

$$.58 \times 7.625" = 4.42"$$

Look up this E.T. (4.42) in Figure 10-3. Note the fire rating in excess of two hours. A 58% solid block is more expensive than the 53% solid block. And the 58% solid block weighs more, making it more expensive to lay. Make sure your bid covers these extra costs.

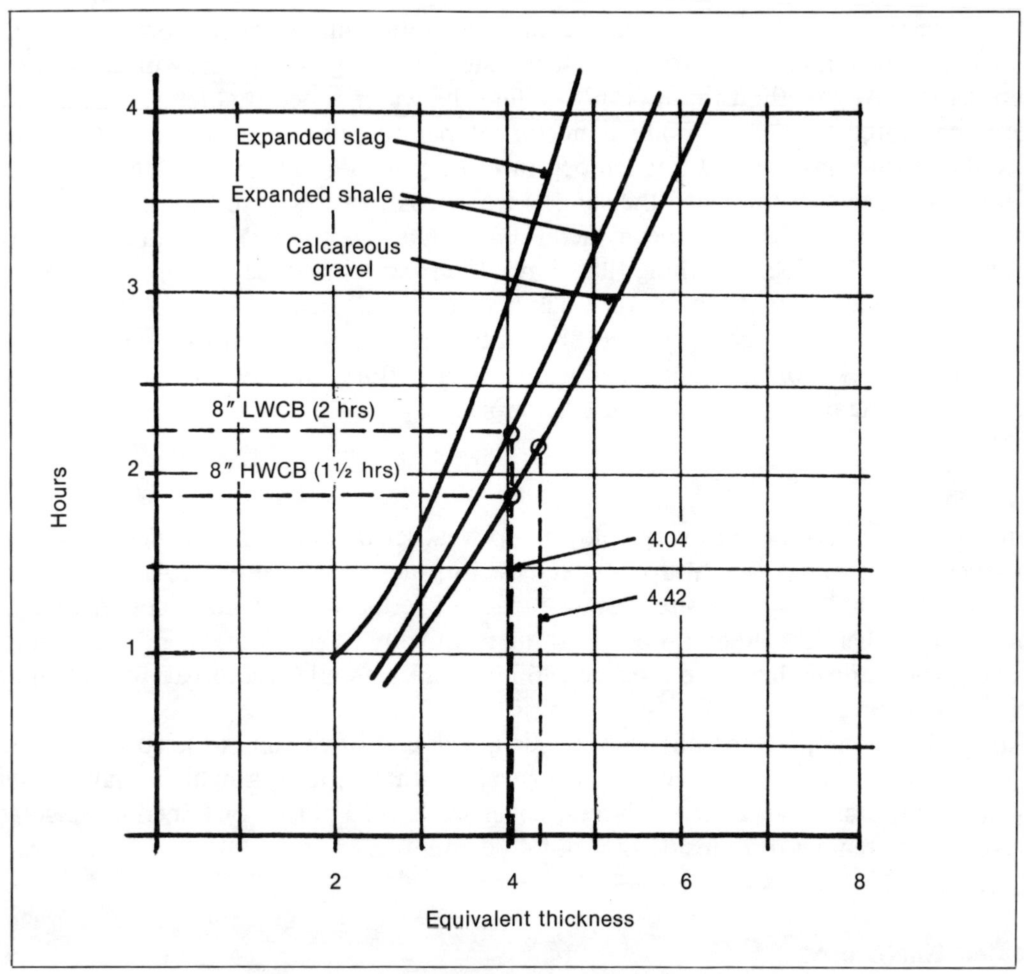

Fire resistance ratings
Figure 10-3

Cold Weather Construction

Masons work slower in cold weather. Consider these higher labor costs carefully when you're bidding work to be done in the winter.

Cold, wind, rain, snow, and ice increase labor costs and raise the cost of construction. Laying off your crews in cold weather may not be the solution. Overhead continues even when work doesn't. And most of your bricklayers will have no income during bad-weather shutdowns. Progressive masonry contractors have learned how to deal with bad weather. As an estimator, you should know what can be done to minimize the higher labor costs associated with it.

Heating Materials

Ideally, the temperature of the mortar on the mortar boards should be between 70 degrees F and 120 degrees F. This may require heating the water, the sand, or the masonry units. You may have to heat all three.

It's easiest to heat the water. Heating only the water will be satisfactory if the other construction materials aren't frozen. (Heat water in a 55-gallon drum with a fire or heat from below). Any method that doesn't pollute the water is acceptable. The mixing water should be heated enough to produce mortar temperatures between 40 and 120 degrees F. Once the mortar has reached this temperature, keep it there for every batch.

Heat the masonry sand when the sand is frozen. An easy way to heat sand is to shovel it over a section of a large diameter metal pipe (such as a culvert). Then build a slow-burning fire in the pipe. Anything that thaws the sand without scorching it is O.K.

If the temperature of dry brick or block is below 20 degrees F, it should be heated before use. Wet frozen masonry units should be thawed. Heat at least enough to keep the brick or block from cooling the mortar too fast. But you may find that production goes faster if the masonry is warmed even more.

Cover Walls

Your crews can work even in very cold, damp weather if they have an enclosed construction site that's kept above 40 degrees. In practice, of course, you can't afford to put a plastic bubble over the site. Balance mason productivity against the cost of protection. If there's a premium on finishing as quickly as possible, spend some time planning for bad weather. I've used everything from a simple windbreak to a completely enclosed structure.

Above 32 degrees, cover walls with plastic at the end of the day to keep water out of the masonry. From 32 to 20 degrees, cover walls with plastic or a light insulation blanket to delay heat loss. From 20 to 0 degrees, cover walls with plastic or a medium insulation blanket so the temperature inside is about 40 degrees.

Heated Enclosures

Enclosures and windbreaks are effective but have to be custom-designed for each job. They can be anything from a single insulation blanket to an elaborate shelter that protects the entire work area.

Canvas and synthetic coverings make good blankets. Use your ingenuity. Consider strength, durability, flexibility, transparency, fire resistance, and ease of installation. An unheated enclosure is the easiest to build and provides enough protection if the weather isn't too cold. But keep your materials above 32 degrees for 24 hours before they're needed if possible. A heated enclosure for material storage may be necessary.

Scaffolding can be a problem in cold weather. Be sure it's erected, braced and anchored to resist snow and wind loads. Don't let ice or snow build up on the planking.

Cost of Cold Weather Construction

Unfortunately, there's no way to figure the exact extra cost of construction during cold weather. For one thing, you can't be sure how cold the weather will be. But I've found that costs usually run about 10% to 15% higher in the winter months than they do during the spring or fall. Most of my jobs are in Ohio. I can imagine that winter costs would be higher in areas with more severe winter weather.

The only published figures I've ever seen on the subject appeared in a 1975 study by the National Association of Home Builders: *HUD's 1975 Survey of Home Builder's All-Weather Building Practices.* That study surveyed the cold weather experience of 2,500 home builders. These builders were asked to report the average increase in labor time for the three worst weather months compared to the three best weather months. For laying block foundation walls, the builders reported increased labor costs as follows:

North	15%		Desert west	2%
Mid-south	9%		Northwest	15%
Deep south	15%		South coast	2%
Mountain west	16%			

Testing

Many jobs now require load-bearing masonry walls for maximum strength. When maximum strength is essential, the specifications will probably require masonry testing. Be sure to include the cost of these tests in your bid.

Where prism testing is required, the test prisms should be representative samples of the actual composition of the wall. Each test prism should be built under a masonry contractor's supervision using the masons, materials, and workmanship used (or scheduled to be used) in the building. Make the prisms as much like the actual walls as possible. Be consistent with the mortar and grout, the thickness and tooling of joints, and the moisture content of the units at the time of laying.

If several tests are required, get a sub-bid from a testing laboratory.

Utilities

Water, power and sometimes heat are needed to lay brick or block. They're not always furnished free. Make the cost of any of these services part of your bid. Even if water and power are provided by the general contractor, you may need to provide hoses and extension cords.

Clean-Up

Assume that you'll be required to clean up your trash and remove it from the job site. Include those costs in your bid also.

Other Miscellaneous Costs

There may be many other costs in your bid. Review the following list before submitting the final quotation:

1)	Photographs	5)	Parking
2)	Permits	6)	Sanitary convenience
3)	Plans	7)	Watchman
4)	Travel		

CHAPTER ELEVEN

Masonry Take-Off and Estimate

 novice estimator looking at a set of plans for a fair-sized job may be overwhelmed by the complexity. The immediate reaction may be, "Where do I start?" The job really isn't as complicated as it looks at first glance. Just take it a step at a time. Start by paging through the plans one sheet at a time.

Get Friendly with the Plans

Layout Drawings
The first plans are usually layout drawings, sometimes referred to as *civil* or *site* drawings. These plans probably show masonry items such as retaining walls, brick paving, mechanical buildings, garages, stone garden walls, and monuments. Some of these items may not be obvious. If you can mark on the plans, highlight any masonry you find on the civil sheets so you won't overlook it later. Most general contractors expect that these items will be included in your bid.

The Floor Plans

The floor plans are the next series of plans. They'll usually include a plan for each floor level and quite often for intermediate levels. Start your estimate with the foundation plan and proceed one floor at a time.

Foundation plans are the hardest to take off, especially materials in the exterior walls. The facing material on the exterior walls is usually carried on a ledge just below the grade line. The take-off will be complicated if the ground around the building isn't level. The brick ledge will probably run at several elevations. To make an accurate take-off, you've got to know the elevation of each level. This information will be on an elevation, cross section, structural drawing, or maybe even a topographical drawing.

The floor plans will show the wall construction of the exterior and interior walls. Find the area of each wall by taking lengths from the floor plans and heights from the wall sections.

Here's why you use floor plans to measure the perimeter of exterior walls:

1)   You can take advantage of duplication. Multi-story buildings often have identical floor plan layouts. There's no need to measure every floor. But it's good practice to include a take-off sheet for each floor, even if you only duplicate the numbers from another sheet. Transfer all the totals to separate lines, one for each duplicate floor, in the recap. See the sample take-off sheet, Figure 11-1.

2)   Floor plans at upper floors will indicate the amount of setback and will show the decrease in perimeter measurement. This is a good place to pick up the parapet walls (at the setbacks). See the sample elevation sheet, Figure 11-2.

3)   The floor-by-floor take-off will be very useful when ordering and stocking materials if you win the job.

Finish Schedule

After the floor plans, you'll find the finish schedule. This will show the type of masonry materials used, such as structural glazed tile, exposed concrete block, sound block, face brick, or stone facing. Use a colored pencil to mark the rooms or areas where these materials occur. Make a separate take-off for each of these materials.

Door and Window Schedule

The next series of plans will probably be the door and window details and schedule. You'll refer to these drawings frequently. Mark the plan sheet numbers on your work sheet or make up a reference table showing what materials are listed on what pages. This makes it easier to find what you're looking for. Use the door and window detail drawings to find the opening size you have to deduct from each wall area. These drawings also show special details such as lintel construction, flashing location, sill materials, and the size and shape of masonry units at jambs.

Elevations

Elevations are very important to the estimator. They show story heights and the masonry needed, especially above and below openings. Notes on the elevations usually indicate the type of masonry, the masonry patterns, and the location of control and expansion joints.

MASONRY QUANTITY SURVEYS

123 Beech Drive
Cincinnati, OH 45123

DATE

SHEET   OF

EST. BY

BID DUE

BLDG. ___________________________   OWNER _______________________

LOCATION ________________________   ARCHITECT ____________________

PLAN NOS. ____________ DATE ________   GEN. CONTR. _________________

EXT. WALLS   3RD FLOOR

3RD FLOOR SAME AS 2ND FLOOR

REPEAT 2ND FLOOR TOTALS IN RECAP

Sample take-off sheet for duplicate floor
Figure 11-1

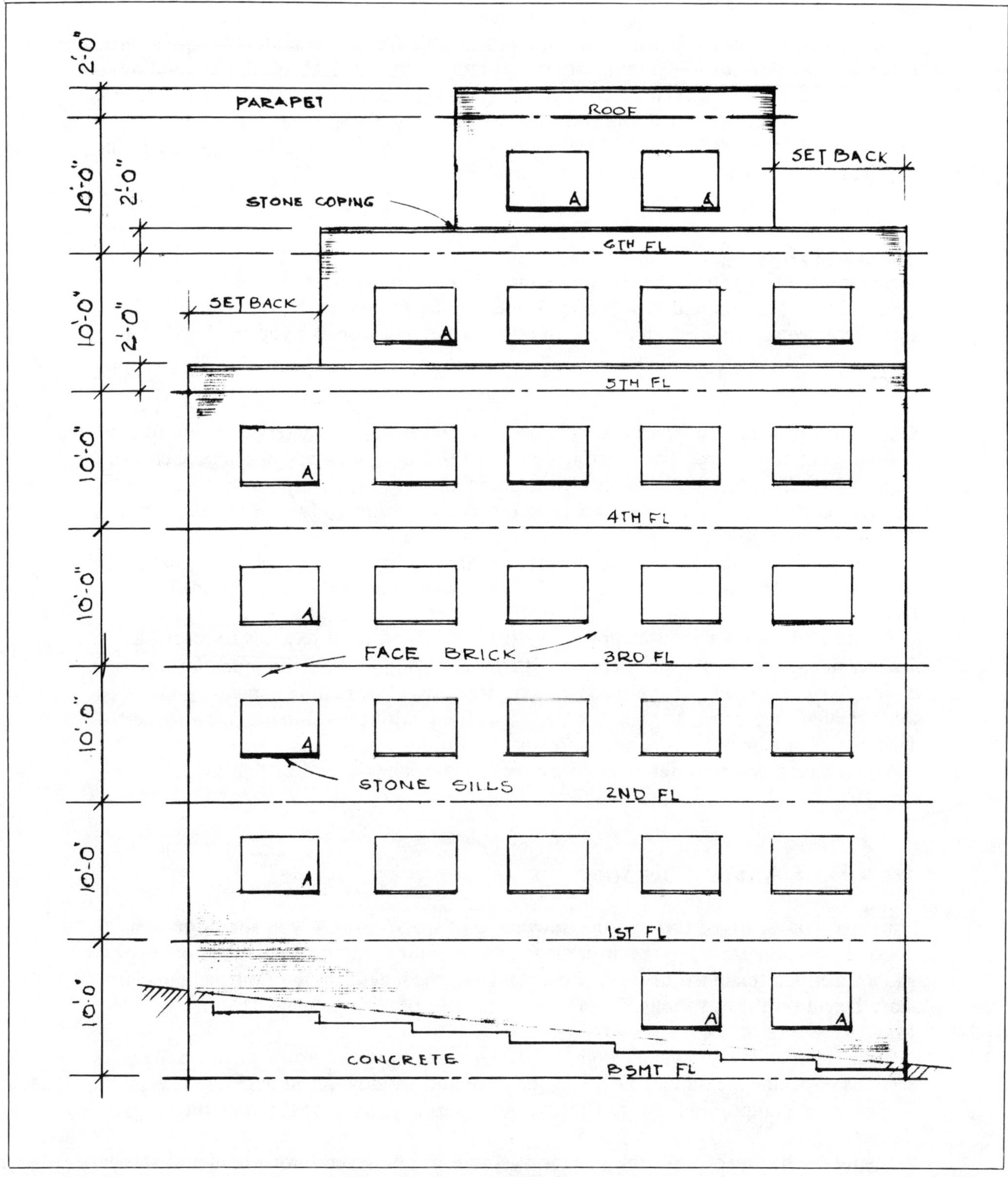

Sample elevation
Figure 11-2

Wall Sections

Wall sections are probably the most important details for the estimator. Sections through exterior walls show details of masonry construction, the materials used, the bonding, the location of flashings, special construction at spandrels, bond beams, and so on.

The sections through partition walls will usually show the thickness, the type of material, height of wall, and the location of bond beams. They'll often note fire ratings required in areas such as stairwells and corridors.

Structural Drawings

Structural drawings show the size of beams. Masonry walls often end under beams, especially in corridors and stair shafts. Remembering to deduct the amount of masonry that these beams displace can reduce an estimate enough to make you the low bidder.

Specifications

Once you've studied the areas and volumes, start reviewing the description and quality of the materials to be used. The specifications spell this out. Masonry usually appears in *section 4* of the specs. But you have to examine all sections. Be especially alert for masonry cost items in the sections headed *General Conditions, Special Conditions, and Instruction to Bidders*.

Items such as flashing, caulking, insulation, and waterproofing probably won't appear in section 4. It's your job to understand clearly what items have to be included in your bid.

Figure 11-3 shows a specification take-off sheet. Use a form like this to record an abstract of the architect's specifications. It's never wrong to have too much information about the specifications. If the specifications are unusual or require something that's unreasonable, photocopy the entire section and file it with the estimate. Then request a clarification or eliminate from your bid what you don't understand.

You'll find a complete set of masonry specifications at the end of this chapter.

How Do I Attack This Job?

Now that you've paged through the drawings and specifications, you should have a good idea of what this job requires. Generally, masonry materials are taken off in square feet. Calculate the area of face brick from the length on the floor plan and the story height on the elevations. Then deduct the area of the openings. Do this floor by floor.

Take the plan measurements from each floor plan. Find the story height on the wall sections. Opening measurements are in the door and window schedules.

Figure the parapet walls the same way, but separately, because the construction is different.

Figure the basement walls the same way. There will be several horizontal and vertical measurements where the wall is stepped at the transition between brick masonry and concrete masonry.

MASONRY QUANTITY SURVEYS

123 Beech Drive
Cincinnati, OH 45123

DATE *12/20/87*
SHEET *1* OF *1*
EST. BY *RVK*
BID DUE

BLDG. *OFFICE BLDG* OWNER ___________

LOCATION ___________ ARCHITECT ___________

PLAN NOS. *1-4* DATE *12-1-87* GEN. CONTR. ___________

Specification Section _____ *4* _____ Date ___________ Addenda ___________

Face Brick	Size	*MODULAR*	Allowance	*$210 00 /M*			
Common Brick	Size	*MODULAR*	Material	*CONCRETE*			
Glazed Tile	Size	*8 x 16 8W*	Material	*CER. GL.*			
Concrete Block	Size	*8 x 16*	Material	*HW & LW*			
Exp. Joints	Type	*—*	Material	*—*			
Control Joints	Type		Material	*PVC*			
Fill	Walls	*GRANULAR*	Material	*VERMICULITE*			
Flashing	Furnished By	*MASON*	Material	*PLASTIC*			
Caulking	Furnished By	*OTHERS*	Material	*—*			
Parging	Thickness	*½" ON BRICK*					
Anchors	Type	Galv.	WT.	Spacing	H	V	
Ties	Type	Galv.	WT.	Spacing	H	V	
Reinforcing	Type *TRUSS*	Galv. *✓*	WT. *9 ga*	Spacing	V	*16"*	
PC Concrete	Sills	Copings	Lintels	Facing			
Stone	Sills *LS*	Copings *LS*	Trim *—*	Facing *—*			
Bond Beams	Fill Furn. By	*MASON*					
P.C. Lintels	*OVER ALL OPENINGS*						
Cleaning	Materials	*DETERGENT*					
Workmanship	Bond	*RUNNING*	Joints	*CONCAVE*			
Waterproofing	*NONE*						
Special							
Alternates							

Specification take-off sheet
Figure 11-3

Accumulate these net areas to find the total area. Then measure the backup material just as you measured the facing material. Figure the stone coping with the parapet take-off. List the stone window sills and lintels with the window opening deductions. In the sample estimate in this chapter, I'll show how these items are measured and listed on the take-off sheets.

Masonry is usually priced by the unit: face brick, concrete block, glazed tile, and so on. But some masonry items are priced by the linear foot (bond beams, precast lintels, stone sills, and stone coping). And some items are priced by the square foot (waterproofing, parging, and cut stone facing). It's easiest if you take off the materials the same way prices are quoted. Years ago, cement was bought by the barrel, stone by the perch, clay tile by the ton — and calculations were cranked out by hand. It's much simpler now.

Forms

Only three forms are needed for masonry take-off: the specification take-off sheet, the take-off sheet, and the summary sheet.

The *specification take-off sheet* (Figure 11-3) is for making an abstract of the specs. It's simply a handy reference.

The *take-off sheet* is used to list areas, quantities and calculations. If you're like me, you won't be able to resist adding special notes to the take-off sheet. It's also used to recap the various masonry items into table form.

On larger jobs, the recap may require many sheets. To avoid rewriting descriptions on all sheets, clip the first two columns off of all the sheets except the bottom sheet. You'll see this system used on the recap sheets in the sample estimate.

The *summary sheet* is used to itemize all masonry items for pricing.

Use the sample forms I've provided if you like. Have a local printer reproduce a few hundred copies and bind them into a pad for convenience. If you don't like my forms, make up your own with a ruled tablet. Use any form that works for you.

Before you do anything else, write a sheet number at the top of the take-off sheet. One of the most serious mistakes you can make is to lose a page of the take-off. Number the sheets as you go. That way you'll know immediately if one sheet is missing.

It's a good habit to fill out the heading of each sheet, especially the date, the plan numbers and identification of the area taken off.

Order of Take-Off

When you've given all the plan sheets and specs a once-over, it's time to begin estimating. To avoid mistakes and omissions, you're going to work very systematically, taking things in the same order every time. Find a good order that seems natural to you and follow it on every estimate. Once you're comfortable with a sequence, it should become second nature to you. If there's more than one estimator in your office, try to use the same sequence. That makes checking the take-offs and recap much easier.

Many estimators like to take off the materials in the order of construction, except for masonry on the civil drawings. It's best to get these out of the way before tackling the main building. Here's the sequence I recommend:

- Civil drawings
- Foundation walls
- Exterior walls, floor by floor
- Parapet walls, floor by floor
- Penthouse structures
- Interior (partition) walls, floor by floor

Record items on the take-off sheet one at a time. Use only standard abbreviations. Any masonry estimator who reviews your figures should be able to understand what you've done.

There may be many take-off sheets. But the summary sheets will seldom exceed two pages — even for very large (million dollar) masonry projects.

Scaling Dimensions

Always check the accuracy of the plan scale. Sometimes plans are reproduced at something other than the original size. That makes the scale wrong. A good place to check this is on the main floor plan. Scale off the overall length of the building. Then read the overall length on the plan. It's not uncommon for these dimensions to disagree. Use the scaled dimensions only if you know they're accurate.

If you're scaling off hundreds of lineal feet at one time, check the overall measurement with a plan measure wheel. These wheels are the size and shape of a stopwatch and have a reset button on the stem. But a small wheel protrudes from the bottom. Roll this wheel along the plan to measure distances. When you carefully trace plan distances with the wheel, the dials on the face show the length.

Wheels are available for measuring distances drawn in several scales — 1/8" = 1'0", 1/4" = 1'0", and 1/2" = 1'0". The most common scale used by estimators for measuring floor plans is 1/8" = 1'0".

Measuring is tedious work. Dropping a hundred feet is easy. A hundred lineal feet could be as much as a thousand square feet and several thousand dollars. Good estimators don't make mistakes like this. Work carefully. Don't allow distractions. Avoid working under time pressure. Have someone check all your figures. If something doesn't look right or doesn't make sense, it's probably wrong.

Perimeter Measurements

It's always easier to list actual plan dimensions on your take-off sheet. But it's usually more convenient to scale them. Buildings with square corners on both the interior and exterior will always have an overlap at four corners.

In the building outlines in Figure 11-4, note that the sum of the exterior dimensions in Buildings A, B, and C each total 300'. Assuming all four buildings are constructed with face brick:

- Building A would have an overlap of 4" at four external corners. The actual lineal feet of brick is 300' minus 1'4", or 298'8".

- Building B has an overlap of 4" at five external corners and one internal corner. So the net overlap would again be 1'4". The actual wall length would be the same as above.

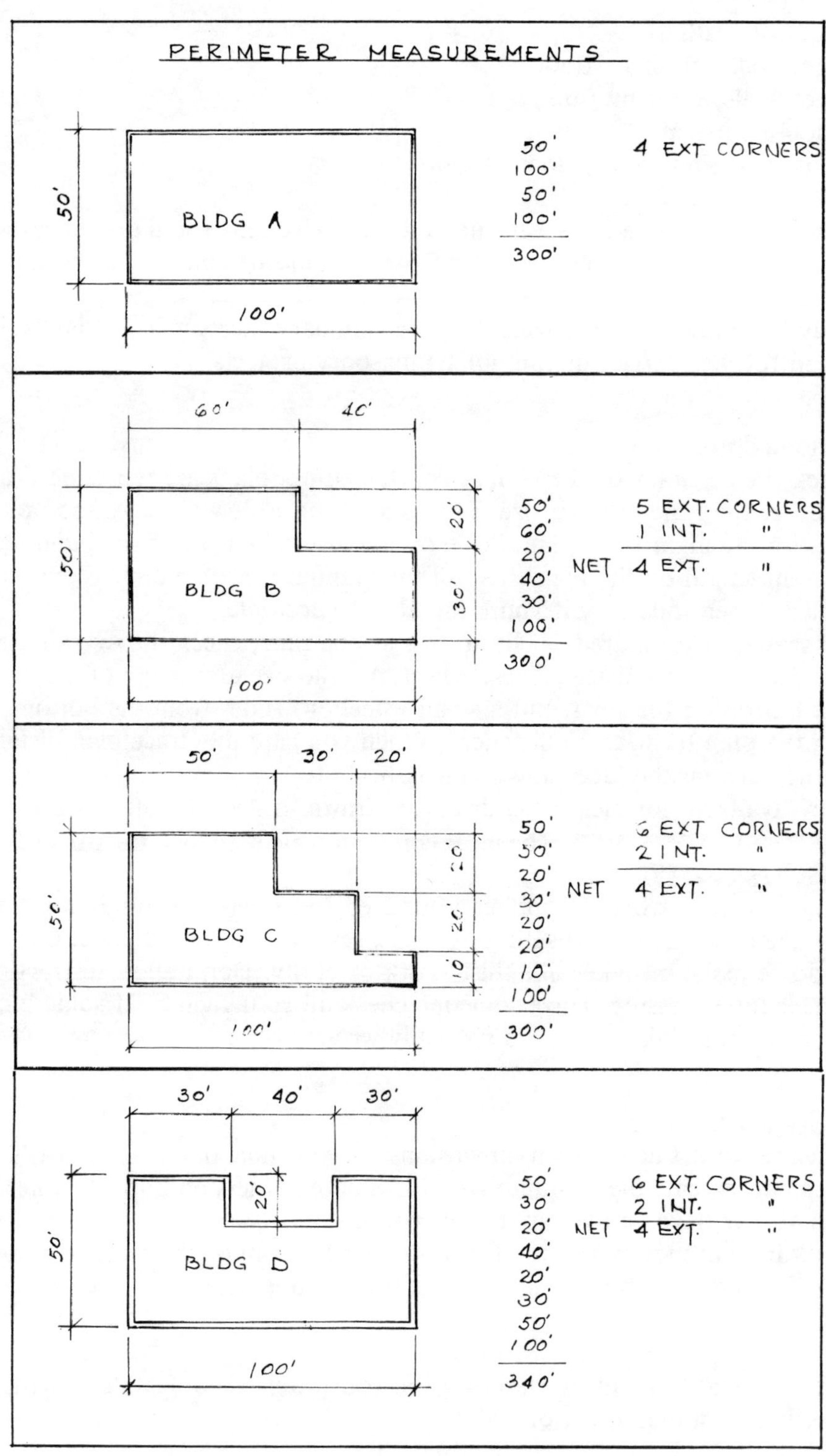

Perimeter measurements
Figure 11-4

- Using the same method, Building C will have a net overlap of four corners. The overlap at an internal corner balances the overlap at an external corner.

- In Building D, exterior dimensions add up to 340'. It has six external corners and two internal corners — again a net overlap of four corners, or 1'4".

Waste Allowance

The overlap at corners will be the same on short walls as it is on long walls. That's why no percentage allowance for overlap will fit all jobs. The waste in the buildings in Figure 11-4 will be small. But since you'll never have a job without some waste, my suggestion is to increase the price (not the quantity) of the face brick by 3% in the summary. The wasted brick must be paid for, but there's no reason to add 3% to the labor cost. You'll see this 3% added to the cost in the summary sheet of our sample estimate later in this chapter.

Of course, you can't ignore the extra cost of labor for building corners. The more corners, the higher the labor cost. Use good judgment when estimating corners, piers, and pilasters. If the production rate for one mason laying brick in a wall with few corners is 560 brick per day, the rate will be less if the wall has many corners. The adjustment will depend on the quantity of work at corners compared to the overall quantity of brickwork.

The extra cost of building corners or other building details, such as quoins, corbels, or dentils, can be accounted for by measuring the areas and listing the item in the summary as:

ITEM	UNIT	QUANTITY	MATERIAL		LABOR		WORK	TOTAL
			Unit	Amount	Unit	Amount		
QUOINS @ CORNERS P.O.	SF	200						

Waste allowance for backup material— The same lineal measurements used for the facing material can be used for the backup material. See Figure 11-5. The waste allowance for backup material is a little greater than for brickwork. It's good practice to add 2% or 3% to the cost of the concrete block when pricing in the summary.

Adjust the cost of labor to allow for corner construction. It's similar to building piers or pilasters in brickwork. The more corners there are, with their more time-consuming workmanship, the less brick or block laid — and the greater the cost. Concrete block is usually available locally, so running short of material isn't as crucial as it is for glazed tile or face brick.

When scaling the lengths of concrete block walls, round the dimension between corners up to the next whole or half masonry unit. For example:

Scaled dimension	Use
17'0"	17'4"
12'0"	12'0"
23'6"	24'0"
52'6"	52'8"

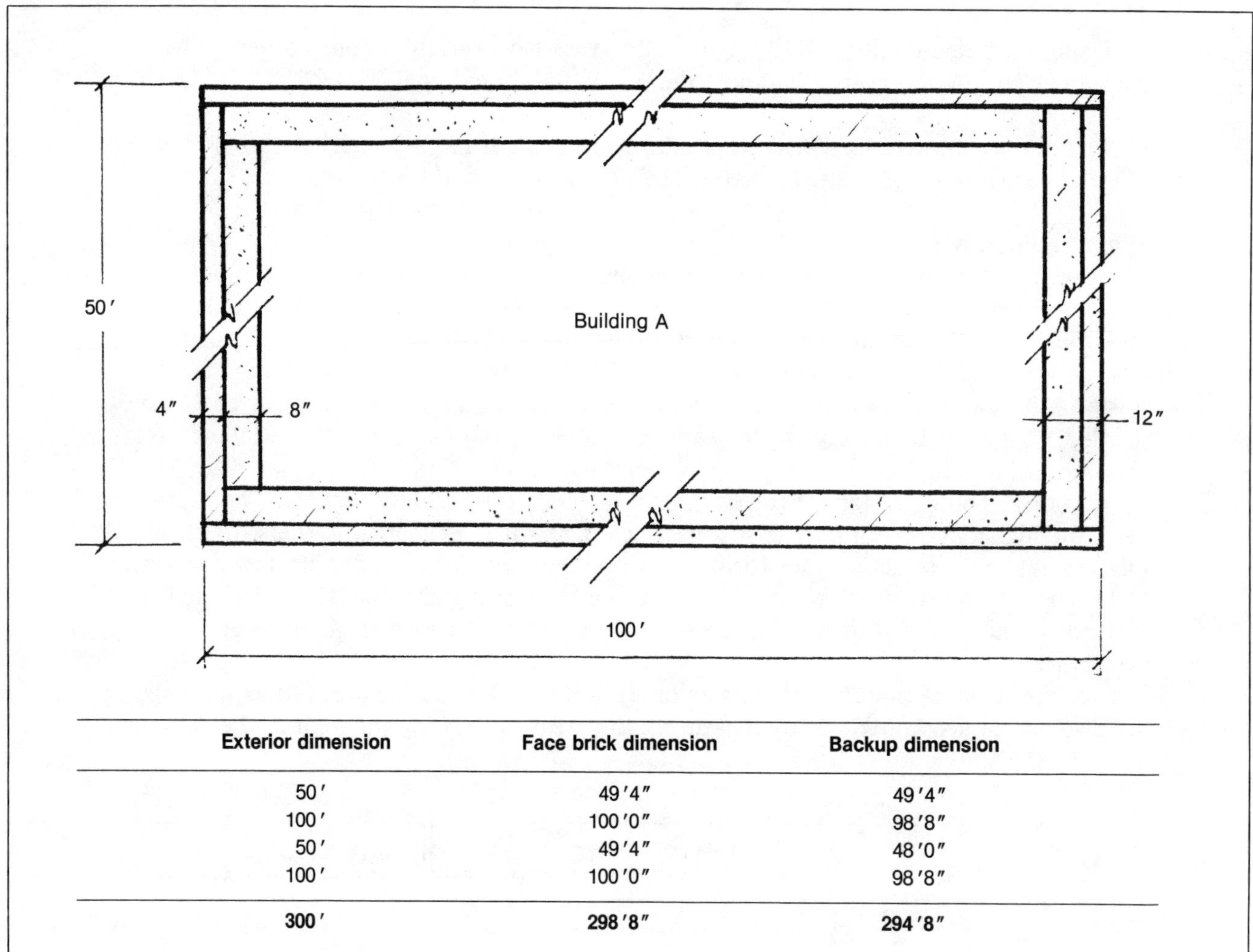

Exterior dimension	Face brick dimension	Backup dimension
50'	49'4"	49'4"
100'	100'0"	98'8"
50'	49'4"	48'0"
100'	100'0"	98'8"
300'	**298'8"**	**294'8"**

Typical detail showing the amount of lap involved when using perimeter dimensions
Figure 11-5

When scaling the lengths of structural glazed tile walls, the dimension should include the length of the wall plus a minimum of 4'' lap at corners (interior and exterior). It also should be rounded up to the next whole tile length. See Figure 11-6. Rounding to the next whole or half unit can be important. Consider our sample take-off in Chapter 2.

Finding the Vertical Dimension

The horizontal dimensions are probably the most important part of a take-off. But it takes two dimensions to calculate an area.

Find the height, or vertical dimension, by studying the wall sections, cross sections through the building, and dimensions shown on wall elevations. Sometimes you can find these vertical dimensions by comparing sea level elevations, floor elevations, or top of wall elevations. For example, if a floor plan shows a first floor elevation of 110'0'' and a second floor elevation of 120'0'', you can assume that the story height is 10'0''.

6T Series

	Scaled dimension	Lap at corners	Total dimension	Use
	6′9″	4″	7′ 1″	8′0″
	7′0″	4″	7′ 4″	8′0″
	8′7″	4″	8′11″	9′0″
	9′2″	4″	9′ 6″	10′0″

8W Series

	Scaled dimension	Lap at corners	Total dimension	Use
	6′9″	4″	7′ 1″	8′0″
	7′0″	4″	7′ 4″	8′0″
	8′7″	4″	8′11″	9′4″
	9′2″	4″	9′ 6″	10′8″

Measurement allowance for scaling structural glazed tile
Figure 11-6

Recording Wall Areas

To make a take-off of wall areas, you need both the horizontal and vertical dimensions. Many estimators would record a wall 40' long and 10' high on the take-off sheet like this:

$$40' \times 10' = 400 \text{ SF}$$

The system I use is slightly different. The dimensions for this wall area are recorded on the take-off sheet vertically, like this:

$$\frac{10^{\underline{o}}}{40^{\underline{o}}}$$

$$\widehat{400}$$

The Sample Take-Off

Let's go through a take-off based on the sample plans in Figures 11-7 through 11-11. The task at hand is to record the masonry items and accessories on take-off sheets, arranged and identified so that it's easy to compile a summary ready to price.

Earlier I suggested that you follow the procedure of taking off the civil drawings first. Civil drawings usually show masonry construction such as retaining walls, brick paving, mechanical buildings, and garages.

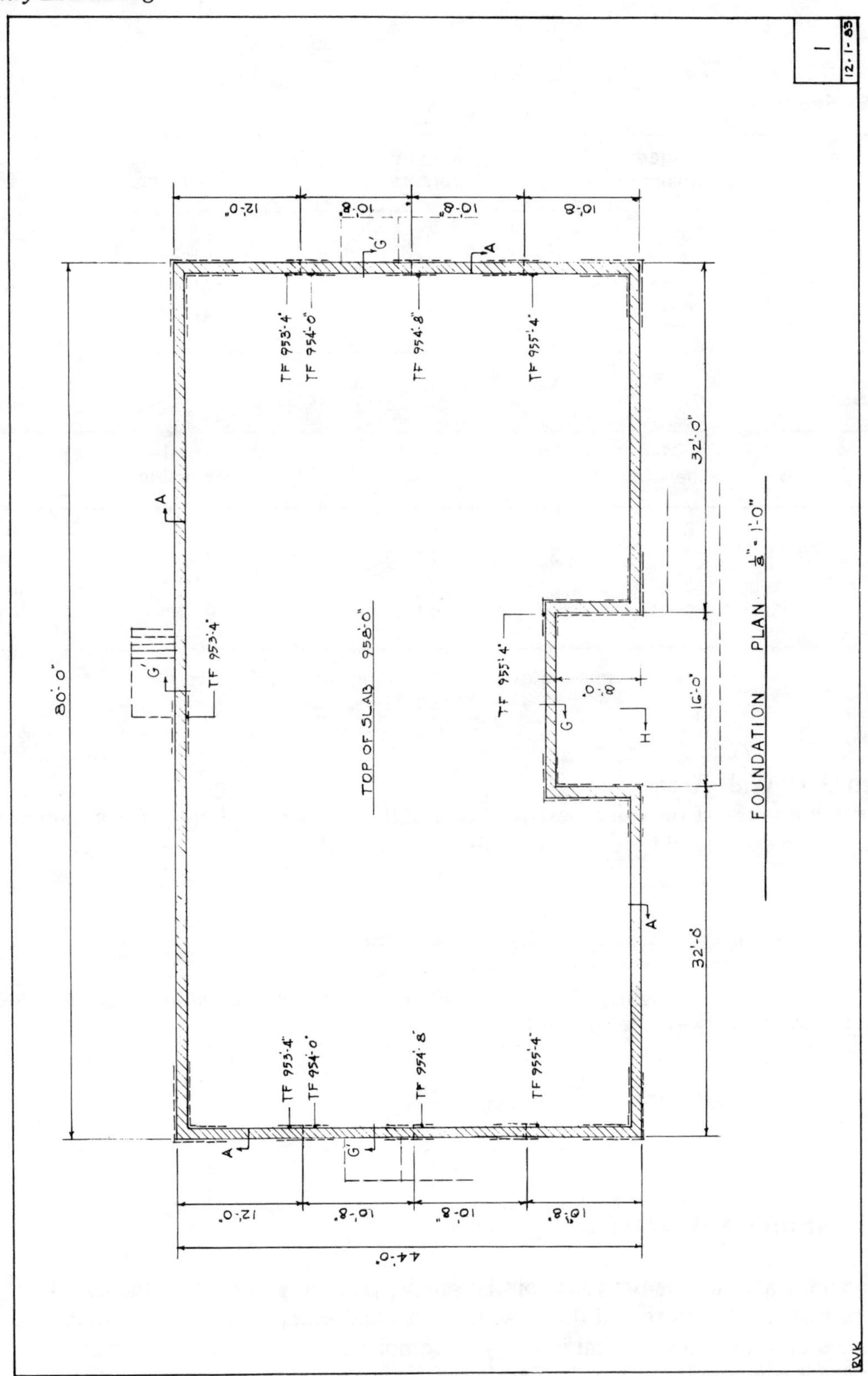

Foundation plans (sheet 1)
Figure 11-7

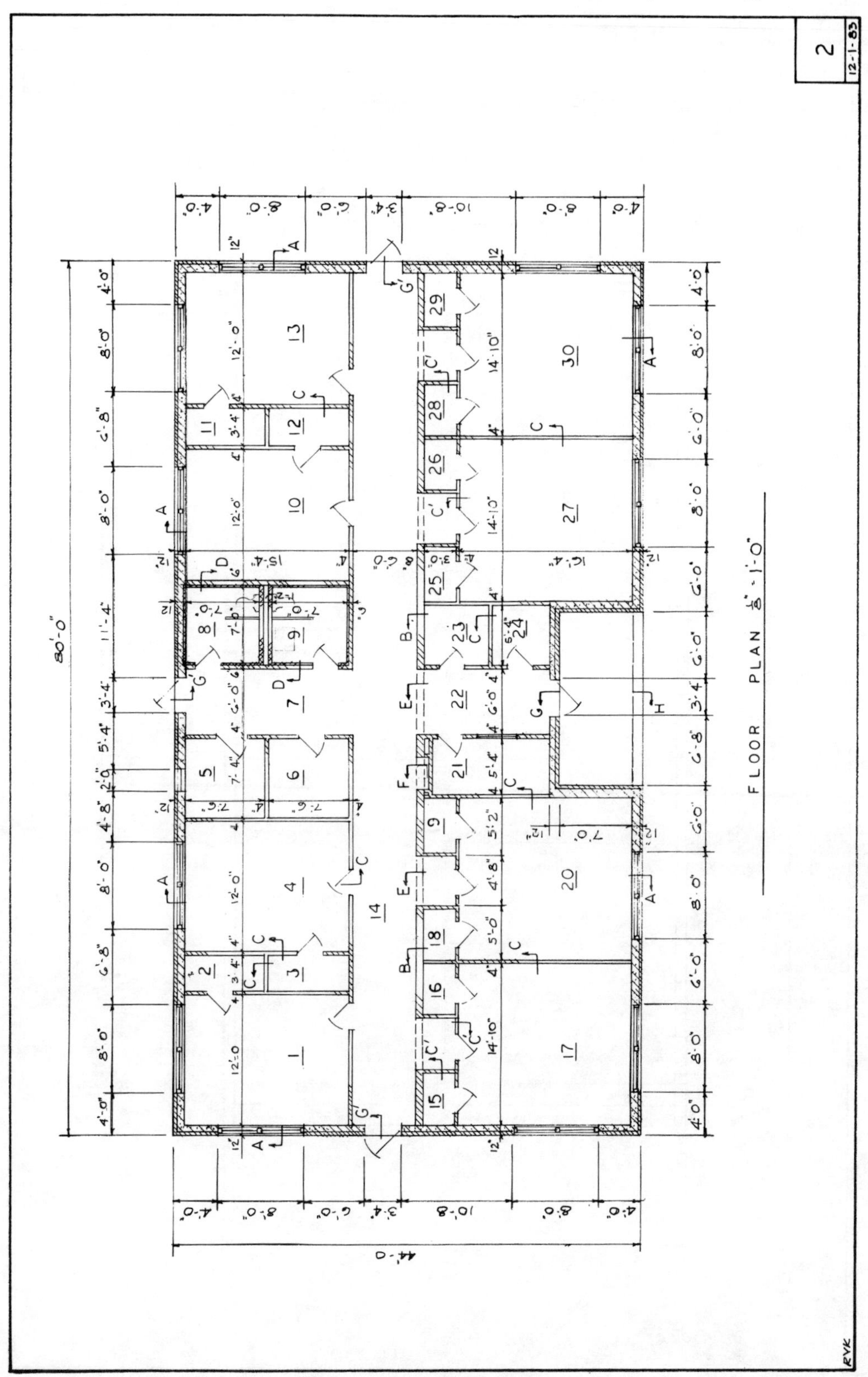

Floor plans (sheet 2)
Figure 11-8

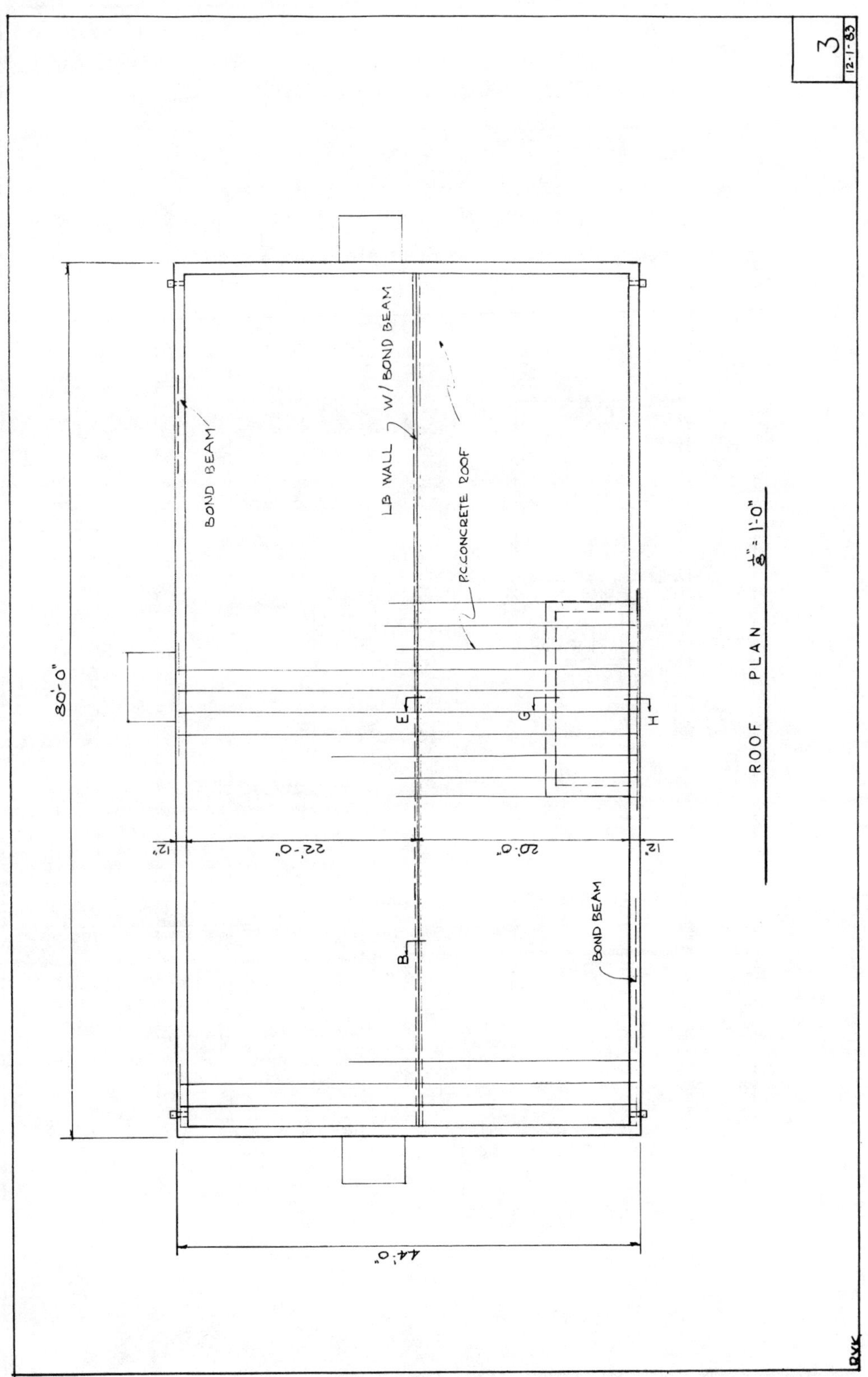

Roof plan (sheet 3)
Figure 11-9

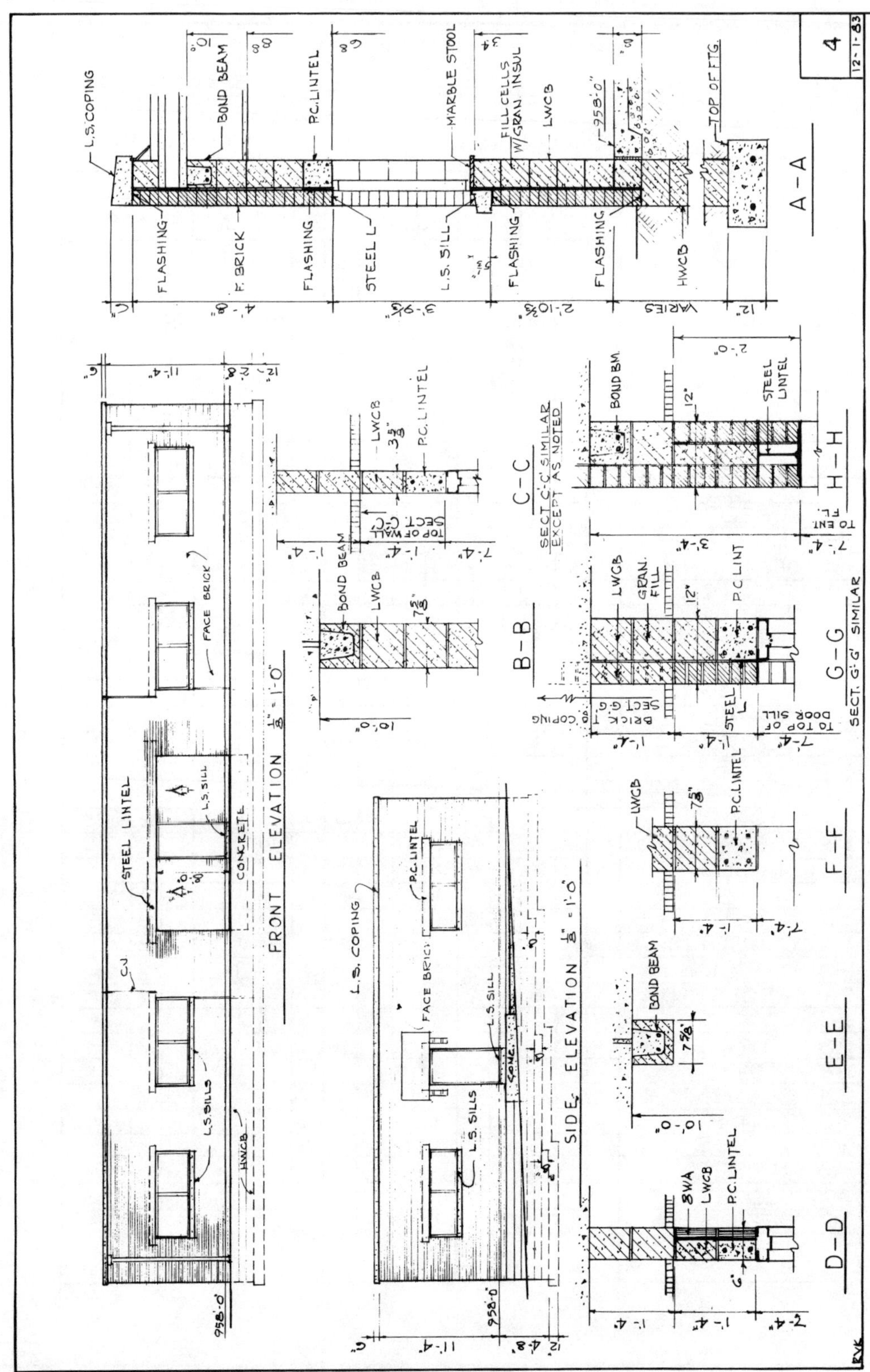

Elevations and details (sheet 4)
Figure 11-10

ROOM FINISH SCHEDULE																
		FLOOR					WALL								CLG.	
		BASE			FIN.		N		E		S		W		FINISH	
		NONE	COVED (GL.)	4" VINYL	CONCRETE	VINYL ASB.	LWCB	GL. TILE	LWCB	GL. TILE	LWCB	GL. TILE	LWCB	GL. TILE	EXPOSED	12'x12" ACOU.
NO.	ROOM	1	2	3	1	2	1	2	1	2	1	2	1	2	1	2	HGTH.
1	OFFICE			3		2	1		1		1		1			2	8'-8"
2	CLOSET			3		2	1		1		1		1			2	"
3	CLOSET			3		2	1		1		1		1			2	"
4	OFFICE			3		2	1		1		1		1			2	"
5	FURNACE	1			1		1		1		1		1		1		10'-0"
6	JANITOR	1			1		1		1		1		1		1		"
7	CORRIDOR			3		2	1		1		1		1		1		8'-8"
8	M. TOILET		2			2		2		2		2		2		2	"
9	W. TOILET		2			2		2		2		2		2.		2	"
10	OFFICE			3		2	1		1		1		1			2	"
11	CLOSET			3		2	1		1		1		1			2	"
12	CLOSET			3		2	1		1		1		1			2	"
13	OFFICE			3		2	1		1		1		1			2	"
14	CORRIDOR			3		2	1		1		1		1			2	"
15	CLOSET			3		2	1		1		1		1			2	"
16	CLOSET			3		2	1		1		1		1			2	"
17	OFFICE			3		2	1		1		1		1			2	"
18	CLOSET			3		2	1		1		1		1			2	"
19	CLOSET			3		2	1		1		1		1			2	"
20	OFFICE			3		2	1		1		1		1			2	"
21	RECEPTION			3		2	1		1		1		1			2	"
22	LOBBY			3		2	1		1		1		1			2	"
23	STORAGE			3		2	1		1		1		1			2	"
24	STORAGE			3		2	1		1		1		1			2	"
25	CLOSET			3		2	1		1		1		1			2	"
26	CLOSET			3		2	1		1		1		1			2	"
27	OFFICE			3		2	1		1		1		1			2	"
28	CLOSET			3		2	1		1		1		1			2	"
29	CLOSET			3		2	1		1		1		1			2	"
30	OFFICE			3		2	1		1		1		1			2	"

5

12-1-83

Room finish schedule (sheet 5)
Figure 11-11

The plans for this sample take-off don't include civil drawings. Because of the wide range of masonry items that can be involved, it's hard to show a typical take-off. Let me suggest that good judgment, detailed descriptions, and accurate measurements will yield good results. The important thing is to be sure that these items get into the summary.

Foundation Walls

Look at the foundation plan, Figure 11-7. One of the first things you'll notice is the notations (TF 953'4'', for example) at various locations around the perimeter of the building. This shows that the *top of footing* (or TF) elevations and the depths of footings vary.

Section A-A on plan sheet 4 (Figure 11-10) shows that the face brick extends 8'' below the floor level, a convenient place to terminate the top of the foundation walls. The only masonry remaining below the brick level is 12'' heavy weight concrete block (HWCB).

The foundation take-off (Figure 11-12A) lists only one item, 12'' HWCB, of various heights.

The first height, 2'0'', is determined by subtracting the shallowest TF (955'4'') from the level of the bottom of the face brick.

Top of slab elev.	958'0''
	− 0'8''
Bottom of f. brick elev.	957'4''
Shallowest TF	− 955'4''
	2'0''

Here's how to find the linear dimension:

$$\text{Perimeter:} \quad 80' + 44' + 80' + 44' = 248'$$
$$\text{Two offsets at } 9' \quad\quad\quad\quad\quad + \ 18'$$
$$266'$$

The next three sets of calculations show the amount of block in the areas where the top of footings are deeper.

$$\frac{955'4'' - 954'8''}{10'8'' + 10'8''} \qquad \frac{0^8}{21^4} = 15 \text{ SF}$$

$$\frac{955'4'' - 954'0''}{10'8'' + 10'8''} \qquad \frac{1^4}{21^4} = 29 \text{ SF}$$

$$\frac{955'4'' - 953'4''}{12'0'' + 80'0'' + 12'0''} \qquad \frac{2^0}{104^0} = 208 \text{ SF}$$

The foundation area is 784 square feet (SF). Remember, the numbers in ovals are extensions. The numbers in small circles refer to the explanations in Figure 11-12B. For each completed take-off sheet in this sample estimate, I'll include a key that explains

MASONRY QUANTITY SURVEYS

123 Beech Drive
Cincinnati, OH 45123

DATE 12/20/87
SHEET 1 OF
EST. BY RVK
BID DUE

BLDG. OFFICE BLDG   OWNER

LOCATION   ARCHITECT

PLAN NOS. 1 TO 4 DATE 12/1/87   GEN. CONTR.

FOUNDATION

			12"HWCB		①
			2^0		②
			248		③
			18		
			266^0		④
			(532)		⑤
			0^8		
			21^4		
			(15)		
			1^4		⑥
			21^4		⑦
			(29)		⑧
			2^0		
			104^0		
			(208)		
			784		⑨
			4		⑩

Foundation take-off (sheet 1)
Figure 11-12A

(1) 12" HWCB
     12" heavyweight concrete block

(2) 2^0
     Height of wall: 2'0"

(3) 248 + 18
     Two wall measurements, lineal feet

(4) 266^0
     Total lineal feet of walls

(5) 532
     Extension: height of wall x total of lengths
     2'0" x 266'0" = 532 SF

(6) 1^4
     Height of wall: 1'4"

(7) 21^4
     Length of wall: 21'4" (10'8" + 10'8")

(8) 29
     Extension
     1'4" x 21'4" = 29 SF

(9) 784
     Total of extensions: total square feet

(10) ✗
      Check with slash indicates arithmetic is checked and transferred

Foundation take-off explanations
Figure 11-12B

how I arrived at the numbers on the take-off. Figure 11-12A is the foundation take-off; Figure 11-12B is the explanations. Item 9 in Figure 11-12B shows that 784 is the total of the extensions — the total square feet of block needed.

Exterior Walls

Now we'll take off the exterior walls. Look at Figure 11-8, the sample floor plan.

Face brick— On the exterior wall take-off sheet, Figure 11-13A, under the heading *4"*
F.Brk, 12'0" is shown as the vertical dimension. This is the sum of all the individual dimensions shown on Section A-A in Figure 11-10:

$$2'10\text{-}2/3" + 3'9\text{-}1/3" + 4'8" = 11'4"$$

That 11'4", plus the additional 8" below floor level, totals 12'0" for the height of the face brick on the take-off sheet. The entry for 4" face brick looks like this:

$$\frac{12^{\underline{0}}}{248^{\underline{0}}}$$
$$\boxed{2976}$$

The 248'0" below the line is the total perimeter of the building, taken from the floor plan in Figure 11-8:

$$44'0" + 80'0" + 44'0" + 80'0"$$

The perimeter dimension (248'0") is also used for the length of the 8" lightweight concrete block (LWCB) backup, limestone coping, bond beam, and flashing.

The oval around a number indicates that it's an extension (height times length). The number within the oval, 2976, is the square foot area. Look at Figure 11-13A and 11-13B.

Concrete block— The height of the 8" LWCB backup is also taken from Section A-A in Figure 11-10, except that the 8" thickness of the roof slab has been deducted. That makes the height 11'4".

At this point the building is completely enclosed with face brick and 8" LWCB backup. Imagine it as a box (44' wide, 80' long, and 12' high) with all four walls made of face brick and block backup. This is a good place to check horizontal and vertical dimensions.

Figuring the adjustments— The next step is to make quantity adjustments for doors, windows, entrances, and so on. These adjustments are usually deductions. But you'll also make additions, such as the face brick at recessed entrances and the additional face brick returns at doors and windows. Look again at Figure 11-13A. The small circled numbers to the left of the various columns show the number of additions or deductions.

MASONRY QUANTITY SURVEYS

123 Beech Drive
Cincinnati, OH 45123

DATE 12/20/87
SHEET 2 OF
EST. BY RVK
BID DUE

BLDG. *OFFICE BLDG*   OWNER ______
LOCATION *135 9TH AVE DAYTON, O.*   ARCHITECT ______
PLAN NOS. *1 TO 4* DATE *12/1/87*   GEN. CONTR. ______

EXT. WALLS, ② ③ ④ ⑤ ⑥ ⑦ ⑧ ⑨

	4" F.BRK CB B/U	② 8" LWCB B/U w/GF	③ LS COPING 14×6 w/FLASH	④ BOND BM 8×8 D.O.	⑤ FLASH @FL 18"W	⑥ LS DR SILL 5½×7¾ w/FLASH	⑦ LS WD SILL 5½×5⅓ w/FLASH	⑧ MARBLE STOOL 8×0¾	⑨ P.C. LINT 8×8 D.O. w/FLASH
①	13'-0"	11'-4"							
	248'-0"	248'-0"	248'-0"	248'-0"	248'-0"				
	(2976)	(2811)			+ 32'-8"				
					281				
	9'-4"	9'-4"							
	32'-8"	32'-8"							
	(305)	(305)							
	2'-0"								
	16'-0"								
	(32)								
	3313								
⑩ ENT 16'-0"×7'-4"	① 117				① 16				
⑪ " 16'-0"×9'-4"		① 149							
⑫ DR 3'-6"×7'-4"	④ 97	④ 97				④ 14			④ 19
⑬ WD 8'-0"×3'-9⅓"	⑫ 362						⑫ 96	⑫ 96	⑫ 112
⑭ " 8'-0"×3'-4"		⑫ 320							
⑮ G.S 7'-4"×8'-8"		① 63							
⑯	576	629							
⑰	2737	2487	248	248	265	14	96	96	131
⑱		+ 44	⑲						
		2531							
⑳									

Exterior wall take-off (sheet 2)
Figure 11-13A

(1) 4" F. BRK, (CB B/U)
     4" face brick, concrete block backup

(2) 8" LWCB B/U
     8" lightweight concrete block backup

(3) L.S. COPING, 14" x 6", W/FLASH
     Limestone coping, 14" wide x 6" high (outside dimensions) with flashing as specified

(4) BOND BM, 8 x 8, D.O.
     Bond beam, 8" wide x 8" high, Difference Only. (The difference between the cost of the material
     it replaces and the cost of the bond beam)

(5) FLASH @ FL 18" W
     Flashing at floor line 18" wide

(6) L.S. DR SILL, 5-1/2 x 7-3/4 W/FLASH
     Limestone door sill, 5-1/2" wide x 7-3/4" high, with flashing

(7) L.S. WD SILL, 5-1/2 x 5-1/3, W/FLASH
     Limestone window sill, 5-1/2" wide x 5-1/3" high, with flashing

(8) MARBLE STOOL, 8 x 0-3/4
     Marble stool, 8" wide x 3/4" high (thick)

(9) P.C. LINT, 8 x 8, D.O., W/FLASH
     Precast lintel, 8" wide x 8" high, Difference Only. (The difference between the cost of the
     material it replaces and the cost of the precast lintel)

Note: Items 10 to 15 inclusive are deductions from the gross quantities

(10) ENT., 16^0 x 7^4
     Entrance 16'0" wide x 7'4" high
     Deduct 1 opening: 117 SF from 4" F. BRK
     Deduct @ 1 opening: 16 LF of FLASH @ FL, 18" W

(11) ENT., 16^0 x 9^4
     Entrance 16'0" wide x 9'4" high
     Deduct 1 opening: 149 SF from 8" LWCB

Exterior wall take-off explanations
Figure 11-13B

(12) DR, 3^4 x 7^4
Door 3'4" wide x 7'4" high
Deduct 4 doors: 97 SF from 4" F. BRK and 8" LWCB
Add @ 4 doors: 14 LF of L.S. DR SILL
$4 \times 3^4 = 13^4$ (use 14 LF)
Add @ 4 doors: 19 LF of P.C. LINT
$4 \times 4^8 = 18^8$ (use 19 LF)

(13) WD 8^0 x $39^{1/3}$
Window 8'0" wide x 3'9⅓" high
Deduct 12 windows: 362 SF from 4" F. BRK
Add @ 12 windows: 96 LF of L.S. WD SILL
$12 \times 8^0 = 96$ LF
Add @ 12 windows: 96 LF of MARBLE STOOL
Add @ 12 windows: 112 LF of P.C. LINT
$12 \times (8^0 + 1^4) = 112$ LF

(14) WD, 8^0 x 3^4
Window, 8'0" wide x 3'4" high
Deduct 12 windows: 320 SF from 8" LWCB

(15) 2" CG1S, 7^4 x 8^8
2" ceramic glazed one side, 7'4" wide x 8'8" high
Deduct 1 wall: 63 SF from 8" LWCB
(Note that the 8" LWCB material deducted above is replaced with 6" LWCB on Figure 11-15A
(Sheet 3)

(16) 576, 629, 16
Deductions from gross quantities

(17) 2737, 2487, 248, 248, 265, 14, 96, 96, 131
Net quantities

(18) +44
This quantity transferred to this sheet from Figure 11-15A (Sheet 3)

(19) ⫽
The check with the double slash indicates that this quantity was transferred twice, once to
Figure 17A (recap 1) and again to Figure 19A (recap 3)

(20) ⫽
The check with the double slash indicates that this quantity was transferred twice, to recaps 1
and 3

Exterior wall take-off explanations
Figure 11-13B (continued)

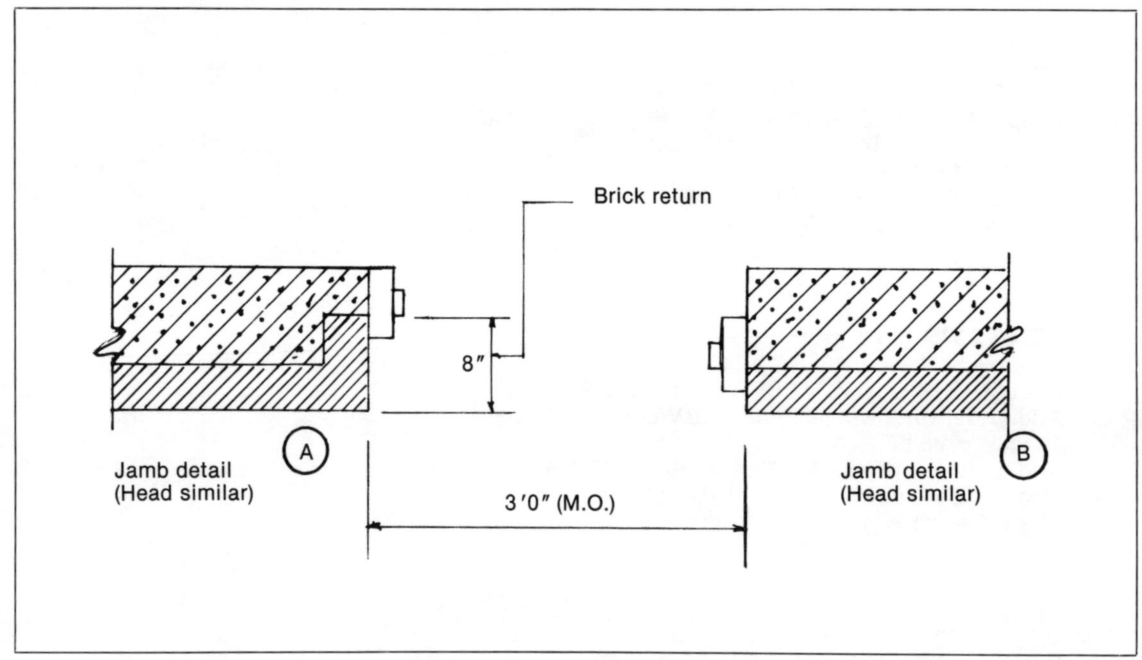

Typical jamb and head details
Figure 11-14

The jamb details for this building are shown in Figure 11-14, detail B. If they were designed like detail A, you'd have to add an additional quantity to your take-off sheet under 4'' face brick. If the offset dimension were 8'', the perimeter of the opening 17'0'', and the number of openings 12, the take-off calculation would look like this:

$$\frac{0^{\underline{8}}}{12 \times 17^{\underline{0}}}$$
$$\boxed{136}$$

The exterior wall take-off includes three more sets of measurements which show the additional face brick and LWCB in the entrance:

$$\frac{9^{\underline{4}}}{32^{\underline{8}}} \quad \frac{9^{\underline{4}}}{32^{\underline{8}}} \quad \frac{2^{\underline{0}}}{16}$$
$$\boxed{305} \quad \boxed{305} \quad \boxed{32}$$

Let's look at the first two dimensions. The height (9'4'') is found by adding 8'0'' and 1'4'' from Section G-G in Figure 11-10. The length (32'8'') is the sum of the lengths of the three entrance walls (16'0'', 8'4'' and 8'4''). The gross area (305) is added in the appropriate columns, under *4'' F. Brick* and *8'' LWCB*.

The only face brick left unaccounted for is an area of hanging wall over the entrance. See Section H-H on Figure 11-10. It's the third additional dimension in Figure 11-13A, with an extension of 32 square feet.

To complete the take-off, we have to deduct for openings. This will reduce the gross area to a net area of exterior masonry. *But it isn't necessary to make the extensions during the take-off.*

The deductions are shown on Figure 11-13A as item numbers 10, 11, 12, 13 and 14.

Item 10 shows a face brick deduction, 16'0'' wide and 7'4'' high. The length is taken from the floor plan (Figure 11-8) and the height from Section H-H of Figure 11-10. There's also a deduction of 16 linear feet of flashing.

Item 11 shows a deduction from the *8'' LWCB* column, 16'0'' wide, but in this case 9'4'' high. Section H-H shows why. The 2'0'' of backup material over the opening is already included in the take-off as 8'' LWCB. This material should be deducted and other material (4'' LWCB and 4'' face brick) added back in. So the height of the deduction is 9'4'' (7'4'' plus 2'0''). The 2'0'' of face brick has already been added.

Because there are so many items on the exterior wall take-off, it takes two sheets. Figure 11-15A is the second sheet of exterior wall take-off (sheet 3). The 1'4'' of 4'' LWCB is added to the take-off on that sheet. Look at the column headed 4'' LWCB.

Item 12 is a deduction of four door openings, 3'4'' wide and 7'4'' high. The small circled number 4 on the left side of the door sill column indicates that there are four openings. This is a convenient place to pick up other masonry items related to the door opening: the limestone door sills and the precast concrete lintels.

Even though these items are recorded with the outs, they are to be added to the take-off. The width of the opening will determine the length of the sill or lintel.

- The length of the slip sill will be equal to the width of the opening.

- The length of the lug sill should be 2'' longer than the slip sills.

- The length of the lintel should be 16'' longer than the width of the opening (8'' on each side).

Item 13 shows a deduction of face brick for 12 windows 8'0'' wide and 3'9⅓'' high. Also, an addition of 12 window sills, 12 marble stools and 12 lintels. See Section A-A on Figure 11-10. You may find it helpful to check with a colored pencil as you take off the items. It saves time to make the extensions later.

Item 14 shows the deductions for the backup material. Section A-A will show why. Note that lintels are regarded as part of the backup. A correction for the difference in cost between 8'' LWCB and 8'' x 8'' precast lintel is made in the summary.

Item 15 is an adjustment to the 8'' LWCB. The exterior wall of room 8 shown on the floor plan (Figure 11-8) shows a 12'' wall made up of 4'' face brick, 6'' LWCB, and 2'' glazed tile (glazed one side or *CG1S*). The backup for this wall is already taken off as 8'' LWCB. A large scale plan of rooms 8 and 9 is shown in Chapter 2, Figure 2-20.

A section of wall 7'4'' long and 8'8'' high is deducted from the 8'' LWCB. An equal area of 6'' LWCB is added back into the take-off. See item 3 on take-off sheet 3, Figure 11-15A.

The 2'' of CG1S will be included with the interior wall take-off. See Item 6 on Figure 11-16A.

MASONRY QUANTITY SURVEYS

123 Beech Drive
Cincinnati, OH 45123

DATE
SHEET 3 OF
EST. BY
BID DUE

BLDG. ___________________ OWNER ___________________

LOCATION ___________________ ARCHITECT ___________________

PLAN NOS. ___________ DATE ___________ GEN. CONTR. ___________________

			12" LWCB (2-UNITS)	4" LWCB B/U	6" LWCB B/U W/G.F.				
		①			8^{8}				
					7^{4}				
					(64)				
			1^{4}						
			32^{8}						
			(44)						
			1^{4}						
			16^{0}						
			(22)						
			44	22	64				
			4	+ 44					
				66					
				4	4				
			④	⑤	⑥				

Ext. Walls ② ③

Second exterior wall take-off (sheet 3)
Figure 11-15A

(1) 12" LWCB, (2-UNITS)
12" lightweight concrete block, 2-units: 4" LWCB + 8" LWCB. See Section G-G on plan sheet 4 (Figure 11-10)

(2) 4" LWCB, B/U
4" lightweight concrete block backup. See Section H-H on plan sheet 4 (Figure 11-10)

(3) 6" LWCB, B/U
6" lightweight concrete block backup
(The backup block in the exterior wall at room 8 behind the 2" CG1S)

(4) 44
Total square feet transferred to 4" LWCB, Figure 11-15A (Sheet 3) and 8" LWCB, Figure 11-13A (sheet 2)

(5) 22 + 44 = 66 SF
Total square feet, transferred to Figure 11-18A (Sheet 6)

(6) 64
Total square feet, transferred to Figure 11-18A and Figure 11-19A

Exterior wall take-off explanations
Figure 11-15B

MASONRY QUANTITY SURVEYS

123 Beech Drive
Cincinnati, OH 45123

DATE ___
SHEET 4 OF ___
EST. BY ___
BID DUE ___

BLDG. ___________________   OWNER ___________________

LOCATION ________________   ARCHITECT ________________

PLAN NOS. ________ DATE ________   GEN. CONTR. ________

INT. WALLS — ② ③ ④ ⑤ ⑥ ⑦

	COVE BASE D.O.	BOND BM 8×8 D.O.	4″LWCB	8″LWCB	6″CGIS	6″LWCB	4″CGIS	4″LWCB	2″CGIS	P.C. LINT 4×8 D.O.	P.C. LINT 8×8 D.O.
①			10⁰	10⁰	8⁸	1⁴	8⁸	1⁴	8⁸		
	36⁸	78	259⁴	78⁰	36⁸	36⁸	14⁸	14⁸	7⁴		
	14⁸		(2594)	(780)	(318)	(49)	(128)	(20)	(64)		
	7⁴										
	58⁸										
				8⁸					10⁰		
				98⁰					2¹⁰		
				(850)					(20)		
				3444					40		

#		size	4″LWCB	8″LWCB	6″CGIS					P.C. LINT 8×8
⑧	DR	2⁸×7⁴	(12) 234							(12) 48
⑨	"	3⁴×7⁴	(13) 317		(2) 48					(13)(2) 70
⑩	OPNG	4⁸×9⁴		(4) 174						
⑪	"	6⁰×9⁴		(1) 56						
⑫	D.F.	3⁴×7⁴		(1) 24						(1) 5
⑬	WD	4⁰×4⁰	(1) 16							(1) 6
				567	254	48				

	COVE	BOND	4″LWCB	8″LWCB	6″CGIS	6″LWCB	4″CGIS	4″LWCB	2″CGIS	P.C.	P.C.
	59	78	2877	526	270	49	128	40	64	124	5
			+ 40		✓			✓	+270		
			+ 270						334		
			3187								
	✓	✓	✓	✓	—	✓	✓	—	✓	✓	✓
			⑭		⑮				⑯		

Interior wall take-off (sheet 4)
Figure 11-16A

(1) COVE BASE, D.O.
     Ceramic glazed cove base at floor line, D.O. (Difference Only)

(2) 6" CG1S
     6" ceramic glazed one side

(3) 6" LWCB
     6" lightweight concrete block (above ceiling to underside of roof slab)

(4) 4" CG1S
     4" ceramic glazed one side

(5) 4" LWCB
     4" lightweight concrete block (above ceiling to underside of roof slab)

(6) 2" CG1S
     2" ceramic glazed one side

(7) P.C. LINT, 4 x 8, D.O.
     Precast lintel, 4" wide x 8" high, Difference Only

Note: Items 8 to 13 inclusive are deductions from the gross quantities, with additions of associated materials.

(8) DR 2^8 x 7^4
     Door 2'8" wide x 7'4" high
     Deduct 12 doors: 234 SF, from 4" LWCB
     Add @ 12 doors: 48 LF of P.C. LINT, 4 x 8

(9) DR 3^4 x 7^4
     Door 3'4" wide x 7'4" high
     Deduct 13 doors: 317 SF from 4" LWCB, and 2 doors: 48 SF, from 6" CG1S.
     Add @ 15 doors: 70 LF of P.C. LINT, 4 x 8
     $15 \times (3^4 + 1^4) = 70$ LF

(10) OPNG, 4^8 x 9^4
     Opening 4'8" wide x 9'4" high
     Deduct 4 openings: 174 SF from 8" LWCB
     (@ entrances to rooms 17, 20, 27 and 30)

Interior wall take-off explanations
Figure 11-16B

(11) OPNG 6^0 x 9^4
      Opening 6'0" wide x 9'4" high
      Deduct 1 opening: 56 SF @ corridor 22, Section E-E

(12) D. F. 3^4 x 7^4
      Drinking fountain recess 3'4" wide x 7'4" high
      Deduct 1 opening: 24 SF from 8" LWCB
      Add @ 1 opening: 5 LF of P.C. LINT. 8 x 8

(13) WD 4^0 x 4^0
      Window 4'0" wide x 4'0" high
      Deduct 1 opening: 16 SF from 4" LWCB
      Add @ 1 opening: 6 LF of P.C. LINT, 4 x 8
      1 x (4^0 + 1^4) = 5^4 Use 6 LF

(14)   2877 Net SF 4" LWCB
        40 Transferred from Item 5
     270 Transferred from Item 2
     ————
   3187 Total SF 4" LWCB transferred to Figure 11-18A (sheet 6)

Note: Item 2 (6" CG1S) is broken down into 2" CG1S and 4" LWCB and transferred to Items 14 and 16

(15) 270 transferred to Item 14 (See note above)

(16)   64 net SF 2" CG1S
     270 net SF 2" CG1S transferred from Item 15 (See note above)
     334 Total SF 2" CG1S transferred to Figure 11-18A (sheet 6)

Interior wall take-off explanations
Figure 11-16B (continued)

Parapet Walls

Section A-A on sheet 4 (Figure 11-10) shows a small parapet and coping, which was taken off with the exterior walls. This was done for convenience. If the parapet walls were higher or the construction was different, it would be better to keep them separate.

Parapet walls on many buildings are reinforced. Some have face brick on two faces, others have different thicknesses. There are buildings with parapets on only three sides, and some with parapets on the front wall with short returns at the ends.

The important thing is to get all the masonry required listed on your take-off sheet.

Penthouse Structures

The plan used for this take-off doesn't show any structures on the roof. But if there were, I wouldn't have a special take-off for the penthouse. Just use the same procedure you use for taking off exterior walls. Consider this take-off an opportunity to be sure all masonry items shown on the roof are included in the summary.

Interior Walls

The layout of the interior (partition) walls is shown on the floor plan in Figure 11-8. These walls are detailed on Figure 11-10 as Sections B-B, C-C, D-D, E-E, F-F and G-G.

The 4'' LWCB is taken off in two calculations:

$$\frac{10^{0}}{259^{4}} \qquad\qquad \frac{8^{8}}{298^{0}}$$

The height 10'0'' is obtained from Section C-C:

$$7'4'' + 1'4'' + 1'4'' = 10'0''$$

The height 8'8'' is obtained from Section C'-C':

$$7'4'' + 1'4'' = 8'8''$$

In offices 17, 20, 27 and 30, the walls at the closets and entrances don't go to the bottom of the slab. You can usually find this information in the specifications.

For the take-off of 8'' LWCB and bond beam, examine Section B-B. The length of this wall is apparent: 80'0'' minus 2'0'' is 78'0''. Section E-E and F-F show the conditions at heads of openings. I'll discuss this later with the outs.

This takes care of all the walls except those around the two toilets, rooms 8 and 9. The glazed tile in these rooms extends from floor to ceiling and the concrete block from the ceiling to the bottom side of the slab. See Section D-D. The 6'' walls are recorded in two calculations:

$$\frac{6''\ \mathrm{CG1S}}{8^{8}} \qquad\qquad \frac{6''\ \mathrm{LWCB}}{1^{4}}$$
$$\frac{}{36^{8}} \qquad\qquad\qquad \frac{}{36^{8}}$$

The 4'' walls at the pipe space are recorded in two calculations similar to the 6'' walls above:

$$\frac{4'' \text{ CG1S}}{\underset{14^{8}}{8^{8}}} \qquad \frac{4'' \text{ LWCB}}{\underset{20^{0}}{1^{4}}}$$

You can record the 2'' CG1S along the exterior wall in one calculation:

$$\frac{2'' \text{ CG1S}}{\underset{7^{4}}{8^{8}}}$$

It takes a little ingenuity to visualize the construction of the exterior wall behind the 2'' CG1S. My guess is that the architect intended this wall be 12'' thick, the same thickness as exterior walls in other parts of the building. So you can assume that it's to be built of three layers of masonry materials: 4'' face brick, 6'' LWCB, and 2'' CG1S.

Adjust these quantities just like we adjusted the quantities for the exterior wall take-off.

The room finish schedule on plan sheet 5 (Figure 11-11) shows that rooms 8 and 9 will be finished in glazed cove base. This is recorded in the first column on take-off sheet 4, Figure 11-16A. The total lineal feet is 58'8''. The dimensions are the same as we used for the lineal dimension of the CG1S items mentions earlier.

One small item of masonry remains to be taken off. At both ends of the pipe space between rooms 8 and 9, a 1'0'' section of 4'' LWCB, 10'0'' high, is added to the take-off. It's the second entry in the second column headed *4'' LWCB* in Figure 11-16A. The totals from both columns headed *4'' LWCB* are combined below the line at the bottom of the first column.

Now we're ready to adjust for openings in the interior walls. See items 8, 9, 10, 11, 12 and 13 on take-off sheet 4, Figure 11-16A. Most of these adjustments are deductions. But again, there are masonry items related to the openings that are additions. The additions in this case are the precast lintels over the openings. These are recorded by using a small circled number on the left side of the appropriate column. The number in the small circle is the number of openings of that size.

Item 8 on Figure 11-16A shows 12 doors 2'8'' wide and 7'4'' high. The area of 4'' LWCB deducted is:

$$12 \times 2'8'' \times 7'4'' = 234 \text{ SF}$$

The length of 4'' precast lintels added is:

$$12 \times (2'8'' + 1'4'') = 48 \text{ LF}$$

The 1'4'' added to the opening width indicates the additional length (8'' each side) for bearing.

Items 9 to 13 are recorded the same way.

Recap

Before you're ready to recap, make sure that the take-off is complete and that you've made and checked the extensions. Extensions should be done and checked on a calculator. To identify the items checked, put a dot above or to the right of the extension. It's easier to see the dot if it's made with a colored pencil. A check mark at the bottom of the column indicates all items in that column have been checked. Now you're ready to recap.

The recap is a compilation of all like items to find the total. That total is then multiplied by a factor to convert square feet to pieces.

On recap 1 (Figure 11-17A), the four items *w/ flash* (with flashing) are struck out. They were taken off along with the major items for convenience. Now they're being separated and transferred to recap 3 as a major item.

Similarly, *w/ G.F.* (with granulated fill) on recaps 1 and 2 (Figure 11-18A) have been separated and transferred to recap sheet 3 (Figure 11-19A).

The Summary

After the items on the recap sheets have been totaled, extended and checked, they're listed on the summary sheet (Figure 11-20A). I find it convenient to list the items in groups: items to be priced by the piece (pcs) in one group, by the linear foot (LF) in another group, square foot (SF) in another group, and so on.

The material prices listed are based on quotations from material suppliers. These prices should include all expenses connected with the quotation, including delivery, unloading, sorting, mixing, and storing.

The labor unit prices listed are based on my judgment and experience with production rates on jobs similar to this job. Use the production rate and the applicable labor rate to find the labor unit cost. We covered production in Chapter 8.

After these items are extended, checked and totaled, sales tax is added to the materials and fringe benefits to the labor. That's your bare cost of doing this job.

No job can be completed without tools and equipment. These costs should be added to the bare costs. Other miscellaneous costs, such as licenses, surveys, pictures, legal fees, tests, mileage, bonds, cold weather protection, electric, water, and clean up, should also be added. And no estimate is complete without adding overhead and profit.

Sharp competition may tempt you to shave your price. If you've got a good crew and are running out of work, it's tempting to accept a slim profit just to stay busy. Sometimes that's irresistible. But I don't advise it. After all, you're running a business, not a charity.

Sample Stone Take-Off

To give you some experience with stone take-off, visualize the office building shown in Figure 11-10 as being faced with limestone instead of face brick. Also, see Figure 11-21.

A stone take-off is very similar to a face brick take-off. The take-off forms are the same, measuring is the same, and the recording procedure on the take-off sheet is the same. The only change is that the column heading is *4" L.S.* (limestone) instead of *4" F. BRK.* (face brick). The take-off is also similar for other unit masonry facing materials, such as architectural concrete block, panel brick, fieldstone, granite, and glazed concrete units.

MASONRY QUANTITY SURVEYS

123 Beech Drive
Cincinnati, OH 45123

DATE
SHEET 5 OF
EST. BY
BID DUE

BLDG. _______________________ OWNER _______________________

LOCATION _______________________ ARCHITECT _______________________

PLAN NOS. _____________ DATE _____________ GEN. CONTR. _______________________

RECAP (1 of 3)

		12"HWCB FOUND	4" F.BRK CB B/U	8"LWCB B/U w/G.F.	L.S. COPING 14x6	BONO BM 8x8 D.O. w/FLASH	FLASH @ FL 18" WI	L.S. DR SILL 5½ x 7¾ w/FLASH	L.S. WD SILL 5½ x 7¾ w/FLASH	MARBLE STOOL 8x0¾	P.C. LINT 8x8 D.O. w/FLASH
(1)		784'									
(2)	EXT. WL (2)		2737'	2531'	248'	248'	265'	14'	96'	96'	131'
	EXT. WL (3)										
(4)	INT WL (4)					78'					
(3)		784 ×1.125 882	2737 × 6.75 18,475	2531 ×1.125 2848	248	326	265 ×1.5 398	14	96	96	131
FOUND.(1)											

Recap 1 (sheet 5)
Figure 11-17A

(1) W/FLASH.
These items transferred to sheet 7, Figure 11-19

(2) 2737•, 2531•, etc.
The dot after each quantity indicates that the transfer has been checked

(3) Conversion factors used to convert net square foot areas to pieces and net lineal feet to square feet

(4) These quantities have been transferred to summary sheet 8, Figure 11-20A

(5) 2531 (SF) x 1.125 = 2848 pcs

(6) 265 (LF) x 1.5 = 398 SF

(7) To avoid having to rewrite the description on all sheets of the recap, clip the sheets on the dotted lines (except the last sheet)

Recap 1 explanations
Figure 11-17B

MASONRY QUANTITY SURVEYS

123 Beech Drive
Cincinnati, OH 45123

DATE
SHEET 6 OF
EST. BY
BID DUE

BLDG. ___________________________   OWNER _______________________

LOCATION ________________________   ARCHITECT ____________________

PLAN NOS. __________ DATE __________   GEN. CONTR. _________________

RECAP   (2 of 3)

		4"LWCB B/U	6"LWCB B/U W/G.F.	COVE BASE	4"LWCB INT.	8"LWCB INT.	6"LWCB INT.	4"CGIS INT.	2"CGIS INT.	P.C. LINT 4×8 D.O.	P.C. LINT 8×8 D.O.
FOUND. (1)											
EXT. WL (2)											
EXT. WL (3)		66	64								
INT. WL (4)				59	3187	526	49	128	334	124	5
		66	64	59	3187	526	49	128	334	124	5
		×1.125	×1.125	×.75	×1.125	×1.125	×1.125	1.125	×1.125		+131
		75	72	45	3586	592	56	144	376		136

Recap 2 (sheet 6)
Figure 11-18A

(1) W/G.F.
     With Granular Fill (See separate item on Figure 11-19A (sheet 7)

(2) 64 (SF) x 1.125 = 72 pcs

(3) 59 (LF) x .75   = 45 pcs

(4) +131 transferred from Figure 11-17A (sheet 5)

Recap 2 explanations
Figure 11-18B

MASONRY QUANTITY SURVEYS

123 Beech Drive
Cincinnati, OH 45123

DATE _______
SHEET **7** OF
EST. BY
BID DUE

BLDG. _______________________ OWNER _______________________

LOCATION _____________________ ARCHITECT _____________________

PLAN NOS. __________ DATE __________ GEN. CONTR. _______________

RECAP   3 of 3

		FLASH @ COPING 12"W	FLASH @ DR SILL 12"W	FLASH @ WD SILL 8"W	FLASH @ P.C. LINT 12"W	—①	②—	FILL 8" LWCB W/ G.F.	FILL 6" LWCB W/ G.F.	—③	
FOUND.①											
EXT. WL②		248	14	96	131			2531			
EXT. WL③									64		
INT. WL④											
④		248 ×1.0	14 ×1.0	96 ×.67	131 ×1.0			2531 ×1.125	64 ×1.125		
⑤		248 +398	14 ⊬	65 ⊬	131 ⊬			2848	72		
⑥		+ 14 + 65									
⑦		+ 131 856									
⑧		⊬	—	—	~			⊬	⊬		

Recap 3 (sheet 7)
Figure 11-19A

(1) Flashing, transferred from Figure 11-17A (sheet 5)

(2) Fill, 8" LWCB, W/ G.F.
    Fill 8" lightweight concrete block with granular fill

(3) Fill, 6" LWCB, W/ G.F.
    Fill 6" lightweight concrete block with granular fill

(4) Conversion factors for converting lineal feet to square feet

(5) +398, transferred from Figure 11-17A (sheet 5)

(6) + 14, + 65, + 131, transferred from Figure 11-19A (sheet 7)

(7) 856, total square feet of flashing

(8) These items transferred to Figure 11-20A (sheet 8)

Recap 3 explanations
Figure 11-19B

MASONRY QUANTITY SURVEYS

123 Beech Drive
Cincinnati, OH 45123

DATE
SHEET *8* OF
EST. BY *RVK*
BID DUE

BLDG. _OFFICE BLDG_   OWNER __________

LOCATION __________   ARCHITECT __________

PLAN NOS. _1 TO 4_ DATE _12/1/87_   GEN. CONTR. __________

| | | (1) | MATERIAL | | (2) LABOR | | (3) | |
ITEM	UNIT	QUANTITY	Unit	Amount	Unit	Amount	WORK	TOTAL
(4) F. BRICK †210⁰⁰/M	PCS	18 475	.217	4010	.36	6651	560	
12" HWCB FOUND.	✓	882	.742	655	2.00	1764	106	
8" LWCB B/U	✓	2 848	.753	2145	1.18	3361	170	
6" LWCB B/U	✓	72	.585	43	1.13	82	177	
4" LWCB B/U	✓	75	.481	36	1.05	79	191	
8" LWCB INT.	✓	592	.753	446	1.42	841	141	
6" LWCB INT.	✓	54	.585	33	1.36	77	147	
4" LWCB INT.	✓	3 586	.481	1725	1.27	4554	158	
2" CG.S INT. 8WA	✓	376	2.450	922	1.43	538	140	
4" CG.S INT. 8W	✓	144	2.690	388	1.43	206	140	
(5) MORTAR (S) BRK	✓	18 475	.026	481	—	—		
" " BLK	✓	8 563	.056	480	—	—		
CLEAN BRK	✓	18 475	.004	74	.04	739		
" BLK	✓	6400	—	—	.03	192		
(6) COVE BASE 8W50A P.O.	✓	45	2.240	101	.70	32		
FILL 8" LWCB W/G.F.	✓	2848	.390	826	.25	712		
(7) " 6" LWCB "	✓	72	.190	14	.17	12		
REINF. 12" EXT.	LF	2714	.099	269	—	—		
" 8" INT.	✓	415	.090	38	—	—		
(8) " 6" INT.	✓	252	.087	22	—	—		
" 4" INT.	✓	2351	.086	203	—	—		
(9) BOND BM 8×8 D.O.	✓	326	.823	269	1.01	330		
P.C. LINT 4×8 D.O.	✓	124	1.709	212	.88	110		
" 8×8 D.O.	✓	136	3.820	520	2.08	283		
LS DR SILL 5½×7¾"	✓	14	8.880	125	2.50	35	80	
LS WD SILL 5½×5⅓	✓	96	6.300	605	2.08	200	96	
LS COPING 14×6	✓	248	11.660	2892	4.00	992	50	
MARBLE STOOL 8×0¾	✓	96	10.000	960	1.74	167	115	
FLASHING	SF	854	.200	172	—	—		
PARGING	✓	2737	.100	274	.30	822		
				18,940		22779		
		TX		947		7517	FRGS 33%	(10)
				19,887		30296		
				4		19887	MTL	(11)
						50183		
						5018	T&E 10%	
						55201		
						2208	O.H. 04%	
						57409		
		BID $61,900 00				4593	P. 08%	
						62,002		(12)

Summary (sheet 8)
Figure 11-20A

(1) Quantities in this column were transferred here from Figures 11-17 through 11-19 (Sheets 5, 6, 7)

(2) See Chapter 8, Production. Examples show how labor units are calculated

(3) See tables in Chapter 8

(4) $210.00/M is the purchase price of the face brick per 1,000 units. The material unit price used is .217 per brick. This includes 3% allowance for waste (no allowance for waste in the labor column)

(5) See Chapter 5, Mortar. Examples show how mortar unit prices are calculated. Calculations should be made for each size unit. In this example an average unit price (.026) was used

(6) Cove Base was taken off in lineal feet and converted to pieces. The price in the material unit price column is the difference between the cost of the cove base unit (8W50A) and the cost of the unit it replaces (8WA)

(7) Fill 6" LWCB W/G.F. Fill 6" lightweight concrete block with granular fill. See Chapter 6, Masonry Accessories

(8) The quantities of the various sizes of reinforcing required were determined from the materials erected:

	12" EXT	8" INT	6" INT	4" INT
	882	592	56	3518
	2848		376	144
	75			
	72		- 72	- 304
pcs.	3877	592	360	3358
(*)	x .7	x .7	x .7	x .7
LF	2714	415	252	2351

(*) Factor: Reinforcing figured in alternate courses with 6" lap
1.333/2 x 1.05 = 0.7

(9) BOND BEAM. See Chapter 6

(10) FRGS 33%: Fringes 33%. See Chapter 8

(11) MTL: Material + 5% sales tax

(12) Total estimate, materials, labor, tools and equipment, overhead and profit: $62,002.00.

Bid $61,900.00

Summary explanations
Figure 11-20B

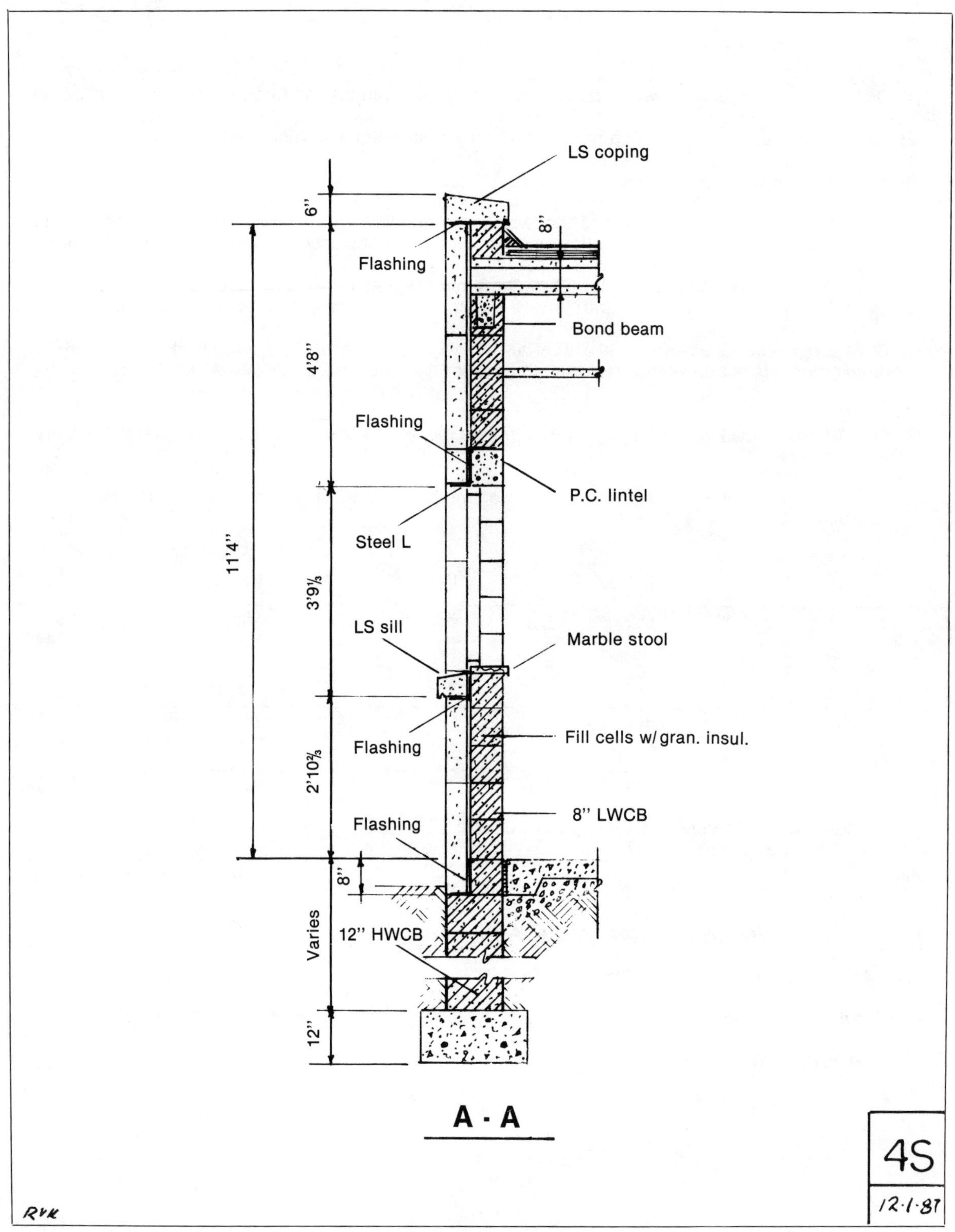

Limestone facing detail
Figure 11-21

Figure 11-22 shows the take-off sheet for the limestone. All other items and numbers are the same as for the face brick take-off.

The net totals from this sheet are transferred to the revised recap sheet, Figure 11-23, then summarized on the revised summary sheet, Figure 11-24A. Notice that there are several new items in the summary (items 1 through 6). They're explained in Figure 11-24B.

Alternate Bids

It isn't unusual for architects to request alternate bids. Sometimes the alternate bids will affect the entire exterior of a building, or the interior of a building, or only a portion of it.

Alternate bids usually require extra work for the estimator. Check the plans and specifications for any alternates that will affect your bid. Keep separate any part of the take-off that's affected by alternates so you can use the same take-off quantities for the alternate as you used for the base bid. This applies to additions, deductions, omissions and replacements.

Bidding documents will describe the alternate bids desired. For example:

Alternate A: Omit Wing A in its entirety.

If Alternate A is accepted, deduct from the base bid the sum of ________________ dollars ($).

For the estimator, this means making up another bid price for Wing A. By keeping this portion of the take-off separate, you can save a lot of repetition.

For the contractor, it means that the alternate bids will be considered along with the base bid to determine who gets the contract.

Some architects encourage alternate proposals with the base bid. These may include alternate construction methods, alternate materials, and alternate equipment.

It's not uncommon to see the words *or equal* in specifications. If you submit a bid based on a material equal to the item named in the specs, be ready to show that your choice is an acceptable substitute. Reputable brand names are usually acceptable, though sometimes certification will be necessary.

MASONRY QUANTITY SURVEYS

123 Beech Drive
Cincinnati, OH 45123

DATE 12/29/87
SHEET 2 OF
EST. BY RVK
BID DUE

BLDG. _OFFICE BLDG_ OWNER __________

LOCATION _35 9TH AVE. DAYTON, O._ ARCHITECT __________

PLAN NOS. _1 TO 4_ DATE _12/1/87_ GEN. CONTR. __________

EXT. WALLS

		4" LS CB B/U	8" LWCB B/U W/G.F.	LS COPING 14×16	BOND BM 8×8 D.O.	FLASH @ FL 18" W	LS DR SILL 5½×7¾	LS WD SILL 5½×5⅓	MARBLE STOOL 8×0¾	P.C. LINT 8×8 D.O.
		12°	11⁴ W/FLASH				W/FLASH	W/FLASH		W/FLASH
		248°	248°	248°	248°	248°				
		(2976)	(2811)			+ 32				
						281				
		9⁴	9⁴							
		32.8	32.8							
		(305)	(305)							
		2°	3116							
		16°								
		(32)								
		3313								
ENT	16°×7-*	(1) 117				(1) 16				
"	16°×9⁴		(1) 149							
DR	3⁴×7½	(4) 97	(4) 97				(4) 14			(4) 19
WD	8°×3¹⅓	(12) 362						(12) 96	(2) 96	(12) 112
"	8°×3⁴		(12) 320							
2°G15	7⁴×8⁸		(1) 63							
		576	629			16				
		2737	2487	248	248	265	14	96	96	131
			+ 44							
			2531							

Limestone take-off sheet
Figure 11-22

MASONRY QUANTITY SURVEYS

123 Beech Drive
Cincinnati, OH 45123

DATE 5R
SHEET OF
EST. BY
BID DUE

BLDG. ___________________________ OWNER ___________________________

LOCATION ________________________ ARCHITECT ________________________

PLAN NOS. __________ DATE __________ GEN. CONTR. ______________________

RECAP   1 of 1

		12" HWCB FOUND.	4" LS CB B/U	8" LWCB B/U w/G.F.	LS COPING 14×6 w/FLASH	BOND BM 8×8 D.O.	FLASH @ FL. 18" W	LS DR SILL 5½×7¾ w/FLASH	LS WO SILL 5½×5½ w/FLASH	MARBLE STOOL 8×0¾	P.C. LINT 8×8 D.O. w/FLASH
FOUND. (1)		784									
EXT. WL (2)			2737	2531	248	248	265	14	96	96	131
EXT. WL (3)											
INT. WL (4)					78						
		784 ×1.125 882	2737	2531 ×1.125 2848	248	326	265 ×1.5 398 ↵	14	96	96	131 ↵
		↵	↵	↵	↵	↵	—	↵	↵	↵	—

Limestone recap sheet
Figure 11-23

MASONRY QUANTITY SURVEYS

123 Beech Drive
Cincinnati, OH 45123

DATE

SHEET *8R* OF

EST. BY *RVK*

BID DUE

BLDG. _OFFICE BLDG._   OWNER_______________

LOCATION _______________

PLAN NOS. _1 TO 4_ DATE _12-1-87_   ARCHITECT_______________

GEN. CONTR. _______________

	ITEM	UNIT	QUANTITY	MATERIAL		LABOR		WORK	TOTAL
				Unit	Amount	Unit	Amount		
①	4" LS FACING	SF	2737	LS	27388.	3.92	10729	51	
	12" HWCB FOUND.	PCS	882	.742	655	2.00	1764	100	
	8" LWCB B/U	"	2848	.753	2145	1.18	3361	170	
	6" LWCB B/U	"	72	.585	43	1.13	82	177	
	4" LWCB B/U	"	75	.481	36	1.05	79	191	
	8" LWCB INT.	"	592	.753	446	1.42	841	141	
	6" LWCB INT.	"	56	.585	33	1.36	77	147	
	4" LWCB INT.	"	3586	.481	1725	1.27	4554	158	
	4" CGIS INT. 8W	"	144	2.690	388	1.43	206	140	
	2" CGIS INT. 8WA	"	376	2.450	922	1.43	538	140	
②	MORTAR (S) LS	CF	55	1.862	103	—	—		
	" " BLK	PCS	8563	.056	480	—	—		
③	CLEAN LS	SF	2737	.027	74	.27	739		
	" BLK	PCS	6400	—	—	.03	192		
	COVE BASE 8W50A D.O.	"	45	2.240	101	.70	32		
	FILL 8" LWCB W/G.F	"	2848	.290	826	.25	712		
	" 6" LWCB "	"	72	.190	14	.17	12		
④	REINF. 8" EXT.	LF	2714	.090	245	—	—		
	" 8" INT.	"	415	.090	38	—	—		
	" 6" "	"	252	.087	22	—	—		
	" 4" "	"	2351	.086	203	—	—		
	BOND BM 8×8 D.O.	"	326	.823	269	1.01	330		
	P.C. LINT 4×8 D.O.	"	124	1.709	212	.88	110		
	" 8×8 D.O.	"	136	3.820	520	2.08	283		
	LS DR SILL 5½×7¾	"	14	—	(*)	2.50	35	80	
⑤	LS WD SILL 5½×5⅓	"	96	—	(*)	2.08	200	96	
	LS COPING 14×6	"	248	—	(*)	4.00	992	50	
	MARBLE STOOL 8×0¾	"	96	10.000	960	1.74	167	115	
	FLASHING	SF	856	.200	172	—	—		
⑥	STONE ANCHORS	PCS	1506	1.000	1506	—	—		
					39526		26035		
	(*) INCLUDED IN LS		Tx 5%		1977		8592		FRGS 33%
	PRICE ABOVE				41503		34627		
					✗		41503		MTL
							76130		
				$			7613		T&E 10%
				BID 93,900 00			83743		
							3350		O.H. 04%
							87093		
							6968		P 08%
							94,061		

Limestone summary sheet
Figure 11-24A

(1) F. Brick is changed to 4" L.S. Facing
Unit: square feet
Quantity: 2,737 SF
Material: LS (lump sum) $27,388.00
   This lump sum figure for material includes all the limestone on the building: facing, door sills, window sills and coping
   Limestone fabricators usually make their own take-off of the project and quote a lump sum figure for all material, delivered and unloaded at the job site. An aggressive estimator can usually acquire quantities of the various sizes and shapes from the fabricator's estimator to check his quantities and to help him price the labor. 4" L.S. facing will be priced by the square foot
   L.S. sills, coping, etc. will be priced by the lineal foot. See Chapter 8

(2) Mortar: Limestone (in lieu of brick). See Chapter 5
Material: See Chapter 4
Labor: Included in production. See Chapter 8

(3) Clean: Limestone (in lieu of brick)
Material: Stiff brush, soap and water
Labor: 240 - 400 SF, one mason, per day

(4) Reinf. 8" Ext.
   The 12" masonry reinforcing shown on the summary sheet will not be required. This reinforcing will be priced as 8" exterior reinforcing

(5) Stone anchors
   The limestone facing is anchored to the backup with special stone anchors. See Chapter 4. The material, size and shape will determine the cost, and fabricators are always anxious to quote prices
   Parging is not required, so use this space to add the new item, Stone Anchors.

(6) L.S. Dr Sill   5-1/2 x 7-3/4
   L.S. Wd Sill   5-1/2 x 5-1/3
   L.S. Coping   14 x 6
   The material for these items is already included in the lump sum price in item (1)
   The labor for these items will remain the same
   After making a few calculations, the labor and material columns are retotaled and the numbers "below the line" are revised for a new bid price

Summary sheet explanations
Figure 11-24B

<u>INDEX</u>

PROJECT REQUIREMENTS

____

BIDDING REQUIREMENTS

____

Instructions to Bidders and General Conditions
Supplementary Instructions to Bidders
Supplementary General Conditions

SPECIFICATIONS

____

Division 1 - General Requirements

____

    Section 01200 - Special Conditions

Division 2 - Site Work

____

    Section 02100 - Demolition
           02200 - Earthwork
           02500 - Paving
           02480 - Landscaping

Division 3 - Concrete

____

    Section 03300 - Concrete

Division 4 - Masonry

____

    Section 04100 - Mortar and Masonry Accessories
           04200 - Unit Masonry

Division 5 - Metals

____

    Section 05100 - Structural and Miscellaneous Metals
           05100 - Metal Joists
           05300 - Metal Deck
           05400 - Cold Formed Metal Framing
           05500 - Metal Fabrications

Division 6 - Wood and Plastic

Section 06100 - Carpentry and Millwork

Division 7 - Thermal and Moisture Protection

Section 07110 - Foundation Waterproofing
        07175 - Water Repellant Coating
        07200 - Insulation
        07256 - Sprayed On Fireproofing
        07400 - Preformed Metal Roofing
        07600 - Flashing and Sheet Metal
        07900 - Sealants

Division 8 - Doors, Windows and Glass

Section 08100 - Hollow Metal Work
        08200 - Aluminum Doors and Frames
        08300 - Special Doors
        08700 - Finish Hardware
        08800 - Glass and Glazing

Division 9 - Finishes

Section 09200 - Lath and Plastering
        09250 - Drywall
        09330 - Quarry Tile
        09500 - Acoustical Tile
        09600 - Slate Flooring
        09680 - Carpeting
        09900 - Painting

Division 10 - Specialties

Section 10900 - Miscellaneous Specialty Items

Division 11 - Equipment

Section 11400 - Kitchen and Food Service Equipment

Divisions 12, 13, 14 - None Required

Division 15 - Mechanical

Section 15005 - Mechanical General Requirements
15050 - Basic Materials and Methods
15500 - HVAC Summary
15510 - HVAC Piping and Specialties
15549 - HVAC Insulation
15550 - Heating Materials and Equipment
15580 - Cooling Materials and Equipment
15588 - Air Distribution
15559 - Testing Adjusting & Balancing
15400 - Plumbing General Requirements
15420 - Drainage and Vent Piping
15430 - Domestic Water and Propane Gas Piping
15440 - Plumbing Fixtures
15499 - Plumbing Insulation

Division 16 - Electrical

Section 16005 - Electrical General Requirements
16100 - Electrical Materials and Methods
16163 - Distribution Panels and Panelboards
16040 - Lighting Fixtures
16850 - Electric Heat

SECTION 04100   MORTAR AND MASONRY ACCESSORIES

PART 1   GENERAL

1.01   WORK INCLUDED

A.   Specifications for mortar materials, anchors, ties, joint reinforcement, concealed in-wall flashing and other accessories for masonry work.

B.   Mortar mix.

1.02   WORK FURNISHED BUT INSTALLED BY OTHERS

A.   Dovetail inserts imbedded in concrete for lateral support of masonry installed in Section 03300 - Cast-In-Place Concrete.

B.   Mortar and masonry accessories installed in Section 04200 - Unit Masonry.

1.03   RELATED WORK

A.   Section 02500 - Paving: Setting materials for masonry paving.

B.   Section 04200 - Unit Masonry.

C.   Section 07200 - Insulation: Cavity wall insulation furnished for installation in Section 04200.

D.   Section 07600 - Flashing and Sheet Metal: Metal in-wall flashing furnished for installation in Section 04200 at the following locations:

1.   At heads of all openings.
2.   At soffits.
3.   Where flashing spans air space within walls.
4.   At all locations where flashing will be sight-exposed.

E.   Section 07900 - Sealants: Sealant in control joints.

F.   Section 10990 - Miscellaneous Specialties: Metal accessories for fireplace furnished for installation in Section 04200.

1.04   SYSTEM DESCRIPTION

A.   Use Type S ASTM C270 mortar for exterior work.

B.   Use Type N ASTM C270 mortar for all other work.

1.05   PRODUCT DELIVERY, STORAGE AND HANDLING

A.   Protect materials in a dry place, off ground and under cover.

B.   Protect reinforcement from elements; immediately before placing, reinforcement shall be free from loose rust or from ine
or other materials that will destroy or reduce bond.

PART 2   PRODUCTS

2.01   MORTAR MATERIALS

A.   Portland cement: ASTM C150, Type I, non-staining cement,
natural gray color.
1.   Type III cement may be used as protection requirement
for laying masonry in cold weather as specified in
Section 04200.

B.   Lime: Hydrated lime shall be Type S, ASTM C207.

C.   Sand: Sand shall conform to ASTM Specification C144.

D.   Mixing water: Water shall be clean, potable, and free of
organic or other deleterious material.

E.   Mortar for fire-rated masonry construction: Provide mortar
of type which has been tested and listed for the fire-resistance
classification indicated.

F.   Mortar for fire brick and clay flue liner in fireplace: ASTM
C105.

G.   Admixtures: No anti-freeze compounds or admixtures shall be
permitted in mortar.

H.   Masonry cement: At Contractor's option in lieu of cement-sand-
lime site mix mortar, Masonry cement shall be Type II ASTM C-91
"Brixment" by Louisville Cement Company, Columbia Masons Mortar
or Richmortar. Packaged product must comply with each mortar
type required as described in "System Description" Part 1 of this
section.

I.   Mortar pigment for use on 1/2 of brick sample panel of exterior
brick: Provide lime and alkali-proof mineral oxides of color
selected, mixed in accordance with manufacturer's directions.
Limitations by weight of cement: 3% for carbon black, 10% for
other pigments. Mortar color shall be selected from manufacturer's full range.

2.02   MASONRY ACCESSORIES

A.   Anchors and ties: Zinc-coated steel (ASTM 153) at interior work;
      copper coated (ASTM B227) at exterior walls and veneers.
      1.   Wire-mesh ties shall be minimum 16 gauge, 1/2 inch mesh, in
            strips 1-inch narrower than the width of partition or wall.
      2.   Wire ties not specified otherwise shall be minimum 10 gauge
            wire, zee-shaped or looped at both ends.
      3.   Corrugated or crimped ties shall be minimum 7/8 inch wide,
            16 gauge sheet steel, not less than 6 inches long.
      4.   Dovetail-type masonry anchors and compatible dovetail
            inserts shall be minimum 16 gauge sheet steel, 7/8 inch
            wide, turned up 1/4 inch at the end or have a 1/2 inch
            diameter hole located within 1/2 inch of the end.
      5.   Rigid steel anchors shall be of not less than 1 inch by 1/4
            inch by 24 inches long with each end turned up not less than
            2 inches.

B.   Joint reinforcement:
      1.   Reinforcing of the proper width for partition and wall
            thickness shall be manufactured by one of the following:
            a)   Dur-O-Wal
            b)   AA Wire Products Company
            c)   National Wire Products Corp.
      2.   Reinforcement shall be zinc-coated, cold drawn steel wire
            per ASTM A-82; minimum 9 gauge deformed wire side rods and
            9 gauge wire cross rods welded to side rods.
            a)   Reinforcement for masonry foundations, masonry parti-
                  tions and all other non-cavity masonry walls shall be
                  the truss type.
            b)   Reinforcement for cavity walls shall be either ladder
                  or truss type and of type specifically manufactured for
                  cavity wall construction; or #6 rectangular ties
                  specifically manufactured for cavity wall construction.
      3.   Provide special formed "L" shapes at corners, "T" shapes at
            intersection of walls and partitions.

C.   Bond breaker strips: 15 lb. asphalt or coal tar roofing felt per
      ASTM D226 or D227 respectively.

D.   Premolded control joints: Solid rubber, neoprene or polyvinyl
      chloride with durometer hardness of 60 to 80, designed to main-
      tain lateral stability in masonry wall.

E.   Plastic in-wall flashing: Minimum 0.020" thick, uniform flexible
      sheet of polyvinyl chloride, plasticers and other modifiers -
      Nervastral, Wascoseal, Lexsuco Membrane or BFG flexible vinyl;
      furnish plastic flashing at all locations not specified to be metal.

F.   Reinforcing rods: Steel rods for masonry reinforced with rod reinforcement shall be Grade 60, ASTM A615. Bars No. 3 or larger shall be deformed.

G.   Wire screening over insulation in auditorium acoustic walls: USG Junior Diamond Mesh Lath, with manufacturer's standard coating of black asphaltum paint. Equal products by Inland-Ryerson, Wheeling, National Gypsum and Georgia-Pacific shall also be acceptable.

H.   Compression seal at expansion joint: Watson-Bowman or Acme.

2.03   MIXES

A.   Comply with ASTM C270 proportion specifications except that lime/cement ratio (by volume) for Type N mortar shall be limited to 1 part lime per part of Portland Cement.

B.   Mixing mortar: Mix all cementitious material and sand in a mechanical batch mixer for a minimum of 5 minutes. Adjust the consistency of the mortar to the satisfaction of the mason but add only as much water as is compatible with convenience in using the mortar. All mortar shall be used within 2-1/2 hours of the initial mixing. It shall not be used after it has begun to set. Retemper mortar during 2-1/2 hour period as required to restore workability.

SECTION 04200   UNIT MASONRY

PART 1   GENERAL

1.01   WORK INCLUDED

    A.   Masonry walls, veneer, precast lintels, bond beams and partitions.

    B.   In-wall flashing, weeps.

    C.   Date stone.

    D.   Building in access panels in masonry walls.

    E.   Coordinate with built-in work of other trades.

    F.   Masonry cleaning.

1.02   WORK INSTALLED BUT FURNISHED BY OTHERS

    A.   Section 02100 - Mortar and Masonry Accessories.

    B.   Section 05200 - Metal Joists: Anchorages for metal joists embedded in masonry.

    C.   Section 05300 - Metal Roof Deck: Anchorages for metal deck embedded in masonry.

    D.   Section 05400 - Cold Formed Metal Framing: Veneer ties at steel studs. (Anchors for veneer ties installed to studs in Section 05400.)

    E.   Section 05500 - Metal Fabrications: Work specified therein that is embedded in masonry.

    F.   Section 07200 - Insulation: Cavity wall insulation; acoustical insulation within auditorium walls.

    G.   Section 07600 - Flashing and Sheet Metal: Metal counter flashing and metal in-wall flashing.

    H.   Section 08300 - Special Doors: Access panels in masonry walls.

    I.   Section 10990 - Miscellaneous Specialties: Metal fireplace accessories.

1.03   RELATED WORK

A.   Section 02500 - Paving: Masonry paving. *We will include*

B.   Section 07175 - Water Repellent Coating. *by others*

C.   Section 07200 - Insulation: Insulation on inside face of masonry walls. *Labor only*

D.   Section 07400 - Preformed Metal Roofing: Saw-cutting of reglet into brick for counterflashing of metal roof. *by others*

E.   Section 07900 - Sealants: Sealant in control joints. *by others*

F.   Section 09600 - Slate Flooring: Slate hearth at fireplace. *by others*

1.04   SYSTEM DESCRIPTION

A.   Type and location of masonry units:
1.   Face brick: Exposed exterior and interior brick.
2.   Building brick: All concealed brick back-up.
3.   Scored concrete masonry: At exposed concrete masonry partitions where indicated.
4.   Scored, ceramic-faced concrete masonry: Base where scheduled.
5.   Hollow lightweight load bearing units: Typical in all locations unless otherwise noted on drawings.

1.05   MOCK-UP

A.   Sample wall panels: Before the installation of any masonry materials, erect at the job site, sample wall panels 4'-0" long by 4'-0" high of face brick, acoustical face brick in Auditorium, and scored concrete masonry with ceramic faced concrete masonry base. Panels shall show the proposed color range, texture, bond, mortar joint and workmanship of masonry materials. Use specified colored mortar on 1/2 of panel of exterior face brick. No masonry work shall be done until the Architect has approved the sample panels. Erect panels at the earliest possible date after contract signing.

B.   The approved panels shall become the standard of comparison for all masonry work built of the materials that the approved panels include. The panels shall not be altered, moved or destroyed until the work is complete.

    C.   Upon completion of all masonry work and upon approval of Architect, remove sample panels in their entirety.

1.06   REFERENCES

    A.   "Recommended Practices for Laying Concrete Block," by Portland Cement Association.

    B.   "Specifications for Design and Construction of Load-Bearing Concrete Masonry," by National Concrete Masonry Association.

    C.   "Technical Notes," by Brick Institute of America.

1.07   SUBMITTALS

    A.   Submit five individual samples showing extreme variations in color and texture of the following materials:
1. Face Brick
2. Scored concrete masonry.
3. Ceramic faced concrete masonry.

    B.   Samples of granite for date stone.

    C.   Submit layout of incised date on date stone.

1.08   DELIVERY, STORAGE AND HANDLING

    A   Store materials under cover in a dry place and in a manner to prevent damage or intrusion of foreign matter. During freezing weather protect all masonry units with tarpaulins or other suitable material.

    B.   Additional requirements for concrete masonry.
1. Only units which have been properly cured to the specified moisture content, (40 percent of maximum absorption), shall be delivered to the job. Questionable units will be tested and shipment will be rejected if the average moisture content of five (5) standard units, selected from shipment at random by the Architect's Representative is found to exceed Specification limits.
2. Units delivered to the job shall be stacked in a dry place, off the ground on a prepared plank platform, and in a manner to promote circulation of air through and around the block. Method of stacking shall be approved by the Architect. The stacked units shall be protected by a shed roof or tarpaulins, arranged to allow for circulation of air around and above the units.

3. Units of moisture content exceeding Specification Requirements shall not be built into the work. The Architect may at any time require a recheck on moisture content and units containing excess moisture shall be dried down to the acceptable maximum, either by further air drying or the use of heat, before being used. No extension of time for completion will be allowed due to delay caused by failure of the Contractor to maintain stored units at the acceptable moisture content.

4. All units must be carefully handled at all times. Units with chipped edges, spalls, or other damage to their appearance which would show in the finished wall, shall not be built into the work.

1.09   ALTERNATES

A. Refer to Section 01100 for alternates.

PART 2   PRODUCTS

2.01

A. Face brick:
1. Provide allowance for face brick as specified in Section 01020. ⟵
2. Special shapes: Provide special shapes as shown on drawings. Match face brick in color and texture. ⟵

B. Building brick:
1. ASTM C62, Grade SW for exterior work; Grade NW for interior work.
2. Color, texture: Selected from manufacturer's standards.

C. Concrete masonry units:
1. Hollow load-bearing units: ASTM C90, Grade N, Type I; cured minimum 14 days if cured at atmospheric pressure.
2. Weight: Lightweight, expanded shale Aggregate per ASTM C331.
3. Fire-rated masonry: Provide fire-rated units meeting the approval of the State of Ohio, Division of Factories and Buildings and meeting the hourly ratings indicated on drawings.
4. Exposed faces: Manufacturer's standard color and texture.
5. Size: Nominal face dimensions of 16" long x 8" high, unless otherwise shown.
6. Scored units: Center scored for 8" x 8" appearance.

7. Special shapes: Provide where shown and required for lintels in scored block walls, and other special conditions.
    a) Provide grooved unit for premoulded control joints where no face brick occurs.
    b) Provide square-edge block for outside corners.
8. Concrete masonry lintels in scored block walls and bond beams: Lintel block units of size indicated with minimum ultimate compressive strength of concrete for <u>block of f'c = 3,000 psi.</u>
9. Glazed units: Ceramic faced concrete masonry units with center score, size as detailed, by Burns & Russel Co. or Nabso Glazed Products; one plain color from manufacturer's full line of standard colors. Ceramic facing shall meet ASTM C744.

D. Precast concrete lintels:
1. Concrete: f'c = 3,000 psi minimum.
2. Reinforcement: 60,000 psi yield strength, deformed bars.
3. Exposed surfaces: smooth, free of cracks, chips, broken edges.
4. Cure properly before setting.
5. Mark top of lintels to properly identify.

E. Masonry cleaner: <u>Sure Klean Vana Trol. No. 600 Detergent and/or No. 101 Lime Solvent</u> as recommended for each type of masonry by the manufacturer, Process Solvent Company. Verify type of <u>cleaner with manufacturers of glass and aluminum in glazed openings adjacent to brick.</u>

F. Fireplace masonry:
1. Shell: Concrete masonry specified herein.
2. Firebrick: Low duty refractory brick, ASTM C64; color and texture selected from manufacturer's standards.
3. Flue liner: Clay flue liner, ASTM C315; size and shape as indicated.
4. Surrounds at openings: Slate, ASTM C-629; 3/4" thick; size as indicated; color and texture selected from manufacturer's full range.

G. <u>Date stone:</u> ASTM C615, meeting standards of National Building Granite Quarries Assn., Inc. (NBGQA); <u>color as selected</u> by Architect from manufacturer's full range; incise date as indicated.

PART 3   **EXECUTION**

3.01   INSPECTION

A.   Examine surfaces upon which masonry will be installed for defects that will adversely affect execution and quality of work.

B.   Do not start work until unsatisfactory conditions are corrected.

3.02   INSTALLATION, GENERAL REQUIREMENTS

A.   Allowable tolerances:
   1.   Vertical surfaces: Variation from plumb shall not exceed 1/4" in 10', 3/8" in a story height or 20' maximum, 1/2" in 40' or more.
   2.   Horizontal coursing: Variation from level shall not exceed 1/4" in length of building.
   3.   Cross-sectional dimension: Variation shall not exceed minus 1/4" or plus 1/2" from dimensional thickness.

B.   Coordinate layout and work with mechanical and electrical trades as well as all other general construction trades for their materials and equipment embedded in or penetrating masonry construction, and for sequence of installation.

C.   Lay out walls in advance for accurate spacing and uniform joints.
   1.   Avoid less than half-size units at corners, jambs.
   2.   Lay out vertical courses on story poles.
   3.   Provide sufficient line blocks to maintain level joints.

D.   Pattern bond:
   1.   1/4-running bond at scored concrete masonry.
   2.   Acoustical "garden-wall" bond, as detailed, in auditorium.
   3.   Running bond at all other masonry unless otherwise indicated.

E.   Masonry walls, partitions: Extend to structure above unless otherwise noted. Where not so required, terminate partition not less than 2" above suspended ceiling.

F.   Control joints: Provide continuous vertical control joints as detailed:
   1.   In exterior walls: Where indicated on drawing.
   2.   In interior partitions: Spaced not to exceed 30'-0" on center.
   3.   Do not continue joint reinforcement across control joint.
   4.   Extend control joint through bond beam unless otherwise noted.

5. Install premoulded joint filler in collar joint where face brick occurs; in grooved concrete masonry unit at all other locations; provide 3/8" open joint at brick veneer.

G. Expansion joint: Install compression seal as detailed.

H. Masonry partition abutting other masonry partitions or exterior masonry wall: Bond in or anchor rigidly with rigid steel straps at 16" centers vertically except where control joint is indicated at intersection.

I. Masonry which faces on or abuts concrete: Attach with dovetail anchors spaced not to exceed 16" vertically, 24" horizontally.

J. Anchor brick to masonry back-up with corrugated or crimped ties specified in Section 04100 spaced 24" o.c. each way. Do not extend wall reinforcing into brick.

K. Cold weather masonry construction: Protect masonry when the air temperature is 40 degrees and falling.
   1. Construct in accordance with International Masonry Industry All Weather Council standards indicated in applicable building code.
   2. Frozen work: Remove and replace; do not build on frozen work.
   3. Use of admixtures or antifreeze agents shall not be permitted.

L. Except walls directly over load-bearing walls, masonry shall not be placed on structural floors until the concrete is at least twenty-eight (28) days old and all shoring has been removed.

M. Soffit: Construct as detailed; assure secure attachment to overhead support structure.

N. Colored mortar for 1/2 of sample panel of exterior face brick: Tool joints at the wetness recommended by the mortar color manufacturer. Do not tool joint when too wet.

3.03   LAYING MASONRY

A. Mortar bed and end joints:
   1. Lay brick in full bed joints with ends buttered sufficiently to fill end joints.
   2. Lay hollow concrete masonry units with full mortar coverage on horizontal and vertical face shells; lay with wider edges up.

3. For all exterior walls of brick with concrete masonry backup, apply a uniform parge coat of mortar, approximately 1/2" thick, to the concealed face of the backup to prevent penetration of water. Apply parge coat and bring the facing up to level, two backup courses at a time to permit proper bedding of metal wall ties. Care shall be taken to work parging snug around wall ties.

4. Joint width; Nominal 3/8 inch; variation up to 5/8" shall be permitted to adjust coursing and to minimize cutting at openings providing such variation is gradual to minimize visual contrast in widths of adjacent joints.

5. Joint configuration:
   a) Joints in masonry surfaces to be finished with other construction: flush.
   b) All sight-exposed joints: tool concave.
   c) At scored concrete masonry, tuckpoint scores to match setting joints.

B. Wet brick masonry having manufacturer's stated absorption rate more than 0.025 oz. per square foot prior to laying; otherwise lay brick only when dry.

C. Do not wet concrete masonry units.

D. Joint reinforcement: Provide in horizontal joints of all concrete masonry walls and partitions as follows:
   1. First bed joint below top course of masonry.
   2. First bed joint above and below openings.
   3. Second bed joint above and below openings -- extended 2'-0" beyond each side of opening.
   4. Spaced not to exceed 16" on center vertically for entire length and height of partition or wall.
   5. At continuous reinforcement in curved walls, clip interior leg of reinforcement to achieve curve.

E. Bearing support: Fill hollow masonry units with concrete under wall supported beams or lintels a minimum 3 courses vertically and 24" horizontally each side of bearing, and where else required.

F. The open space at expansion or control joints shall be kept free of mortar by using a continuous wood or metal strip temporarily set on the wall.

G. Parapets: Parapets above roof line shall be brick masonry throughout with face brick exterior and building brick on interior wythes. Provide continuous joint reinforcement 8" on center.

H. Built-in work: Coordinate work with that of other sections so
    that all connecting work shall be properly located and installed.
    1. Build in panel boxes, access panels, anchors, grounds,
        flashing, expansion joints and all other necessary in-
        cidental work.
    2. Steel lintels: Firmly and solidly bed in mortar; install
        asphalt paper slip plane at control joints.
    3. Fill in solid with mortar behind all metal door frames.
    4. Provide caulking spaces of 1/4 inch wide by 3/4 inch deep
        around wall openings or as indicated on drawings.
    5. Fill cores at vertical reinforcing.
    6. Anchor masonry sills as detailed.

I. Joints at ledge angles: Cut brick immediately below ledge angles.
    to prevent bearing of ledge angles on masonry below. Do not
    install mortar at joint immediately below ledge angles; leave
    open for caulking by others.

J. Stopping and resuming work:
    1. Cover tops of walls with non-staining waterproof coverings
        when work is not in progress. When work is resumed, clean
        top surface of all loose mortar. In drying weather thor-
        oughly wet top surface except for walls of concrete masonry
        units.
    2. Stop off horizontal run of masonry by racking back each
        course one-half masonry unit in length. Toothing shall not
        be permitted.
    3. Clean faces and point joints at end of each working day all
        masonry work that is to be sight-exposed. Holes resulting
        from removal of line pins shall be filled. Use a $1\frac{1}{2}$"-2"
        wheel-type grinder, not a disc-type grinder, if grinding of
        dried mortar is necessary.

3.04 FLASHING

A. Install metal flashing, furnished in Section 07600, which is
    embedded in masonry; form drips at heads of all openings, at
    soffits, and other locations where masonry does not occur immedi-
    ately below flashing; seal penetrations in flashing with mastic.
    Refer to Section 04100 for locations of metal flashing.

B. Install plastic in-wall flashing on bed of mortar, seal penetra-
    tions in flashing with mastic. Terminate flashing 1/2" from face
    of wall. Refer to Section 04100 for locations of plastic flashing.

    C.   Weeps: Provide weeps spaced 24" apart horizontally in head joints of first course above flashing. Form weeps with 5/16" diameter oil-soaked braided cotton sash cord; remove cords at completion of work.

    D.   Extend flashing at window sills to first head joint past sills and turn up 1".

3.05   ADDITIONAL REQUIREMENTS FOR CAVITY WALLS

    A.   Keep cavity clean of mortar during construction; use wood strip in cavity and raise at every other course.

    B.   Install horizontal joint reinforcement at the spacing specified above if continuous type; if rectangular ties, space 16" o.c. vertically and 32" horizontally.

    C.   Insulation: Strike flush mortar at exterior (cavity) face of interior wythe and apply insulation with mastic specified firmly and securely to this surface. Apply insulation per manufacturer's recommendations fitted tightly against joint reinforcement and all edges buttered and butted. Maintain clear space between face of insulation and outer wythe of masonry.

    D.   Install metal flashing continuously with all splices carefully sealed at the following locations:
        1.   At base of wall where cavity terminates.
        2.   Beneath window sills.
        3.   Above heads of windows, entrances and door frames; form drips.
        4.   At other lintels or other horizontal interruptions of the cavity.
        5.   Where else indicated or noted on drawings.
        6.   Do not use non-metal flashing in cavity walls.

    E.   Provide weeps in exterior wythe not more than 24" on center at all flashing locations.

3.06   CONCRETE MASONRY AND PRECAST LINTELS

    A.   Provide precast or formed-in-place masonry lintels wherever openings over 1'-0" wide occur without structural steel or other supporting lintels. Provide formed-in-place masonry lintels in all scored concrete masonry walls.

B.   Reinforcement: Unless otherwise indicated provide one reinforcing bar for each 4" width of wall thickness of size number
not less than the number of feet of the opening width.

C.   Bearing: Minimum 8" at each jamb unless otherwise indicated.

D.   Precase lintels: Thoroughly cured before handling and installation.

E.   Formed-in-place masonry lintels:
1.   Construct proper shoring to provide level platform true to
proper elevation and of sufficient strength to support load
without visible deflection. Shoring shall remain minimum 7
days after lintel is poured.
2.   Lay masonry units with full mortar coverage all abutting
edges, reinforcing steel placed accurately and supported in
cavity. Pour concrete and rod carefully to ensure complete
filling of cavity, proper embeddment of reinforcing without
displacement. Screed off excess concrete to level top
surface.

F.   Lay first course of masonry above lintel in full mortar bed.

G.   Install formed-in-place masonry lintels to match adjacent vertical and horizontal coursing.

H.   Install asphalt paper slip plane under all lintels at control
joints.

3.07   ADDITIONAL REQUIREMENTS FOR CERAMIC FACED MASONRY

A.   Rake setting mortar 1/4" and allow to dry; then tuckpoint raked
joints and scores at same time. Do not use smeared grout method
to fill joints.

B   Keep glaze clean: With clean, soft, damp rags, wipe off at once
all mortar smears, spatters. Do not allow hardening.

3.08   ADDITIONAL REQUIREMENTS FOR BRICK VENEER ON STEEL STUDS

A.   Install veneer ties in brick veneer at 16" vertically. Keep all
ties horizontal into joints. If Burke ties are used, drive a 16d
galvanized nail behind each tie to make tight in anchor.

B.   Maintain detailed space between sheathing and brick; keep free of
mortar similar to cavity walls.

3.09   ADDITIONAL REQUIREMENTS FOR FIREPLACE

A.   Construct fireplace in strict accordance with building code, referenced standards and as detailed.

B.   Install firebrick and clay flue liner with specified fire resistant mortar.

C.   Install metal lintel, damper and other related accessories ← furnished in Section 05500.

D.   Slate surrounds at openings:
1.   Install slate on bed of 1:3 mix of portland cement and mason's sand.
2.   Tamp slate firmly into mortar; level and remove any excess mortar.
3.   Lift slate and butter a paste of neat portland cement to the back, then tamp back into place.
4.   Make joints 1/4" to 1/2" wide; point with 1:2 grout mixture on same day that slate is installed. Clean all grout and cover and protect slate.

3.10   <u>DATE STONE AND TIME CAPSULE</u>

A.   <u>Install</u> time capsule furnished in Section 05500

B.   <u>Install</u> date stone as detailed.

3.11   ACOUSTICAL INSULATION

A.   Acoustical insulation in auditorium masonry walls; <u>Install</u> insulation with joints butted tight; <u>install wire screening</u> against insulation as detailed.

3.12   ADJUSTMENT AND CLEANING

A.   Cut out defective mortar joints; refill solidly with mortar and tool to match adjacent work.

B.   Clean exterior masonry:
1.   Use extreme care to protect adjacent glass and aluminum surfaces to prevent run-down of masonry cleaning materials onto these surfaces.

CHAPTER TWELVE

Calculating Unit Prices

nit prices can be a boon to an estimator — or a disaster. If your unit prices are accurate and you use them in the right situations, they can save you hours of time. But if they're not accurate or you use them inappropriately, they can cost you much more than the value of the time you save.

The tables in this chapter won't be accurate for your work, of course. But you can (and should) use them as guides for compiling your own unit costs. Be sure you use the current material and labor costs for *your* area. And if you follow my suggestions for when to use unit costs, you can save time — and money.

There are several ways to compile unit prices. The two most common ways are *cost per unit* and *cost per square foot*. I used both methods to calculate the unit prices in the tables in this chapter. I started by calculating the cost per unit, then multiplied by the number of units per square foot to convert to cost per square foot. My unit prices include all the costs to erect the various units in place. Yours should too.

But what do you do with your unit prices after you've compiled them? With unit prices at your fingers, you can make fast and logical decisions about construction methods. Your office staff can use them to budget money for labor, materials, taxes, accessories, and so on. Unit prices are helpful for making up your monthly invoices. And architects like to use them when comparing competitive costs or alternate bids. But if you quote unit prices for alternate bids, be sure they're appropriate for the particular situation.

There are many ways to use unit costs, but there's one situation where you don't want to use them: Unit prices aren't meant to be used for estimating. You can use them to check your estimates after they're done — *after* you've done the take-off and followed all the estimating steps I recommend in this manual.

In Chapter 1, I stressed that your estimates should be *exact* — as exact as the information available permits. Unit prices are exact, too, but only for the average job. And very few, if any, of your jobs will be average. No single figure can apply to all the conditions you'll be facing on your jobs.

As useful as unit prices can be, they can also be dangerous. Unit prices can be misleading. They can lull you into believing that they cover all of your costs. Here's an example. A masonry estimator I know did a favor for an architect who wanted a quick alternate bid for some concrete block partitions. He made his take-off from a floor plan the architect provided — and he made it carefully and checked it for errors. Since there were only a few items involved, he used his unit prices as a quick, easy way to arrive at a bid price. The contractor was pleased to be awarded the contract — until he discovered that the work was on the twelfth floor. The unit prices didn't include the extra cost for hoisting.

The point here is that the estimator, in his rush to give the architect his quick estimate, took a shortcut. He used unit prices and overlooked a very important step in the estimating process. If he had taken the time to make an abstract of specifications describing the change and make a note of the plan numbers, he probably would have noticed the note about the floor level.

Unit Prices for Additions and Deductions

Quite often an architect will ask for an estimate of the cost for deducting from, or adding to, work under contract. With a simple take-off and unit prices, you can make the estimate he requested. But there's one catch. Many masonry contractors feel that they're entitled to the profit on "deduct" changes. If you agree, you'll need two sets of unit prices, one for additions and one for deductions. The deduction unit price will be less than the addition unit price by the amount of your profit.

The Unit Price Tables

Figure 12-1 shows the data I used to calculate unit prices. The calculations show the cost of the masonry unit materials plus the cost of the reinforcing and wall ties. Making a table like this should be your first step in calculating unit prices.

Figures 12-2 and 12-3 show how I compiled unit prices for face brick. The calculations show the proportionate cost of mortar, cleaning, reinforcing and wall ties. They also show the applicable sales tax on the materials and the fringes added to labor costs, as well as other costs for tools and equipment, overhead and profit.

Figures 12-4 to 12-7 show my unit prices for concrete masonry units, including lightweight, heavyweight and various special concrete masonry units.

Unit	Face size	Material cost	Units per SF of wall	Units laid per 8 manhours	Weight per unit	Type N mortar (cubic yards per 1,000 units)
Face brick						
4" solid	$2\frac{2}{3}$ x 8	$150.00/M	6.75	560	5.3	.515
4" solid	$2\frac{2}{3}$ x 12	245.00/M	4.50	459	7.8	.713
4" solid	$3\frac{1}{8}$ x 12	265.00/M	3.75	423	9.2	.738
4" solid	4 x 12	350.00/M	3.00	291	12.5	.781
4" solid	8 x 8	630.00/M	2.25	238	14.0	.692
4" solid	12 x 12	1975.00/M	1.00	157	30.2	1.035
6" solid	4 x 12	600.00/M	3.00	250	13.5	1.119
6" hollow	4 x 12	590.00/M	3.00	340	10.8	.676
8" solid	4 x 12	720.00/M	3.00	172	20.0	1.456
8" hollow	4 x 12	710.00/M	3.00	196	16.0	.676
LWCMU						
4"	8 x 16	.481 each	1.125	180	18.0	1.019
6"	8 x 16	.585 each	1.125	168	24.0	1.146
8"	8 x 16	.753 each	1.125	161	27.0	1.146
10"	8 x 16	1.051 each	1.125	148	33.0	1.273
12"	8 x 16	1.094 each	1.125	137	37.0	1.273
HWCMU						
4"	8 x 16	.349 each	1.125	166	25.0	1.019
6"	8 x 16	.446 each	1.125	148	33.0	1.146
8"	8 x 16	.502 each	1.125	137	37.0	1.146
10"	8 x 16	.716 each	1.125	107	46.0	1.273
12"	8 x 16	.742 each	1.125	92	52.0	1.273
4-flute						
4"	8 x 16	.656 each	1.125	130	33.0	1.223
6"	8 x 16	.686 each	1.125	122	36.0	1.376
8"	8 x 16	.779 each	1.125	115	39.0	1.376
10"	8 x 16	.938 each	1.125	77	55.0	1.528
12"	8 x 16	1.109 each	1.125	74	61.0	1.528
Striated						
4"	8 x 16	.402	1.125	148	26.0	1.019
8"	8 x 16	.548	1.125	118	39.0	1.146
Scored						
4"	8 x 16	.373	1.125	155	26.0	1.019
6"	8 x 16	.470	1.125	143	32.0	1.146
8"	8 x 16	.520	1.125	124	39.0	1.146
Embossed						
4"	8 x 16	.583	1.125	135	26.0	1.019
8"	8 x 16	.730	1.125	109	39.0	1.146
12"	8 x 16	.976	1.125	75	54.0	1.273
Split						
4"	8 x 16	.602	1.125	151	33.0	1.019
8"	8 x 16	.741	1.125	95	46.0	1.146
Sound						
4"	8 x 16	1.761	1.125	144	18.0	1.019
Slump						
8"	4 x 16	.670	2.250	176	13.0	.955

(continued on following page)

Data used to calculate unit prices
Figure 12-1

Unit	Face size	Material cost	Units per SF of wall	Units laid per 8 manhours	Weight per unit	Type N mortar (cubic yards per 1,000 units)
Structural glazed tile						
2"	5⅓ x 12	.830	2.250	150	6.0	.331
4"	5⅓ x 12	1.060	2.250	150	10.2	.467
6"	5⅓ x 12	1.540	2.250	137	16.0	.622
2"	8 x 16	1.950	1.125	142	13.6	.408
4"	8 x 16	2.120	1.125	142	21.0	.589
Glazed concrete block						
2"	8 x 16	2.710	1.125	144	13.0	.408
4"	8 x 16	2.880	1.125	144	22.0	1.019
8"	8 x 16	3.260	1.125	136	32.0	1.146
Glass block						
4"	8 x 8	4.00	2.25	240	6.0	.498
4"	12 x 12	10.00	1.00	180	16.0	.743

Reinforcing: Standard · Truss · Mill Galvanized

4" standard	$ 89.00 per 1,000 LF
6" standard	90.00 per 1,000 LF
8" standard	93.00 per 1,000 LF
10" standard	98.00 per 1,000 LF
12" standard	103.00 per 1,000 LF
10" standard drip	101.00 per 1,000 LF
12" standard drip	106.00 per 1,000 LF
14" standard drip	113.00 per 1,000 LF

Veneer wall ties — Galvanized Steel

4" veneer	$25.00 per 100

Masonry unit	Reinforcing (cost per unit standard @ 16")	Reinforcing (cost per unit drip @ 16")	Wall ties (cost per unit @ 1 per 2⅔ SF)
4 x 8 x 16	.063		
6 x 8 x 16	.064		
8 x 8 x 16	.066		
10 x 8 x 16	.069		
12 x 8 x 16	.073		
8 x 4 x 16	.033		
4 x 2⅔ x 8	.011		.014
4 x 2⅔ x 12	.016		.021
4 x 4 x 12	.024		.032
6 x 4 x 12	.024		
8 x 4 x 12	.025		
4 x 5⅓ x 12	.032		
6 x 5⅓ x 12	.032		
4 x 8 x 8	.032		
4 x 12 x 12	.047		
Cavity wall			
4 + 2 + 4 10" drip		.072	
4 + 2 + 6 12" drip		.075	
4 + 2 + 8 14" drip		.080	

Data used to calculate unit prices
Figure 12-1 (continued)

MATERIAL

Item	Face brick 2⅔ x 8 6.75	Face brick 2⅔ x 12 4.50	Face brick 4 x 12 3.00	Face brick 8 x 8 2.25	Face brick 12 x 12 1.00	
						— ①
Material	.155	.253	.361	.649	2.035	— ②
Mortar (N)	.025	.034	.037	.033	.046	— ③
Clean	.004	.005	.008	.010	.022	— ④
Reinforcing (wall ties*)	.014*	.021*	.032*	.042*	.094*	— ⑤
	.198	.313	.438	.734	2.197	
Tax (5½%)	.011	.018	.025	.041	.121	
Net cost per unit	.029	.331	.463	.775	2.318	

LABOR

Production	**560**	**459**	**291**	**238**	**157**	— ⑥
Erect	.357	.436	.688	.841	1.274	— ⑦
Clean	.038	.056	.084	.112	.250	— ⑧
	.395	.492	.772	.953	1.524	
Fringes (33%)	.131	.163	.255	.315	.503	— ⑨
Net cost per unit	.526	.655	1.027	1.268	2.057	

TOTAL COST

Material plus labor	.735	.986	1.490	2.043	4.375	
Tools and equipment, overhead, profit	.177	.237	.358	.491	1.050	— ⑩
Cost per unit	.912	1.223	1.848	2.534	5.425	
Cost per SF	$6.16	$5.55	$5.55	$5.71	$5.43	— ⑪

Unit prices for 4″ face brick
Figure 12-2A

① Number of units per square foot.

② Cost of material per unit. Brick cost includes 3% allowance for waste.

③ Cost of mortar. See Chapter 5.

④ Cost of material required to clean one unit.

⑤ Cost of wall reinforcing prorated for one unit, usually installed in horizontal masonry courses spaced 16" vertically. See Chapter 6. Also, cost of wall ties prorated for one unit, usually installed in horizontal masonry courses at one tie per 2⅔ square feet, or one tie each 16" vertically and 24" horizontally.

⑥ Production: The number of units a mason can install in one day. See Chapter 8.

⑦ Erect: The labor cost to erect in place one unit. See Chapter 8.

⑧ Clean: The labor cost to clean one face of one unit. See Chapter 7. If masonry walls are exposed on two faces, the extra charge should be added here.

⑨ Fringes: The cost added to labor for fringe benefits. See Chapter 8.

⑩ Tools and equipment, overhead, profit: The total cost of miscellaneous charges expressed as a percentage of material plus labor. In the following examples, I used 24%.

⑪ Cost per SF: The total cost to erect in place one square foot of the particular masonry. This is calculated by multiplying the cost per unit by the number of units per square foot.

Explanations for unit prices
Figure 12-2B

MATERIAL

Item	6" face brick (s) 4 x 12 3.00	6" face brick (h) 4 x 12 3.00	8" face brick (s) 4 x 12 3.00	8" face brick (h) 4 x 12 3.00
Material	.618	.608	.742	.732
Mortar (N)	.053	.032	.063	.032
Clean	.008	.008	.008	.008
Reinforcing	.024	.024	.025	.025
	.703	.672	.838	.797
Tax (5½%)	.039	.037	.047	.044
Net cost per unit	.742	.709	.885	.841

LABOR

Production	250	340	172	196
Erect	.800	.589	1.163	1.021
Clean	.084	.084	.084	.084
	.884	.673	1.247	1.105
Fringes (33%)	.292	.223	.412	.365
Net cost per unit	1.176	.896	1.659	1.470

TOTAL COST

Material plus labor	1.918	1.605	2.544	2.311
Tools and equipment, overhead, profit	.461	.386	.611	.555
Cost per unit	2.379	1.991	3.155	2.866
Cost per SF	$7.14	$5.98	$9.47	$8.60

Unit prices for utility face brick
Figure 12-3

MATERIAL

Item	4" LWCMU 8 x 16 1.125	6" LWCMU 8 x 16 1.125	8" LWCMU 8 x 16 1.125	10" LWCMU 8 x 16 1.125	12" LWCMU 8 x 16 1.125
Material	.481	.585	.753	1.051	1.094
Mortar (N)	.048	.054	.054	.060	.060
Clean	--	--	--	--	--
Reinforcing	.063	.064	.066	.069	.073
	.592	.703	.873	1.180	1.227
Tax (5½%)	.033	.038	.049	.065	.068
Net cost per unit	.625	.741	.922	1.245	1.295

LABOR

Production	180	168	161	148	137
Erect	1.112	1.191	1.243	1.352	1.460
Clean	.030	.030	.030	.030	.030
	1.142	1.221	1.273	1.382	1.490
Fringes (33%)	.377	.403	.421	.457	.492
Net cost per unit	1.519	1.624	1.694	1.839	1.982

TOTAL COST

Material plus labor	2.144	2.365	2.616	3.084	3.277
Tools and equipment, overhead, profit	.515	.568	.628	.741	.787
Cost per unit	2.659	2.933	3.244	3.825	4.064
Cost per SF	$3.00	$3.30	$3.65	$4.31	$4.58

Unit prices for lightweight concrete masonry units
Figure 12-4

MATERIAL

Item	4" HWCMU 8 x 16 1.125	6" HWCMU 8 x 16 1.125	8" HWCMU 8 x 16 1.125	10" HWCMU 8 x 16 1.125	12" HWCMU 8 x 16 1.125
Material	.349	.446	.502	.716	.742
Mortar (N)	.048	.054	.054	.060	.060
Clean	--	--	--	--	--
Reinforcing	.063	.064	.066	.069	.073
	.460	.564	.622	.845	.875
Tax (5½%)	.026	.030	.035	.047	.049
Net cost per unit	.486	.594	.657	.892	.924

LABOR

Production	166	148	137	107	92
Erect	1.205	1.352	1.460	1.870	2.174
Clean	.030	.030	.030	.030	.030
	1.235	1.382	1.490	1.900	2.204
Fringes (33%)	.408	.457	.492	.627	.728
Net cost per unit	1.643	1.839	1.982	2.527	2.932

TOTAL COST

Material plus labor	2.129	2.433	2.639	3.419	3.856
Tools and equipment, overhead, profit	.511	.584	.634	.821	.926
Cost per unit	2.640	3.017	3.273	4.240	4.782
Cost per SF	$2.97	$3.40	$3.69	$4.77	$5.38

Unit prices for heavyweight concrete masonry units
Figure 12-5

MATERIAL

Item	4" striated 8 x 16 1.125	8" striated 8 x 16 1.125	4" scored 8 x 16 1.125	6" scored 8 x 16 1.125	8" scored 8 x 16 1.125
Material	.402	.548	.373	.470	.520
Mortar (N)	.048	.054	.048	.054	.054
Clean	--	--	--	--	--
Reinforcing	.063	.066	.063	.064	.066
	.513	.668	.484	.588	.640
Tax (5½ %)	.029	.037	.027	.032	.036
Net cost per unit	.542	.705	.511	.620	.676

LABOR

Production	148	118	155	143	124
Erect	1.352	1.695	1.291	1.399	1.613
Clean	.032	.032	.032	.032	.032
	1.384	1.727	1.323	1.431	1.645
Fringes (33%)	.457	.570	.437	.473	.543
Net cost per unit	1.841	2.297	1.760	1.904	2.188

TOTAL COST

Material plus labor	2.383	3.002	2.271	2.524	2.864
Tools and equipment, overhead, profit	.572	.721	.546.	.606	.688
Cost per unit	2.955	3.723	2.817	3.130	3.552
Cost per SF	$3.33	$4.19	$3.17	$3.53	$4.00

Unit prices for special concrete masonry units
Figure 12-6

MATERIAL

Item	4" 4-flute 8 x 16 1.125	8" 4-flute 8 x 16 1.125	10" 4-flute 8 x 16 1.125	4" split 8 x 16 1.125	8" split 8 x 16 1.125
Material	.656	.779	.938	.602	.741
Mortar (N)	.058	.065	.066	.048	.054
Clean	--	--	--	--	--
Reinforcing	.063	.066	.069	.063	.066
	.777	.910	1.073	.713	.861
Tax (5½%)	.043	.051	.060	.040	.048
Net cost per unit	.820	.961	1.133	.753	.909

LABOR

Production	130	115	77	132	95
Erect	1.539	1.740	2.598	1.516	2.106
Clean	.035	.035	.035	.031	.031
	1.574	1.775	2.633	1.547	2.137
Fringes (33%)	.520	.586	.869	.511	.706
Net cost per unit	2.094	2.361	3.502	2.058	2.843

TOTAL COST

Material plus labor	2.914	3.322	4.635	2.811	3.752
Tools and equipment, overhead, profit	.700	.798	1.113	.675	.901
Cost per unit	3.614	4.120	5.748	3.486	4.653
Cost per SF	$4.07	$4.64	$6.47	$3.93	$5.24

Unit prices for special concrete masonry units
Figure 12-7

Figure 12-8 shows how unit prices for structural glazed tile units are compiled and Figure 12-9, glazed concrete and glass block unit prices.

Figures 12-10 and 12-11 show the unit prices for composite walls. Composite walls are a combination of two or more different size units, such as face brick with concrete block backup. Obviously, the only practical way to make up a unit price for such a wall is by adding the unit price per square foot of the single wall wythes. For example, to calculate the unit price per square foot of a composite wall made up of 4'' face brick and 4'' LWCMU, add together the unit price per square foot of each wythe ($6.04 + $2.88 = $8.92).

Figure 12-12 (unit prices for cavity walls) is also compiled by combining the unit price per square foot of the single wall wythes. Notice the additional cost for the cavity wall drip reinforcing.

MATERIAL

Item	2" SGT 5⅓ x 12 2.25	4" SGT 5⅓ x 12 2.25	6" SGT 5⅓ x 12 2.25	2" SGT 8 x 16 1.125	4" SGT 8 x 16 1.125
Material	.830	1.060	1.540	1.950	2.120
Mortar (N)	.016	.022	.030	.020	.028
Clean	--	--	--	--	--
Reinforcing or wall ties*	.042*	.032	.032	.084*	.063
	.888	1.114	1.602	2.054	2.211
Tax (5½%)	.049	.062	.089	.113	.122
Net cost per unit	.937	1.176	1.691	2.167	2.333

LABOR

Production	150	150	137	142	142
Erect	1.334	1.334	1.460	1.409	1.409
Clean	.014	.014	.014	.027	.027
	1.348	1.348	1.474	1.436	1.436
Fringes (33%)	.445	.445	.487	.474	.474
Net cost per unit	1.793	1.793	1.961	1.910	1.910

TOTAL COST

Material plus labor	2.730	2.969	3.652	4.077	4.243
Tools and equipment, overhead, profit	.656	.713	.877.	.979	1.019
Cost per unit	3.386	3.682	4.529	5.056	5.262
Cost per SF	$7.62	$8.29	$10.20	$5.69	$5.92

Unit prices for structural glazed tile
Figure 12-8

MATERIAL

Item	2" GLCB 8 x 16 1.125	4" GLCB 8 x 16 1.125	8" GLCB 8 x 16 1.125	4" glass block 8 x 16 2.25	4" glass block 12 x 12 1.00
Material	2.710	2.880	3.260	4.000	10.000
Mortar (N)	.020	.048	.054	.024	.035
Clean	--	--	--	--	--
Reinforcing or wall ties*	.084*	.063	.066	.032	.063
	2.814	2.991	3.380	4.056	10.098
Tax (5½%)	.155	.165	.186	.224	.556
Net cost per unit	2.969	3.156	3.566	4.280	10.654

LABOR

Production	144	144	136	240	180
Erect	1.389	1.389	1.471	.834	1.111
Clean	.027	.027	.027	.014	.030
	1.416	1.416	1.498	.848	1.141
Fringes (33%)	.468	.468	.495	.280	.377
Net cost per unit	1.884	1.884	1.993	1.128	1.518

TOTAL COST

Material plus labor	4.853	5.040	5.559	5.408	12.172
Tools and equipment, overhead, profit	1.165	1.210	1.335.	1.298	2.922
Cost per unit	6.018	6.250	6.894	6.706	15.094
Cost per SF	$6.78	$7.04	$7.76	$15.09	$15.10

Unit prices for glazed concrete block and glass block
Figure 12-9

MATERIAL

Item	8" face brick F2S (s)	4" face brick 2⅔ x 8 6.75 (a), (b)	4" face brick 4" LWCMU	4" face brick 2⅔ x 8 6.75 (c)	4" LWCMU 8 x 16 1.125 (d) (e)
Material		.155		.155	.481
Mortar (N)		.025		.025	.048
Clean		.004		.004	--
Reinforcing		.033(a)		-- (c)	.066(d)
		.217		.184	.595
Tax (5½%)		.012		.011	.033
Net cost per unit		.229		.195	.628

LABOR

Production		571(b)		560	191(e)
Erect		.351		.357	1.048
Clean		.038		.038	.030
		.389		.395	1.078
Fringes (33%)		.129		.131	.356
Net cost per unit		.518		.526	1.434

TOTAL COST

Item	8" face brick F2S (s)	4" face brick 2⅔ x 8	4" face brick 4" LWCMU	4" face brick 2⅔ x 8	4" LWCMU 8 x 16
Material plus labor		.747		.721	2.062
Tools and equipment, overhead, profit		.180		.174	.495
Cost per unit		.927		.895	2.557
Cost per SF	$ 6.26	$6.26	$6.04	$6.04	$2.88
	6.26		2.88		
	$12.52		$8.92		

Notes: (a) Reinforcing - ½ the cost of 8" reinforcing
(b) Production - for 8", facebrick wall
(c) Reinforcing - included with B/U
(d) Reinforcing - for 8" wall
(e) Production - for B/U, running bond

Unit prices for composite walls
Figure 12-10

MATERIAL

Item	4" face brick 6"LWCMU (c)	6" LWCMU 8 x 16 1.125 (a), (b)	4" face brick 8" LWCMU (s)	4" face brick 4 x 12 3.00 (d)	8" LWCMU 8 x 16 1.125 (e), (f)
Material		.585		.361	.753
Mortar (N)		.054		.037	.054
Clean		--		.008	--
Reinforcing		.069(a)		-- (d)	.073(e)
		.708		.406	.880
Tax (5½%)		.039		.023	.049
Net cost per unit		.747		.429	.929

LABOR

Production		178(b)		291	171(f)
Erect		1.124		.688	1.170
Clean		.030		.084	.030
		1.154		.772	1.200
Fringes (33%)		.381		.255	.396
Net cost per unit		1.535		1.027	1.596

TOTAL COST

	4" face brick 6"LWCMU (c)	6" LWCMU 8 x 16 1.125 (a), (b)	4" face brick 8" LWCMU (s)	4" face brick 4 x 12 3.00 (d)	8" LWCMU 8 x 16 1.125 (e), (f)
Material plus labor		2.282		1.456	2.525
Tools and equipment, overhead, profit		.548		.350	.606
Cost per unit		2.830		1.806	3.131
Cost per SF	$6.04(c)	$3.19	$5.42	$5.42	$3.53
	3.19		3.53		
	$9.23		$8.95		

Notes: (a) Reinforcing - for 10" wall
(b) Production - for B/U, running bond
(c) Cost for 4" FB per SF - taken from Figure 12-10
(d) Reinforcing - included with B/U
(e) Reinforcing - for 12" wall
(f) Production - for B/U, running bond

Unit prices for composite walls
Figure 12-11

MATERIAL

Item	4" face brick 2" cav. 4" LWCMU	4" face brick 2" cav. 6" LWCMU	4" face brick 2⅜ x 8 6.75 (s) (a), (b)	4" LWCMU 8 x 16 1.125 (c)	6" LWCMU 8 x 16 1.125 (d)
Material			.155	.481	.585
Mortar (N)			.025	.048	.054
Clean			.004	--	--
Reinforcing			-- (a)	.072(c)	.075(d)
			.184	.601	.714
Tax (5½%)			.011	.034	.040
Net cost per unit			.195	.635	.754

LABOR

Production			532(b)	180	168
Erect			.376	1.112	1.191
Clean			.038	.030	.030
			.414	1.142	1.221
Fringes (33%)			.137	.377	.403
Net cost per unit			.551	1.519	1.624

TOTAL COST

Item	4" face brick 2" cav. 4" LWCMU	4" face brick 2" cav. 6" LWCMU	4" face brick	4" LWCMU	6" LWCMU
Material plus labor			.746	2.154	2.378
Tools and equipment, overhead, profit			.180	.515	.571
Cost per unit			.926	2.669	2.949
Cost per SF	$ 6.25	$6.25	$6.25	$3.01	$3.32
	3.01	3.32			
	$9.26	$9.57			

Notes: (a) Reinforcing - included with B/U
(b) Production - for running bond, cavity
(c) Reinforcing - for 10" cavity wall, drip
(d) Reinforcing - for 12" cavity wall, drip

Unit prices for cavity walls
Figure 12-12

CHAPTER THIRTEEN

An Actual Estimate

his is my actual take-off and estimate of a six-story college campus building. I can't reproduce the plans in this book — they're just too large. But there's a lot to learn here if you take the time to study each page of the take-off. And here's the most important lesson you can learn: Complicated take-offs are just a combination of many simple take-offs. If you've followed along with the sample take-offs throughout the book, you have all the tools you need to do a take-off like this one. It just takes care and confidence.

For this building, it was necessary to take off each floor, one floor at a time. But you can often simplify the procedure. If the next floor is the same as the one you just measured, don't waste time measuring it. But it's a good idea to have a take-off sheet for each floor, even if some of the sheets only say "third floor same as second floor" or "fourth floor same as third floor except . . . ."

Most housing projects are made up of groups of similar buildings. There's no need to measure every building. First analyze the plans, then save yourself a lot of work by making one take-off of each different unit.

The measuring I did in this take-off follows the principles you've read throughout the book. But this one takes you a little further. It shows you how to handle some items I didn't cover in the text, including soldier courses, caulking, sloped brick sills, rigid insulation, rolok caps, curved walls, pavers, 45-degree brick, glazed concrete block, and fireplace items.

You'll also find a little more detail about how to transfer items from the take-off to the recap and summary. And there's an alternate bid included. Notice how flexible the system is. You can use it to make a unit masonry take-off for any type of building.

Go through this take-off carefully. You may find it the most useful part of the book.

MASONRY QUANTITY SURVEYS

123 Beech Drive
Cincinnati, OH 45123

DATE
SHEET *1* OF *34*
EST. BY *RVK*
BID DUE

BLDG. *CARLIN HALL*   OWNER *STATE*
LOCATION *COLLEGE CAMPUS*   ARCHITECT *G-B-B*
PLAN NOS. *A1-A36* DATE *8-87*   GEN. CONTR. *JB INC.*
S1-17

BASEMENT

	4" F.BRK CB Blu	4" CB Blu	8" CB	Soldier D.O.	4" F.BRK Conc Blu	4" CB	8" CB Blu	12" CB	P.C. LINT 4×8
	9^4	9^4	2^0		9^4	2^0	9^4	2^0	
	20^0	20^0	20^0		2^0	8^0	6^0	6^0	
	6^0	2^0	(40)		(19)	-2^0	(56)	(12)	
	6^0	$\overline{22^0}$				6^0			
	2^0	(206)			12^0	(12)			
	$\overline{2^0}$				4^0				
	36^0				(48)				
	(336)								
					2^0				
	10^0	10^0			$\overline{105^0}$		10^0		
	$\overline{105^0}$	10^0			(210)		$\overline{105}$		
	10^0	(100)					(1050)		
	$\overline{115^0}$				$2^{10\frac{2}{3}}$				
	(1150)				$\overline{27^0}$				
					(78)				
	1486	306					1106		
					2^0				
DR $8^0 \times 8^0$	① 64	① 64		① 8	$\overline{20^0}$				
OPNG $18^0 \times 8^{2\frac{2}{3}}$	① 148			① 18	(40)		① 148		
✓ $6^4 \times 4^0$	① 25			① 7			① 25		
LVR $9^0 \times 7^4$	① 66						① 66		
DR 99 $6^4 \times 7^4$	② 46								① 8
DR $6^0 \times 9^4$							① 56		
✓ $8^0 \times 9^0$		① 74							
	349	138					295		
	1137	168	40	33	395	12	811	12	8
	✓	✓	✓	✓	✓	✓	✓	✓	✓

MASONRY QUANTITY SURVEYS

123 Beech Drive
Cincinnati, OH 45123

DATE
SHEET **2** OF
EST. BY
BID DUE

BLDG. _______________   OWNER _______________

LOCATION _______________   ARCHITECT _______________

PLAN NOS. __________ DATE __________   GEN. CONTR. _______________

BASEMENT — 2

	8" CB	LEDGEL CAULK FLASH	CAULK @ SLAB 2 SIDES	12" CB	8" CB	P.C. LINT 8×8	8" CB 1½ HR 8×8	4" CB 8×8	4" CB	6" CB
	w/5@24 8°			12°	12°		9^{4}	9^{4}	12°	12°
	29°	108	29	34	39		219	8	2	6
	(232)	20	34	20	44		− 8	(75)	(24)	(72)
		128	238	54	14		211			
			211	(648)	141		(1970)	3^{4}	2^{8}	
			8		238			7		
			2		− 20		3^{4}	(24)	(22)	
			6		218		14			
			528		(2616)		(47)			
					2^{8}		2017	99	46	
					211					
					(563)					
					6°					
					10 ⟍ 3239					
					(60)					
DR	$6^{8}\times7^{4}$							(1) 46		
BM	$1^{\circ}\times1^{4}$			(15) 20	(26) 34					
OPNG	$2^{\circ}\times8^{\circ}$				(1) 16	(1) 4				
DR	$4^{\circ}\times7^{\circ}$				(1) 28	(1) 6				
B91	$3^{\circ}\times7^{\circ}$				(1) 21	(1) 5	(8) 168			
B03	$6^{\circ}\times7^{\circ}$						(3) 126			
FLOOR	$1^{4}\times20^{\circ}$				(1) 26					
BM	36×3^{4}									
				20	125	15	294	46		
	232	128	528	628	3114	15	1729	53	46	72

By others

MASONRY QUANTITY SURVEYS

123 Beech Drive
Cincinnati, OH 45123

DATE ___________
SHEET **3** OF ___
EST. BY ___________
BID DUE ___________

BLDG. ___________________________ OWNER ___________________________

LOCATION ________________________ ARCHITECT ________________________

PLAN NOS. __________ DATE __________ GEN. CONTR. ______________________

1ST FLOOR

Metal stud	4" F.BRK MS B/U	4" F.BRK MS B/U	SOLDIER	SPL BRK SILL	C.J.	EXP. JT	SLOPE SILL	4" F.BRK CB B/U	SPL BRK SILL	LEDGE L
			D.O.	[trapezoid] $2\frac{2}{3}$			[shape]		[shape] 4"	4" CAULK
	$14°$	$4\ 5^3$		W/FLASH	$4°$	$4°$		0^8	W/FLASH	FLASH
	$5°$	$170°$	$170°$	$170°$	4	1	16^4	16^4	45	71
	(70)	16^4	16^4	16^4	(16)	(4)	$105°$	$105°$		72
		186^4	$45°$	186^4			121^4	121^4		224
	$10°$	(829)	$105°$		5^4			(81)		57
	4		336^4		2					28
	(40)	$14\ 5^3$			(11)					11
		$71°$								36
	12^8	(1026)			$14\ 5\frac{1}{3}$					499
	72				1					
	(912)	5^4			(15)					
		$45°$								
	$16°$	(240)			4^8					
	224				4					
	(3584)	$4°$			(19)					
		$105°$								
	9^4	(420)								
	41									
	(383)	7515								
	4989									

ENT $21° \times 9^4$ (1) 196 (1) 21
✓ $15° \times 9^4$ (1) 140 (1) 15
✓ $10° \times 9^4$ (1) 93 (1) 10
@ GRAT. $44° \times 4°$ (1) 176
✓ $28° \times 3^4$ (1) 93
                        698 + 46

	4" F.BRK	4" F.BRK	SOLDIER	SPL BRK	C.J.	EXP. JT	SLOPE	4" F.BRK	SPL BRK	LEDGE L
	4989	1817	383	187	61	4	122	81	45	499
		4989			4	4				
		6806			65					
		4	4	4	4		4	4	4	4

MASONRY QUANTITY SURVEYS

123 Beech Drive
Cincinnati, OH 45123

DATE 4
SHEET OF
EST. BY
BID DUE

BLDG. ___________________ OWNER ___________________

LOCATION ___________________ ARCHITECT ___________________

PLAN NOS. ___________ DATE ___________ GEN. CONTR. ___________________

1ST FLOOR — 2

12" CB CONC B/U	4" F. BRK INSUL.	2" RIGID CORN	45° BRK MS B/U	4" F. BRK CR B/U	4" F. BRK B/U w/#8@24"	8" CB BM 8×8	BOND B/U	4" CB CB B/U ON 11" CURVE	4" F. BRK HDRS CS
3"	1"	1"	9"	12°	12'	12'		8°	14°
35°	72	72	2	57°	28	28	28	3	33	32
(117)	224	224	(19)	(684)	11	11	28	(24)	(462)	
	28	28			39	39	56			
	11	11			(494)	(494)				
	335	335								
	(447)	(447)			8°	12°				
					3	9°				
	2°	2°			3	(108)				
	57	57			6°					
	(114)	(114)			(48)	10°				
						36				
	14°	14°			14°	(360)				
	2×8°	36°			9					
	(224)	(504)			8	14°			14°	
					17	4			39	
					(238)	(56)			(546)	
	785	1065			780	1018				

interior

exterior

Totals:

117	785	1065	19	684	780	1018	56	24	1008	32
✓	✓	✓	✓	✓	✓	✓	✓	✓	✓	✓

MASONRY QUANTITY SURVEYS

123 Beech Drive
Cincinnati, OH 45123

DATE ___________
SHEET *5* OF ___________
EST. BY ___________
BID DUE ___________

BLDG. ___________   OWNER ___________

LOCATION ___________   ARCHITECT ___________

PLAN NOS. ___________ DATE ___________   GEN. CONTR. ___________

AUDITORIUM   (DEDUCT ALT G-1)

4" F. BRK CB BLU ON RAD. 8°	4" F. BRK CB BLU 8°	8" CB BLU w/ #5 P @ 4" 16-8	BOND BM D.O.	SLOPE SILL w/FLASH	ROLOK SILL	F. BRK BLU	45° BRK D.O. 8°	C.J. 10°	ROLOK CAP 17" W w/FLASH	4" F. BRK BRK BLU w/FLASH 0-10 2/3
104°	76	180	180	180	180	180	4	2	14	14
(832)	(608)	(1200)					(32)	(20)		(13)
										1-1/3
										150°
										(167)
										180
LVRE 6°x6-8 (1) 40 (1) 40										
	40	40								
832 568	1160	180	180	180	180	32	20	14	180	
832										
1400										
— 4	5	5	5	5	5	5	5	5	5	

$C = 2\pi R$
$A = \pi R^2$

MASONRY QUANTITY SURVEYS

123 Beech Drive
Cincinnati, OH 45123

1" Pea gravel
2" Insul.
Membrane Flash

DATE
SHEET 6 OF
EST. BY
BID DUE

BLDG. ___________________ OWNER ___________________

LOCATION ___________________ ARCHITECT ___________________

PLAN NOS. ___________ DATE ___________ GEN. CONTR. ___________________

AUDITORIUM (DEDUCT ALT G-1)

	SAW CUT PAVERS	4" F.BRK BRK B/U w/FLASH 3⁴	8" BRK B/U 2⁸	SOLDIER	P.C. CONC SILL 5×5	ROLOK CAP 20" W W/FLASH	12" BRK B/U 1⁴	PAVER #1	PAVER #2	F. BRK SCREEN W/MET. SCR 2" INSUL 14 5⅓	F. BRK Do ON CURVE 18 5⅓
	101	18º	18º			150	150	52⁶ × 39⁶	π × 17 × 17	62º	60
	101	(60)	(48)				(200)	(2074)	(908)	(896)	(1107)
	202										
								$\frac{\pi \times 27 \times 27}{2}$		interior	interior
								(1146)			
								3220			

Metal screen by others

	SAW CUT PAVERS	4" F.BRK	8" BRK	SOLDIER	P.C.	ROLOK	12" BRK	PAVER #1	PAVER #2	F. BRK	F. BRK
LVRE	6º × 6⁸			(1) 6	(1) 6						
STAIR	7º × 6º							(2) 84			
COLOR	π × 16 × 16							(1) 805			
	202	60	48	6	6	150	200	2331	908	896	1107
Perim	240										
	442										
	✓	✓	✓	✓	✓	✓	✓	✓	✓	✓	✓

Sect 02500
Separate Summary

MASONRY QUANTITY SURVEYS

123 Beech Drive
Cincinnati, OH 45123

DATE
SHEET 7 OF
EST. BY
BID DUE

BLDG. ___________________________ OWNER ___________________________

LOCATION ________________________ ARCHITECT ________________________

PLAN NOS. __________ DATE __________ GEN. CONTR. ______________________

AUDITORIUM   (DEDUCT ALT G-1)

		8" CB PART	P.C. LINT 8×8	4" F.BRK Conc B/u	4" F.BRK BRK B/u	45° BRK	Rolok 12" W w/ FLASH	4" BRK FILL		
		14⁰		4⁰	2⁸	2⁸		2⁸		
		113⁰		20⁰	20⁰	1	20⁰	20⁰		
		(1582)		31⁰	20⁰	(3)	31⁰	31⁰		
				51⁰	31⁰		51	51		
				(204)	31⁰			(136)		
					102					
					(272)					
DR	3⁰×6⁸	(1) 20	(1) 5							
✓	6⁰×6⁸	(2) 80	(2) 16							
LVRE	4⁰×4⁰	(2) 32	(2) 12							
		132	33							
		1450	3.3	204	272	3	51	136		
		₄	₄	₄	₄	₄	₄	₄		

MASONRY QUANTITY SURVEYS

123 Beech Drive
Cincinnati, OH 45123

DATE
SHEET *8* OF
EST. BY
BID DUE

BLDG. _______________________ OWNER _______________________

LOCATION _______________________ ARCHITECT _______________________

PLAN NOS. ___________ DATE ___________ GEN. CONTR. _______________________

AUDITORIUM   BASE BID   (ADD BACK IN   ALT G-1)

		4' F.BRK CB BLU	8" CB BLU w/1# g 2¾"	4" F BRK CONC. BLU	2" RIGID INSUL					
		8⁸	8⁸	1⁴	1⁴					
		66⁰	66⁰	66⁰	66⁰					
		(572)	(572)	(88)	(88)					

This sheet (8)
(a) *Do not include in base bid*
(b) *Deduct from Alt G-1*

		572	572	88	88					
		✗	✗	✗	✗					

MASONRY QUANTITY SURVEYS

123 Beech Drive
Cincinnati, OH 45123

DATE
SHEET **9** OF
EST. BY
BID DUE

BLDG. _______________   OWNER _______________

LOCATION _______________   ARCHITECT _______________

PLAN NOS. _______ DATE _______   GEN. CONTR. _______________

1ST FLOOR INTERIOR

12"CB	8"CB	6"CB	6"GLCB	8"GLCB	8"CB	8"GLCB	P.C. LINT 6×8	4"F.BRK INT.	P.C. LINT 8×8	4"CB B/U	P.C. LINT 4×0
12⁸⁻	4⁰	13⁴⁻	0⁸	0⁸	13⁴⁻	0⁸		7¹₃		10⁰	
20	98	340⁰	307	15	15	83		6⁰		98	
(254)	(392)	16⁰	33	(10)	(200)	(56)		(43)		(980)	
		3.54	16								
12⁸⁻	(4747)	356			14⁰			10⁻²₃			
117		(238)			57			98			
−20	14⁰				(798)			(1002)			
97	13⁰										
(1229)	(182)				3⁴			7⁰			
					10			4			
					(34)			(28)			
1621	4929										
					1032			1073			

BM 77⁰×0⁸	① 51										
DR 6⁰×0⁸					② 8						
∨ 3⁰×6⁰	⑥ 108	⑥ 12					⑥ 30				
∨ 5⁰×6⁰	⑩ 300	⑩ 33					⑩ 70				
∨ 3⁰×6⁸					① 20			⑤ 100	① 5	⑤ 100	⑤ 25
∨ 6⁰×6⁸								① 40		① 40	① 8
	459	45			20	8		140		140	
254	1621	4470	193	10	1012	48	100	933	5	840	33
	4			4	1621	10					
					2633	58					
4	—	4	4	—	4	4	4	4	4	4	4

MASONRY QUANTITY SURVEYS

123 Beech Drive
Cincinnati, OH 45123

DATE _______
SHEET 10 OF _______
EST. BY _______
BID DUE _______

BLDG. _______________________ OWNER _______________________

LOCATION _____________________ ARCHITECT ___________________

PLAN NOS. ___________ DATE ___________ GEN. CONTR. _________________

2ND FLOOR

4" F. BRK MS B/U		LEDGE L	2" RIGID INSUL	4" F BRK CONC B/U	4" F. BRK C B B/U	C. J.	8" CB B/U w/ 1" &8 @ 24"	SOLDIER D.O.	SPL BRK SILL	8" CB B/U
$0\frac{5\frac{1}{3}}{}$	$12\frac{8}{-}$		$2\frac{8}{-}$	$2\frac{5\frac{1}{3}}{}$	$12\frac{8}{-}$	$15\frac{1\frac{1}{3}}{}$	$12\frac{8}{-}$			$8\frac{0}{-}$
37	56°	56°	56°	56°	56	3	56°	142	37	2 x 4°
(17)	- 4°	56	(150)	(137)	(710)	(46)	(710)	87		(64)
	52	219						39		
14°	659	57	$12\frac{8}{-}$	$12\frac{8}{-}$	8°	8°		50		8°
219	226		4	4	2 x 4°	3		318		8°
(3066)	$1\frac{1\frac{1}{3}}{}$	614	(51)	(51)	(64)	(24)				(64)
$13\frac{9\frac{1}{3}}{}$	56	(63)								
57			$1\frac{4}{-}$	$1\frac{4}{-}$	8°	14°				128
(786)	$7\frac{1\frac{1}{3}}{}$		56	56	8°	7				
	142°		(75)	(75)	(64)	(98)				
$3\frac{4}{-}$	1010		$1\frac{4}{-}$	8°	11°	4°				
226			57	2 x 8°	2 x 16°	6				
(754)	6°		226	(128)	(352)	(24)				
	87		283							
4623	(522)		(378)	8°						
	6°		654	2 (16)	1190	192				
	22°									
	(132)	1386		$1\frac{4}{-}$						
				57°						
				226						
WD $45\frac{0}{-} \times 3\frac{6\frac{2}{3}}{}$	(1) 160			283				(1) 45	(1) 45	
○ WD $8\frac{0}{-}$ R	(1) 20			(378)						
4" F. BRK $6\frac{0}{-} \times 6\frac{0}{-}$				2 72						
	180			72			+ 45	+ 45		
4623	2206	614	654	785	1118	192	710	363	82	128
4	4623									
	6829									

MASONRY QUANTITY SURVEYS

123 Beech Drive
Cincinnati, OH 45123

DATE
SHEET *11* OF
EST. BY
BID DUE

BLDG. ___________________ OWNER ___________________

LOCATION ___________________ ARCHITECT ___________________

PLAN NOS. ___________ DATE ___________ GEN. CONTR. ___________________

2ND FLOOR

4"CB	12"CB	BOND BM 8x8	4"F.BRK CB B/U ON R	8"CB B/U ON R	4"F.BRK CB B/U ON R	FLASH @ Roof	ROLOK CAP 20"W	P.C. LINT 8x8	6"CB INT.	P.C. LINT 6x8	8"CB INT.
6^{0}	10^{8}		8^{0}	8^{0}	INT 8^{0}				14^{0}		14^{0}
2×6^{0}	14^{0}	39^{0}	39^{0}	38^{0}	33^{0}	22^{0}	14^{0}		256^{0}		49^{0}
(72)	(150)		(312)	(304)	(264)				11		(686)
									7		
									$\overline{274^{0}}$		
									(3836)		
DR $9^{0} \times 6^{8}$									(1) 60	(1) 11	
✓ $5^{0} \times 6^{8}$								0 7	(14) 500	(14) 105	(1) 33
BM $224^{0} \times 0^{8}$											(1) 49
OPNG $10^{0} \times 10^{0}$											(1) 100
									560		182
72	150	39	312	304	264	22	14	7	3276	116	504
✓	✓	✓	✓	✓	✓	✓	✓	✓	✓	✓	✓

MASONRY QUANTITY SURVEYS

123 Beech Drive
Cincinnati, OH 45123

DATE
SHEET *12* OF
EST. BY
BID DUE

BLDG. ______________________________ OWNER ______________________________

LOCATION ____________________________ ARCHITECT ___________________________

PLAN NOS. ___________ DATE __________ GEN. CONTR. _________________________

2ND FLOOR

		4"F. BRK CB B/U INT.	4"CB B/U	8"CB INT.	8"CB B/U	P.C. LINT 8×8	P.C. LINT 4×8	12"CB
		10 2⅔	10°	4°	14°			14°
		46°	46°	46°	11°			20°
		5	9	9	(154)			(280)
		9	55°	55				
		16	(550)	(220)				
		11						
		87°		14°				
		(890)		85°				
				56				
				− 20				
				121				
				(1694)				
				1914				
DR	5°×6⁸	(2) 66			(1) 33	(1) 7		
✓	3°×6⁸	(3) 60	(3) 60	(1) 20		(1) 5	(3) 15	
		126	60	20	33			
		754	490	1894	121	12	15	280
		✓	✓	✓	✓	✓	✓	✓

MASONRY QUANTITY SURVEYS

123 Beech Drive
Cincinnati, OH 45123

DATE
SHEET 13 OF
EST. BY
BID DUE

BLDG. _______________________ OWNER _______________________

LOCATION _______________________ ARCHITECT _______________________

PLAN NOS. __________ DATE __________ GEN. CONTR. _______________________

3RD FLOOR

4"CB INT.	12"CB INT.	4"F.BRK MS BIV	BRICK SILL △ 2⅔	SOLDIER D.O.	RECES'D SOLDIER 3"x8" ↑/C SOLID	FLASH @ ROOF	C.J.	LEDGEL	4"F.BRK INT.	P.C. LINT 8x8	8"CB INT.
10⁸	10⁸	12⁰					8⁸		8⁸		3⁴
7⁰	22⁰	409⁰			104⁰	68⁰	4⁰	409⁰	65⁰		65⁰
7	(235)	(490 8)				10	3		(564)		(217)
10						78	4				
24							3				12⁰
(256)							14				98⁰
							(122)				(1176)
											1393
DR 3²x6⁸									(2) 40	(3) 15	(3) 60
BM 140⁰x1⁴											(1) 186
WO 38²x3⁵²⁄₃		(2) 270	(2) 76	(2) 76							
v 37⁰x6⁰		(1) 222	(1) 37	(1) 37							
v 45⁰x3⁴²⁄₃		(1) 160	(1) 45	(1) 45							
LVRE 4⁹x6⁵²⁄₃		(1) 30	—	(1) 5							
WO 104⁰x3⁶²⁄₃		(1) 369	(1) 104	(1) 104							
v 45²x3⁴²⁄₃		(1) 160	(1) 45	(1) 45							
LVRE 5⁵x6⁰		(1) 32	—	(1) 6							
		1243							40		246
256	235	3665	307	318	104	78	122	409	524	15	1147
✓	✓	✓	✓	✓	✓	✓	✓	✓	✓	✓	✓

MASONRY QUANTITY SURVEYS

123 Beech Drive
Cincinnati, OH 45123

DATE
SHEET *14* OF
EST. BY
BID DUE

BLDG. ________________________   OWNER ________________________

LOCATION ________________________   ARCHITECT ________________________

PLAN NOS. ____________ DATE ____________   GEN. CONTR. ________________________

3RD FLOOR

		4" CB	P.C.								
		B/U	LINT								
			4 x 8								
		8⁸									
		65									
		(564)									
DR 3⁰ x 6⁸ ②	40 ② 10										
		40	70								
		524	10								
		✗	✗								

MASONRY QUANTITY SURVEYS

123 Beech Drive
Cincinnati, OH 45123

DATE ___
SHEET *15* OF ___
EST. BY ___
BID DUE ___

BLDG. ___________________________ OWNER ___________________________

LOCATION ___________________________ ARCHITECT ___________________________

PLAN NOS. ___________ DATE ___________ GEN. CONTR. ___________________________

4TH FLOOR

		4" F. BRK MS B/U	BRICK SILL, □=2⅓	SOLDIER D.O.	RECES'D SOLDIER 3x8 SOLID	C.J.	LEDGE L	4" F. BRK INT.	4" CB B/U	8" CB INT.	12" CB INT.
								8⁸⁻	8⁸⁻	3⁴⁻	10⁸⁻
								57	57	57	22
								(494)	(494)	(190)	(235)
		REPEAT FROM 3RD FLOOR								12⁰⁻ 118⁸⁻	
		3665	307	318	104	122	409			(1416)	
										1606	
OR 3⁰⁻x6⁸⁻								② 40	② 40	③ 60	
BM 185⁰⁻x1⁴⁻										① 246	
								40	40	306	
		3665	307	318	104	122	409	454	454	1300	235
		✓	✓	✓	✓	✓	✓	✓	✓	✓	✓

MASONRY QUANTITY SURVEYS

123 Beech Drive
Cincinnati, OH 45123

DATE
SHEET *16* OF
EST. BY
BID DUE

BLDG. ___________________________   OWNER ___________________________

LOCATION ___________________________   ARCHITECT ___________________________

PLAN NOS. ___________ DATE ___________   GEN. CONTR. ___________________________

4TH FLOOR

		4"CB	P.C. LINT 8x8	P.C. LINT 4x8							
		12⁰									
		8⁰									
		(96)									
DR 3⁰ x 6⁸		③ 15	② 10								
		96	15	10							
		✗	✗	✗							

MASONRY QUANTITY SURVEYS

123 Beech Drive
Cincinnati, OH 45123

DATE _______
SHEET *17* OF _______
EST. BY _______
BID DUE _______

BLDG. _______________________ OWNER _______________________

LOCATION _____________________ ARCHITECT ____________________

PLAN NOS. __________ DATE __________ GEN. CONTR. _______________

5TH FLOOR

		4" F. BRK MS B/U	BRICK SILL	SOLDIER	RECES'D SOLDIER	C.J.	LEDGE L			
		REPEAT FROM 3RD FLOOR								
		3665	307	318	104	122	409			
		3665	307	318	104	122	409			
		✓	✓	✓	✓	✓	✓			

MASONRY QUANTITY SURVEYS

123 Beech Drive
Cincinnati, OH 45123

DATE
SHEET *18* OF
EST. BY
BID DUE

BLDG. _______________________   OWNER _______________________

LOCATION _______________________   ARCHITECT _______________________

PLAN NOS. ____________ DATE ____________   GEN. CONTR. _______________________

5TH FLOOR

		4" F.BRK INT.	4" CB B/U	8" CB	12" CB	4" CB	P.C. LINT 8×8	P.C. LINT 4×8			
		8^8	8^8	3^4	10^8	10^8					
		58°	58°	58°	22°	27°					
		(503)	(503)	(194)	(235)	(288)					
				12°							
				96°							
				(1152)							
				1346							
DR	$3^\circ × 6^8$	② 40	② 40	③ 60			③ 15	② 10			
BM	$160^\circ × 1^2$			① 213							
		40	40	273							
		463	463	1073	235	288	15	10			
		4	4	4	4	4	4	4			

MASONRY QUANTITY SURVEYS

123 Beech Drive
Cincinnati, OH 45123

DATE 19
SHEET   OF
EST. BY
BID DUE

BLDG. __________   OWNER __________

LOCATION __________   ARCHITECT __________

PLAN NOS. __________ DATE __________   GEN. CONTR. __________

6TH FLOOR

	4' F. BRK MS B/U	BRICK SILL	SOLDIER D.O.	C.J.	BRICK SILL	LEDGE L	4" F. BRK INT.	4' CB B/U	8" CB	P.C. LINT 4×8
		2⅔								
	13^4			13^4			9^4	9^4	1^4	
	236			14	182	228	58	58	58	
	(3147)			(187)			61	61	61	
							119	119	119	
	0^8						(1111)	(1111)	(159)	
	182									
	(122)									
	3269									
WD 30°×3 $6^{⅔}$	(1) 106		(1) 30	(1) 30						
✓ 45°×✓	(1) 160		(1) 45	(1) 45						
LVR 5⁵×6°	(1) 33		—	(1) 6						
DR 3°×6⁸							(7) 140	(7) 140		(7) 35
✓ 10×8							(1) 80	(1) 80		
	299						220	220		
	2970	75	81	187	182	228	891	891	159	35
	✓	✓	✓	✓	✓	✓	✓	✓	✓	✓

MASONRY QUANTITY SURVEYS

123 Beech Drive
Cincinnati, OH 45123

DATE 20
SHEET ____ OF
EST. BY
BID DUE

BLDG. ____________________ OWNER ____________________

LOCATION ____________________ ARCHITECT ____________________

PLAN NOS. ____________ DATE ____________ GEN. CONTR. ____________________

6TH FLOOR

		12"CB	4"CB	8"CB	4" Fire Brick	Slate 1"×5"	Ash Pit C.O. Door 20×16	L 6"×4"×¼" 4 8 Lg	Damper 4°	Flue Lining 16"×20"	Temp. Glass Door
		10^8	10^8	10^8	3^0						10^0
		22	22	74^0	5^0	26^0	1	2	2	1	
		(235)	(235)	(790)	(15)			(10)		(10)	
					4^0						
					2^6						
					(10)						
					25						

DR 3^0×6^8

By others

| | | 235 | 235 | 790 | 25 | 26 | 1 | 10 | 2 | 10 | |
| | | ✓ | ✓ | ✓ | ✓ | ✓ | ✓ | ✓ | ✓ | ✓ | ✗ |

MASONRY QUANTITY SURVEYS

123 Beech Drive
Cincinnati, OH 45123

DATE
SHEET *21* OF
EST. BY
BID DUE

BLDG. ________________________ OWNER ________________________

LOCATION ______________________ ARCHITECT ____________________

PLAN NOS. __________ DATE __________ GEN. CONTR. ________________

6TH FLOOR

		CAST CONC. HEARTH $3^0 \times 4^0 \times 0^8$		12" CB	4" CB	8" CB	L $4" \times 4" \times \frac{1}{4}"$ 5^0 Lg	FILL	SPARK ARRESTER	WTR PRF CEM CAP $8" \times 9^0$
				4^0	1^4	34		6^0		
		1		2×3^0	2×4^0	18^0	1	$0^6 \times 5^0$	1	1
				㉔	⑪	㊀	⑤	⑮		
						$\dfrac{6^0}{114}$		$\dfrac{6^0}{0^6 \times 2^0}$		
						㊳		⑥		
						128		21		

		1		24	11	128	5	21	1	9
		4		4	4	4	4	4	4	4

MASONRY QUANTITY SURVEYS

123 Beech Drive
Cincinnati, OH 45123

DATE ______
SHEET **22** OF ______
EST. BY ______
BID DUE ______

BLDG. ______________________   OWNER ______________________

LOCATION ______________________   ARCHITECT ______________________

PLAN NOS. ______ DATE ______   GEN. CONTR. ______________________

ROOF

		4" F.BRK CB B/v	8" CB B/v	12" CB	8" F.BRK	BOND BM 8×8	8" CB 4" hi	P.C. LINT 8×8			
		$12\frac{8}{-}$	$12\frac{8}{-}$	$0\frac{8}{-}$	$1\frac{4}{-}$		1 C				
		$84\frac{8}{-}$	$84\frac{8}{-}$	$84\frac{8}{-}$	$84\frac{8}{-}$	$44\frac{8}{-}$	$44\frac{8}{-}$				
		$84\frac{8}{-}$	$84\frac{8}{-}$	$84\frac{8}{-}$	$84\frac{8}{-}$	$44\frac{8}{-}$	$44\frac{8}{-}$				
		$169\frac{4}{-}$	$169\frac{4}{-}$	$169\frac{4}{-}$	$169\frac{+}{-}$	$89\frac{+}{-}$	$89\frac{+}{-}$				
		(2145)	(2145)	(113)	(226)						
			$2\frac{8}{-}$	$2\frac{8}{-}$							
			$3\frac{4}{-}$	$20°$							
			(9)	(54)							
			$14°$	167							
			$20°$								
			(280)								
			2434								
DR	$3°×6\frac{8}{-}$	② 40	②1 60					②1 15			
WD	$3\frac{4}{-}×1\frac{6}{-}$	① 5	① 5					① 6			
✓	$4°×3°$	111 36	111 36					111 18			
✓	$4°×1\frac{#}{-}$	1 5	1 5					1 6			
		86	106	~~167~~							
		2059	2328	167	226	90	90	+ 45			
		↵	↵	↵	↵	↵	↵	↵			

MASONRY QUANTITY SURVEYS

123 Beech Drive
Cincinnati, OH 45123

DATE
SHEET 23 OF
EST. BY
BID DUE

BLDG. ______ OWNER ______

LOCATION ______ ARCHITECT ______

PLAN NOS. ______ DATE ______ GEN. CONTR. ______

BASE BID RE-CAP (SHEET 1 OF 6)

	4"F.BRK CB B/U	4"F.BRK MS B/U	4"F.BRK CONC B/U	SOLDIER D.O.	BRICK SILL 2 2/3 W/FLASH	BRICK SILL	BRICK SILL 4" W/FLASH	BRICK CORN 45° D.O.	4"F.BRK ON CURVE EXT.	4"F.BRICK ON CURVE INT.
BSMT	1137		395	33						
"										
1ST FL	81	6806		383	187	122	45			
"	780	684	785					19	546	462
AUD.	1400							32		
"				6						
"			204					3		
"										
1ST FL										
2ND FL	1118	6829	785	363	82					
"									312	264
"										
3RD FL		3665		318	307					
"										
4TH FL		3665		318	307					
"										
5TH FL		3665		318	307					
"										
6TH FL		2970		81	75					
"										
"										
ROOF	2059									
→	6575	28,284	2169	1820	1265	122	45	54	858	726
	× 6.8	× 6.8	× 6.8	× 6.8	× 1.5	× 13.5	× 1.5	× 4.5	× 6.8	× 6.8
	44,710	192,332	14,750	—	1898	1647	68	—	5835	4937
	① ✓	② ✓	③ ✓		④ ✓	⑤ ✓	⑥ ✓		⑦ ✓	⑧ ✓
		MS TIES	DVTL SLOT	D.O.	D.O.	D.O.	D.O.	D.O.	D.O.	
		× .375	× .75	× 6.8	× 1.5	× 13.5	× 1.5	× 4.5	× 6.8	
		10,607 ✓	1627 ✓	12,376 ✓	1898 ✓	1647 ✓	68 ✓	243 ✓	5835 ✓	
			DVTL TIES		FLASH	FLASH	FLASH			
			× .375		× 1.0	× 2.5	× 1.0			
			814 ✓		1265 ✓	305 ✓	45 ✓			

ALT G-1 (bracketing AUD. through 1ST FL rows)

no need to repeat all these items

Cut off on dotted line and list them on sheet 6 of 6 only

see back side for accumulation of F. Brick items ① to ⑱ sh 23A

SHEET 23A

BACK SIDE OF SHEET 23 (FACE BRICK ITEMS ① TO ⑱)

ITEM	4" F. BRK EXT.	4" F. BRK INT.	4" F. BRK ON CURVE D.O. EXT.	4" F. BRK ON CURVE D.O. INT. SCREEN	
①	44710				
②	192332				
③	14750				
④	1898				
⑤	1647				
⑥	68				
⑦	5835		5835		
⑧	—	4937	4937		
⑨	6516				
⑩	810				
⑪	126				
⑫	3482				
⑬	1845				
⑭	—	4570		4570	SCREEN
⑮	—	5646		5646	SCREEN ON CURVE
⑯	345				
⑰	—	27330			
⑱	3074				
	277438	42483	10,772 pcs	10,216 pcs	
	42483				
	319,921 pcs				

MASONRY QUANTITY SURVEYS

123 Beech Drive
Cincinnati, OH 45123

DATE 24
SHEET 24 OF
EST. BY
BID DUE

BLDG. _______________________ OWNER _______________________

LOCATION _____________________ ARCHITECT ___________________

PLAN NOS. __________ DATE __________ GEN. CONTR. ____________

BASE BID   RE·CAP   SHEET 2 of 6

ALT G-1

	BRICK PROV'D HDR CS D.O.	BRICK SILL [diagram] W/FLASH	ROLOK CAP 8"W W/FLASH	Com. Brk B/U [diagram 1⁵⁄₁₈]	ROLOK CAP 17"W W/FLASH	4"F. BRK BRK B/U W/FLASH	8" Com Brk B/U	ROLOK CAP 20"W W/FLASH	12" Com BRK B/U	4"F. BRK SCREEN INT. 2" INSUL.
BSMT										
"										
1ST										
"	32									
AUD.		180	180	180	14	180				
"						60	48	150	200	896
"						272				
"										
1ST										
2ND								14		
"										
"										
3RD										
"										
4TH										
"										
5TH										
"										
6TH		182								
"										
"										
ROOF										
	32	362	180	180	14	512	48	164	200	896
	×1.0	×18.0	×4.5	×22.5	×9.0	×6.8	×13.6	×11.25	×20.4	×5.1
	—	6516	810	4050	126	3482	653	1845	4080	4570
		(9) ✓	(10) ✓	✓	(11) ✓	(12) ✓	✓	(13) ✓	✓	(14) ✓
	D.O.	D.O.	D.O.		D.O.			D.O.		D.O.
	×1.5	×18.0	×4.5		×9.0			×11.25		×5.1
	48	6516	810		126			1845		4570
	✓	✓	✓		✓			✓		✓
		FLASH	FLASH		FLASH	FLASH		FLASH		2" INSUL
		×2.5	×1.0		×1.5	×1.0		1.5		×1.0
		905	180		21	3482		246		896
		✓	✓		✓	✓		✓		✓

see back side for accumulation of special items sheet 24A

SHEET 24A

BACK SIDE OF SHEET 24   (RE-CAP OF SPECIAL ITEMS)

COM BRK	SOLDIER	SILL	ROLOK	FLASH
4050	12376	1898	810	1265
653	943	1647	126	305
4080	48	68	1845	45
925		6516	345	905
9708	13,367	10,129	468	180
			3594	21
				3482
				246
				51
				2696
				100
				9296

MASONRY QUANTITY SURVEYS

123 Beech Drive
Cincinnati, OH 45123

DATE
SHEET 25 OF
EST. BY
BID DUE

BLDG. ___________________ OWNER ___________________

LOCATION ___________________ ARCHITECT ___________________

PLAN NOS. ___________ DATE ___________ GEN. CONTR. ___________________

BASE B10   RE-CAP   (SHEET 3 of 6)

Margin note (left side, along dotted cut line): No need to repeat all these items — Cut on dotted line and list them on sheet 6 of 6 only

4" F.BRK SCREEN ON CURVE (w/ FLASH)	ROLOK 12" W	COM BRK FLL	4" F.BRK INT.	SOLDIER REC'D 3×8 1c SOLID D.O.	FIRE BRICK	8" F.BRK	4" CB B/U	8" CB	4" CB
							168	40	12
								3114	46
							24		
1107									
	51	136						1450	
			933				840	2633	
								504	72
			754				490	1894	
			524	104					256
							524		
			454	104			454	1300	
									96
				104					
			463				463	1073	288
			891				891	159	
					25			790	235
								128	11
						226			90
1107	51	136	4019	312	25	226	3854	13085	1106
×5.1	×6.75	×6.8	×6.8	×4.5	×6.8	×13.6	×1.125	×1.125	×1.125
5646	345	925	27,330	—	170	3074	4336	14,721	1245
(15) ✓	(16) ✓	✓	(17) ✓		✓	(18) ✓	✓	4,801	✓
								19,552	
D.O.	D.O			D.O.			8" DUR	✓	
×5.1	×6.75			×4.5			×1.125		
5646	345			1404			4336	8" DUR	4" DUR
✓	✓			✓			✓	×1.125	×1.125
								14721	1245
2" INSUL	FLASH			SOLID				✓	✓
×1.0	×1.0			×1.5					
1107	51			468					
✓	✓			✓					

MASONRY QUANTITY SURVEYS

123 Beech Drive
Cincinnati, OH 45123

DATE
SHEET 26 OF
EST. BY
BID DUE

BLDG. ___________________________   OWNER ___________________________

LOCATION ________________________   ARCHITECT _______________________

PLAN NOS. ___________ DATE _________   GEN. CONTR. ____________________

BASE BID RE-CAP   (SHEET 4 of 6)

	8"CB B/U	12"CB	8"CB w/ #8@24	8"CB SCOR'D	4"CB SCOR'D	6"CB	6"GLCB	8"GLCB	P.C. LINT 4x8	P.C. LINT 8x8
	811	12							8	
		628	232	1779	53	72				15
		117	1018							
			1160							
										33
		254				4470	193	58	33	5
	128		710							
	304	150				3276				7
	121	280							15	12
		235	1147							15
		235							10	
									10	15
		235							10	15
									35	
		235								
		94								
	2328	167								45
	3692	2572	4267	1729	53	7818	193	58	121	162
	×1.125	×1.125	×1.125	×1.125	×1.125	×1.125	×1.125	×1.125		
	4154	2894	4801	1946	60	8795	218	66		
	4	4	4	4	4	4	4	4	4	4
	12"TAB	12"DUR	8"DUR	8"DUR	4"DUR	6"DUR	6"DUR	8"DUR		
	×1.125	×1.125	×1.125	×1.125	×1.125	×1.125	×1.125	×1.125		
	4154	2894	4801	1946	60	8795	218	66		
	4	4	4	4	4	4	4	4		
			#8 ROD	FILL						
			×.56	×.28						
			2390	1195						
			4	4						

Cut off on dotted line
(see note sheet 25)

See back side for accumulation of reinforcing items — sheet 26A

324

SHEET 26A

BACK SIDE OF SHEET 26 (RE-CAP OF REINFORCING ITEMS)

8" DUR	4" DUR	12" TAB	12" DUR	6" DUR
4336	1245	4154	2894	8795
1472	60			218
4801				
1946				
66				
12,621	1305	4154	2894	9013
× .7	× .7	× .7	× .7	× .7
8835	914	2908	2026	6310
✓	✓	✓	✓	✓

CONVERT UNITS TO LF

$$PCS \times 1.333 \times \frac{10.5}{10} \times .5 = .699 \quad (use\ .7)$$

MASONRY QUANTITY SURVEYS

123 Beech Drive
Cincinnati, OH 45123

DATE ___
SHEET **7** OF ___
EST. BY ___
BID DUE ___

BLDG. ___________________

OWNER ___________________

LOCATION ___________________

ARCHITECT ___________________

PLAN NOS. ___________ DATE ___________

GEN. CONTR. ___________________

BASE BID   RE-CAP   (SHEET 5 of 6)

		P.C. LINT 6×8	BOND BM 8×8	P.C. CONC SILL 5×5	LEDGE L D.O. FLASH	C.J. D.O.	2" RIG'D INSUL (SET ONLY)	FLASH @ ROOF	SLATE SURROUND 1"×5'	ASH PIT DOOR 20×16	LS 6"×4"×4"
					128						
					499	65					
			56				1065				
			180			20					
				6							
		100			614	192	654				
		116	39					22			
					409	122		78			
	TRIM				409	122					
					409	122					
					228	187					
									26	1	10
			90								
		216	365	6	2696	830	1719	100 ×1.00	26	1	10
		↵	↵	↵	↵	↵	−100 +896 +1107 3722 ↵	100 ↵	↵	↵	− +5 15 ↵
					FLASH ×1.0 2696 ↵						

MASONRY QUANTITY SURVEYS

123 Beech Drive
Cincinnati, OH 45123

DATE _______
SHEET _**78**_ OF _______
EST. BY _______
BID DUE _______

BLDG. _______________________ OWNER _______________________

LOCATION _______________________ ARCHITECT _______________________

PLAN NOS. _______ DATE _______ GEN. CONTR. _______________________

BASE BID RE-CAP (Sheet 6 of 6)

SHEET NO.	FLOOR	DAMPER 4" Lg	FLUE LINING	CONC. SLAB 3⁰ × 4⁶ × 0⁸	LS 4×4×¼	MORTAR FILL	SPARK ARRESTR	CEMENT CAP 1" × 8"		
						CF	LF			
1	BSMT									
2	"									
3	1ST									
4	"									
5	AUD.					↑				
6	"			ALT G·1	DEDUCT	THESE	ITEMS			
7	"					↓				
8	"									
9	1ST									
10	2ND									
11	"									
12	"									
13	3RD									
14	"									
15	4TH									
16	"									
17	5TH									
18	"									
19	6TH									
20	"	2	10							
21	"			1	5	21	1	9		
22	ROOF									
		2	10	1	5	21	1	9		
		↙	↙	↙	↙	↙	↙	↙		

MASONRY QUANTITY SURVEYS

123 Beech Drive
Cincinnati, OH 45123

DATE 29
SHEET OF
EST. BY
BID DUE

BLDG. ___________________________ OWNER___________________________

LOCATION ________________________ ARCHITECT _______________________

PLAN NOS. ____________ DATE ______ GEN. CONTR. _____________________

RE·CAP   ALT G·1   (OMIT AUDITORIUM)   SHEET 1 OF 3

		4"F.BRK CB B/U		BOND BM 8x8	SLOPE SILL w/FLASH	ROLOK CAP 8"W	Com BRK FLL	45° BRK D.O.	C.J. D.O.	ROLOK CAP 17"W	4"F.BRK BRK B/U w/FLASH
5	AUD.	1400		180	180	180	180	32	20	14	180
6	"										60
7	"							3			272
8	"	(−572)									
		828		180	180	180	180	35	20	14	512
		×6.8		×1.0	×18.0	×4.5	×22.5	×4.5		×9.0	×6.8
		5631		180	3240	810	4050	—	—	126	3482
		3240		✓	✓	✓	653			✓	✓
		810					4080				
		126					925				
		3482			D.O.	D.O.	—	D.O.	D.O.	D.O.	
		1688			×18.0	×4.5	9708	×4.5	×1.0	×9.0	
		789			3240	810		158	20	126	
		345			✓	✓	✓	✓	✓	✓	
		4570									
		5646									
		24,327			FLASH ×2.5	FLASH ×1.0				FLASH ×1.5	FLASH ×1.0
		✓			450	180				21	512
					✓	✓				✓	✓

MASONRY QUANTITY SURVEYS

123 Beech Drive
Cincinnati, OH 45123

DATE
SHEET 30 OF
EST. BY
BID DUE

BLDG. __________________________ OWNER __________________________

LOCATION __________________________ ARCHITECT __________________________

PLAN NOS. __________ DATE __________ GEN. CONTR. __________________________

RE-CAP   ALT G-1 (OMIT AUDITORIUM)   SHEET 2 OF 3

		8" Com Brk B/U	Soldier	P.C. Conc Sill 5×5 D.O.	Rolok Cap 20"W w/Flash	12" Com Brk B/U	4"F. Brk Screen 2" Insul	4"F. Brk Screen	8" CB Int.	P.C. Lint 8×8	4"F. Brk Conc B/U
5	AUD.										
6	"	48	6	6	150	200	896	1107			
7	"								1450	33	204
8	"										(-88)
		48	6	6	150	200	896	1107	1450	33	116
		×13.6		×1.0	×11.25	×20.4	×5.1	×5.1	×1.125	×1.0	×6.8
		653	—	6	1688	4080	4570	5646	1632	33	789
		✓		✓	✓	✓	✓	✓	✓	✓	✓
			D.O.		D.O.		D.O.	D.O			DVTL SLOT
			×6.8		×11.25		×5.1	×5.1			×.75
			41		1688		4570	5646			87
			✓		✓		✓	✓			✓
					FLASH		2" INSUL		8" DUR		DVTL ANG
					×1.5		×1.0		×1.125		×.375
					225		896		1632		44
					✓		✓		✓		✓

MASONRY QUANTITY SURVEYS

123 Beech Drive
Cincinnati, OH 45123

DATE ______
SHEET 31 OF ______
EST. BY ______
BID DUE ______

BLDG. ______________________   OWNER ______________________

LOCATION ____________________   ARCHITECT __________________

PLAN NOS. __________ DATE __________   GEN. CONTR. ______________

RE-CAP   ALT. G-1 (OMIT AUDITORIUM)   SHEET 3 OF 3

		ROLOK 12" W	4" COM BRK FILL		8" CB B/U w/ #8@24"	2" RIGID INSUL	ROLOK D.O.	SOLDIER D.O.	SCREEN D.O.	FLASH	8" DUR
		w/ FLASH									
5	AUD				1160						
6	"										
7	"	51	136								
8	"				(−572)	(−88)					
		51	136		588						
		×6.75	×6.8		×1.125						
		345	925		662	—					
		✓	✓		✓						
		D.O.			8" DUR		810	—	4570	450	1637
		×6.75			×1.125		126		5646	180	662
		345			662		1688		10,216	21	
		✓			✓		345		✓	512	2294
		FLASH			#8 ROD		2969			225	✓
		×1.0			×.56		✓			51	
		51			330					1439	
		✓			✓					✓	
					FILL						
					×.28						
					165						
					✓						

MASONRY QUANTITY SURVEYS

123 Beech Drive
Cincinnati, OH 45123

DATE
SHEET 32 OF 34
EST. BY *RYK*
BID DUE

BLDG. CARLIN HALL   OWNER STATE

LOCATION COLLEGE CAMPUS   ARCHITECT G-B-B

PLAN NOS. A-1 TO A-36   S-1 TO S-17   DATE AUG. 87   GEN. CONTR. JB INC.

SUMMARY BASE BID   SHEET 1 OF 2

ITEM	UNIT	QUANTITY	MATERIAL Unit	MATERIAL Amount	LABOR Unit	LABOR Amount	WORK	TOTAL
F. BRICK @ $260 ⁰⁰	PCS	319 921	.268	85 738	.39	124 770	560	
COM BRICK	✓	9 708	.091	884	.36	3495	600	
FIRE BRICK	✓	170	.557	95	.72	123		
4" CB B/U	✓	4336	.481	2086	1.19	5160		
4" CB	✓	1245	.481	599	1.20	1494		
6" CB	✓	8795	.585	5145	1.29	11346		
8" CB B/U	✓	4154	.753	3128	1.34	5567		
8" CB	✓	19522	.753	14701	1.36	26550		
12" CB	✓	2894	1.094	3166	2.17	6280		
8" CB SCOR. 8×8	✓	1946	.783	1524	2.25	4379		
4" CB SCOR. 8×8	✓	60	.511	31	1.37	83		
8" GLCB	✓	66	3.586	237	1.49	99		
6" GLCB	✓	218	3.377	737	1.43	312		
MORTAR BRK EXT.	✓	297024	.051	15149	—	—		
" " INT.	✓	42483	.051	2167	—	—		
" CB	✓	43238	.058	2508	—	—		
CLEAN BRK	✓	319921	.004	1280	.04	12797		
" CB	✓	32429	—	—	.02	649		
TIES @ METAL STUDS	✓	10607	—	—	.15	1592		
" " CONCRETE	✓	814	.10	82	.05	41		
DVTL SLOT	LF	1627	.14	228	—	—		
SOLDIERS D.O.	PCS	13367	—	—	.09	1204		
SILL @ $600 ⁰⁰ D.O.	✓	10129	.618	6260	.12	1216		
BRICK ON CURVE D.O.	✓	10772	—	—	.10	1078		
BRICK SCREEN D.O.	✓	10216	—	—	.15	1533		
ROLOK CAP D.O.	✓	3594	—	—	.08	288		
FLASHING	SF	9296	—	—	.15	1395		
2" RIGID INSUL.	✓	3722	—	—	.25	931		
REINF ROD #8	LF	2390	—	—	.50	1195		
FILL 8" CB W/ CONC.	PCS	1195	.50	598	.50	598		
4" REINF. TR.	LF	914	.082	75	—	—		
6" " "	✓	6310	.083	524	—	—		
8" " "	✓	9835	.087	769	—	—		
12" " "	✓	2026	.095	193	—	—		
12" " TAB	✓	2908	.240	698	—	—		

(CONT'D NEXT PAGE)

MASONRY QUANTITY SURVEYS

123 Beech Drive
Cincinnati, OH 45123

DATE
SHEET 33 OF 34
EST. BY
BID DUE

BLDG. ___________________________ OWNER___________________________

LOCATION ________________________ ARCHITECT________________________

PLAN NOS. __________ DATE __________ GEN. CONTR. _____________________

SUMMARY BASE BID   SHEET 2 OF 2

ITEM	UNIT	QUANTITY	MATERIAL		LABOR		WORK	TOTAL
			Unit	Amount	Unit	Amount		
P.C. LINT 4x8	LF	121	1.71	207	.88	107		
" " 8x8	✓	162	3.82	619	2.08	337		
" " 6x8	✓	216	2.69	582	1.69	365		
BOND BEAM 8x8	✓	365	.83	303	1.01	369		
PC CONC. SILL 5x5	✓	6	1.54	10	.87	6		
" " FLOOR–FIRE PL.	EA	1	—	20	—	100		
ASH PIT DOOR	✓	1	—	—	—	10		
FIRE PLACE DAMPERS	✓	2	—	—	—	30		
SPARK ARRESTER	✓	1	—	—	—	40		
LEDGE LS	LF	2696	—	—	1.00	2696		
FIREPLACE LS	✓	15	—	—	1.00	15		
C.J.	✓	830	—	—	1.00	830		
SLATE SURROUND 1"x5"	✓	26	—	—	2.00	52		
FLUE LINING 16" X 20"	✓	10	15.00	150	10.00	100		
CEM. WASH @ CAP	✓	9	1.00	9	2.00	18		
DATE STONE 2"x8"x24"	EA	1	—	500	—	50		
SAMPLE PANEL	✓	1	—	150	—	200		
				151 152		219 500		
		SALES TAX 5½%		8314		72 435	FRGS 33%	
				159 466		291 935		
						159 466	MTL	
						451 401		
						36 113	T&E 8%	
						487 514		
						19 501	OH 4%	
						507 015		
						40 562	P 8%	
						547 577		

MASONRY QUANTITY SURVEYS

123 Beech Drive
Cincinnati, OH 45123

DATE
SHEET 34 OF 34
EST. BY
BID DUE

BLDG. _______________________ OWNER_______________________

LOCATION _______________________ ARCHITECT_______________________

PLAN NOS. ___________ DATE ___________ GEN. CONTR. _______________________

SUMMARY   ALT G-1 (OMIT AUDITORIUM)   SHEET 1 OF 1

ITEM	UNIT	QUANTITY	MATERIAL		LABOR		WORK	TOTAL
			Unit	Amount	Unit	Amount		
F. BRK	PCS	26 327	.268	7056	.39	10268		
COM. BRK	✓	9708	.091	884	.36	3495		
8" CB B/U	✓	662	.753	499	1.34	888		
8" CB	✓	1632	.753	1229	1.36	2220		
MORTAR BRK	✓	26327	.051	1343	—	—		
" CB	✓	3294	.058	192	—	—		
CLEAN BRK	✓	26 327	.004	106	.04	1054		
" CB	✓	3294	—	—	.02	66		
DVTL ANC	✓	44	.10	5	.05	3		
DVTL SLOT	LF	87	.14	13	—	—		
SILL D.O.	✓	3240	.618	2003	.12	389		
BRICK SCREEN D.O.	✓	10216	—	—	.15	1533		
ROLOK CAP D.O.	✓	2969	—	—	.08	238		
FLASHING	SF	1439	—	—	.15	216		
REINF. ROD #8	LF	330	—	—	.50	165		
FILL 8" CB W/ CONC	PCS	165	.50	83	.80	83		
8" REINF. TR.	LF	2294	.087	200	—	—		
BOND BEAM 8x8	✓	180	.83	150	1.01	182		
C.J.	✓	20	—	—	1.00	20		
P.C. CONC SILL 5x5	✓	6	1.54	10	.87	6		
P.C. LINT 8x8	✓	33	3.82	127	2.08	69		
				13 900		20 895		
		SALES TAX 5½%		765		6896	FRGS 33%	
				14665		27791		
						14665	MTL	
						42456		
						3397	T&E 8%	
						45853		
						1835	OH 4%	
						47688		
						3816	P 8%	
						$ 51,504		

GLOSSARY

A

Accelerator: In masonry, any ingredient added to mortar to speed drying and solidifying.

Admix: Any material other than water, aggregate, lime, and cement that is added to mortar or grout to improve the quality.

Adobe brick: An unfired clay brick dried in the sun.

Aggregate: The sand or gravel in mortar.

Ashlar masonry: Masonry made up of rectangular units of various sizes, generally larger in size than a brick, having squared bed, bonded together, and laid in mortar. Ashlar masonry may be coursed, random or patterned.

B

Backup: Units behind, or backing up, other masonry construction, such as concrete block in a wall composed of face brick and block.

Bat: An end portion of a brick, approximately a half brick.

Batter: Masonry that is receding or sloping back in successive courses; the opposite of a corbel.

Bed joint: The horizontal mortar joint upon which the masonry units are laid.

Belt course: A continuous horizontal band of masonry, such as window sills which are made continuous; sometimes called *string course* or *sill course*.

Bond: To tie the various wythes of a masonry wall by lapping one unit over another; the pattern formed by the exposed faces of the unit; also, the adhesion of mortar to the units.

Bullnose: Unit with rounded edges. Jamb and sill units are commonly bullnosed for safety. Standard radius is 1''.

Buttering: Placing mortar on a masonry unit with a trowel.

C

Cavity wall: A construction of masonry laid up with a continuous air space between the wythes. The wythes are usually tied together with metal ties or bonding units.

Ceramic color glaze: An opaque colored glaze of satin or gloss finish obtained by spraying the clay body with a compound of metallic oxides and burning at high temperatures, fusing the glaze to the body, making them inseparable.

Clay: A natural mineral aggregate consisting essentially of hydrous aluminum silicate. It is plastic when sufficiently wetted, rigid when dried, and can be vitrified or fired to a high temperature.

Closer: The last masonry unit laid in a course. It may be whole or a portion of a unit. Sometimes spelled *closure*.

Closure: Supplementary or short length units used at corners or jambs to maintain bond patterns. (See *Closer.*)

Collar joint: The vertical longitudinal joint between wythes of masonry.

Common bond: Brickwork laid up of stretchers and headers exposed in the face of the wall. Sixth course headers are most common.

Composite wall: Multiple wythe construction in which at least one of the wythes is dissimilar to the other, *i.e.,* block and brick.

Coping: The material or units used to form a cap or finish on top of a wall, pier, or pilaster to protect the masonry below from the penetration of water from above.

Corbel: A shelf or ledge formed by projecting courses of masonry cut from the face of the wall.

Cramp: A U-shaped metal fastening to hold adjacent units of masonry together, as in a wall coping or a stone slab.

Culling: Sorting brick for size, color and/or quality.

Cut joints: Masonry bed and head joints cut flush with trowel.

D

Dampproofing: The layer of moisture-impervious material in the joints of masonry at locations susceptible to water penetration. Also, to plaster a basement wall and apply bituminous material to the plaster.

Dentil: The clogged or tooth-like members which project under a cornice, used for decorative effect.

Dog's tooth: Brick laid so their corners project from the face of the wall.

Double brick: A solid masonry unit whose nominal dimensions are 4" x 5⅓" x 8."

Drip: Groove or slot cut beneath and slightly behind the forward edge of a projecting stone member, such as a sill or coping, to cause water to drip off and deter it from penetrating the wall.

Dutch arch: In masonry, a brick arch which is flat at both the top and bottom, constructed with ordinary bricks which are not worked to a wedge shape but are laid so as to slope outwards from the middle of the arch.

E

Efflorescence: A whitish powder sometimes found on the surface of masonry, caused by the deposition of soluble salts.

Equivalent thickness: Average thickness of solid material in a wall or partition. It is found by taking the total volume of the wall unit, subtracting the volume of core spaces and dividing this volume by the area of the face of the unit.

Exfoliation: Scaling or flaking off the surface.

F

Fat mortar: Mortar containing a high percentage of cementitious components. It is a sticky mortar which adheres to a trowel.

Fire clay: A clay which is highly resistant to heat without deforming; used for making brick.

Fireproofing: To cover steel with masonry or other materials to retard fire damage.

Fire wall: Any wall built for the purpose of restricting or preventing the spread of fire in a building; a wall of solid masonry which subdivides a building to prevent the spread of fire. Such a wall begins at the foundation of the building and extends continuously through all stories to, and above, the roof.

Flagging: A pavement made of stone slabs is known as flagging or flagstone.

Flashing: A thin impervious material placed in mortar joints and through air spaces in masonry walls to prevent water penetration and/or provide water drainage; also, manufacturing method to produce specific color tones on brick.

Flue liner: A fireclay core of lining for a chimney.

Freestone: Stone with no tendency to split in any preferential direction; usually stone that is fine grained, good for carving.

French arch: In masonry, a type of bonded arch which is flat at both top and bottom, having the bricks sloping outward from a common center.

Fringe benefits: The portion of the worker's wages paid into trust funds administered by the unions. These are paid by the employer and cover such things as pension, health and welfare, and construction advancement program.

Frog: A depression in the bed surface of a brick.

G

Granite: An igneous rock composed chiefly of feldspar but containing also some quartz and mica.

Gross area: The width times length of the unit in the bearing plane. Net area is the gross area times percent solid.

Grout: Mixture of cementitious material and aggregate which is proportioned to produce pouring or pumping consistency without segregation of the material.

Gypsum: Soft mineral consisting of hydrous calcium sulfate. The raw material from which plaster is made.

H

Header: A masonry unit laid across a wall with the end surface exposed. Headers are usually used as bonders.

Hollow brick: One whose net cross-sectional area in any plane parallel to the bearing surface is less than 75% of the gross area.

Hollow concrete masonry unit: One whose net cross-sectional area in any place parallel to the bearing surface is less than **75% of the gross area.**

Hydrated lime: Quicklime to which sufficient water has been added to convert the oxides to hydroxides.

I

Imperviousness: The ability of masonry to reject the penetration of moisture, acids, dirt, etc.

J

Jack arch: One having horizontal or nearly horizontal upper and lower surfaces. May also be called a *flat* or *straight arch.*

Jumbo brick: A brick whose dimensions are $3\frac{5}{8}$'' x $2\frac{3}{4}$'' x 8''.

K

Kerf: A serrated back on a masonry unit for easy spitting.

Keystone: The wedge-shaped piece at the top of an arch, which locks all other members together.

King closer: A brick cut diagonally to have one 2'' end and one full-width end.

L

Laying overhand: Building the face of a wall from scaffold on the other side.

Lime: A caustic, highly infusible, white substance produced by the action of heat on limestone, shells or other forms of calcium carbonate. The heat drives out the carbonic acid and moisture, leaving only the quicklime.

Lime putty: Hydrated lime in a plastic form ready to be added to mortar.

Lintel: A horizontal member over an opening used to support the load above; steel angles or steel plates welded to I-beams and precast concrete lintels are examples.

Load-bearing wall: Any wall which, in addition to supporting its own weight, supports the building above it.

M

M factor: Heat transfer calculations accounting for thermal storage due to mass.

Masonry: A built-up construction or combination of masonry units set in mortar or grout.

Modular brick: Brick whose nominal dimensions are based on the 4'' module.

N

Net area: Gross area times percent solid. Gross area is the area obtained by multiplying the width times the length of the unit in the bearing plane.

Nogging: In masonry, the filling in with bricks of the spaces between timbers, such as studding in walls and partitions.

Nominal dimension: A dimension which may be greater than the specified masonry dimension by the thickness of a mortar joint.

Norman brick: A brick whose dimensions are $3\frac{5}{8}$'' x $2\frac{1}{4}$'' x $11\frac{5}{8}$''.

Norwegian brick: A brick whose dimensions are $3\frac{5}{8}$'' x $2\frac{3}{4}$'' x $11\frac{5}{8}$''.

O

Oolitic limestone: A calcite-cemented calcareous stone formed of shells and shell fragments, non-crystaline in character.

Outs: A term used by estimators to indicate a deduction from the whole area, as openings in a wall.

P

Panel brick: A brick whose dimensions are 3⅝'' x 7⅝' x 7⅝'', (8-square) or 3⅝'' x 11⅝'' x 11⅝'' (12-square).

Parge: To back-plaster masonry units.

Parget: A term used by architects when referring to plaster or stucco work.

Pier: An isolated column of masonry.

Pilaster: That portion of a wall which may serve as either a vertical beam or a column, or both. In reinforced masonry, the pilaster may or may not project beyond either face of the wall.

Plumb rule: A narrow board having a plumb line and bob on one end or more commonly having a bubble in a tube. It is used for establishing vertical lines.

Pressed brick: A high-grade brick which is molded under pressure, as a result of which it has sharp edges formed by the meeting of two surfaces and a smooth face, making it suitable for exposed surface work.

Prism: A small masonry assemblage made with masonry units and mortar, primarily used to predict the strength of full scale masonry members.

Q

Quantity survey: An inventory compiled for the purpose of estimating the amount of materials and labor required to complete a construction operation.

Queen: A half brick made by cutting a whole brick in two, lengthwise. See *Soap*.

Quicklime: The solid product remaining after limestone has been heated to a high temperature. The process of producing lime is known as lime burning.

Quoin: A unit finished on the face and end, usually a glazed tile unit. Also, projecting courses of brick at the corners of buildings as ornamental features, or large squared stones set at angles or corners of a building.

R

R value: The amount of resistance to heat flow between the warm side and the cold side of a building section.

Raked joint: In brick masonry, a type of joint which has the mortar scraped out to a specified depth and tooled while the mortar is still green.

Reinforced masonry: Masonry units, reinforced with steel, grout and/or mortar, combined together to resist forces.

Roman brick: A brick whose dimensions are 3⅝'' x 1⅝'' x 11⅝''.

Rowlock: In masonry, a term applied to a course of bricks laid on edge, the end of the brick showing on the face of the brick wall. Also *Rolok* or *Rowlok*.

Rubble masonry: Masonry walls built of unsquared or rudely squared stones, irregular in size and shape; also, uncut stone used for rough work, such as for backing of unfinished masonry walls.

S

Salmon brick: Relatively soft, under-burned brick, so named because of its color.

Salt glaze: A gloss finish obtained by the thermochemical reaction of the silicates of the clay body with vapors of salt.

Sandstone: A sedimentary rock consisting usually of quartz cemented with silica, iron oxide or calcium carbonate.

Scale: As used in this book, a measuring devise or ruler, such as architects scale, engineers scale. (To scale: to measure)

Scale, drawn to: A system, designating a unit of measurement, such as 1/8'' ⁵ 1'0''.

Scored block: A unit with a groove in the middle of the block, giving it a half unit effect.

Scutch: In masonry, a bricklayer's cutting tool, used for dressing and trimming brick to a special shape.

Shale: Rock formed from hardened clay used in making brick.

Shear wall: A wall which resists horizontal forces applied in the plane of the wall.

Skintled brickwork: In masonry, an irregular arrangement of bricks with respect to the normal face of the wall. The bricks are set in and out so as to produce an uneven effect on the surface of the wall. Also, a rough effect caused by mortar being squeezed out of the joints.

Slag concrete: A concrete in which blast-furnace slag is used as an aggregate. Relatively light in weight.

Snecked masonry: A term applied to rubble walls in which the stones are roughly square but of irregular sizes and not arranged in courses.

Soap: A masonry unit of normal face dimensions, having a nominal 2'' thickness.

Solid brick: One whose net cross-sectional area in any plane parallel to the bearing surface is 75% or more of the gross area.

Sound Transmission Class (STC): The ability of a wall to stop the transmission of sound from one of its sides to the other, expressed in decibels.

Spall: A small fragment broken from the face of a masonry unit.

Standard brick: A brick whose dimensions are 3⅝'' x 2¼'' x 8''.

Story pole: A marked pole for measuring masonry coursing during construction.

T

Temper: To moisten and remix to a proper consistency.

Tinker's dam: In plumbing, a small dam made to enclose a spot which is to be flooded with solder.

Toothing: In masonry construction, allowing alternate courses of brick to project like teeth and provide for a good bond with any adjoining brickwork which may follow.

Travertine: Dolomitic limestone.

Trig: The bricks laid in the middle of a wall between the two leads to overcome the sag in the line.

U

U factor: The calculated thermal conductance between the warm side and the cold side of a building section, expressed in Btus.

Unit masonry: A type of construction made up of masonry units, such as brick, clay, tile, glazed tile, concrete block, glass block, or stone, laid up with or without mortar.

V

Veneer: A single wythe of masonry for facing purposes, not considered as contributing to the structural value of the wall or surface.

Vermiculite: A mineral closely related to mica, having the ability, when heated, of expanding to form lightweight material with insulating properties.

Vitrified: That characteristic of a clay product resulting when the temperature in the kiln is sufficient to fuse all the grains and close all the pores of the clay, making the mass impervious.

Voussoir brick: Building brick made especially for construction arches. Such bricks are so formed that the face joints radiate from a common center.

W

Wall tie: A bonder or metal piece that connects wythes of masonry to each other or to other materials.

Wythe: Each continuous vertical section of masonry, one unit in thickness.

Abbreviations

A

A	Area (πr^2)
ACI	American Concrete Institute
AIA	American Institute of Architects
ANSI	American National Standards Institute
ASTM	American Society for Testing and Materials

B

BBC	Basic Building Code
BF	Board feet
BIA	Brick Institute of America
BN	Bullnose
BOCA	Building Officials Conference of America
B/U	Backup
Btu	British thermal unit

C

C	One hundred, circumference ($2 \pi r$)
CB	Concrete block
CF	Cubic feet
CMU	Concrete masonry unit
C.O.	Clean out
CSI	Construction Specification Institute
CWT	One hundred weight, 100 pounds
CY	Cubic yard

D

do	Ditto
D.O.	Difference only
DR	Door

E

EA	Each
E.T.	Equivalent thickness

F

F	Fahrenheit
F1S	Faced one side
FB	Face brick
FL	Floor
FIP	Foam in place
FR	Fire rating
FTG	Footing
FTI	Facing Tile Institute

G

G.F.	Granular fill
GLCMU	Glazed concrete masonry unit
GSA	General Service Administration
G1S	Glazed one side
G2S	Glazed two sides
GYP	Gypsum

H

HC	Horizontal cell
HRS	Hours
HWCMU	Heavyweight concrete masonry unit

I

I	I beam
I.D.	Inside diameter
IMI	Internal Masonry Institute
IUBAC	International Union of Bricklayers and Allied Crafts

K

KIP	One thousand pounds

L

lb	Pound
LB	Loadbearing
LF	Lineal feet
LFP	Loose fill, perlite
LFV	Loose fill, vermiculite
Lg	Long
LS	Lump sum
L.S.	Limestone
LWCMU	Lightweight concrete masonry units

M

M	One thousand, mass coefficient
MCAA	Mason Contractors Association of America
MIN.	Minimum

N

NCMA	National Concrete Masonry Association
NO.	Number

O

o.c.	On centers, center to center
OH	Overhead

P

P.C.	Precast, Portland Cement
pcf	Pounds per cubic feet
PCS	Pieces
PIC	Polyisocyanurate foam board
PSB	Polystyrene bead foam board
PSE	Polystyrene extruded foam board
psf	Pounds per square foot
psi	Pounds per square inch
PSI	Polystyrene foam bead molded inserts
PU	Polyurethane foam board

Q

qt	Quart
Q	Quarter

R

r	Radius
R	Thermal resistance
RD	Round

S

Sc	Scored
SF	Square feet
SGT	Structural glazed tile
Sm	Smooth
SPEC	Specification
SQ	Square
STC	Sound transmission class
SY	Square yard

T

T	Ton
TC	Terra cotta
T&E	Tools and equipment

U

U	Thermal transfer coefficient
UBC	Uniform Building Code

V

VC	Vertical cell

W

W	Window, wide, weight
WD	Wood
WP	Waterproofing

Weights of Materials

Material	Weight (lb per CF)
Ashlar Masonry	
Granite	165
Limestone	160
Sandstone	140
Brick Masonry	
Common brick	120
Pressed brick	140
Soft brick	100
Concrete Masonry	
Cement, cinder	100
Cement, slag	130
Cement, stone	144
Dry Rubble Masonry	
Granite	130
Limestone	125
Sandstone	110

Material	Weight (lb per CF)
Earth, Excavated	
Clay, dry	63
Earth, dry	76
Sand, gravel, dry	90-105
Mortar, Rubble	
Granite	155
Limestone	150
Sandstone	130
Minerals	
Clay, marl	137
Granite (165-190)	175
Gypsum	159
Limestone (135-180)	165
Marble (155-170)	165
Pumice	40
Quartz	165
Sandstone (140-150)	147

Weights of Materials

Material	Weight (lb per CF)
Shale	175
Slate	175
Soapstone	169

Metals

Material	Weight (lb per CF)
Aluminum	165
Brass	534
Copper	556
Gold	1,205
Iron, cast	450
Iron, steel	490
Iron, wrought	485
Lead	710
Silver	656
Zinc	440

Bituminous

Material	Weight (lb per CF)
Coal, anthracite	97
Coal, bituminous	84
Coke	75

Various Liquids

Material	Weight (lb per CF)
Gasoline	42
Ice	57.2
Oil	57
Snow	8
Water	62.5

Timber

Material	Weight (lb per CF)
Ash, white	40
Cedar	22
Cypress	30
Elm	45
Fir, Douglas	32
Hemlock	29
Hickory	49
Maple, hard	43
Maple, soft	33
Oak	45
Pine, white	26
Pine, yellow	44
Redwood	26
Spruce	27

Various Building Materials

Material	Weight (lb per CF)
Cement, portland, loose	90
Cinders	40-45
Lime, loose	55-60
Mortar, set	103
Sand	100
Slag, machine	96

Lime Putty

A CF of lime putty weighs approximately 80 pounds.

A CF of lime putty is made from 45.8 pounds of hydrated lime.

A CF of lime putty is made from 27.3 pounds of quicklime.

A 12-quart bucket holds approximately 30 pounds of lime putty.

A CF of lime putty is approximately 2.7 12-quart buckets.

A CF of lime putty is approximately 6.5 No. 2 shovels.

Hydrated Lime

Hydrated lime weighs 40 pounds per CF.

A 50-pound bag of hydrated lime makes 1.09 CF lime putty.

45.8 pounds of hydrated lime make 1 CF lime putty.

170 pounds of hydrated lime makes the same quantity of putty as 100 pounds of quicklime.

A CF of lime putty made from hydrate weighs about 83 pounds.

Quicklime

Quicklime weighs 55-60 pounds per CF.

27.3 pounds of quicklime will make 1 CF of lime putty.

100 pounds of quicklime will make 3.69 CF of lime putty.

100 pounds of quicklime will make as much putty as 170 pounds of hydrate.

A CF of putty made from quicklime weighs slightly over 80 pounds.

Sand

A CY of sand weighs approximately 2,700 pounds.

A ton of sand is approximately 3/4 of a CY.

A CF of sand weighs approximately 100 pounds.

A 12-quart bucket holds approximately 40 pounds of sand.

A ton of sand contains approximately 20 CF of sand.

Mathematics For Calculating Areas

Triangle

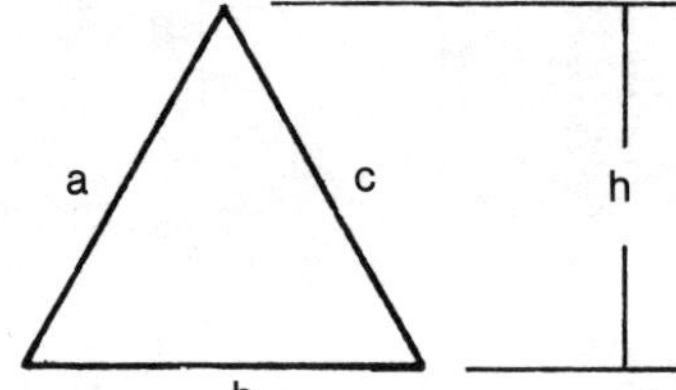

Area (area)

$A = \frac{1}{2}bh$

Right triangle

A triangle whose sides are in the proportion of 3-4-5 will give a right angle (90°), often used in surveying and laying out of buildings.

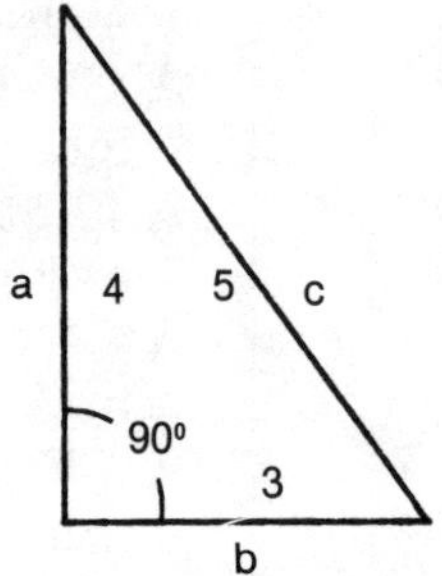

$A = \frac{1}{2}ab$

$c = \sqrt{a^2 + b^2}$

Square, Rectangle,
Parallelogram (shown)

(opposite sides parallel)

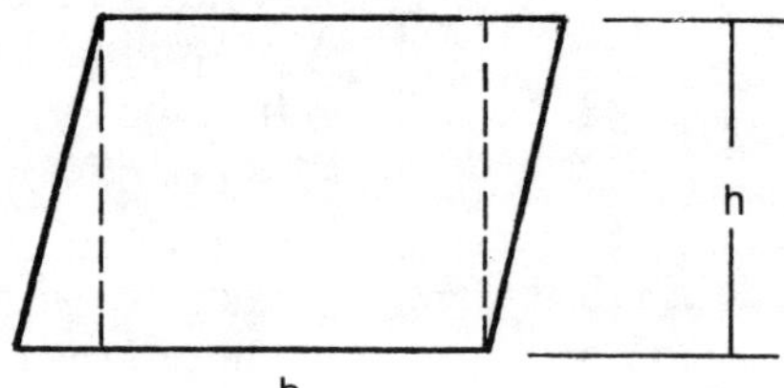

A (area)

$A(sq) = bh$

$A(rect) = bh$

$A(par) = bh$

Trapezoid
(2 sides parallel)

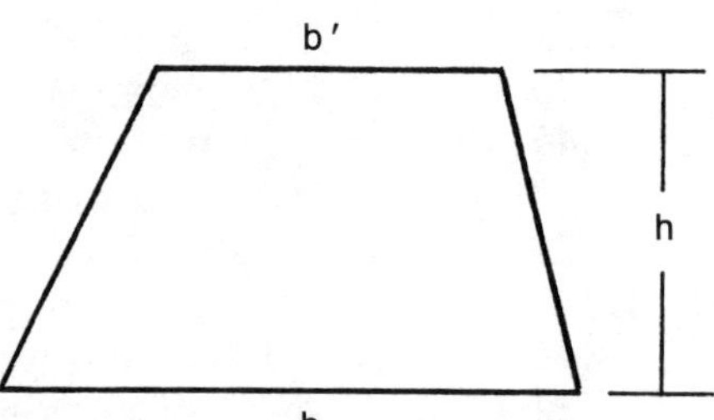

A (area)

$A = \frac{1}{2}(b + b')h$

Trapezium
(no sides parallel)

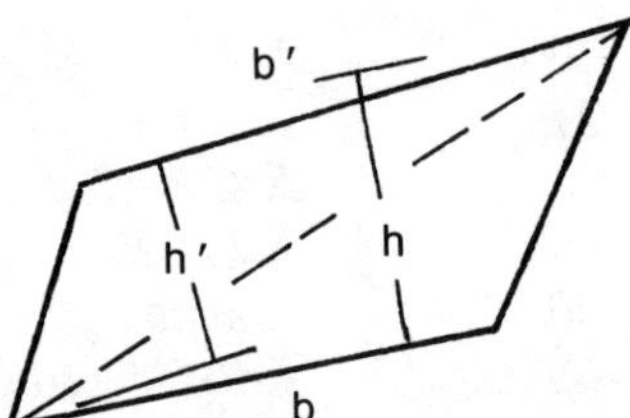

$A = \frac{1}{2}(bh + b'h')$

Mathematics For Calculating Areas (Continued)

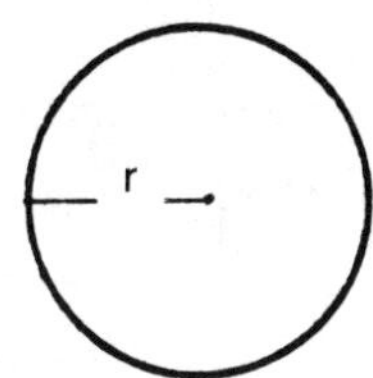

A   (area)
C   (circumference)
R   (radius)
π (3.1416)
$A = \pi r^2$
$C = 2\pi r$

Circle

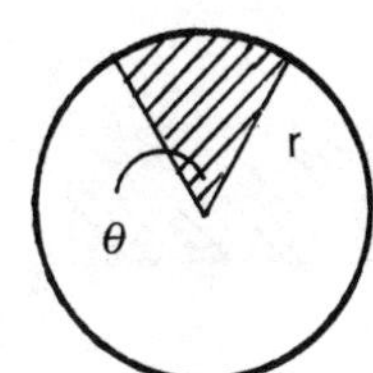

θ (angle, degrees)

$$A = \frac{\pi r^2 \theta}{360}$$

Section of circle

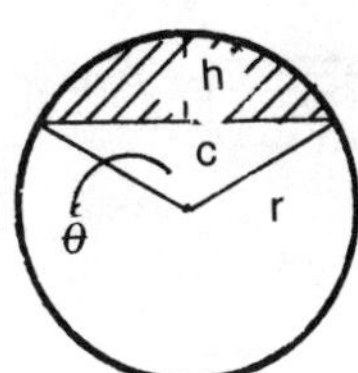

$$A = \frac{\pi r^2 \theta}{360} - \frac{c(r - h)}{2}$$

Segment of circle

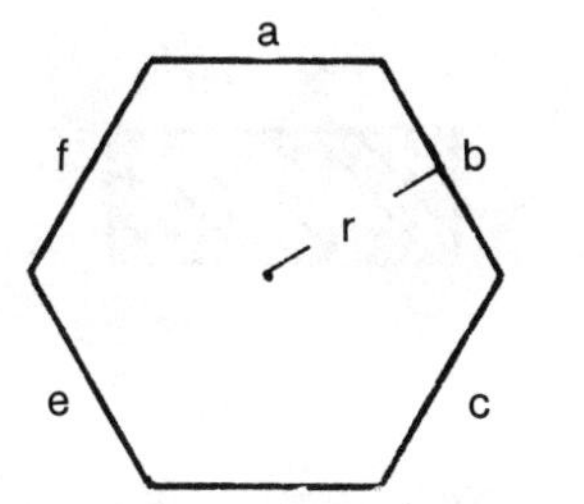

r (radius)

$A = r \times \tfrac{1}{2}$ sum of sides

$A = r/2(a + b + c + d + e + f)$

Polygon
(hexagon shown)

Commonly Used Architectural Symbols

< Angle	× By, times	— Minus, deduct
′ Feet	+ Plus, add	± Plus or minus
″ Inches, quotation, ditto	π Pi (3.1416)	✔ Check, ditto
□ Square	North	✔ Check with transfer
□′ Square feet	@ At	Result of an extension
° Degree	% Percent	√ Square root
Σ Summation	/ Per, with	₵ Centerline
θ Degrees in an angle		# Number (when written before numerals)

Pound (when written after numerals)

Material Symbols

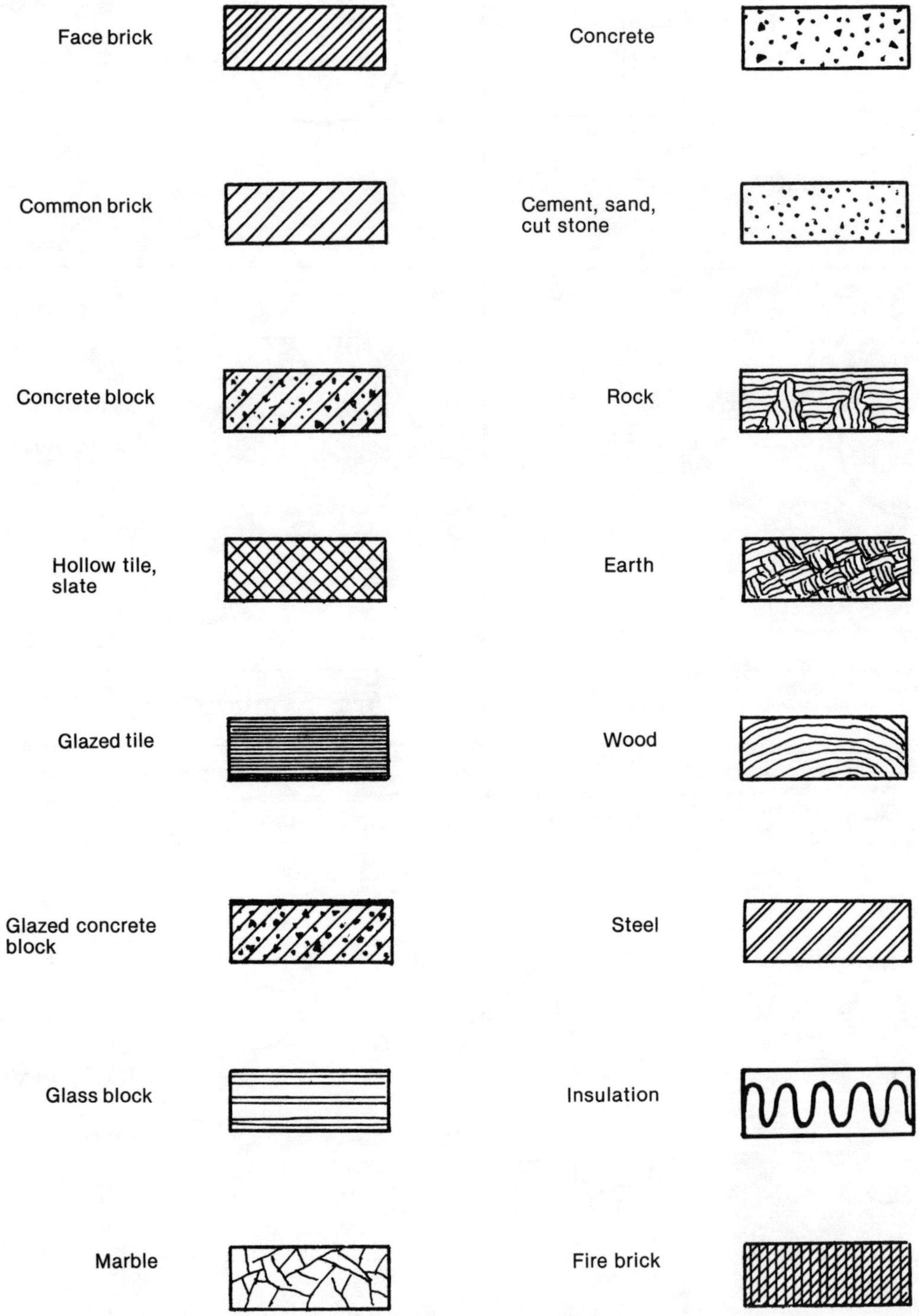

Face brick		Concrete	
Common brick		Cement, sand, cut stone	
Concrete block		Rock	
Hollow tile, slate		Earth	
Glazed tile		Wood	
Glazed concrete block		Steel	
Glass block		Insulation	
Marble		Fire brick